Between Kant and Hegel

Texts in the Development of Post-Kantian Idealism

SUNY Series in Hegelian Studies
Quentin Lauer, S.J., Editor

Between Kant and Hegel

Texts in the Development of Post-Kantian Idealism

Translated and Annotated by
George di Giovanni
and
H.S. Harris

with two essays by the Translators

State University of New York Press

Published by
State University of New York Press, Albany

© 1985 State University of New York

Printed in the United States of America

For information, address State University of New York
Press, State University Plaza, Albany, N.Y., 12246

Library of Congress Cataloging in Publication Data
Main entry under title:

Between Kant and Hegel.

  (SUNY series in Hegelian studies)
  Bibliography: p.
  1. Philosophy, Modern — 18th century — Addresses, essays,
lectures.   2. Philosophy, Modern — 19th century — Addresses,
essays, lectures.   3. Philosophy, German — 18th century —
Addresses, essays, lectures.   4. Philosophy, German — 19th
century — Addresses, essays, lectures.   I. Di Giovanni,
George, 1935-   .   II. Harris, H.S. (Henry Silton),
1926-   .   III. Series.
B2741,B485   1985   142'.3   84-16252
ISBN 0-87395-984-1
ISBN 0-87395-983-3 (pbk.)

10 9 8 7 6 5 4 3 2 1

CONTENTS

PREFACE

This volume was born in what was at first only a strategic decision to combine two mutually compatible (but more limited) projects. On the one hand, there was a desire to fill one of the most important lacunae in the philosophical tradition as it exists for English speaking readers, by providing an anthology from the crucial generation of German thinkers between Kant and Hegel; on the other hand, a desire to make available the few important essays from the *Critical Journal* of Schelling and Hegel that were still untranslated. But there was hardly enough material in this second project to make a proper book by itself. The problem with the first project, on the other hand, was to reduce it to the dimensions of a single volume appropriately. Coalescing the two projects resolved both problems at once. The first offered the larger material context required by the second, while the focus provided by the *Critical Journal* supplied the first with the limit that it needed.

The resulting volume, however, has an organic unity that the original purely strategic decision could not have provided by itself. The remarkable coherence of the philosophical experience documented by the texts in this volume is something which the translators came to appreciate only in the process of working on them. It is the lesson that *we* learned.

Kant's critical philosophy was determined by three factors. There was, first, the desire to establish philosophy on a sound scientific basis; second, the awareness of the limitations of human reason; and third, the belief that a science of philosophy could be established all the same, in spite of these limitations, using the 'subject' as principle. Now, in the first period of the reception of critical philosophy, which is documented in the first part of this volume, the tone was set by K. L. Reinhold. Reinhold was a product of the Enlightenment, and his almost instantaneous success in making the *Critique* popular among his contemporaries was due to a large extent to his ability to re-state it in terms drawn from the Enlightenment tradition which they could all understand. The universally accepted assumption was that philosophy must be based on the 'facts of consciousness'. Dissensions arose only in respect to the nature of these supposed facts, or the possibility of ever establishing the truth about them with any degree of certainty. As Reinhold now re-interpreted the *Critique*, the latter had uncovered a new and infallible source of 'original facts' that could resolve all past philosophical dissensions, and finally set philosophy on a scientific, systematic basis. Reinhold's interpretation, in other words, stressed the first and third element of critical philosophy to the prejudice of the second. Of course Reinhold paid abundant lip service to Kant's pronouncements about the limitations of human reason. But in fact there was in him not the least trace of the new 'critical skepticism', or the belief that reason is at odds with itself precisely *qua* reason, that animated the *Critique*. In this respect Reinhold's interpretation was a very conservative one. It forced critical philosophy back into the conceptual straight-jacket of the Enlightenment. How much it was still vulnerable, when viewed in this way, to the attacks of the skepticism of the Enlightenment type was amply demonstrated by the *Aenesidemus* of Schulze.

The appearance of the *Aenesidemus* precipitated Fichte's statement of his version of critical philosophy. Fichte, and also Schelling soon after, contributed a new and much more romantic note to the debate surrounding the *Critique*. They also provided a new definition of 'fact of consciousness', and re-stated the problem of the relationship that Kant had assumed between 'appearances' and 'thing-in-itself' in strictly subjective terms, as a relationship between the 'conscious' and the 'unconscious'. The latter move was one which Reinhold had already anticipated; but it remained for Fichte and Schelling to exploit it in full. Yet, for all their differences from Reinhold, the interpretation of critical philosophy given by Fichte and Schelling was no less conservative than his. It was still based on the belief that we can escape from the limits of conceptualization, and ground the edifice of philosophical reason on some sort of immediate infallible 'fact'. Although they were now parading it in a more dynamic form, dressed up in the execrable language of the Absolute, Fichte and Schelling were still bound to the intuitionism of classical philosophy.

The originality of Hegel's interpretation of critical philosophy can only be appreciated when this is recognized. Hegel was the first to take seriously the skeptical aspect of the *Critique*, which was after all its most revolutionary one. He understood that reason is antinomic by nature. It *has* to enter into conflict with itself, since it is capable of reflecting upon its concepts, and hence is constantly creating a distance between itself and itself. On the other hand, by the very fact that reason recognized its inner discord, it has already overcome it. *It knows how to contain it.* This, if any, is the fundamental 'fact' of consciousness on which philosophy has to capitalize in order to establish itself as genuine science. To take this as the starting point of philosophy, however, as Hegel eventually did, was to reverse the whole thrust of the previous interpretations of critical philosophy. It was to commit philosophy to the circle of conceptualization, whereas all previous philosophy had tried to transcend it. The task of philosophy was now to abide by the conflicts of reason in order to deepen their significance, and ultimately turn them into constructive means of the life of spirit. Kant had of course implicitly defined a programme of this sort. Criticism was for him a way of living at the very limit of thought, by recognizing that limit and ensuring that it is never transcended. But Kant still hankered after a supposed intellectual intuition that would have removed the limit—as if the labour of the concept could yield only the second best truth, or the only truth *for us*. The difference in Hegel is that for him that labour is *all* that there is, and to try to escape it through some mystical intuition only leads to nihilism.

This position of Hegel is only to be found fully elaborated in the *Phenomenology* and in the *Logic*. It is not to be found in the essays from the *Critical Journal* translated in the second part of this volume. Yet these essays are significant, because they show Hegel precisely as he is reflecting on the nature of skepticism, both new and old. The break from Schelling's intuitionism was still to come, but the reconstruction of the history of skepticism that Hegel was now attempting provided the falling stone that eventually precipitated the latter developments, as the actual facts show. For even now Hegel perceived that the truth of skepticism (of ancient skepticism at least, for Hegel put no more store by the skepticism of the Enlightenment type than he did by Reinhold) is that there is *no* criterion by which to distinguish between true appearance and false. At this time Hegel could just as well use his insight to justify the kind of negative logic with which he routinely prefaced his lectures on metaphysics. The function of this logic was to unmask the contradiction inherent in any conceptual construct, and thereby clear the way for the intuition on which the metaphysics supposedly depended. But Hegel only had to realize that the sought for criterion lies precisely *in* the debate between one philosophical position and another, between skepticism and dogmatism, and ultimately between philosophy and unphilosophy, in order to make that supposed intuition superfluous.

The texts in the second part of this volume document some of Hegel's earliest public reflections on critical philosophy, and on the debate surrounding it. They herald his eventual shift of concern away from the 'content' of philosophical debate to the 'debate' itself. Together with the texts in the first part they represent one aspect of the story of the events that run from Kant to Hegel. The whole story, as we see it, consists in Hegel's return to a Kant freed from his Enlightenment encumbrances, after Hegel's break from Schelling's intuitionism has allowed him to shake off those encumbrances himself. Neither the texts, nor the two introductory essays (either singly or together) give the full story, of course. They only hint at it; we only hope that the hint is more than just a vague gesture.

In another respect too the present volume is limited. The focus provided for it by the *Critical Journal* has resulted in a bias that should not be overlooked or minimized. What happened in Germany in the twenty-five years following the publication of the *Critique of Pure Reason* (1781) is far more complex than this selection of texts can reveal; there are important figures and groups who are here omitted, and in some instances what is included can hardly provide an adequate sample of the author's range and significance. There is scope left for at least another volume of texts that would reflect the moral side of the debate represented here. At any rate, the present volume ought to be read in conjunction with the translations by Cerf and Harris, Peter Heath, and Fritz Marti, of other early texts from Fichte, Schelling, and Hegel.

The complete absence in this volume of F.H. Jacobi is to be regretted. But the reader will soon realize that repetitive long-windedness is a common fault in this generation of writers; and Jacobi suffered from it more than most of them (as Hegel's summaries and citations in *Faith and Knowledge* rather cruelly underline). Jacobi was an influential thinker—not least upon Coleridge. But his first appearance in English dress must wait upon another occasion.

Except in the case of one previously published essay, we have each gone over the other's work carefully; but only the Schelling essay is a collaborative effort in the full sense. There the first draft and the final revision of the text is by di Giovanni; but a second draft was made, and finally the footnotes were added by Harris. Elsewhere we have operated more independently, and each of us bears the final responsibility for his own decisions. Because of this independence some variations in terminology will be observed; but we hardly feel that this calls for apology, since even one translator working alone could not maintain terminological uniformity in rendering such a varied group of writers (at least not without awkward artificialities, and perhaps not without serious distortions).

We should mention, on the other hand, three instances in which we deliberately chose to be consistent. The distinction between *wissen* and *erkennen* (and their derivatives) is in German to a large extent idiomatic. But in Hegel it assumes philosophical significance, and for this reason we decided to retain it in English *as far as possible* by translating the two terms with 'knowledge' and 'cognition' (and their derivatives) respectively. But 'cognition' and 'cognizing' can be terribly artificial in English; so, in the other (non-Hegelian) texts we have been prepared to shift back to 'knowledge' and 'knowing' whenever the awkwardness became unbearable, provided that there was no obvious advantage in abiding by the convention. (This happened especially in the excerpts from Aenesidemus and from Beck). The same applies to *Verhältnis* and *Beziehung*. In this case too the distinction acquires a technical meaning in Hegel, and we have tried to preserve it by translating *Verhältnis* as 'relation' and *Beziehung* (apart from rare and unimportant exceptions) as 'connection' or 'reference'. In any event, 'relation' as it is being used in English nowadays is too broad a term for *Beziehung*; the epistemological bias of our texts requires a narrower concept such as 'connection' or 'reference'. The translation of *ich* also presented a problem. 'I' can be awkward. 'Self', which is the translation adopted by Heath and Lachs, does not really translate *ich*. Moreover, it carries psychological connotations that are completely out of place in certain contexts (notably in Fichte). The term is obviously a technical one which our authors use with meanings that vary considerably and since in English the *natural* way of rendering philosophical technical terms is *Latin*, we finally opted for ego. This translation also has the advantage of reminding the reader of the Cartesian background of the German philosophical *ich*.

All the internal references to the texts translated in this volume are by the pagination of the original text (which is printed in the margin of our text).

It remains for us to make due acknowledgements. We shall do this under separate initials below. To all those mentioned, and to the others, some of whom we may not remember, we wish to express our heartfelt thanks.

George di Giovanni   H.S. Harris
McGill University   York University
Montreal   Toronto

I wish to thank McGill University for a research grant that helped defray some of the expenses incurred in the work of translation and in the preparation of the final manuscript; my colleagues in the German Department, Profs. H. Richter and J. Schmidt, who answered innumerable questions about German usage; Dr. Manfred Kuehn, who helped track down some very obscure references; Mrs. Laurie McRobert, who read and commented on an early draft of the Beck text; and Dr. Laura Zagolin, who did the same for the other texts for which I am responsible. Most of all I wish to thank my collaborator in this project, H.S. Harris, who went over all my texts with a fine toothcomb, detected many inaccuracies and made innumerable stylistic suggestions. If Reinhold, Schulze, Fichte, Maimon and Beck have as good a command of colloquial English as they show in this volume, it is due to a large extent to him. I am responsible of course for any mistake.

G. di G.

The editing and preparation of the final manuscript of the *Critical Journal* essays was supported by two research grants from Glendon College (York University) for which I am very grateful. Most of this final editorial work was done by Anne Harris (who also helped in lots of other ways). The «Introduction for the *Critical Journal*» and the «Scepticism» essay were typed by Ruth Koski Harris; «Scepticism, Dogmatism and Speculation» and the «Krug» essay were typed first by Ida Sabag and again by Anne Harris. Stephen Boos helped with the Bibliography. To all of them, my thanks.

For the text of the essays from the *Critical Journal* I have used the reprint published in 1957 (Georg Olms Verlagsbuchhandlung, Hildesheim). But I have also consulted both the critical edition, edited by H. Buchner and O. Pöggeler (*Hegel, Gesammelte Werke*, Vol. IV, Hamburg: Meiner, 1968) and the French translation of the «Introduction» and the «Skepticism» essay by B. Fauquet (Paris: Vrin, 1972). From these two sources I derived much of the information in the footnotes; and the pioneer work of Fauquet was an immense help in the making of the English version. (I wish that I had discovered N. Merker's Italian translation - Bari, Laterza, 1970 — sooner. He was the real pioneer, but I did not know it).

The translation of the «Introduction» for the *Critical Journal* was first published in the *Independent Journal of Philosophy*, III (1979). It appears here by kind permission of the editor, Dr. George Elliot Tucker. Dr. Tucker deserves my thanks also for his careful examination of the translation at the time of its first appearance. Many of his helpful suggestions were adopted then and are preserved now.

To George di Giovanni I owe a debt of a different kind. It is true that he went over my other contributions in the way that Dr. Tucker went over the "Essence of Philosophical Criticism"; and I am grateful for that. But the insights I have gained from his own contributions to this volume (and from our discussions about it) into what Hegel called the "revolution" to be expected from the perfecting of the Kantian system are much more important. I have written about that "revolution" for years without any proper grasp of its context. I trust that I am only the first of many readers to owe this debt to George; and I would wish their gratitude to be directed to the right address—as mine is.

George being on sabbatical leave in Belgium at the time, the task of correcting proofs and preparing the index fell to my lot (which was only fair since he did most of the work in the earlier preparation of the manuscript). I have received valuable assistance in both tasks from Carol and Anne Harris and from Pierre Bruneau and James Devin. The index was typed by Ruth Koski Harris. I am very grateful to all of them.

H. S. H.

PART

I

The Critical Philosophy
and its First Reception

The Facts of Consciousness

George di Giovanni

1. A Critical Misunderstanding

FEW PHILOSOPHERS WERE as badly misunderstood by their contemporaries as Kant was. In part at least the misunderstanding was due to his success, for Kant had identified himself so well with the issues of the day that he easily gave the impression that he was still working within the limits of his contemporaries' assumptions, though he was in fact revolutionizing them.

We must remember the intellectual and cultural context within which Kant's critical philosophy was born.[1] By 1770, the year of Kant's *Dissertatio*, the Wolffian rationalism that had been the dominant force of the German Enlightenment in its early stage had already been on the decline for many years. Opposition to it had been restricted at the beginning to the precincts of academic life, and had come mainly from the followers of Christian Thomasius (1655-1728), who were the pietist inheritors of the theological anti-intellectual tradition that had once begotten Martin Luther. By the middle of the century, however, this same rationalism was already suffering from the effects of forces that had sprung up outside the universities. Most important among them was the sudden and quick spread among the educated public, at first *via* the French *philosophes*, of the ideas and practices of British empiricism and of British natural science. Hume's skepticism followed in the wake of these, and at the same time, imported as munition in the attempt to stem its spread, came the 'common sense' philosophy of Reid, Oswald, and Beattie. In the course of the general and often confused debate that ensued, the very idea of doing philosophy in systematic form fell into disrepute.

Traditional metaphysical issues gave way more and more to aesthetic, psychological, and practical concerns, thus accentuating the trend away from speculation in favour of anthropology that had characterized the Enlightenment from its beginning. The 'popular philosophers', of whom Moses Mendelssohn (1729-1786) was undoubtedly the finest example, were the by-product of this weakening of the academic regime. They were moralistic thinkers whose main preoccupation was the ethical and aesthetic education of the individual. Finally, a new generation of defenders of the faith had arisen who eyed with suspicion, not just the rationalism of the academic philosophy, but philosophy and reason as such. They were quick to realize that they could now use the newly imported empiricism and skepticism to press their case against the claims of reason. At their instigation the philosophical debate about the relation of the 'truths of fact' to the 'truths of reason' had been extended to implicate also the theological issue of how 'faith' stood with respect to 'reason'. In this connection the names of Georg Hamann (1730-1788) and Friederich Heinrich Jacobi (1743-1819) immediately come to mind. And so does that of Johann Gottfried Herder (1744-1803), though in his case some important reservations must be entered, for unlike Hamann and Jacobi, Herder never opposed philosophy or reason *per se*; he was only opposed to the kind of synthesis between faith and reason that the academic rationalists advocated.

Dissension and doubt were, in brief, the key-notes of the intellectual situation at the time when Kant's *Critique of Pure Reason* made its appearance. In the universal confusion that reigned, the one assumption that all parties would have been willing to accept was that philosophy must restrict itself in its investigations to the 'facts of consciousness'. It is no surprise, therefore, that when Kant announced his Copernican revolution, his contemporaries took the announcement as just the start of one more round in the general debate that was already being waged about the nature and content of those 'facts', or that they expected this round to be just as inconclusive as the previous ones. Yet Kant was claiming that he had stemmed the tide of skepticism once and for all; further, that he had re-introduced in philosophy the conceptual rigor of Wolffian rationalism[2]; and to top it all, that he had finally settled the long-standing dispute between faith and reason to the satisfaction of all sides. These claims appeared to Kant's contemporaries just as scandalous as they were unexpected. And in the added confusion that followed, the fact that he had given to the presumed 'facts of consciousness' an extra dimension of meaning went unnoticed.

The change introduced was just as subtle as it was important. Kant had recognized that the facts of consciousness need not be exclusively *about* consciousness, just because they *pertain* to it. On the contrary, all conscious activities must be understood as in one way or another directed to an object which, if it is ever actually given, stands related to those activities as a distinct term. Hence, to reflect upon them and to establish their requirements is the same as to define the structure of a possible objective world in outline form. Kant did not express himself in these words, of course, yet this was the clear implication of his often repeated claim that the possibility of the objects of experience can be established *a priori* through a reflection upon the requirements of thought, but that these objects must be *given* to thought in actual experience all the same.[3] And from this insight three important consequences followed, all of which were clearly perceived by Kant. In the first place, it followed that although Kant could still accept the

Cartesian principle that philosophy must begin with self-consciousness, he did not also have to accept the Cartesian conclusion that all knowledge consists in a reflection upon the *ego* and its content. On the contrary, the *ego* is for Kant an empty intention that needs an extra-conceptual content to have significance, just like any other thought.[4] In other words, although Kant could maintain that all consciousness requires self-consciousness, he did not have to reduce the consciousness of an object to the consciousness *of the consciousness* of that object. Secondly, it followed that although Kant restricted our knowledge of the 'thing-in-itself', outside consciousness to its appearances *in* consciousness, he still could retain this presumed 'thing' as the object at least of an ideal possibility.[5] In fact, he *had* to retain it on both theoretical and existential grounds—on the one hand, as we have just seen, as a means for conceptualizing the irreducibility of consciousness to self-consciousness; and on the other, in order to avoid restricting the possibilities of self-consciousness to the limits of theoretical thought. The 'thing-in-itself' actually played for Kant a double role. It stood both for all that we cannot excogitate on the strength of pure thought alone, and hence must accept simply on the blind testimony of the senses; and for what we do, perhaps, freely produce through the power of thought, yet are unable to recognize because of our dependence on the senses. Finally, Kant was able to clarify the distinction between thought and sensation, which both the empiricists and the rationalists had muddied, by assigning to sensation a special existential role in experience. As Kant was to say in a letter to his disciple Sigismund Beck: "Knowledge is the representation through *concepts* of a *given* object as such. . . [hence] for knowledge, two sorts of representations are required: (1) intuition, by means of which an object is given and (2) conception, by means of which an object is thought."[6] Intuition, in other words, is where the abstract intentions of thought are finally realized. It provides the existential touchstone for the whole process of cognition. But since our only intuition is sensible, it follows that for us at least this touchstone is provided by the senses. The problem of cognition, as Kant had now redefined it, consists precisely in showing how thought intentions can be, and are in fact, realized in objects given in sense experience.

These consequences clearly followed from Kant's basic premise. But they were precisely the sort that his contemporaries, accustomed as they were to think of consciousness as an inner theatre in which, so to speak, a private show is being staged, were unable to appreciate. And Kant made things even more difficult for them by introducing an impossible ambiguity in the very statement of his central position. Kant was in fact defending, not one, but two theses; and he often drew consequences from one that were possible only on the basis of the other. One thesis is the one stated in the letter to Beck. It assumes an original empty reference to the 'thing-in-itself' which is only to be realized, however, when restricted to the appearances of this intended 'thing' in experience, i.e., when the latter is redefined to mean 'possible object of experience in general',[7] The only implication of this thesis is that we know the intended 'thing' only as 'it appears to us', not as it is 'in-itself'. The other thesis, on the other hand, is that in knowing the 'thing' as it only appears to us, *we do not know it at all*. And the problem with this thesis—quite apart from the fact that it is not at all identical with the first—is that Kant could not defend it without at the same time denying himself the right to maintain the other. For the thesis implies that the world of appearances is somehow illusory— which is precisely what the skeptics held. It implies that sensations are purely private, subjective events. This is indeed what everybody in Kant's time thought—the empiricists as well as the rationalists. But if this is all that sensations were, how could Kant ever expect to find *given* in them the very objects that we represent *a priori* through the universalizing intentions of thought? On the view of the nature of sensation implied by Kant's second thesis, the problem of how to realize thought-intentions in sense data becomes just as intractable as, on the same view, would be the problem of how to realize them in the 'thing-in-itself'.

The ambiguity presented Kant with an impossible choice. Either he granted that sensations are not altogether 'blind'; that they include, even *qua* sensations, a reference to the object of cognition. If he made this move, however, he would have had to concede, because of the special existential character of sensations, that we do have *some* knowledge of the 'thing-in-itself'. Kant would have had to reject, in other words, his second thesis. Or he granted that strictly speaking thought-intentions are never resolved in sensation, but only in the syntheses that the imagination specially constructs for thought, in accordance with its rule, out of raw sense data. This is the line of argument that Kant officially followed.[8] Its obvious implication, however, was that the spatio-temporal objects that constitute the content of experience are only imaginary entities—that strictly speaking we have no *direct* intuition of them as 'objects'. But this was a position which Kant tried hard to distance himself from because he identified it with Berkeley.[9]

In other words, whichever option he adopted, Kant would have had to modify his critical position from the ground up. There were other options open, of course. For instance he could have simply dismissed the very idea of the 'thing-in-itself' as too abstract and hence deceptive. He could have re-stated the problem of how consciousness transcends itself (as indeed it must) in terms of the relation that consciousness bears within itself to its own pre-conscious, natural past. And since this relation, as we have just said, is part of consciousness itself, he could have conceded that we cannot investigate what consciousness is without at the same time considering its natural and social history (i.e., to use Kant's language, without implicating the 'thing-in-itself'). This is the line of investigation which Hegel was eventually to explore. But Hegel belongs to the final stage of German Idealism, and our task is simply to consider the first events that led from Kant to the subsequent idealism. As far as Kant's contemporaries were concerned, Kant's critical position appeared to be simply perverse. To them it seemed that Kant was trying to refute Berkeley, using Berkeley's principles as his ground. It was this confusion in their mind that led finally, as we shall have to see, to the collapse of the critical system.

Warning of the impending disaster came to Kant early enough. It arrived in the form of a long manuscript, entitled *Essay in Transcendental Philosophy*,[10] that was sent to him on the recommendation of his friend Markus Herz by its author Solomon Maimon.[11] In the *Essay* Maimon had developed a form of critical philosophy which, in spite of its bizarre features, clearly illustrates the problem that Kant faced.[12] Maimon compared sensations to the "differentials" of infinitesimal calculus because, just like these mathematical entities, they are ideal, vanishing quantities that we never actually perceive, but which we assume nonetheless in order to explain how the objects that we do experience ever come to be. These objects are the product of a synthesis that is carried out among the sensations, in accordance with the rule of the categories, at a pre-conscious level of existence. The process becomes conscious only in the imagination. It is here that we finally find the objects, and we then try to explain them by positing their ideal infinitesimal components, and the process of synthesis by which they are produced. Hence, to the question whether we actually perceive the order of the categories in the sense-content of experience (*quid facti*), Maimon answers in the negative. 'Sensations' are only ideal entities. Whatever the process of categorization required before our objects finally appear in the imagination, that process is not given to us *in* the objects themselves. The order that these exhibit can be immediately explained in terms of the synthesis which is most appropriate to the imagination—i.e., according to the psychological laws of association. It would be different, of course, if we were able to analyze their content into their infinitesimal components. But since this is something which we patently cannot do, we must be satisfied with an ideal construction on the one hand, and a merely psychological explanation on the other. For the same reason, we should also answer in the negative the question whether we have any right even to assume that the world of experience is ordered according to the categories (*quid iuris*). But Maimon avoids this conclusion by postulating that our intellect is only a finite aspect of God's mind. Because of this continuity of our intelligence with the divine, we are then justified to take our ideal constructions to be partial images of the perfect resolution of the world into all its infinitesimal elements that God has already accomplished *ab aeterno*. In laying down this postulate, Maimon thought that he was reconciling Kant's critical philosophy with Leibniz's metaphysics.

Kant did not reply to Maimon directly. He acknowledged to Herz, however, that nobody had so far understood him as well as this character previously unknown to him. The very fact that Kant had taken the time to read Maimon's bulky manuscript (much of it at any rate), and to write comments which he was now sending to Herz with the clear understanding that he would pass them on to Maimon, indicated that his compliment was meant seriously.[13] Kant gave no sign, however, of having appreciated the strength of the criticism implicit in Maimon's *Essay*. He limited himself to pointing out that Maimon had indeed gone back to Leibniz, even though Leibniz himself had never explicitly concerned himself with the issue of the harmony between the faculties of the mind; nor had he ever held, for that matter, that the human intelligence is an aspect of the Divine Intellect. But Kant granted that the issue was implicit in Leibniz's metaphysics, and Maimon was simply bringing it to light. In revealing the Spinozistic implications of that metaphysics, moreover, Maimon was refuting it (so Kant thought) by a *reductio ad absurdum*. As for his own position, Kant simply reiterated it, stressing the distinction between thought and sensation to the point of reducing the latter to the level of a pre-conscious, quasi biological event—apparently unaware of the fact that in so doing, he was playing into the hands of Maimon. For to the extent that sensations are only pre-conscious events, to that extent they cannot be brought within the circle of consciousness without being idealized; and to the extent that they are idealized, they lose their privileged existential status. The supposed connection between the categories and sensations then becomes the object of an inference, not a directly perceivable fact of consciousness.

Kant never saw the problem. Or more precisely, inasmuch as he saw it, he tried to deal with it by interjecting between thought and sensations the schemata of the imagination and the ideas of reason, thus postponing the problem without really resolving it. Unwittingly he was already sliding either into the phenomenalism that Beck was later to develop, or into the idealism which Fichte will soon advocate. A possible alternative would have been to assume an attitude of utter skepticism with respect to the whole issue of the relation of the categories to empirical experience. This is precisely the position that Maimon was to adopt in his second major book, *Essay towards a New Logic or Theory of Thought*, which he published in 1794.[14] By that time, however, Kant's *Critique* was no longer the only object of Maimon's concern. For in 1789, one year before the publication of Maimon's first *Essay*, an event had occurred that was to alter the tone and character of the debate surrounding Kant's work. The event was the publication of Reinhold's *Essay towards a New Theory of the Human Faculty of Representation*.[15] It was this book that occasioned the famous skeptical attack of Schulze against the critical philosophy, which in turn set in motion the series of events that eventually led to post-Kantian idealism. It is to these events that we must now turn.

2. The Compounding of the Misunderstanding: Karl Leonhard Reinhold's Philosophy of the Elements

When Jenisch wrote to Kant in 1787, announcing that his critical philosophy was being talked about everywhere, he left no doubt as to the cause of this sudden popularity.[16] It was due to the influence of a series of open letters concerning the *Critique of Pure Reason* that a certain Karl Leonhard Reinhold had just published in the *Teutscher Merkur*.[17] Kant did not fail to acknowledge the debt that he owed to the author of the letters. He thanked him warmly for his contribution to the spread of his ideas in a letter of December 28, 1787;[18] and for a time at least he entertained the illusion that he had found in Reinhold a spokesman who would advance the cause of his system among the public, while he busied himself completing it. Reinhold, as we shall see, did not live up to Kant's expectation. On the contrary, he eventually turned against the very idea of 'critique', thus coming round full circle to his original position. For Reinhold's first reaction to the *Critique of Pure Reason* had been quite negative; he had even authored an anonymous letter defending Herder's *Ideas for a Philosophy of History* against Kant's severe criticism of it.[19] His acceptance of the critical philosophy was sudden and laden with emotional overtones, exhibiting all the earmarks of a conversion.[20] As things turned out, it was to be only the first of a series of philosophical conversions (Reinhold had undergone a religious conversion from Catholicism to Protestantism earlier) whose frequency quickly became the butt of endless jokes. A charitable interpretation of these philosophical wanderings is that Reinhold remained until the end a man of the Enlightenment, for whom the ultimate aim of reason was not the building of a system of thought, but the moral education of mankind. Even after his conversion to critical philosophy, Reinhold's principal reason for recommending it to the public in his *Kantian Letters* was the advantages that it supposedly offered to the cause of morality and religion. And although at one point he did turn to system-building for the sake of his moral goal, Reinhold could feel no repulsion against shifting from system to system as long as, in these changes, he remained faithful to the goal itself. At the end, still for the sake of that goal, Reinhold felt compelled to abandon the idealistic movement altogether, and even to join forces with Jacobi's party against it.

Reinhold's first systematic statement of his position, and of its place with respect to that of Kant, came with his appointment to a chair of philosophy which had recently been established at Jena with the express purpose of promoting the philosophy of Kant. This first statement was followed by a stream of essays and occasional pieces, and by five major volumes (which included many of the essays that he had already published)—all in a very short period of time. In the course of this voluminous output Reinhold was forced, under the pressure of polemical debate, to introduce some changes in his original position. But the changes only reflected his heightened awareness of the original-ity of his system with respect to that of Kant. We shall now consider what Reinhold thought his own contribution to critical philosophy was; how he sought to realize it and what innovations he actually brought to it.

(a) From Critique to Philosophy of the Elements

Reinhold viewed the history of philosophy as a process directed towards the final complete revelation of truth. The way to this final disclosure is made up of a series of partial revelations, each occasioned by the attempt to resolve the problems that the previous revelation has occasioned because of its limitedness. And since the process thus unfolds organically, each stage building upon the previous one, the history of a particular system of thought is also the measure of its truth. Its statement of the problem of 'truth', and its success in addressing itself to it, is itself a sign of how close the system is to the final revelation. Moreover, since truth is by nature self-revelatory, we should expect that the closer a philosophy is to that final stage, the greater is also its power to command assent. Reinhold distinguished in this respect between the 'validity' of a philosophy and its 'binding power', i.e., its effectiveness. A philosophy is universally valid (*gültig*) to the extent that it unfolds the implications inherent in its premises in a coherent fashion. It is then indeed capable of commanding assent, but only hypothetically, i.e., on condition that its premises have already been accepted. It is universally binding (*geltend*), on the other hand, to the extent that its premises are of such a nature that nobody can avoid accepting them once they have been made public. The final philosophy, as Reinhold envisaged it, should command assent precisely in this unconditional sense.[21]

Now, whether one measured the philosophy of his age by the criterion of history, or by that of its binding power, there was no doubt in Reinhold's mind that the stage was set for a final break-through. For after Hume, the central issue of philosophy had been, not just whether some particular doctrine or other was true, but whether truth itself was possible. No further radicalization of its central problem could be achieved. Philosophy was thus left with the choice either of transforming itself once and for all into genuine science, or of forever relinquishing its claim to knowledge. It so happened, moreover, that the existing schools of thought had so re-defined and buttressed their positions in reaction to Hume, that together they exhausted the only logically possible avenues to the resolution of the problem that he had posed. And since every school, in defining its position, had in fact implied the partial truth of a second school which, in turn, implied the partial truth of still a third, yet this third invariably turned out to contradict the first, it followed that in the present situation the unprejudiced observer was being denied access even into the philosophical *problem* of truth. In this respect too philosophy was faced with an ultimate choice. Either it must find a way out of its present impasse, or it must resign itself to perpetual irrelevancy. The case of Kant's critical philosophy presented a final paradox. For Kant had in fact resolved the Humean doubt; he had broken the impasse in which the warring schools of thought had landed themselves, by unscrambling and reconciling their many claims and counter-claims. One would have expected, therefore, that his philosophy would command universal assent. But in fact it did not—and this circumstance was another indication that the age was indeed in labour with the final revelation of truth, but that it had still to bring it forth.[22]

What was it, then, that had gone wrong with the critical philosophy? To answer this question Reinhold introduces a new distinction. We must distinguish between two levels of philosophy.[23] At one level it is concerned with the possibility and the structure of the objects of human cognition and desire. At this level philosophy is basically metaphysics; it includes as particular sciences the metaphysics of sensible nature, the metaphysics of the ideal objects that transcend sensible nature; and the theory of desires. At the other level, which is the more fundamental one, it is concerned, not with the *objects* of consciousness, but with *consciousness* itself—specifically, with its basic fact which is 'representation'. Here the goal of philosophy is to establish the possibility of all the particular sciences of metaphysics, first by identifying the primitive facts of consciousness upon which each particular science is based, and then by validating the genuiness of these facts by relating them to the one fundamental fact of representation. This level of philosophy divides into two others. The first begins with 'representation', which it expresses in what Reinhold calls the 'principle of consciousness'; it then proceeds to identify the general faculty of representation, its essential properties, and the consequences that these have for consciousness as a whole. The three particular faculties of representation, viz., 'sensibility', 'understanding' and 'reason', are deduced at this level. The second begins by assuming these particular faculties, and then proceeds to examine their special properties. On their basis it develops a theory of cognition which, together with the general theory of representation developed at the previous level, constitutes the theory of the faculty of representation as a whole. It is this theory that provides for philosophy as a whole, and especially for metaphysics, the science of the foundations of knowledge.

With all these distinctions behind him, Reinhold is ready to explain what went wrong with critical philosophy. Kant had recognized that the possibility of metaphysics can be established only by reflecting upon the conditions of the consciousness of its objects. This had been his great insight. But in putting it into practice Kant had stayed very close—*too close*—to the objects themselves; he had appealed to the facts of consciousness that justify them on an *ad hoc* basis alone—whenever a special problem arose, and only to the extent that it was required to resolve that particular problem. Kant had proceeded *critically* rather than *systematically*, in other words. He had given the fragments of a foundational theory of cognition, without ever bothering to identify the fundamental fact of consciousness that makes cognition itself possible, let alone trying to build upon it systematically. Of course this way of proceeding was only to be expected from someone who was doing pioneer work. But now that Kant's spade-work had been done, the need for a complete grounding of science was all the more apparent. And if philosophy was to survive, there was no choice but to satisfy it. Reinhold's idea of a Philosophy of the Elements that would lay down systematically and exhaustively the foundations of all knowledge was his answer to this need.[24]

This was how the idea of surpassing the master by grounding his doctrines on a more secure basis was born. Fichte was to be motivated by it as well; and after Fichte, Schelling too—except that in his case the immediate object of the reforming zeal will be Fichte. We shall have to see how successfully Reinhold's Philosophy of the Elements finally fulfilled its declared goal. One point can already be made, however. The theme of 'system' and 'systematization' is a genuinely Kantian one. It had been Kant, not Reinhold, who had insisted in the first place on the need to develop the principles of metaphysics into an exhaustive system.[25] It had been Kant again, not Reinhold, who had first thought that this task of systematization could be accomplished in short order, and *once and for all*. This expectation is actually Cartesian in origin, for once the assumption has been made that the object of philosophy is the 'facts of consciousness', and that these facts are the property of everyone, it follows that an "inventory of all our possessions through *pure* reason"(the phrase is Kant's)[26] can be easily carried out provided that the proper principle is made available. Reinhold thought that Kant had failed to deliver this principle, and he was only trying now to succeed where his master had failed. Yet, even at this point he was already parting company with Kant. For it is true, as Reinhold had been perceptive enough to recognize, that Kant's principal concern had always been with the objects of consciousness. He had been able to dodge the kinds of problems that the relation of understanding to sensibility entailed precisely because, in spite of all his talk about consciousness and its conditions, he had restricted himself for the most part to the analysis of the concept of experience in general presupposed by our physico-mathematical sciences. He had never given a phenomenological description of consciousness that could have provided an existential basis for that concept. This description is what Reinhold now wanted to provide. The problem, however, was that the description did not have to lead necessarily to the kind of system that Kant had had in mind. What happened, as we shall see, is that in altering the method of the *Critique*, Reinhold ended up undermining its very idea.

(b) The Theory of the Faculty of Representation

Parts II and III of *Essay towards a New Theory of the Human Faculty of Representation* contain the only complete exposition of the Philosophy of the Elements that Reinhold ever provided. Parts II and III were re-stated in an abbreviated and somewhat modified form in a later essay.[27] Part II develops the General Theory of Representation. Part III contains the special Theory of Cognition instead; this is undoubtedly the most interesting part of Reinhold's work, because it is here that he diverged most radically from Kant, and where he made his significant contribution to the later idealistic theory of consciousness. The whole Theory unfolds in 138 propositions, as if *more geometrico*. It is clear, however, that this formal supra-structure does not in any way affect the content of the Theory, which consists rather in a description of the principal components and properties of consciousness as seen by Reinhold. In spite of its claims to perfect self-evidence, the Theory never really convinced anyone—presumably not even its author, who ended up by repudiating it.[28]

In Reinhold's opinion, the most important result of the General Theory of Representation was that it established what Kant had simply asserted without ever proving, viz., that although the 'thing-in-itself' (or for that matter, the 'self-in-itself') necessarily exists, it cannot be known, and that our knowledge is therefore restricted only to appearances. The Theory begins with the claim that "representation is distinguished in consciousness by the subject from both subject and object, and is referred to both."[29] This is Reinhold's notorious 'principle of consciousness', which he takes to express an obvious and indubitable fact of all consciousness. The terms 'subject' and 'object', as they enter in the statement of the principle, are to derive their meaning from the principle itself. By 'object' we mean, at first, anything that can be made present to the subject in representation; by 'subject', *where* the representation occurs. These are only very general definitions, but Reinhold quickly moves to narrow them down by introducing two distinctions. The first is between those conditions of representation that are required in order for an object to be at all present in consciousness, and those that apply only to the representation of some particular object.[30] Reinhold's Theory will be exclusively concerned with the first set of conditions; the second set is the object of metaphysics. The second distinction is between those conditions that pertain to representation as its constituent elements, and those that pertain to it only because they belong to its process of coming to be.[31] Now, since Reinhold's Theory must restrict itself to what is immediately evident, it has no choice but to abstract completely from this second set of conditions. They occur *before* consciousness proper comes to be, and hence are not open to direct inspection. And since 'subject' and 'object', understood in the special sense of the 'self' and the 'thing' 'in-itself' respectively, belong to this second set of conditions, the Theory will have to abstract from them too. What we are left with is simply 'subject' and 'object' inasmuch as they are present, in a form yet to be specified, in representation itself.

This first abstraction from anything external to consciousness is only programmatic in character. The next step will be to show that the abstraction is a necessary condition of *all* human cognition, even though— paradoxically enough—that there *is* an 'in-itself' apart from consciousness is a truth that resists every attempt at reduction. Reinhold sets in motion this line of considerations by introducing still another distinction. He now distinguishes (rather laconically, considering how much depends upon it) between the 'material' of representation and its 'form'. By the 'material' (*Stoff*) he means that component of representation that makes it 'something given'.[32] It entails an element of receptivity on the part of the subject in which the representation is found; and for this same reason it also necessitates a reference to a term external to consciousness. The idea of this 'in-itself', which is presumably responsible for the material of representation, only arises in the act through which the material is being referred to it. It does not contain anything over and above what this referring puts into it. On the other hand, without it the material could never be transformed into 'representation' proper. And to say this is already to have introduced the concept of 'form'.[33] For the material of representation consists of a manifold which is brought to a unity precisely in the process of being referred to its transcendent object. And this unification is done according to conditions set by the subject itself, i.e., according to a 'form' which is the product of the subject, and which entails the presence in the latter of an element of 'spontaneity', just as the 'material' entails the presence in it of an element of 'receptivity' instead. Because of its informing function, the subject can refer the representation back to itself as its product. On the other hand, because of the material present in its representation, it can also distinguish the representation from itself. But again, because of its own informing presence to it, it equally distinguishes it from the transcendent object—something that it could not do on the basis of receptivity alone. Thus the subject can refer the representation to itself and to the object, yet distinguish it from both at the same time.

This is then Reinhold's first major conclusion: the 'in-itself' whether we mean by it the 'self' or the 'thing', *must* be posited.[34] Reinhold has actually said nothing that Kant had not already made clear, though Reinhold now repeats it in a language fraught with useless and often dubious distinctions. The basic point is that the 'in-itself' is required in order to maintain *within* consciousness the distinction between consciousness itself, and what consciousness is about, without which the process of referring and distinguishing required by representation is not possible. Though an empty concept, it plays a crucial role in the theory of consciousness all the same.

Nor does Reinhold really improve on Kant with his other proof, by which he tries to establish that this same 'in-itself' can never be known by us—though in this case the clumsiness of his argument has at least the merit of making all the more obvious the ambiguity that was inherent in Kant's notion of 'appearance', and the disastrous effects that it had for the critical theory of knowledge. The core of Reinhold's argument is brief enough.[35] Since form and matter are both required for the representation of anything, and whatever cannot be represented cannot be known, anything for which a corresponding matter cannot be found, or to which we cannot apply the form of representation, cannot be known. But the object, *qua* 'thing-in-itself', is not susceptible to the form of representation. (It is precisely the term external to it). Nor can a material be had for the subject *qua* self 'in-itself', for the subject is present in representation only as a source of spontaneous activity. It follows that neither the object nor the subject, can be known 'in-itself'.

This is a most peculiar argument, for it draws from its premises a conclusion which is the direct opposite of the one that we should have expected. It is granted *ex hypothesi* that the object 'in-itself' is not a representation; nor is the subject 'in-itself' the product of its own spontaneity. On the other hand, it is also granted *ex hypothesi* that we have in sensation a material which corresponds to the object 'in-itself', and to which the subject imparts the form of representation by referring it to its transcendent object. But since knowledge occurs by means of representation, it follows on these assumptions that we *do* have knowledge of the object 'in-itself' — though restricted to the limits allowed by the material available in sensation. And the same applies for the self 'in-itself'. This is an obvious conclusion to be drawn, and if Reinhold did not see it, it is because he was still operating, even more so than Kant had, on the empiricist assumptions concerning the nature of sensations. Reinhold wants to hold both (1) that sensations are private events, as the empiricists did, and (2) that they constitute our most primitive representations of a transcendent object, without realizing that to the extent that he asserts (1), he must also deny (2). What his position really amounts to is that sensations are our first *objects* of representation (even though he still calls them 'representations'). On this assumption, however, the same difficulty arises referring to sensations the representations that *we* have of them as arises referring the sensations to the presumed object 'in-itself'. The same problem recurs, though in a different form, that had arisen in Kant relating understanding to sensation.

Reinhold actually suggested a possible way out of this difficulty, but he did so only unwittingly, in his Theory of Cognition, and at the price of breaking away from Kant altogether. This last part of his general Theory only comes after the concept of 'faculty' has been unfolded in all its details, and the model of the mind presupposed by critical philosophy has been re-introduced in its entirety around it. The immediate preparation for it is a reflection upon the conditions that make consciousness 'clear and distinct'; they provide the basis for the transition from the general Theory of Representation to the particular Theory of Cognition. As we must now see, Reinhold begins to make his break from Kant precisely as he lays them down.

Although consciousness cannot be identified with representation, there is according to Reinhold no consciousness without representation, nor any representation without consciousness.[36] Now, we must distinguish between 'pure' and 'empirical' representations. Empirical representations are those that derive their material, not from consciousness itself, but from some presumed source external to it. Pure representations, on the other hand, have as their object the process of representation itself; in their case, therefore, the required material is derived *a priori* through a simple reflection upon consciousness. A perfect example of 'pure representation' is Reinhold's own representation of 'representation in general'. Its object is all the representations that can ever be found in consciousness; its material, or the part in it that corresponds to this object, is the concepts 'form' and 'material'; and its form is the presentation of these two concepts precisely as the components, not of some particular representation or other, but of the principle that defines what any representation is. Nothing is added to consciousness by this representation except a heightened awareness of itself *qua* consciousness. Consciousness is said to be clear precisely to the extent that, to any representation (pure or empirical) that it has of an object, it adds a second (pure) representation that reflectively represents the first as the representation of that object. And it is said to be *distinct* to the extent that it adds still a third representation which reflectively represents the first as the product of the representing subject. In short, the clear and distinct consciousness of an object is a consciousness self-consciously aware of the fact that it is a subjective representation of that object.

The stage is thus set for the Theory of Cognition. For all that is needed for cognition proper to occur is a further reflective modification of consciousness that leads to the representation of its object as something distinct from representations; in cognition the object of consciousness is represented (or *determined*, as Reinhold puts it) precisely as object. There are three basic ways, however, in which this can occur, viz., by representing the object (1) as 'thing-in-itself', i.e., as the ultimate term of reference that can only be represented under the determination of 'not being known'; (2) as the *immediate* term of reference of an intuition, i.e., inasmuch as the manifold of sensation given in consciousness through the presumed affection of the 'thing-in-itself' is referred to an object in general, without the latter being in any way represented or in any way specified; (3) as the point of reference that objectively determines the unity of consciousness without transcending its limits, i.e., as a term of reference that transcends any single representation that the subject has of its object, yet still falls within consciousness. In cognition we begin with the indeterminate object of intuition (2); and we represent it to ourselves as the possible unified appearance *in* consciousness (3) of the 'thing-in-itself' (1). We thus obtain our first concept of an object of experience; and we proceed to add content to it by abstracting one by one the components of the manifold given in intuition, and by reflectively representing them as the determinations of that object. In this process of attribution, our 'empirical concepts' are generated. The process is controlled from its very beginning, however, by the 'pure concepts' of the understanding (i.e., the categories) that reflectively define our concept of an object in general. Thus cognition is the process by which, given an original intuitive 'representation', we reflectively represent it to ourselves once more, first by identifying its material components and explicitly attributing them to it (this is what the sciences of nature do); and then by identifying the conditions that make it a representation in the first place, and by explicitly attributing them to it (this is the task of philosophy). In a word, cognition is the process of explication and clarification of the content of consciousness.

Here we have it stated in simplified form, Reinhold's move away from Kant. For Reinhold has in effect reduced objective consciousness to a reflective modification of self-consciousness—a move that Kant himself had always avoided. Reinhold has relativized the distinction between the form and content of experience, between its a priori and a posteriori elements, which for Kant was absolute. On Reinhold's definition of pure and empirical concepts, the difference that separates the two is simply a difference in the degree of clarity and distinctness that each enjoys. There is no representation, whether pure or otherwise, that does not include both a form and a material. And if for some representations, viz., those that are 'pure' in a special sense, the material is said to be derived a priori, this is so only because in their case the fact that it consists only in a modification of consciousness has been made explicit. But sensations are modifications of consciousness just as well, even though in their case this fact is only obscurely apprehended. In either case, whether the representation is 'pure' or not, cognition still implies only an awareness on the part of consciousness of its own content qua consciousness.

There is of course no problem of a transition from thought to sensation on this model of consciousness, for there is nothing contained in one level of consciousness (according to it) that is not contained in all the others. Nor is there any room left for the 'thing-in-itself', even though Reinhold thought to have finally proved its existence. For the only significant difference with respect to consciousness that the model still allows is the difference between a consciousness that is explicitly aware of itself, and a consciousness that is not. The only problem left is where to draw the line of demarcation between the two, and how. The centre of philosophical interest has been shifted away from the relation between consciousness and the 'thing-in-itself', where Kant had still left it, to the relation between the explicit and the implicit, between consciousness and the 'unconscious'. And it is here that it will remain throughout the evolution of post-Kantian idealism. Reinhold's contribution to the shift is that he provided the model of consciousness required by it. But as we have just seen, the price that he had to pay for it was that he had to abandon the very distinction between thought and sensation on which the master's theory of cognition depended. Reinhold had in effect made his way back to Leibniz—just as Solomon Maimon had already done (but deliberately in his case) in his *Essay in Transcendental Philosophy*.

(c) After Reinhold

Reinhold never noticed what was really original in his Theory of Cognition. Of course we cannot blame him for not seeing what was in store in the future. But he should have recognized at least that, whatever his Theory accomplished, it certainly did not ground anything that Kant had done. There simply was no continuity between his project and Kant's. He once complained against Kant for not having adequately defined the concept of consciousness, and for having restricted its 'transcendental unity ' to the level of conceptualization alone—as if the *ego* which is the principle of that unity were not present at all levels of consciousness, including that of sensation.[37] An objection of this sort makes sense only on the assumption that the *ego* is a center of real life—a monad in Leibniz's sense. And Reinhold should have known that this is not what Kant had meant by it. He should have known that Kant's only aim had been the examination of the *formal* conditions of experience, and that to this end the only *ego* that he needed (indeed, the only *ego* that was possible) was a formal principle of thought. If Reinhold found this *ego* insufficient, it is because he, unlike Kant, was interested in consciousness itself. He was not really grounding Kant's system but doing something completely different.

As far as our story is concerned, the important point is that Fichte, while meditating on the philosophy of the Elements, saw what its author had missed.[38] He saw that the problem after Reinhold was to discover a method that would allow us to do indeed the kind of concrete description of consciousness that Reinhold had attempted, but with the conceptual rigor that Reinhold had only postured without ever really achieving. To the empiricists' objection that his principle of consciousness did not demand assent, because it only reported a supposed fact, Reinhold had replied that *his* fact of consciousness had special intuitive power; to state it was the same as to give assent to it.[39] Coming from Reinhold, the reply relied on the empiricist assumption that consciousness is, so to speak, an inspection of given facts. Fichte saw it, on the other hand, as a statement of the problem that idealism was to resolve. Is there a fact so constituted that to express it, is the same as to grant that it exists? What would this fact be like? By answering these questions, Fichte thought that he would complete the model of consciousness that Reinhold had initiated; he would thus uncover precisely the point in consciousness where intuition and reflection, the unconscious and the conscious, meet.

3. The Skeptical Attack

Before turning to Fichte, however, we must consider another event that occurred right after Reinhold's last major statement of the Philosophy of the Elements. It too had its influence on the shaping of the new idealism. The event was the anonymous publication in 1792 of a book that represented the reaction of established skepticism against the recent popularity of Kant. The book proved to be so successful that for a time at least it seemed to turn the tide of public opinion against critical philosophy once more, in favour of skepticism.

The book, whose author was Gottlob Ernst Schulze (1761-1833),[40] purported to be the record of a correspondence between two characters, one of whom (named after the classical skeptic Aenesidemus) is trying to dissuade the other (Hermias) from his recently found faith in critical philosophy. The correspondence includes five letters all together. Aenesidemus' major attack against Kant and Reinhold comes in a treatise that is appended to the third letter. In the second letter, as a preparation for the attack to come, Aenesidemus reminds Hermias of what the tenets of skepticism truly are.[41] As he tells him, the skeptics have never denied that we might be able in the future to obtain knowledge of the 'things-in-themselves', or for that matter, that perhaps we already possess it. Nor have they ever denied that in the future we might succeed in establishing the true limits of human knowledge, or that perhaps we have already done so in the past. Or again, they have never denied that nature might have equipped us with *non-scientific* means sufficient to attain certainty about these matters, and about any other matter that affects our existential welfare. The skeptics' only claim has always been that at the present moment, and without prejudice to what might happen in the future, *science* cannot say anything definitive about the 'things-in-themselves' and about the limits of human cognition. According to Aenesidemus, the claim still holds true for the present day; there is nothing that either Kant or Reinhold have done to affect its validity. This is what he will try to demonstrate. And to show the falsity of the belief that the skeptics are not qualified to enter into any debate, because they are said not to grant principles and hence not to be able to abide by binding conclusions, Aenesidemus states in the letter that accompanies his treatise (the third in the series) the two principles which he takes as fundamental, and which he expects to be judged by.[42] They are: (1) There are representations in us that have certain characteristics in common, yet differ from each other in many other ways; (2) logic is the criterion of truth; any reasoning about matters of fact can lay claim to validity only to the extent that it conforms to its rule. Finally, Aenesidemus denies that Reinhold's position is the same as Kant's, and although his attention will be mostly directed to Reinhold's Theory, he will also deal with Kant on his own.[43]

Aenesidemus begins by conceding that Reinhold is right in thinking that the only adequate foundation of science is a theory of representation.[44] It is precisely a theory of this sort that Locke and Hume tried to develop in their essays. This is as far as Aenesidemus is willing to go the way of Reinhold, however. In his opinion, Reinhold's theory has gone wrong in its very foundation. It is not true, for instance, that the 'principle of consciousness' expresses the most fundamental fact of consciousness.[45] The principle includes such complex concepts as 'distinguishing' and 'referring' which obviously presuppose, in order to have any meaning for us, our previous consciousness of much simpler facts. One cannot distinguish a representation from the subject and the object, yet refer it to both, as the principle stipulates, without already being conscious of the said object and subject. And one could not be already conscious of them by means of a representation understood as defined by Reinhold's principle, for the need to presuppose the consciousness of them in order to represent them would simply re-assert itself. According to Aenesidemus, Reinhold's principle only applies to one segment of representations, namely, to 'thoughts'. But it does not apply to 'intuitions', which are a form of consciousness that does not imply (again, according to Aenesidemus) any distinction between subject and representation at all. At any rate, Reinhold has used 'subject', 'object', 'distinguishing' and 'referring', without first defining their meaning, even though they happen to be some of the most difficult concepts in philosophy. This is hardly the proper way to proceed when one is laying down a principle that should command universal assent. And even if the principle were self-evident, as Reinhold claims, still it would be subject to the law of contradiction; it would not be in other words, the *first* of philosophy.

Reinhold's introduction of the concept of 'faculty' provides Aenesidemus with the occasion for turning his attention to Kant, for the assumption of faculties as conditions of experience is what he takes to be the point that Reinhold and Kant have in common, and also the point where they differ most from Hume.[46] Kant's critical philosophy and the Philosophy of the Elements of Reinhold differ because each begins from a different supposed fact. For Reinhold this fact is representation; for Kant, it is the presence in experience of synthetic *a priori* judgements ("synthetic necessary judgments," as Aenesideumus prefers to call them, since he challenges the whole idea of 'a priority'). Now, although these two facts do not amount to the same thing, they both lead to the same assumption of a subject 'in-itself', which supposedly lies behind experience, and is equipped with the appropriate faculties that make Reinhold's 'representations' possible on the one hand, and Kant's 'judgements' on the other. This assumption leads them both to absurd consequences. Either the assumed subject is something that exists really (as both Kant and Reinhold often seem to say) or it is a mere idea. In the first case, Kant and Reinhold would be inferring from a presumed effect — viz., the 'synthetic necessary judgements' in one case, and the 'representations' in the other — its supposed cause, using as the basis for the inference an assumed cause-effect relationship between the two. But the inferred cause, i.e., the 'self-in-itself', is nowhere to be found in experience. Hence Kant and Reinhold would be contravening the central critical tenet that thought-categories cannot be used to establish the existence of objects that are not given in experience. In the second case, even if we granted that the idea of a 'self-in-itself' would hypothetically explain the supposed facts in question, since Kant and Reinhold have both sharply distinguished between 'logical' and 'real' truth, we would still be lacking an adequate existential foundation for a science of experience. Finally, in either case, whether we take the causal inference to have real or merely logical significance, we would still be acting on the assumption that there *are* in experience judgements of the kind that Kant requires, or representations as defined by Reinhold. But this is precisely the assumption that Hume refused to accept. And since the arguments that either Kant or Reinhold offers on its behalf have no intrinsic validity, it follows that their alleged refutation of skepticism is only a case of *petitio principii*. Here is where the ultimate difference between Kant and Reinhold on the one hand, and Hume on the other, lies. They simply take for granted precisely what Hume doubted.

This is in essence Aenesidemus' defence of Skepticism. The list of detailed objections against Reinhold, however, (and occasionally against Kant as well) is by no means exhausted. For instance, Reinhold has distinguished between the material and form of representation, and has attributed the material to the 'thing-in-itself', and the form to the mind.[47] Aenesidemus points out that, on the contrary, there is no reason why the order should not be reversed, why the subject should not be the cause of the material, and the 'thing' of the form. And there is still a third possibility open.[48] The *whole* representation could be related to *both* subject and object, but to each in a different way: to the subject, as to a substratum in which it inheres as property; to the object, as to a 'thing' which it signifies as sign. Self-consciousness, for instance, is clearly a case in which, since subject and object are *ex hypothesi* the same, there is nothing in the representation that cannot be attributed with equal right to both. This is an important case for Aenesidemus because he obviously regards self-consciousness to be the basic form of consciousness. He also assumes that this is a thesis that he shares with critical philosophy. And since Reinhold's theory of representation implies the directly opposite view, namely, that self-consciousness is only a particular case of consciousness, it follows that Reinhold is once more contravening the very principles on which critical philosophy supposedly rests.

Aenesidemus also objects to Reinhold's handling of the 'thing-in-itself'. On this issue he feels that skepticism is clearly on the side of common sense. For skepticism does not deny (any more than common sense does) either that it is possible in principle to acquire knowledge of that 'thing', or that in some particular instances this knowledge has already been realized. Its contention is that science is still unable, in its present stage of development, either to define the limits of that possibility, or to determine the extent to which it may, already have been realized. It also claims that it can explain how common sense comes by its certainty about things 'in-themselves' without thereby having to grant that they really exist. This is a point to which Aenesidemus likes to revert over and over again, obviously because he feels that it is a particularly strong one. It is directed to both Kant and Reinhold. In Aenesidemus' opinion, by categorically denying knowledge of the 'thing-in-itself', they have both landed themselves in a paradoxical situation. For we cannot even raise the question whether we can cognize things outside us or not, without presupposing that they exist, i.e., without implying some knowledge of them.[49] The critical position regarding the nature of truth is riddled with inconsistencies. On the one hand, some friends of critical philosophy hold that truth is exclusively a matter of lawfulness.[50] On this assumption, the whole issue of the conformity between 'things' and the mind is abstracted from, and all the objections of skepticism against critical philosophy would lose their meaning. But Aenesidemus claims that it is impossible to resist our natural inclination to assume that truth requires some reference to an outside world; without this reference, our objects would be only an illusion. On the other hand, critical philosophy deliberately stresses the difference between 'illusion' and 'appearance', and claims that the objects of experience are 'appearances' (not merely 'illusion') because their content derives from the outside world. But how can it make this claim, yet also hold that the category of causality cannot be applied to the 'things-in-themselves'—hence, also to the relation that they bear to our senses. It seems that critical philosophy is simply assuming what it pretends to demonstrate, viz., that what we experience is genuine 'appearance'.[51]

Another objection of Aenesidemus is that it is not necessary to assume that the necessity of any of our judgements must derive from its supposed *a priori* forms. It can in every case be based on perception just as well. For instance, the fact that I see a tree at a given place in space, and at a certain moment in time, is just as irrevocable once the seeing has taken place as any supposed *a priori* truth.[52] And the same necessity applies to everything that occurs in consciousness once it has occurred. This factual necessity is the only kind of necessity which is obviously available to us.

The list of objections continues. The basic point, however, has already been made. It is one that we should have expected from the two principles which Aenesidemus put at the very head of his treatise. Truth is to be obtained either through the direct inspection of the content of immediate perceptions, or by reflection upon the results of that inspection. In one case it has real significance, but it remains tied down to some particular event of consciousness; its necessity is the irrational necessity of a brute fact. In the other case, it enjoys indeed universality, but at the price of being merely formal, i.e., of not adding anything new to what we already know. This disjunction is absolute. And the weapon that Aenesidemus uses in order to impose it upon Kant and Reinhold is the Humean assumption, which *he* takes as an obvious and fundamental fact of consciousness, that consciousness is in essence always a 'consciousness about consciousness'; or, as Aenesidemus says in one place, that "every consciousness contains only a fact which is present simply *in us*."[53] Or again, that the only distinction in intuition is between the subject and its representation.[54] On this assumption it follows of course that 'representation' (if we still want to retain the term) is essentially an undifferentiated sensible intuition which is just as necessary as it is irrational. One can try to construct a whole network of relations upon its content through the use of such concepts as 'thing', 'faculty', etc. But since these relations do not affect the content intrinsically, but are only superimposed upon it, it follows that the concepts expressing them have no real truth.

A worse misunderstanding could not have been possible. Aenesidemus had completely missed the point which—other shortcomings apart—made Kant's and Reinhold's position revolutionary. Both had assumed the 'thing-in-itself' because it is needed to retain the intentional distance between representation and object; if this distance is allowed to collapse, the other distance between subject and representation, which is the only one that was evident to Aenesidemus, collapses too. That *both* distances are required for consciousness is for critical philosophy its fundamental fact. And it is one to which Aenesidemus was completely blind. To be sure, Kant and Reinhold had done a lot to hide it from him. But Aenesidemus was so caught up in the prejudices of empiricism that he was not even giving the new philosophy a chance. The instant success that Schulze's book achieved among the learned public was indeed a telling sign of how shallow the popularity that Kant had recently won through the efforts of Reinhold really was.

Kant's and Reinhold's reaction to the book was strangely muted. The silence on the part of Kant could be easily explained by his desire not to embroil himself in another controversy, as he had recently done by responding publicly to Eberhard.[55] He was aware of the book, however, and made known what he thought about it in a letter to Beck, dated December 4, 1792. "Under the assumed name of Aenesidemus," he says, "an even wider skepticism has been advanced, viz., that we cannot know at all whether our representations correspond to anything else (as object), which is as much as to say: whether a representation is a representation (stands for anything). For 'representation' means a determination in us that we relate to something else (whose place the representation takes in us). . . ."[56] Kant's reply was just as brief as it was to the point.

Reinhold's silence is more difficult to explain. The reply finally came in an essay that he prefaced to Tennemann's new translation into German of Hume's *Enquiry Concerning Human Understanding*[57] and which he reproduced, under a new title but otherwise unchanged, in the *Contributions* of 1794.[58] Its tone was quite different from Kant's. Reinhold's aim in the essay is to distinguish between genuine and self-contradictory skepticism. Genuine skepticism presupposes both a well defined notion of truth in general, and some specific actual cognition, on the basis of which it is possible to deny some other kind of cognition *in specific terms*. Genuine skepticism, in other words, does not limit itself to a sterile suspension of belief in general. After Reinhold has made this point, and after he has specified what he means by truth, he proceeds to his key statement: "The *truth* of his [i.e., the true skeptic's] foundation. . . . consists in the agreement of the logically correct concepts of the actual facts of consciousness, manifested to him through feelings [*Gefühle*], and these facts themselves."[59] The implications of this passage are clear. It marks Reinhold's point of retreat into sheer subjectivity. For Reinhold is now parading as the only true skeptic, because he—unlike Hume and Aenesidemus—has defined the area within which alone truth is possible; hence he can consistently deny the knowledge of 'things-in-themselves'. And that area is to be found within the subject itself.

Reinhold establishes it precisely by the distinction between the 'immediately felt facts' of consciousness, and the 'representations' of these facts, which allows him to abide by the general notion of truth as an agreement between 'representation' and its 'object', without thereby having to transcend the subject. The agreement is to be *realized* within it. The same intentional structure of consciousness, in other words, to which Kant had appealed in order to avoid Cartesian subjectivism is now being used by Reinhold to make that very subjectivism consistent with itself.

Aenesidemus had obviously left his mark. This turn to subjectivity should not come to us as a surprise, however. For as we have seen, Reinhold had already whittled away any essential difference between consciousness and self-consciousness, and his interest had been from the start in the subject as a real principle of mental life. Aenesidemus' push was all that was needed to resolve in favour of subjectivism whatever ambiguity there still was in his mind. "The *source* [of the Philosophy of the Elements]," he says in an article published in the second volume of *Contributions*, but written just before the appearance of Fichte's review of Aenesidemus, "*is inner experience insofar as the latter is independent of the outer*, insofar as it consists of the *facts of pure self-consciousness*."[60] Although Kantian echoes can still be heard in this passage, there is no doubt as to its real significance. It represents Reinhold's attempt to erase whatever realistic traces were still to be found in the Philosophy of the Elements, so as to display it again as the only genuine philosophy of subjectivity.

Fichte wrote his review of *Aenesidemus* at the same time as he was reflecting on Reinhold's philosophy. Aenesidemus' insistence that consciousness is fundamentally consciousness of itself obviously struck a receptive chord in him. Reinhold, for his part, presented him with a model of the mind which made direct consciousness a variation of reflective consciousness. To these two elements he added a distinctive idea of his own which, in some respects, put him closer to Kant than Reinhold ever was. And thus the new idealism was born. We must now see just what Fichte's innovation was. But before leaving Aenesidemus, two more passages from his treatise must be noted, because of the way they point to the future. In the first passage, which comes at the end of the treatise, Aenesidemus is arguing that if we were to take critical philosophy seriously, we would commit ourselves to resolving experiences into two parts — a system of universal forms on the one side, and a mass of amorphous, meaningless matter on the other. What would be missed in the process is the richness and originality of the individual objects that actually constitute experience. Aenesidemus proposes, therefore, that we call critical philosophy "formalism"; it is the epithet that best captures its spirit.[61] The second passage is found in the fifth letter, where Aenesidemus is refuting the point often made in defence of critical philosophy, that it promotes the interests of religion and morality better then any other philosophy. Kant's moral proofs of the immortality of the soul and of God's existence appear to him, on the contrary, only as variations on the traditional ones. They are instances once more of the fallacy of drawing existential conclusions from logical premises. And Aenesidemus finally asks: Even supposing that Kant had succeeded in establishing the *fact* − not just the idea−of moral obligation, how could we be sure that the alleged obligation is truly the product of freedom, and not of some irrational force of nature?[62]

Now, whether or not Fichte took the first passage seriously, it actually turned out to be a programmatic statement of his idealism. As for the second, Fichte could not have paid enough attention to it. It turned out to be an announcement, made even before its birth, of how the new idealism was to meet its end.

4. Idealistic Overtures

It fell upon Fichte to turn the tide of philosophical opinion once more against skepticism. The announcement of his new idealism came− only fittingly as it appears in retrospect−in a review of *Aenesidemus* that he published in 1794 in the *Allgemeine Literatur-Zeitung.*[63] To his readers of the time the review must have appeared indeed cryptic. It hinted at a new philosphical principle, and at a new philosophical method, without actually spelling out their nature. Fichte was to do the spelling out only in the *Science of Knowledge* which he published soon after−at first *seriatim*, in preparation for the lectures that he would have to give as the successor to Reinhold's chair of Kantian philosophy at Jena.[64] For us, however, who can read the review with the knowledge of his later work, it is clear that his early pronouncements already contained in principle the whole programme of his new Science.

The review was a *tour de force*. It granted everything to Aenesidemus as well as to Reinhold and Kant, but at the price of denying to each the ground on which he stood. And it did so in the form of a virulent attack on skepticism in general, and on Aenesidemus's in particular. To Reinhold, Fichte grants that the principle of contradiction is only the highest *formal* principle of philosophy, and that as such it presupposes another principle that has *real* significance.[65] To Aenesidemus, on the other hand, he grants that the terms in Reinhold's principle of consciousness are poorly defined; the ambiguity inherent in their meaning is itself an indication that the principle cannot be the highest principle of philosophy.[66] Again, Fichte grants to Reinhold, *contra* Aenesidemus, that the principle of consciousness does not depend for its definition of 'representation' on any abstraction from more particular kinds of representation such as 'intuition', 'concepts', and 'ideas'.[67] On the other hand, he grants to Aenesidemus, *contra* Reinhold, that the principle still depends on some sort of abstraction, for it is derived from a reflection upon the activity of representing which is an empirical fact of consciousness.[68] It follows that Reinhold's principle of consciousness is indeed a *first* principle, but only in a relative sense. i.e., only with respect to the sphere of *empirical consciousness*; and this is the only sphere that Aenesidemus has in mind.[69] It also follows that Reinhold is right in holding that the process of 'distinguishing and referring' that gives rise to 'representing' applies also to 'intuition' (something that Aenesidemus denies) — provided, however, that the 'object' being referred to in this case transcends the limits of empirical consciousness, and that the two activities in question are understood in a very special sense. The object must be identical with these very activities — understood, however, as acts that give rise to consciousness *originally*, and which we become aware of precisely *because* we perform them. Understood in this sense, the acts are not part of any given content of consciousness. And the intuitive awareness that we have of them is nothing at all like 'empirical perception'.[70] Now, as Fichte has just said, Reinhold's principle of consciousness is indeed the first valid principle of the science of the basic facts of consciousness. But it cannot be the principle of the science that tries to establish their possiblity by grounding them on the very operations that give rise to them in the first place. This science must rely on a first principle that is intuitively established in the sense just described. Fichte hints at the possibility that this principle might be the traditional principle of identity, re-stated in such a way as to include an extra dimension of existential significance.[71] He also suggests at the very beginning that this significance is what Aenesidemus had in mind when he declares that the principle of contradiction is the highest in philosophy — a disingenuous suggestion, of course, for Aenesidemus obviously had nothing of the sort in mind.[72] In any event, the question whether Reinhold's principle is analytic (as Reinhold himself claims) or synthetic (as Aenesidemus contends) is to Fichte entirely irrelevant. The significant point is that the act of 'representing' which it expresses has a synthetic function, for it 'differentiates' and it 'connects' at the same time, and that its synthesis could not be possible without previous positing and counterpositing of the terms that have to be synthesized.[73] These 'positing' and 'counterpositing' (so Fichte seems to imply) are the fundamental acts that give rise to consciousness, and make possible the acts of 'distinguishing' and referring in the first place.

Thus Fichte has introduced the two distinctions that will be all-important in his subsequent system, viz., the distinction between *fact* understood as content of consciousness (i.e., as *Tatsache*) and as conscious act (i.e., as *Tathandlung*)[74]; and the parallel distinction between consciousness as the perception of an object, and as the purely subjective awareness that accompanies this perception. We can obtain a few more clues as to the meaning of these distinctions from what Fichte has to say in defence of Kant. Here too, just as he had done for Reinhold, in turning the table against Aenesidemus, Fichte ends up turning it against Kant as well. The defence is based on the assumption that by the 'thing-in-itself' Kant could not have meant anything external to consciousness. Fichte even castigates Aenesidemus for thinking that Kant had had any such idea in mind. In this Aenesidemus had given himself away. He had shown that skepticism is only a form of dogmatism, for like all dogmatism, it is caused by the inability to function without introducing the 'thing-in-itself'—even though it is not being called for, and its very idea is a contradiction in terms.[75] Critical philosophy, on the other hand, is based on the insight that consciousness is necessarily and exclusively 'consciousness *for itself*'. (In fact, this was not Kant's position at all; if anything, it was closer to Aenesidemus'). Consciousness constitutes a circle whose limits we cannot transcend, not just because *we* are unable to reach outside them, but because there is nothing outside them to be reached.[76] This is not to say that one can no longer speak of 'being', of something 'other' than the subject, or a 'non-*ego*'—of Kant's 'thing-in-itself', in other words. But this 'thing' must be understood as included within the circle itself, as a moment of its constant return upon itself. Its being consists precisely in 'being represented'. But if 'being' is thus reduced to a moment of consciousness, it also follows that there is no distinction, strictly speaking, between logical and real truth; the laws of thought are also the laws of being.[77] And Fichte goes on to fault Aenesidemus for thinking that Kant could have ever held that distinction, any more than he could have believed in a 'thing-in-itself'—though Fichte concedes in this regard that Kant was partly responsible for Aenesidemus' misunderstanding, for he had not derived 'space' and 'time' from the *ego*, as he had done for the categories.[78] But this omission was only part of his intention only to prepare for the final science without actually producing it.

Here we have it, in the very passage in which Fichte is supposedly upholding Kant's cause against Aenesidemus, the step from critical to speculative idealism. Fichte has turned against itself Kant's great insight that consciousness is, even *qua* consciousness, already an objective world. He is now using it, not as a means for keeping consciousness open at least in principle to a transcendent being, but in order to enclose it strictly upon itself. Consciousness is now a world unto itself — a divine monad, so to speak. And Fichte's task will be to show that all the distinctions previously based on the assumption of a transcendent 'thing' can be re-introduced within it on its own terms. We get one final clue as to how this task is to be realized from Fichte's parting shot against Aenesidemus. We remember that Aenesidemus had claimed that Kant's arguments for the immortality of the soul and the existence of God were only versions of the old dogmatic proofs. Fichte's reply is that Aenesidemus has failed to notice that Kant has reversed the traditional order between theoretical and practical reason in favour of practical reason. Moral obligation is for Kant a fundamental fact which does not need theoretical justification. On the contrary, the subjective evidence that it provides, and on which moral faith in God and immortality rests, is the only unimpeachable evidence that is possible on Kant's premises.[79] For once, Fichte's statement of the critical position is correct. The gloss that he goes on to add, however, is unmistakably his own. The *ego* is, *because* it is, i.e., it is an absolutely self-positing act; but since this act would not be conscious of itself without objectification, the *ego* must assume its being as if it were given to it ready-made by nature. A conflict is thereby generated between the two fundamental conditions of the existence of the *ego*, namely the requirement for autonomy on the one hand, and the *de facto* restrictions imposed upon the attempt of the *ego* to satisfy this requirement on the other. And since this conflict would end up paralyzing the *ego*, the latter commits itself to the belief that all the means required for its resolution are *in fact* available. In this way moral faith is born. Freedom, or more precisely, the *ego's* act of absolute self-positing, is the fundamental operation of which we are intuitively aware in consciousness; we only become reflectively conscious of it, however, through 'representation', or through other more specialized conceptual means such as the 'categories', or the idea of the 'thing-in-itself'.[80]

Fichte called his new philosophy *Wissenschaftslehre*, or the *Science of Knowledge*. He worked on it until the end of his life, providing in sketch form several versions of it. His first formulation was the only one, however, that came at least close to a complete system; and also the only one that was available to the public at large in his time. In some ways the system resembled Reinhold's Theory. It was an account of the structure of consciousness that leads, at least in its theoretical part, to the deduction of the 'representation' from which Reinhold's Theory begins. As in Reinhold's Theory, the more reflective forms of consciousness are presented on a continuous line with the more immediate ones; each level is obtained through a reflection upon the previous one that objectifies it along with its requirements. Hence the distinction between reflective and intuitive consciousness is removed—in principle at least, if not necessarily in fact.

The resemblance ends here, however; and the difference turns out to be much more radical. Reinhold's Theory begins with the intuitive apprehension of a supposed fact of consciousness, or, in the revised formula that Reinhold gave in response to Aenesidemus, with the reflective representation of something immediately felt. Based on this original apprehension, the Theory proceeds to a systematic inventory of all the supposed *facts of consciousness*, keeping itself within the confines of the latter throughout. The basic problem of Fichte's Science, on the other hand, is to determine precisely how reflective consciousness can arise out of intuitive awareness—how blind 'will' gives rise to 'pure thinking' or 'intelligizing' (*Intelligiren*).[81] And while it is granted from the start that the two, viz., immediate feeling and reflection, must coincide in an absolute act of self-positing, the point where the coincidence finally occurs, or for that matter, where the two originally diverge, remains *ex hypothesi* unconscious. Fichte has now explicitly and deliberately made his own the problem of how consciousness arises from its pre-conscious past to which, as we have seen, Reinhold had *in effect* already reduced the whole problem of the relation of consciousness to the 'thing-in-itself'. But as a result, Fichte's account of the *genesis* of consciousness cannot be just a *description* (no matter how systematic) of its *given* facts. It has to be rather an ideal reconstruction of a process which we must postulate as occurring 'behind its back' (as Hegel will say), but which we can never directly *perceive* as issuing in it. Fichte's constructions must be formalistic because they cannot ever be instantiated in actual experience. In this restricted sense, i.e., because of the formalism of his whole approach to experience, Fichte remained much closer in spirit to critical philosophy than Reinhold ever was. When the latter declared himself for the Science of Knowledge, he gave once more an example of his bad philosophical judgement.[82] He had failed to see that all the complaints that he had lodged against Kant's formalism now applied to Fichte with greater force than ever.

Fichte said that we must distinguish between two series of experiences, viz., those of ordinary consciousness on the one hand, and those that are the product of the philosopher's re-construction of the experiences in the first series on the other. The second series is supposed to explain the first.[83] Since it too, however, falls within the limits of consciousness, the point where ideal reconstruction and concrete experience finally meet escapes consciousness. Philosophy too, in other words, is the result of the original effort by which the *ego*, as it tries to posit itself, ends up alienating itself from itself. Consciousness is this state of alienation, and philosophy is just one more expression of it. This is not to say that the movement of transcendence of consciousness is directed at anything that lies outside it. On the contrary, it is directed precisely at the point of coincidence between subject and object which, as we must assume, consciousness carries within itself all the time — for it is the point where it originates. But to the extent that it is brought back to it, consciousness also ceases to exist as consciousness. This is its problem: it must destroy itself in order to find itself. And since the problem is one that cannot be resolved on theoretical grounds, but must ultimately be dealt with through moral means, philosophy has to become finally an expression of freedom in order to achieve truth; its evidence ultimately rests on moral commitment.

With Fichte philosophy thus turns into ideology; it becomes a work of ideas that derives its truth only from the function that it plays at the service of the will. Implicit in this new philosophical programme, however, are the seeds of a terrible ambiguity. It is the one that Aenesidemus had already detected in Kant's moral theory, and in so doing, as we said, he had unwittingly prophesied the end of post-Kantian idealism even before it was born. It will be Schelling who brings the ambiguity to light in Fichte, and it now remains to see how. But first we must introduce two more characters who also participated in the *Aenesidemus* debate, and who contributed to it while still abiding by its pre-Fichtean tone.

5. The Case for Negative (Anti-dogmatic) Criticism and Phenomenalism

(a) *The Skepticism of Solomon Maimon*

We have already met Solomon Maimon. The story of this strange but interesting man has already been told several times.[84] Born and raised in a Jewish village in Lithuania where the Talmud was his only source of learning, he eventually fled from his place of birth (and from his mother-in-law) in order to seek his fortunes in the university cities. Although unable at first to speak any of the then recognized European languages, he finally succeeded in capturing the attention of the *literati*, and in establishing himself as an author of some repute. After the publication of his *Essay in Transcendental Philosophy*, Maimon was involved in a protracted and often bitter controversy with Reinhold, during which he became more and more skeptical about the results of critical philosophy. When *Aenesidemus* appeared on the scene, it was only natural for him to side with the skeptics. His new reservations about Kant's philosophy were expressed in a book entitled *Essay towards a New Logic or Theory of Thought*,[85] in which he offered a revised form of general logic based on the principles of transcendental logic, and also a new analysis of the faculty of cognition. Appended to the book were six letters addressed to Aenesidemus by a certain Philaletes in which the writer (obviously representing Maimon) states his position with respect to Aenesidemus, Reinhold and Kant. They provide the clearest and also (considering Maimon's normal prolixity) the tersest statement of his skepticism.

The letters are a perfect reflection of the undisciplined genius that Maimon was. They were written in his usual petulant tone, and are replete with comments which, when not trivial, are often dubious and sometimes plainly wrong. Yet the point they finally make against Kant is well-taken; and unlike the criticisms of either Reinhold or Aenesidemus, Maimon has the virtue of respecting the terms of Kant's own statement of the critical problem.

Maimon's point is in brief this. Reinhold is wrong in basing his theory of cognition on 'representation'. 'Consciousness' must be the most generic concept of any theory of cognition. And consciousness consists in the direct *presentation* in sensation of an object which is then *partially* presented in the imagination once more; and in being thus *re*-presented, it is also *determined* (*for* the subject, presumably) as the particular object that it is. The original presentation of the object is intuitive. There cannot be in it any distinction between the object and its presentation, for if there were, it would only be a *re*presentation; since it would then require an external term of reference, we would be forced into an infinite regression from representation to representation. As an original presentation, intuition can only present itself.[86] Moreover, since this presenting occurs *in* consciousness, the possibility that cognition might extend beyond consciousness in order to reach the thing 'in-itself' is precluded from the start. Any supposed knowledge of it is an illusion that arises from the mistake of treating original presentations as if they were re-presentations; since no term of reference can be found for them within consciousness, the imagination conjures one up for them outside it, and this is how the illusion is born. The whole of dogmatism is based on it.[87] Maimon argues against Aenesidemus that skepticism and critical philosophy do not stand at all opposed on the question of the 'thing-in-itself'. Dogmatism simply assumes that the 'things' which we do not directly cognize, but which we can *think* as determined in certain ways in virtue of certain possible relations, are in fact so determined. Skepticism questions the validity of this assumption. Critical philosophy simply goes one step further by denying it altogether. It examines the *a priori* conditions that would be required in order to obtain any actual knowledge of the possible relations between the 'things' in question, and it concludes that any such knowledge is impossible for us in principle.[88] The central problem of philosophy is to determine, rather, whether we have *a priori* concepts of an object of thought in general (i.e., a possible object), and whether we have any right to apply these concepts to objects of knowledge derived *a posteriori*.[89] This question has to be dealt with without transcending the limits dictated by the facts of consciousness.

The principle of contradiction and the forms of thought established by general and transcendental logic are sufficient to determine the object of a representation as 'object in general'.[90] This is, according to Maimon, simply a fact.[91] The principle as well as the forms apply to all representations, at any level of particularity. They presuppose in every case, however, that some object is already given in consciousness. They do not establish whether this object is real, or whether it is not the product of some arbitrary construction of thought instead—that is to say , whether it was ever *presented* to thought on its own, and not produced in the first place through the process of re-presentation.[92] In order to draw this distinction, another principle is required. What is needed is precisely a criterion of what counts as an 'objective synthesis of representations'. Kant did not provide one, according to Maimon. And Maimon is now set to make up for the master's failure by proposing a new principle which he calls "the principle of determinability", and which he considers his single most important contribution to philosophy.[93] According to the principle, two representations constitute together a real objective unity if, and only if, the object of one of them can be present to consciousness as an independent subject, and the object of the other as a determination inhering in this subject. Any other combination of representations—in other words, any combination in which the objects represented could both be present to consciousness as independent subjects, or in which each of the two objects would have to depend on the other—expresses no more than either a formal or an arbitrary unity. What the principle in effect requires of every representation, in other words, is that in order to be objective it must either simply designate an object which is already present to consciousness through some other means than representation, or identify (i.e., re-present) some determination in the object thus designated.

There is nothing in the principle that we would not expect from what Maimon has already said about the requirements of 'representation'. The principle is important to Maimon, however, because it allows him to re-state in his own terms the critical problem of how synthetic *a priori* judgements are possible, and to show how limited Kant's answer to the problem had really been. The problem, according to Maimon, is to establish how it is possible to determine *a priori* the determination of an object, granted that these determinations would have to be *given* in the object itself in order to be objective. How can a representation, which is *ex hypothesi* only a partial *re*-presentation or the mere designation of a presented object, apply to the latter *a priori*?[94] The problem is easy enough to resolve if by the 'object' in question we mean an object of *thought* in general—in which case general and transcendental logic provide, as we have said, a suitable answer. The situation is quite different, however, if what we have in mind is some particular object given to consciousness in actual fact, and not just as a mere possiblility of thought—for in this case, the demand for an *a priori* representation of its determination seems to imply the reversal of the proper order of consciousness; the immediate, intuitive presentation of an object is made to depend on its reflective *re*-presentation. Kant, according to Maimon, had failed to face up to this difficulty in all its generality. He had tried to deal with it piecemeal instead, first with respect to the objects of mathematics, and then with respect to those of the philosophy of nature. But he had never come to grips with the real problem which is whether the objects that we *represent* in *thought* are ever actually *given* in sense experience, and whether they need be so given in order for experience to be possible. This, and no other, was the issue in the dispute between critical philosophy and skepticism. Maimon agrees with Kant that it is indeed possible to represent mathematical objects *a priori*, for the validity of mathematical representations can always be tested by producing ideal objects in the imagination by which they can be measured. He also agrees with him that, to the extent that the objects of sensible experience can be determined mathematically, i.e., quantified, they too can be represented *a priori*. But it does not follow from the fact that *we* can determine them in this way—or that we might even have to do so, for the sake of science, in the imagination—that they are actually *given* in sensation as so determined. Nor does it follow that we can ever *perceive* in sensations the order prescribed by the categories, just because we are capable—again, for the sake of science—of ideally re-constructing their content in the imagination according to that order. On the contrary , granted that sensations are the simple and intuitive mental events that both Hume and Kant have assumed them to be, nothing should be less likely than that we should find realized in them the highly complex structures that thought requires. Actual experience is closer to the way Hume has described it—a play of accidental events that we tend to combine in structured totalities out of habit, or under the influence of some other subjective constraint, but not because of any objective exigencies that we discover in them.

The upshot of Maimon's analysis is that the principles and laws of science can only be instantiated in ideal, not in real experience.[95] This is the basis of his skepticism. Whether or not 'things-in-themselves' can be known is not an issue for Maimon. The significant question for him, rather, is whether it is possible to obtain necessary and universal knowledge or real objects of experience even within the limits prescribed by Kant. And since his answer is negative, Maimon proclaims his philosophy to be a rational form of skepticism—one that accepts the negative (or anti-dogmatic) part of critical philosophy, but rejects its supposed positive results.[96] As long as we share Kant's empiricist prejudice about the nature of sensations, Aenesidemus is right, Kant has only established what the objects of experience must be *if* science is to be possible—not that they are actually so, or that we actually possess scientific knowledge of them. This is a real flaw in Kant's *Critique*, and Maimon must be credited for having been the first to have seen it. He had already exposed it in his earlier *Essay*. But now that he has dropped all the metaphysical assumptions with which he had earlier tried to shoulder the critical system, the skeptical consequences of Kant's prejudice have finally been made clear.

(b) The phenomenalism of Jakob Sigismund Beck

Another who clearly saw Kant's problem but who, unlike Maimon, refused to succumb to the temptation of skepticism was Jakob Sigismund Beck (1761-1840).[97] Unlike Maimon, Beck had a highly disciplined mind, and the solution that he proposed for it proved to be, unlike Maimon's earlier metaphysical hypothesis, a piece of first rate philosophical thinking that still deserves our attention. Beck is best known for his correspondence with Kant in which he elicited from the aging master some of the clearest and tersest statements of his critical position. Kant dedicated much effort to it because, after the disappointments of Reinhold and Fichte, he saw in Beck his last hope for a disciple who would clarify his doctrine, while still remaining faithful to it. As things turned out, Beck too was to be included in the list of those false disciples whom the master publicly rejected;[98] Kant apparently thought that he too had gone the way of Fichte's idealism. Beck had in fact deliberately refused to take that step, and was to continue to do so until the end. In spite of his growing impatience with Kant's inability to see the merit of his interpretation of the *Critique*, he always saw himself with respect to the master's work as an expositor and commentator, never as an innovator.[99] He brought changes to it nevertheless; and although not quite of the nature that Kant himself perhaps thought, they proved to be just as radical all the same. Beck's 'doctrine of the standpoint' (as his philosophy came to be known because of its insistence that the *Critique* be read and understood from the proper 'standpoint') was neither just an elaboration of Kant's philosophy, nor an approximation of Fichte's. It was uniquely Beck's.

Crucial to Beck's standpoint is the recognition of what 'thought' truly is. In thought, as Beck claims, we fix for ourselves a point of reference, i.e., an object, by attributing to it a determination.[100] 'Concepts' are the result of this operation; they represent an object for us precisely in the particular form in which we have 'fixed' its presence in front of us by means of that attribution. Through them we become aware of the process of referring and fixating that we have performed; but they are not identical with it, for they presuppose in every case that the process has already taken place. Hence, if we restrict our investigation into the possiblity of experience to the analysis of concepts alone, we end up assuming as already given the very fact that we are supposed to establish, viz., whether and how concepts represent an object at all. The most that we can attain along this line of investigation is a system of concepts that we claim to be an account of the supposed facts of consciousness without being able to demonstrate it. We can try, as some have done since Kant (notably Reinhold, of course), to anchor the system to some principle that we claim to be the fundamental fact of consciousness. But as long as we have not explained how we ever came to represent it in the first place, whether we choose as fundamental one fact or another remains strictly arbitrary.[101]

The biggest mistake that one can make in interpreting the *Critique* is to think that its categories are only 'concepts'.[102] This is what its commentators have done, according to Beck; and as a result they have forced upon it the impossible task of demonstrating that the categories actually apply to a presupposed content of experience.[103] Kant himself is partly to be blamed for this unfortunate development. He separated too sharply the Transcendental Aesthetic from the Transcendental Analytic, and treated sensibility as if its content were given in consciousness prior to any activity of synthesizing on our part. Thus he gave the impression that experience is a process by which we formally superimpose a network of concepts upon a ready-made content. And once this assumption is made, we are faced by such questions as where the material and the content come from, and why we are justified in referring the concepts to the material, none of which we can answer. In raising these questions "we do not really understand ourselves," as Beck puts it. It was not Kant's intention to be understood literally, however. He only wanted to lead his reader step by step to the special attitude of mind that is required by transcendental philosophy; and to this end he began by adopting the deceptive language and the distinctions to which the reader was already accustomed, in order at the end to wean him from them completely. [104] Unfortunately his strategy backfired; and Beck's intention is now to try to remedy the adverse effects that it has had by openly declaring from the beginning the kind of attitude that he requires from his reader—the 'standpoint', in other words, that the reader must adopt in order to understand the Critique.[105] He must be willing to transcend the limits of the mere analysis of concepts, and to transpose himself in thought into the original, synthesizing activity of 'representing' in virtue of which objects are given to us in the first place. This activity of 'representing'—not any 'representation', however general and obvious its term of reference—is the fundamental fact of consciousness upon which Beck now proposes to base his exposition of transcendental philosophy.[106] Kant's categories must all be re-interpreted as aspects of this fundamental activity.[107]

Thus the aim of Beck's *Standpunktslehre* is to be a descriptive, yet methodical account of how the facts of consciousness are originally given to us. The 'fact' of consciousness *qua* fact—not its concept—is his object.[108] Special use must be made in it of concepts—for although we cannot avoid using them, still we must not rely on them for any representation of the facts that we are trying to uncover. Concepts might be able to lead us to them and, once we possess them, to represent them for us; but they cannot produce them for us. We can only obtain them, ultimately, by exhibiting them in intuition.[109] And this is done through the deliberate, methodical attempt at performing, while observing at the same time, the act by which we attain an object in the first place. It is up to each of us individually, as Beck never tires of repeating, to make this attempt.[110] Hence, the science that Beck is proposing cannot be 'systematic' in Reinhold's sense. It has to be 'methodical', to be sure, because it must first identify the simplest form of 'original representing', and then build the more complex ones upon it; but it cannot be systematic, for it must avoid any principle about consciousness that would imply that we can find a ready-made content in it of which we can make an inventory. Beck's starting point is not at all a principle, but the postulate 'Represent originally' which, as he points out, does not say anything about consciousness, but only stipulates the kind of activity that we must perform to obtain our intended object.[111]

Beck dispenses with any definition of consciousness in general—of the kind with which Reinhold had tried to ground his theory of cognition—because it would have been entirely derivative.[112] His attention is directed from the start to specific cognitive acts instead. In this respect he follows Kant's lead. How far he also diverges from him, however, becomes apparent the moment Beck begins to give his interpretation of the categories. "Quantity," as Beck says, "is the original synthesis (putting together) of the homogeneous that proceeds from the parts to the whole."[113] This synthesis is not exercized upon a manifold previously given in space; it gives rise to a manifold in the first place. Quantity *is* space. And space *is* knowledge.[114] It is the intuiting that yields for us the simplest possible object. 'Intuition' (or 'intuiting', which is the term preferred by Beck) must not be understood as an 'immediate relation to an object'. This is indeed Kant's definition, but it has the disadvantage of implying that something is given in consciousness prior to it, which we then enter in relation with by means of intuition. Intuiting is, on the contrary, the *original* synthesis that establishes the *original* aggregate of parts on which all objectivity is based. Moreover, in the course of this intuiting there arises for us a series of 'now's; and in virtue of these, by synthesizing them in a particular order, and by referring them to the parts of the spatial manifold, we 'fixate' both the new temporal synthesis just produced and the original one; that is to say, we synthesize the (spatial) product of the original synthesis once more by determining it in terms of the (temporal) act that produces it. Beck calls this second thesis the "synthesis of recognition."[115] Both types of syntheses, i.e., the one through which the object is first produced, and the one through which it is first recognized, are repeated with each categorical act, until a completely determined object is finally produced. With this final step, however (which begins with the activity of judging) a new process has already begun. We now begin to fixate the object just obtained by recognizing in it all the elements that *we* have put into it in the previous synthesis. It is here that the process of 'attributing', through which the analytical unities of concepts originate, begins.[116]

What Beck has done, in other words, is to identify Kant's categories with their *schemata*. In this way he has precluded even the logical possibility of an object that could transcend, ideally, the limits of sensible experience. On the other hand, he has introduced a reflective moment (i.e., the act of 'recognition') into the very structure of sensibility. This step resembles the move by which Reinhold and Fichte had extended the 'form-content' distinction, which Kant had laid down *between* thought and sensation alone, to apply at every level of mental activity—i.e., *within* thought and *within* sensation as well. It has at any rate the same effect of undercutting Kant's sharp distinction between *a priori* and a *a posteriori* knowledge, and by the same token to reinforce the immanentism already implicit in the identification of category with *schema*. Every categorical act that follows upon the first spatio-temporal synthesis only adds to it, according to Beck, a new 'fixing' of its product, i.e., a new arrangement of what is already contained there, and a renewed recognition of its dependence upon original 'representing'. For instance, "the category of *reality* is the original synthesis of the homogeneous, a synthesis that proceeds from whole to parts."[117] With this operation too, however, "I generate time"; and as I determine it, and thereby fixate my new synthesis, I give rise to "the original synthetic unity of consciousness – i.e., the unity of the concept through which I think the reality of a thing."[118] The category of causality "is an original positing that fixes the original synthesis of my sensations *qua* successive." Here too, as Beck goes on to say, "the original representing divides into two operations of original synthesis and original recognition. The first consists in the linking together of my sensations, and is further determined in original recognition by the fixing of the time in accordance to which the sequence of the synthesis is fixated."[119] And so on. In every case we never transcend the limits set in the first spatio-temporal synthesis, but only add to it a new awareness of what we have attained in the act of original representing. In this sense Beck can say that all experience, and philosophy in particular, is only a process of self-knowledge, or that to entertain an empty thought like the 'thing-in-itself' is really "not to understand oneself."[120] Beck's immanentism is absolute. The modal categories, with which the process of original representing is brought to a close, leave no doubt about it. "Possibility," Beck says, "consists in the reduction of the mere concept, through which an object is thought to be the original representing in the categories of quantity, quality and relation.[121] The sphere of 'possibility', in other words, which is the object of thought, is ultimately reducible to the sphere of 'actuality', i.e., to the object of the first spatio-temporal synthesis; and the same applies to the sphere of 'necessity'.

This immanentism is what Kant had in mind, as Beck believes, when he distinguished between 'appearances' and 'thing-in-itself', and restricted our knowledge to appearances alone.[122] Yet it is interesting to note that, although Kant was willing to go along with many of Beck's suggestions as to how the material of the *Critique* could be re-arranged to make it more accessible to the public, and even allowed that the Transcendental Aesthetic should come after the Transcendental Analytic, he always insisted that, somewhere at the end of the Analytic, it should be made clear that thought is by itself empty, and that a content must be added to it which is given in sensibility.[123] It is statements of this sort that Beck could not accept because they implied, as he clearly realized, that consciousness cannot be defined simply in terms of consciousness, but that it presupposes an unknowable 'thing-in-itself' distinct from it. They implied, in other words, that in principle at least 'logical possibility' is not co-extensive with 'actuality' as understood by Beck. On the other hand, Beck's unwillingness to grant that any content is given to consciousness could easily give to Kant the impression that he too held, like Fichte, that the *ego* creates its own object.[124] And this is a position that seemed absurd to him.

It must be said in all fairness to Beck that he never sided with Fichte. He steadfastly refused to reduce sensation to an alleged pre-objective state of consciousness as Fichte had done—to some 'raw feel', as we would call it nowadays. Nor did he try to trace the genesis of consciousness back to some primordial preconscious deed. His only intention was to give as accurate a descriptive account of the emergence of an object of consciousness as possible. Since consciousness *begins* with the synthesis of space, so must our account of its origin. There is no more room in it for a theoretical construct like Fichte's '*ego is ego*' than there is for Kant's 'thing-in-itself'. Of course, since in sensation we feel our sense being impinged upon by external things, this fact too must be saved. But it cannot be done by appealing to some supposed factor external to consciousness, as if the impinging began outside it. The event is a particular appearance that belongs to a network of equally particular appearances, and is just as open to direct inspection as any other. Beck represents it *originally* through the category of 'reality'; it occurs as part of the synthesis of the homogeneous that proceeds from the whole to the parts, in which the empirical unity of consciousness is generated.[125] It is clear, however, that if we want to examine the event further, we have to treat it simply as a case of an object (say, a 'table' or a 'chair') affecting another object, viz., my sense organs; and that these are part of the physical world just like any other object.[126] Our study of the event would fall within the domain of a particular science of nature such as psychology or physiology.

Beck's project—it must be noted—is a serious one. It still deserves our attention for its intrinsic philosophical value. It is as consistent an attempt to reduce critical philosophy to phenomenalism as possible. Yet, it is precisely at the level of phenomenal description that the weakness of Beck's position shows up most clearly. For even granted that consciousness begins with the synthesis of 'quantity', and that we cannot transcend the limits of what this synthesis produces; granted also that the synthesis is identical with space; still it is not true to say, with respect to it, that 'I perform it'—not at least in any recognizable sense of these words. The synthesis in question is an anonymous event that occurs indeed in consciousness, but cannot be simply reduced to it. The fundamental fact of consciousness is precisely that we are not originally responsible for all the syntheses that we deliberately develop once consciousness has begun; when this happens we find that, on the contrary, those syntheses have already been originated for us. Consciousness, in other words, is constantly transcending itself—if not in the direction of Kant's 'thing-in-itself' or Fichte's *ego*, certainly towards a nature in which it has its pre-conscious history. For all the inadequacies of Kant's and Fichte's theoretical constructs, their function was at least to express this truth. But it is a truth that Beck apparently never appreciated. He never explained how the *ego* which is supposedly responsible for the synthesis of 'space' that is the basis of all objectivity is the same *ego* that in the synthesis of 'reality' we *find* affected by external things. Like all phenomenalists, he sometimes tends to reduce *esse* to *percipi* (as in the first spatio-temporal synthesis and in the synthesis of the modal categories), and sometimes *percipi* to *esse* (as in the synthesis of 'reality'), without ever explaining how the identity achieved in each case is to be defined, and related to the other. This is the heart of the problem of consciousness, and Beck ends up ignoring it altogether.

One wonders what the history of post-Kantian idealism would have been if Beck, not Fichte, had given shape to it. The merit of the *Standpunktslehre* is that it not only avoids the extravagancies of Fichte's conceptual baggage; it also strips Kant's of many of its rationalistic encumbrances. Perhaps, if Beck had had his way, Kant's *Critique* might have been followed by a renewed attempt at describing the facts of consciousness done in the spirit of empiricism—but with a greater appreciation of what those facts actually are, and with a much more sophisticated conceptual apparatus then the Humean tradition had ever shown before. But Beck did not have his way, after all. As we know, it fell upon Fichte to define the terms of the new round of philosophical debate that followed the Aenesidemus debate.

6. The Larger Story

By the time Fichte appeared on the scene the Enlightenment had already run its course. The French Revolution was the great event of the close of the Eighteenth Century; it shook European society at all levels and inaugurated a new age. Fichte's idealism was just as much a response to the spirit and the exigencies of this new age as to the pressures of philosophical debate. As a product of thought, however, Fichte alone was responsible for it. It is he who defined the terms of the new debate. And the first to challenge him, while accepting at the same time those terms, was Friederich Wilhelm Joseph von Schelling (1775-1854)

The objection that Schelling raised, stated as briefly as possible was this. If Fichte's fundamental thesis, viz., 'ego is ego', is the expression of an absolute identity, why should it not be interpreted to mean 'id is id' just as well? What is there to distinguish an ideal identity from a mere identity of 'being'? Or again, if the event that gives rise to con-sciousness is not itself conscious, why could it not be an accident of blind nature, just as well as an expression of absolute freedom?[127] This was in effect the same as the objection that Aenesidemus had raised against Kant's moral philosophy. If we have no theoretically sufficient justification for a belief to which we are *existentially* bound, how can we be sure that the force of the belief is not due to some irrational factor in our nature? Why can't the belief be just an illusion? But Schelling was now raising the objection, not to exploit it as a reduction *ad ab-surdum* of Fichte's new idealism, but to plead his case for a *Philosophy of Nature* which, as he thought, should complement Fichte's *Science of Knowledge*. Schelling thought that he had found a much more adequate way of formulating the first principle of philosophy than Fichte had done, and that he was thus playing with respect to him the same radicalizing function that Fichte and Reinhold had tried to play with respect to Kant. Fichte's thesis must include its antithesis, i.e., the *ego* must include the non-*ego* as well; or better still, as Schelling was eventually to claim, the fundamental principle of philosophy, the Absolute, must be conceived as the point of indifference between the '*ego=ego*' on the one hand, and the '*id=id*' on the other.

Thus a controversy arose between the first two exponents of the new idealism that could never be resolved on the terms in which it was being waged, for each side ended up yielding to the other simply by stating its own position. As long as Fichte maintained that theory must be based on moral commitment, he also conceded to Schelling the right to defend an alternative view of the phenomenal world to his own. And the same applied to Schelling with respect to Fichte. It was possible, on his view, to construe two parallel pictures of the world—one according to the laws of nature, and the other according to those of freedom—and to show that each was only one aspect of one fundamental unity. As long as he admitted, however, as indeed he had to, that his system of parallel constructions was itself *only* a construction, and that in philosophy the reconciliation of freedom and nature in the Absolute occurs only ideally, he conceded to Fichte that the view he was defending had no stronger theoretical value than Fichte's. Like Fichte's Transcendental Idealism which it was supposed to incorporate, his own system had to rely on extra-conceptual, ultimately pre-rational, evidence. But once the limits of conceptualization had been transcended, what was there to make Fichte's moral intuition any less valid a source of evidence than the kind on which Schelling was now relying?

Our story has actually come full circle. For the problem behind the Fichte-Schelling controversy was still the same as the fundamental problem with which Kant was trying to contend, though in his case the terms in which it was being raised were still scholastic in inspiration. On the one hand, consciousness is a world unto its own, complete with laws and exigencies that cannot be derived from anything that transcends consciousness itself. On the other, consciousness presupposes, precisely *qua* consciousness, a 'thing-in-itself'; without it, it collapses upon itself (as it does on any phenomenalistic account) or runs the risk of being no more than an illusory world. The problem was precisely to reconcile these two apparently irreconcilable requirements. Kant, for his part, never claimed to have given to it a positive solution. His only aim had been to ensure that nothing was said that contradicted either requirement. But even under this restriction, the problem proved too much for him. Fichte and Schelling were now claiming to have resolved it positively. Yet, for all their preposterous talk about the 'Absolute' and 'absolute knowledge', their alleged solution rested on a move that Kant had already seen, but had rejected because of its obvious irrationalistic consequences. Their solution was to make the truth of consciousness depend on intuition. But the problem was that, whether one called it 'intellectual' or not, as long as intuition implied no distance between subject and object, it still escaped consciousness; and hence there was no accounting for it. As the Fichte-Schelling controversy illustrated, the appeal to intellectual intuition could justify one ideal construction as well as any other.

After Fichte and Schelling, the future did not augur well for reason. Nineteenth-century irrationalism can be traced directly back to them. But apart from what the future held in store, one possible avenue of solution still lay open. It is the one we have suggested at the very beginning. One could substitute for the myth-making of Fichte and Schelling (for their 'pragmatic histories') *real history*. One could claim that, although consciousness is autonomous once it has made its appearance in nature, its coming to be there has a history—first in nature itself, and then in the social structures that constitute for man his most proximate natural environment. And this history, however unconscious in its making, can become all the same the object of explicit consciousness. This, as we said, was the avenue that Hegel was to explore. How he did it, however, and with what success, belongs to the larger story of post-Kantian idealism that we can only hint at now.

Notes

1. For the best and most easily available history in English of this period, see Lewis White Beck, *Early German Philosophy, Kant and his Predecessors*, Cambridge, Massachusetts: Harvard University Press, 1969. Beck does not pay enough attention to the influence

in Germany of Scottish "common sense" philosophy, however. See Manfred Kuehn, *Scottish Common Sense Philosophy in Germany*, 1768-1800, Ph.D. Thesis, McGill University, 1980 (but I do not agree with the conclusions of the thesis regarding Kant). A picture of the period that is closer to life can be obtained through some individual biographies and some specialized studies; for instance, W. M. Alexander, *Johann Georg Hamann, Philosophy and Faith*, The Hague: Nijhoff, 1966; Henry E. Allison, *Lessing and the Enlightment*, Ann Arbor: The University of Michigan Press, 1966; Alexander Altmann, *Moses Mendelssohn*, University, Alabama: The University of Alabama Press, 1973 (This is a truly masterly work); Robert T. Clark, Jr., *Herder, His Life and Thought*, Berkeley and Los Angeles: The University of California Press, 1969; Valerio Verra, *F. H. Jacobi, dall'illuminismo all' idealismo*, Torino: Edizioni di Filosofia, 1963.

2. Cf. *Critique*, BXXXVI.

3. E.g. Ibid., A155-156, B194-195; A721-B749.

4. Cf. Ibid., B157-158, note.

5. Cf. Ibid., BXXVI-XXIX

6. January 20, 1792, *Briefwechsel*, Academy Ed., Vol. XI, p. 302. English tr.: Arnulf Zweig, *Kant, Philosophical Correspondence*, 1759-99, Chicago: The University of Chicago Press, 1967, p. 184.

7. *Critique*, B165-166 (§27).

8. Cf. reference in note 6.

9. Cf. *Critique*, B274-275 (*Refutation of Idealism*); Bxl.

10. *Versuch über die Transzendentalphilosophie*, eventually published in Berlin: Voss & Sohn, 1790. *Gesammelte Werke*, ed. Valerio Verra, Vol. II, Hildesheim: George Olms, 1965.

11. Herz to Kant, and Maimon to Kant, April 7, 1789, *Briefwechsel*, Academy Ed., Vol. XI, pp. 14-17.

12. Maimon's doctrine is to be found in Chapter 2 of *Versuch über die Transzendentalphilosophie*.

13. Kant to Herz, May 26, 1789. *Briefwechsel*, Academy Ed., Vol. XI, pp. 48-54. (Kant's compliment is on p. 49). English tr., pp. 150-156.

14. *Versuch einer neuen Logik*, Berlin: bei Ernst Felisch, 1794. See the introductory note to the translation of the Maimon excerpt, below, p. 159.

15. *Versuch einer neuen Theorie des menschlichen Vorstellungsvermögens*, Prague and Jena: Widtmann & Mauke, 1789.

16. May 14, 1787, *Briefwechsel*, Academy Ed., Vol. X, p. 462.

17. The letters appeared in 1786 and 1787, and were re-published in 1790 (with some modifications) as volume I of *Briefe über die Kantische Philosophie*. For the major texts on which the following account of Reinhold is based, see the introductory note to the translation of *Fundament*, below, p. 53, and note 64 to the text of the translation, below, pp. 101-3. For Reinhold's life and work, see Ernst Reinhold, *Karl Leonhard Reinholds Leben und litterarisches Wesen, nebst einer Auswahl von Briefen Kants, Fichtes, Jacobis und andrer philosophierenden Zeitgenossen an ihn*, Jena: Fromann, 1825. Alfred Klemmt, *Karl Leonhard Reinholds Elementarphilosophie, Eine Studie über den Ursprung des spekulativen deutschen Idealismus*, Hamburg: Meiner, 1958; Reinhart Lauth, ed., *Philosophie aus einem Prinzip, K. L. Reinhold*, Bonn: Bouvier, 1974; Angelo Pupi, *La*

Formazione della filosofia di K. L. Reinhold, 1784-1794, Milano: Vita e Pensiero, 1966 (the most historically detailed account of Reinhold's 'Kantian' period); Willhelm Teichner, *Rekonstruktion oder Reproduktion des Grundes, Die Begründung der Philosophie als Wissenschaft durch Kant und Reinhold*, Bonn: Bouvier, 1976 (a philosophical study). See also the recent and very informative article by Daniel Breazeale, "Between Kant and Fichte: Karl Leonhard Reinhold's 'Elementary Philosophy'," *The Review of Metaphysics*, XXXV (1981-1982), 785-821.

18. *Briefwechsel*, Academy Ed., Vol. X, pp. 487-489; English tr., pp. 127-128.

19. See Pupi, *Reinhold*, p. 40. Later on Reinhold felt embarrassed about this essay; cf. Reinhold to Kant, October 12, 1787, *Briefwechsel*, Academy Ed., Vol. X, p. 475.

20. Ibid.

21. Cf. *Theorie*, pp. 66, 71 (§I), 120 (§II).

22. This is in brief the point that Reinhold endlessly belabours in the Preface and Part I of *Theorie*.

23. Cf. Reinhold's description of his Philosophy of the Elements in *Ueber das Fundament des philosophischen Wissens*, Jena: Mauke, 1791, pp.70ff.

24. Ibid., pp. 70, 114ff.

25. *Critique*, AXIII, XX.

26. Ibid., AXX.

27. "Neue Darstellung der Hauptmomente der Elementarphilosophie," *Beiträge zur Berichtigung bisheriger Missverstandnisse der Philosophen*, Vol. I, Jena: Mauke, 1790, pp. 167-254.

28. For a rapid review of the ephemeral Reinholdian school, see Pupi, *Reinhold*, 359-360, note.

29. This is the formulation given in "Neue Darstellung," *Beiträge*, Vol. I, p. 167. In *Theorie*, the formula is somewhat different: "Consciousness compels us to agree that to each representation belongs a represented subject and a represented object, and that both must be *distinguished* from the *representation* to which they belong."

30. *Theorie*, pp. 214ff.

31. Ibid., pp. 202ff; pp. 220ff.

32. Ibid., pp. 230ff, 255ff, 264ff.

33. Ibid., pp. 235ff, 255ff, 267ff.

34. Ibid., p. 299.

35. Ibid., pp. 244ff.

36. I am commenting on Props. xxxviii-xlv, ibid., pp. 321-351. Cf. also "Neue Darstellung," *Beiträge*, Vol. I, pp. 218ff (Props. xxix-xxxiv).

37. Cf. "Ueber das Verhältniss der Theorie des Vorstellungsvermögens zur Kritik der reinen Vernunft" (Concerning the Relation of the Theory of the Faculty of Representation to the Critique of Pure Reason), *Beiträge*, Vol. I, pp. 255-338, pp. 305ff.

38. Cf. the notes that Fichte wrote as he reflected on Reinhold's *Elementarphilosophie*, and the comments on this text by its editor, Reinhart Lauth. *Eigne Meditationen über Elementarphilosophie* (1793-1794), Vol. II 3, *Gesamtausgabe der Bayerischen Akademie*. Also on the same subject, Peter Baumanns, *Fichtes Wissenschaftslehre Probleme ihres Anfangs*, Bonn: Bouvier, 1974, pp. 80-97; Reinhart Lauth, "Genèse du 'fondement de

toute la doctrine de la science' de Fichte à partir de ses 'Méditations personnelles sur l'élementar-philosophie'," *Archives de Philosophie*, XXXIV (1971), pp. 51-79.

39. *Fundament*, pp. 77-78.

40. *Aenesidemus oder über die Fundamente der von dem Herrn Prof. Reinhold in Jena gelieferten Elementar-Philosophie*, n.p.p., 1792; reprinted in *Aetas Kantiana*, Bruxelles: Culture et Civilization, 1969.

41. Ibid., pp. 24ff.

42. Ibid., p. 45.

43. Ibid., pp.96-97.

44. Ibid., pp.53-54.

45. Ibid., pp. 59ff.

46. What follows is a brief summary of the excerpt translated below, pp. 105-33.

47. *Aenesidemus*, pp. 202-203.

48. Ibid., pp. 213ff.

49. Ibid., pp. 261ff.

50. Ibid., pp. 225ff, note; pp. 229-230, note.

51. Ibid., pp. 263ff; pp. 379-381.

52. Ibid., pp. 143-145.

53. Ibid., p. 383.

54. Ibid., pp. 72-73.

55. Cf. below, p. 87, and note 55.

56. *Briefwechsel*, Academy Ed., pp. 100-1. XI, p. 381; English tr., p. 198.

57. *David Humes Untersuchung über den menschlichen Verstand, neu übersetzt von M. W. G. Tennemann, nebst einer Abhandlung über den philosophischen Skeptizismus von Hrn. Prof. Reinhold*, Jena: Akademische Buchhandlung, 1793. Reinhold's essay bears the title: "Ueber den philosophischen Skepticismus" (May 1, 1793).

58. "Ausführliche Darstellung des negativen Dogmatismus oder des metaphysischen Skeptizismus," *Beiträge*, Vol. II, pp. 159-206.

59. Ibid., p. 177

60. "Ueber den Unterschied zwischen dem gesunden Verstande und der philosophierenden Vernunft," *Beiträge*, Vol. II, pp. 1-72, p. 65. Cf. Pupi, *Reinhold*, p. 347.

61. *Aenesidemus*, pp. 386-388.

62. Ibid., pp. 438-439.

63. The references are all to the pagination of *Johann Gottlieb Fichtes Sämmtliche Werke*, I. H. Fichte, ed., 8 vols., Berlin: Veit & Co., 1845-1846, Vol. I. See also the introductory note to the translation, below p. 137. For a recent discussion in English of the Review, see Daniel Breazeale, "Fichte's *Aenesidemus* Review and the Transformation of German Idealism," *Review of Metaphysics*, XXXIV (1981), pp. 545-68. Cf. also some older studies, Martial Guéroult, *L'évolution et la structure de la Doctrine de la Science chez Fichte*, Vol. I, Paris: Société d'Edition, 1930, pp. 143ff. Xavier Léon, *Fichte et son temps*, Paris: Colin, 1954, Vol. I, pp. 239-261.

64. *Ueber den Begriff der Wissenschaftslehre oder der sogenannten Philosophie, als*

Einleidungschrift zu seinen Vorlesungen über diese Wissenschaft, 1794; and *Grundlage der gesammten Wissenschaftslehre, als Handschrift für seine Zuhörer,* 1794. Both can be found in J. G. Fichte, *Gesammtausgabe der Bayerischen Akademie der Wissenschaften,* R. Lauth and H. Jacob, eds., Vol. I, 2, Stuttgart-Bad Cannstatt: Frommann, 1965. An English translation of the *Grundlage* can be found in *Fichte: Science of Knowledge with First and Second Introductions,* ed. and tr. Peter Heath and John Lachs, New York: Appleton-Century-Crofts, 1970; re-issued, Cambridge University Press, 1982. The references to the German text are to Vol. I of the 1845/46 edition. "Science of Knowledge" is the translation of *Wissenschafslehre* set by Heath and Lachs. A more accurate translation would be "Doctrine of Science".

    65. *Review,* p. 5.

    66. Ibid., p. 6.

    67. Ibid., p. 7.

    68. Ibid., p. 8.

    69. Ibid., p. 8.

    70. Ibid., pp. 9-11.

    71. Ibid., p. 5.

    72. Ibid., pp. 5-6.

    73. Ibid., pp. 6-7.

    74. Ibid., p. 8.

    75. Ibid., pp. 13ff, p. 19.

    76. Ibid., pp. 15, 16-17.

    77. Ibid., p. 13.

    78. Ibid., p. 19.

    79. Ibid., pp. 22ff.

    80. Ibid., pp. 23ff. I have expanded Fichte's otherwise cryptic statements.

    81. J. G. Fichte, *Die Wissenschaftslehre in ihrem allgemeinen Umrisse* (1810), vol. II, 1845/46 ed., p. 703. English tr.: Walter E. Wright, *The Science of Knowledge in its general outline* (1810), *Idealistic Studies,* VI (1976), p. 112.

    82. The announcement came in the Preface to *Auswahl vermischter Schriften,* Vol. 2, Jena; Mauke, 1797, pp. x-xi.

    83. *Zweite Einleitung in die Wissenschaftslehre* (1797), (*Second Introduction to the Science of Knowledge*), Vol. I, 1845/46 ed., p. 454. Also found in Vol. I, 4 of the *Gesammtausgabe.* English tr., *Science of Knowledge,* p. 30.

    84. Solomon Maimon, *Lebensgeschichte,* Berlin: Vieweg, 1792/1793; *Gesammelte Werke,* Vol. I; *Solomon Maimon: An Autobiography,* ed. and with an epilogue by Moses Hadas, New York: Schocken Books, 1947; J. Clark Murray, *Solomon Maimon: An Autobiography with Additions and Notes,* Paisley, Alexander Gardner, 1888 (A translation of the *Lebensgeschichte;* parts are omitted). Samuel Atlas, *From Critical to Speculative Idealism: The Philosophy of Solomon Maimon,* The Hague: Nijhoff, 1964. Samuel Hugo Bergman, *The Autobiography of Solomon Maimon with an Essay on Maimon's Philosophy,* London: The East and West Library, 1954; Samuel Hugo Bergman, *The Philosophy of Solomon Maimon,* tr. from the Hebrew by Noah J. Jacobs, Jerusalem: The Magnes Press, Hebrew University, 1967; Martial Guéroult, *La philosophie transcendentale de Solomon Maimon,*

Paris, 1929; Friederich Kuntze, *Die Philosophie Solomon Maimons*, Heidelberg: Carl Winter's Universitätsbuchhandlung, 1912. For a vivid portrait of Maimon seen through the eyes of Moses Mendelssohn, see Altmann, *Moses Mendelssohn*, pp. 360-364.

85. *Versuch einer neuen Logik oder Theorie des Denkens*, Berlin: bei Ernst Felisch, 1794. See the introductory note to the translation of the Maimon excerpt, below, p. 159.

86. Ibid., pp. 319-321, 361-362, 365-366, 401.

87. Ibid., pp. 370ff.

88. Ibid., pp. 375-376.

89. Cf. Ibid., p. 325.

90. Ibid., p. 326.

91. Ibid., pp. 300-301.

92. Ibid., p. 310.

93. Ibid., pp. 20, 310-314; 433ff.

94. Ibid., pp. 429ff.

95. Ibid., p. 438.

96. In a comment made in reply to a critic. The passage is included only in the 1912 edition of *Versuch einer neuen Logik*, pp. 265-266.

97. See the introductory note to the translation of the Beck excerpt, below, p. 205. The best work in English on Beck is Ingrid Wallner, *Jacob Sigismund Beck's Phenomenological Transformation of Kant's Critical Philosophy*, Ph.D. Thesis, McGill University, 1979. There is otherwise very little published on Beck in English, and also in German, apart from general history works. For a general treatment, see Ernst Cassirer, *Das Erkenntnisproblem in der Philosophie und wissenschaft der neueren Zeit*, Vol. III: *Die nach-kantischen Systeme*, Berlin: Bruno Cassirer, 1923, pp. 69-80.

98. Open letter on Fichte's *Wissenschaftslehre*, August 7, 1799. *Briefwechsel*, Academy Ed., Vol. XII, pp. 396-397. English tr., pp. 253-254.

99. Wallner, *Beck's Phenomenological Transformation of Kant's Critical Philosophy*, p. 2.

100. *Einzig-möglicher Standpunkt aus welchem die Kritische Philosophie beurteilt werden muss*, Riga: bei Johann Friederich Hartknoch, 1796, pp. 134-135.

101. Ibid., pp. 135-137.

102. Ibid., p. 140.

103. Cf. Beck's discussion of the distinction between *a priori* and *a posteriori* judgements; Ibid, II, 4.

104. Ibid., p. 6, 45-48 (among many other texts).

105. Ibid., p. 14.

106. Ibid., pp. 124-127.

107. Ibid., p. 140.

108. Ibid., pp. 126, 137.

109. Ibid., pp. 148-149, 152.

110. E.g. Ibid., p. 129.

111. Ibid., p. 124.

112. Ibid., p. 123.

113. Ibid., pp. 140ff.

114. Ibid., p. 150.

115. Ibid., pp. 142ff.

116. Ibid., pp. 185-186. I take this step to follow immediately upon the modal categories, but Beck is not explicit on this point. Cf. "Actuality is the original representing upon which the concept of object directly follows." Ibid., p. 166.

117. Ibid., p. 145.

118. Ibid.

119. Ibid., p. 154.

120. Ibid., p. 160.

121. Ibid., p. 165.

122. Ibid., pp. 149-150, 159.

123. Kant to Tieftrunk, December 11, 1797, *Briefwechsel*, Academy Ed., Vol. XII, pp. 221-223; English tr., pp. 246-248.

124. The claim has been made that in his *Opus Postumum* Kant gives evidence of having been influenced by Beck. (Herman-J. de Vleeschauwer, *The Development of Kantian Thought*, tr. A. R. C. Duncan, London: Nelson & Sons, 1962, pp. 168ff.). It seems to me that if there truly is any influence, it is best seen in the texts dealing with *Selbst-Affektion* and *Erscheinung der Erscheinungen*. I have briefly commented on these texts (in a completely different context) in "Kant's Metaphysics of Nature and Schelling's *Ideas* for a Philosophy of Nature"; *Journal of the History of Philosophy*, XVII (1979) 197-215, cf. pp. 203-206.

125. *Standpunkt*, pp. 146, 151-152.

126. Ibid., pp. 156-157, 162-163.

127. The expression 'id is id' is not Schelling's. I am just trying to simplify in a few words a very complex debate. For the dispute, see the following letters: Fichte to Schelling, November 15, 1800; Schelling to Fichte, November 19, 1800; Fichte to Schelling, December 27, 1800; Schelling to Fichte, May 24, 1801; Fichte to Schelling, May 31, 1801; Schelling to Fichte, October 3, 1801; Fichte to Schelling, January 15, 1802. F. W. J. Schelling, *Briefe und Dokumente*, ed. H. Fuhrmans, Vol. II (Zusatzband), Bonn: Bouvier, 1973. For a lucid and accurate description of Schelling's position, as it took form in his *Darstellung meines Systems der Philosophie* (1801, see H. S. Harris' *Introduction* to the Cerf-Harris translation of Hegel's *Differenz-Schrift: Hegel, The Difference Between Fichte's and Schelling's System of Philosophy*, Albany: State University of New York Press, 1977.

THE FOUNDATION OF PHILOSOPHICAL KNOWLEDGE
By
K. L. Reinhold

Together with some comments concerning the Theory of the faculty of Representation

Jena: At Johann Michael Mauke's, 1791

Translation and Notes By George di Giovanni

Karl Leonhard Reinhold (1758-1823) developed his Philosophy of the Elements in Versuch einer neuen Theorie des Menschlichen Vorstellungsvermögen *(Essay towards a New Theory of the Faculty of Representation)* Prague and Jena, 1789 (2nd ed., 1795); *in two volumes of* Briefe über die Kantische Philosophie *(Letters Concerning the Kantian Philosophy),* Leipzig, 1790 and 1792, in two volumes of Beiträge zur Berichtigung bisheriger Missverständnisse der Philosophen *(Contributions to the Rectification of Misconceptions Hitherto Held by Philosophers),* Jena, 1790 and 1794; *and in* Ueber das Fundament des philosophischen Wissens, Jena. 1794. *What follows is the translation of a substantial excerpt from this latter work. Reinhold begins by claiming that philosophy has so far lacked a proper foundation, and proceeds to examine the attempt to ground it on the principle of contradiction. The translation is from the original edition which is now also available in photo-mechanical reproduction (but without the replies to two reviews of Volume I of the* Beiträge *which were included in the original edition), ed. Wolfgang H. Schrader, Hamburg: Meiner, 1978.*

. . . THE PROPOSITION, 'all that comes to be must have a cause or (what amounts to the same thing) must be an effect', has been demonstrated by a great many from the principle of contradiction. All the proofs so far mustered for it, however, have always presupposed nothing short of what they were supposed to prove, namely, "that the concept 'what comes to be' can only be thought by being characterized as 'effect'."[1] This can never be deduced from the principle of contradiction, which says nothing either about the concept 'coming to be' or about the concept 'effect'; rather, it presupposes that the concept 'effect' is already contained in the concept 'coming to be', or that there is some ground external to the latter that links the characteristic 'effect' to the characteristic 'coming to be'. In the first // case, Kant calls it an "analytical" judgement—one that expresses the union with the subject of a predicate already contained in it *prior* to the judgement[2]; in the second case, he calls it "synthetic" judgement—one that expresses the union with the subject of a predicate not contained in it, but joined to it in virtue of an external ground.[3] And since the principle of contradiction has demonstrative force only *in those cases* where the predicate is already thought in the subject, and its demonstrative force is exhaustive, moreover, only inasmuch as the predicate is exhaustively thought in the subject, Kant restricts its use to the demonstration of *analytical* judgements.[4]

[38]

Whether the concept 'effect' is already included in the concept 'coming to be' has been one of the most important issues of contention in philosophy so far.[5] The question is answered *in the negative* by the defenders of widely different systems, e.g., by Spinoza, Crusius, Hume, and Kant, all of whom deny that 'effect' is included in their respective concepts of 'coming to be'. Others instead, e.g., the Leibnizians, claim to have no other concept of 'coming to be' save one that includes 'effect'. The dispute makes clear this much, however: the principle of contradiction cannot supply the right concept of 'coming to be'; rather,

[39]   it presupposes it, for all the proofs by // which each disputing party wants to establish the necessity or non-necessity of thinking 'coming to be' as 'effect' are derived in each case from the party's concept of 'coming to be'. [It so happens that] the Leibnizian finds the concept of 'effect' in *his* concept of 'coming to be';[6] *consequently*, whether he confuses the principle of *sufficient reason* which is merely logical with the metaphysical *principle of generation*, as he sometimes does, or distinguishes between the two as he does at other times, in either case he demonstrates both principles from the principle of contradiction. Hume, instead, does not find the concept of 'effect' in his concept of 'coming to be', and from this he concludes that the proposition, 'All that comes to be has a cause', is not demonstrable. But of course, in doing this he assumes with the Leibnizians that the demonstrability of the proposition depends on whether the concept 'effect' is already contained in 'coming to be'. Crusius and Kant, on the other hand, although they too fail to find the one concept included in the other, conclude from this no more than that the principle of generation, if it is to be demonstrable, must be demonstrated not from the mere concept 'coming to be' through the principle of contradiction, but *on some other basis*. The use of the principle of contradiction presupposes in every case that what is being predicated

[40]   of a subject as pertaining to // it on the strength of the principle must have already been thought in the concept of the subject; the principle itself, therefore, presupposes the *correctness* of *what has already been thought* without in any way establishing it. I must have already thought 'winged horse' as 'having wings', 'bear' as 'white', 'coming to be' as 'effect', if the contrary of these given predicates is to contradict their subjects, and if the necessity of the predicates is to follow from the impossibility of conceiving a contradiction. From the mere *fact*, however, that the said subjects are being thought with the said predicates, the *correctness* of their being so thought cannot be inferred. I have no basis, besides my or somebody else's arbitrary concepts, for thinking that an actual horse has wings; I am not able, therefore, to establish the *reality* of 'winged horse' from the principle of contradiction either. But I have grounds in actual experience for thinking that a

bear is white, quite apart from its mere concept; hence I can prove the *reality* of 'white bear', not indeed from the principle of contradiction, but from experience. It might be that in actual fact I think 'coming to be' as 'effect'. But if I have no reason to justify my concept save the *fact* that I have it—if there is no ground for it besides the concept itself, then the principle of contradiction will be // of no help to me to prove it is *real*. For the principle presupposes this reality, since I can only apply it insofar as I *actually* think the concept 'effect' in the concept 'coming to be'. If I cannot give the *reason why* I think 'coming to be' as 'effect', then I do not know whether my proposition, 'every coming to be is an effect', which is otherwise very much in conformity to the principle of contradiction, has any more reality than the proposition, 'Every winged horse has wings'. The reason why I think 'circle' to be 'round', i.e., why I conceive 'roundness' and 'circle' in the representation of one and the same object, lies in the immediate representation or *intuition* of a circle; and since this intuition is inseparable from the concept 'circle', everyone can find *in it* the reason why I think 'circle' as 'round'; my judgement is thus universally binding.[7] But the reason why I think 'coming to be' as 'effect' at all is not be found in any intuition which would be inseparable from the concept of 'coming to be'—in an intuition, that is, that would give everyone access to the justification of my concept, and would thus raise it to [the level of] one which is *universally binding*. For many of the leading independent thinkers have found nothing like 'effect' in their concept of 'coming to be'. If I want to justify my // concept, therefore, by appealing to the principle of contradiction, I must cling to the way I *actually think* it, and conclude from the *fact* that I think it as joined to the characteristic 'effect' that it *must* be thought in this way. I must also grant, however, to anyone else whose concept is opposed to mine the right to claim the same about it, viz., that just *because* he *actually thinks* the concept of 'coming to be' without the characteristic '*effect*', it is possible to deny this characteristic of the concept without offence to the principle of contradiction.

For its correct application, the principle of contradiction presupposes a ground different from it; hence it is not at all the *fundamental principle* of philosophy. The ground that it presupposes concerns nothing less than the *reality* of the propositions to which it is applied; these propositions are demonstrable through it only insofar as they do not lack this reality. They *could* never have reality if they contradicted the principle, but they do not have it just because they do not contradict it. A 'white bear' could not exist if the predicate 'white' contradicted the subject 'bear', but it does not exist just because the predicate does not contradict this subject. 'Coming to be' could not // be thought of as 'effect' if this second concept contradicted the first; but

[41]

[42]

[43]

'coming to be' need not be thought as 'effect', and will not actually be so thought, simply because the two can be thought together. Hence the principle of contradiction only expresses the ground of the mere possibility of thought, never of its *actuality*; it expresses the ground of its *necessity*, however, if, and *only if*, a subject is already *actually* being thought through a certain predicate on some ground other than the principle of contradiction. Through the principle of contradiction, therefore, a proposition acquires only *logical truth*; this truth is indeed presupposed in every case of *real* truth, but by itself it never constitutes the latter; on the contrary, it assumes it. Every proposition must conform to the principle, since none can be true that contradicts it. Any proposition that conforms to it can be false, however, for logical truth does not by itself yield real truth; and whenever and wherever the *real ground* for the application of the principle is missing, we cannot substitute a *logical ground* for it, i.e., the simple possibility of being thought. In the Leibnizian philosophy, however, it is the innate representations that constitute the foundation of philosophical knowledge. But since the criterion of an innate representation is its

[44]   absolute necessity and // universality, and the criterion of these, in turn, is the principle of contradiction, it is the latter that provides the scientific foundation for that philosophy. The whole Leibnizian system, therefore, is built on a principle which it misunderstands, and which (in the sense it is used as foundation) is false. There is nothing the system is further from than authentic science; and for all its wealth of philosophical truths (which however it does *not prove*) it is still an untenable, illegitimate system.

The theories on the origin of representations offered by Locke[8] and Leibniz[9] completed the analytical portion of the groundwork that philosophical reason had been busy preparing for the only two *dogmatic* systems that had hitherto been possible, viz., *empiricism* and *rationalism*. The two philosophers laid down, one in the simple representations drawn from experience and the other in innate representations (and their presumed criterion, viz., the principle of contradiction), the only foundation of philosophical knowledge possible for the empiricists [on the one hand] and the rationalists [on the other]. And while their followers were busy disagreeing about the external details and the

[45]   refinements // of their systems, David Hume[10] came along and undertook, and even completed, the work of analysis required for the grounding of *skepticism*. This he did without having had even one predecessor *equal* to those several whom Locke and Leibniz had (for what is Sextus Empiricus in comparison to a Plato or an Aristotle?). For Hume, representations consist originally in mere *impressions* and their *reproductions*; hence he was able to show from the very nature of *representation*, as the source of all knowledge, that knowledge in general

and philosophical knowledge in particular is merely the product of the imagination, and that all [supposed] *objective truth*, i.e., any *real* conformity of representations to their objects, lacks foundation and is quite undemonstrable. Locke as well had taken his simple representations drawn from experience to consist only of inner and outer impressions; but he had assumed that they conformed to their objects, and that they provided therefore a solid basis for the knowledge that they made possible. Being *more consistent* than Locke, Hume confronted this crucial issue about the *conformity* of impressions to their objects; this was what everybody had taken for granted without proof before his time, and he demonstrated that no proof can be offered that is without contradiction. Every possible demonstration of objective truth would call for a // *comparison* between a *representation* and an *object*   [46] different from it; but at the same time this comparison could only take place through representations, and indeed it would have to be between the one representation that consists in the impression itself, and the other through which this impression is represented; consequently, the comparison would never be set up between a representation and an object that is not already a representation. Our concepts of objects get their reality only from the original representations, that is to say, from the *impressions*. Where the impressions get their *reality* from, and whether they have any reality at all, simply cannot be known, for they are the *ultimate thing* that we cognize, and for that reason they cannot be derived from anything more primitive. The concepts of objects are originally only representations of the impressions themselves, and these do not present us with anything besides what they contain. Whether and to what extent there is anything *objective* outside this content that corresponds to it will remain forever unknown; to suppose otherwise would be only an illusion. Suppose that we compare a rose (considered as object) with its representation: then the rose, inasmuch as we *think* it as an object different from the representation, can be nothing else but a *represented impression*; on the other hand, its *immediate* // representation is nothing else but   [47] the *impression* itself. I can never reach out to a rose which would be different from my impression of it, which would not occur in my representation. And should I imagine for a moment that I have attained to the objective rose, I should immediately be overtaken by the reflection that I have simply put the content of a mere representation in place of that imagined object. In other words, if by knowledge we understand the consciousness of the agreement of representation with objects that are different from mere representations, then no knowledge is possible. And no principles are possible if by *principles* we understand propositions expressing the necessary and universal characteristics of objects *of this sort*. And no philosophy is possible if we take *philosophy* to be not just some loose aggregate of unfounded intentions, but science — whether it be the Leibnizian science of *necessary* and *universal* truth as determined by innate representations, or the Lockean science of the *individual* objects which we are to infer from the[11] simple representations originally drawn from experience (and containing the

[48]   immutable characteristics of objects).//

In vain would we offer to the Humean skeptic the *simple representations* of Locke, or following Leibniz, the *principle of contradiction*, as our ultimate criterion of truth and the foundation of philosophical knowledge. His philosophy, founded as it is on the belief that all representations originate from impressions, is a philosophy that destroys all philosophy. He would accept the simple representations as well as the principle of contradiction, but at the same time would show that it is only on the strength of an unfounded assumption that they can be employed as criterion of truth and foundation of knowledge. He would say: "Simple representations can found objective truth and attest to it, only if we *assume* with regard to them precisely what has to be established through them, i.e., their agreement with objects differing from them. And the principle of contradiction can demonstrate the necessity and universality of a judgement, only if in passing the judgement we assume the reality of its subject — the very thing which was to be inferred through the judgement. I might grant that *if*, and *to the extent that*, a predicate is joined to a subject, its contrary does

[49]   not permit to be joined to it as well. The principle // of contradiction presupposes everywhere the validity of this condition; its use is justified by it. But it is precisely the validity of this condition, upon which everything depends, that Leibniz assumes as decided, whereas he ought to have given a proof for it. And he failed to give one because in fact no proof can be given for it. I grant that if ever I think a subject with a certain predicate, I cannot think the same subject with the contrary predicate. How do I know, though, that I was right in thinking the subject with that given predicate? That I *had* to think it as I actually did, and could not have thought it otherwise? How do I know this, except because I have assumed that the object of my representation which is distinct from my representation is independently constituted as I have thought it — just so and not otherwise? In other words, I have presupposed what I believe that I had to establish by applying the principle of contradiction; I have presupposed it because it is only on that assumption that the principle can be applied["]. To the dogmatic skeptic the principle of contradiction can have no other meaning than this: "Insofar as two impressions are joined together in my consciousness, they are not separate in it."

[50]   Thus Leibnizian *rationalism* and Lockean *empiricism* rest on // foundations which their originators simply took for granted, and which

later disciples demonstrated only by arguing in a circle from the systems based upon these assumed foundations. The genetic account of representations upon which Hume based his skepticism refuted the unproven assumptions of Locke and Leibniz, and shook the foundations of their systems. One can well understand, therefore, why no dogmatic representative of philosophy has yet made any attempt to refute Humean skepticism that is worthy of notice; or why no Leibnizian or Lockean has yet attacked the Humean foundation, or at least tried to defend his own system upon new grounds. (Let anyone contrast the well known objections of Plattner against Hume, for instance, with the tenets of his skepticism as I have outlined above, and let him judge *whether they hit the mark*.)[12] In keeping with the law of its progression, philosophical [*philosophierende*] reason had to abandon its two older dogmatic expressions in the face of Humean skepticism. Hume's system now stood as its latest attempt at expression. But the less it had to object to it, the more the so-called *common understanding of man* (*sensus comunis*, 'common sense') or, // more precisely, *judgement* guided by the universally *felt* needs of human nature, was aroused by it. For the new philosophy did more than just attack human pride at its most senstitive side by annulling all its claims to knowledge. By challenging the legitimacy of all the supposed grounds of our duties and rights in this present life, as well as of our hope of a future life, it also threatened to steal the Palladium of mankind. Nothing was more natural than the course that Reid, Oswald, Beattie, and others embarked upon to refute Hume.[13] They summoned the common sense of mankind against him, for it was the only course open to them given the stage of development that philosophy had attained at that time. They appealed in their writings to every FEELING at whose tribunal Hume would necessarily stand convicted—even if he had had much more success defending the rigorous requirements of philosophical reason than he in fact did. These were the feelings that help sustain, even among the majority of cultivated people, the principles produced *by thought*. Some of them, the *moral feelings*, since they are expressions of practical reason, are the only means of orientation that *theoretical* reason has at its disposal in the midst of the // internal dissensions which it cannot avoid while it makes its way TOWARDS the discovery of its *ultimate* grounds (that is, BEFORE the discovery itself). This appeal to common sense, and its intervention, were in fact the only means by which the dogmatists could rescue the dignity of their systems and prevent the spreading of a philosophy that was as detrimental to the interest of mankind as it was to that of the sciences. Yet, indispensable and effective as it was, the role assigned to this *newcomer* in the household of philosophy would eventually have been just as detrimental to the progress of philosophical reason (and consequently,

[51]

[52]

to the interest of mankind and science) if the newcomer had in fact retained or enforced his supremacy there, as for a while he seemed to be doing.

Since the judgements of common sense are determined more by will than by thought, more by inclinations than by insights, since their grounds are more felt than thought, they are to this extent (not seldom indeed) an unfailing remedy against the aberrations of *thought*. Like every medicine, however, they become a deadly poison if they

[53]   are used not as medicine but as nourishment for // the philosophical reason. Feelings can only *proclaim* the falsity of thought, not prove it; that *they* are right, on the contrary, can only be tested through reason. The common understanding of man was all too readily misjudged and misused by the philosophers. They should have let it come forward at the trial of *judgement* simply as the advocate of feelings against philosophical reason, which is the advocate of thought. They would have then settled the dispute between the two to the advantage of both. Instead they mistook it for judgement itself; they ensconced it in a judicial seat, and used its one-sided decisions to snub the reason of philosophy. The proposition: 'This is what common sense says' then became the *first principle* of a would-be new philosophy. Its followers called it "eclectic", because it allowed them the most perfect freedom to agree among themselves on no other principle save that one, and when writing books, to select from any given system anything in it that each felt able to accommodate to common understanding, by which each meant all too readily his own. The common sense of academic teachers established the existence of God, the immortality

[54]   of the soul, // and nominally at least the freedom of the will. (As a matter of fact, it would have proven not to be common sense if it had established the contrary, and had thereby lost for its man his professorial chair and the meagre living attached to it.) The common sense of tough-minded French philosophers established instead the non-existence of God, the mortality of the soul, and the fatalistic necessity of all human activities. In this style of philosophizing the reasons adduced for or against the basic truths of religion and morality were as different in each case, when they were not copied from another writer, as modes of representation can possibly be when they depend not upon well thought-out and universally binding principles, but on differences of temperament, education, talent, and cognition. One professor always attacked the argument of another and the tough mind usually uncovered the weakness of the tender one. The ultimate reason that anyone gave for his opinion was always some proposition which, as he claimed, it would have been just as non-sensical to seek

[55]   to prove as to doubt, since it was a pronouncement of common // sense. Through all these discordant oracles nothing was to become

more contentious, equivocal and doubtful in the end than common sense itself, and soon enough the foundation of popular philosophy suffered no better fate than the foundations of the many edifices erected by they systematizers.

Never had philosophy found itself in a more embarrassing position as regards its foundations, and hence as regards the first among the conditions by which it comes to be philosophy, than at the time when, in the name of common sense, the most complete anarchy reigned, and popularity passed as the criterion of truth. Never before had philosophy fallen as far behind the other sciences and especially behind that erudition which displays itself in *narrations* and *descriptions*. Philosophical reason seemed finally to have come to a standstill when, in the person of a man in whom are combined the systematic spirit of Leibniz and the skeptical one of Hume, Locke's sound faculty of judgement and Newton's creative genius, it made advances such as were never made by any single thinker before. Kant discovered a new *foundation of // philosophical knowledge* that includes the truth found scattered, in one-sided forms, in the previous expositions of that knowledge, yet excludes their falsity. Like all of his predecessors he too assumed *immutability*, which is the hallmark of truth, to be the essential characteristic of the foundation of philosophy as well; unlike Locke, however, who tried to obtain it from the *simples* borrowed immediately from experience, and unlike Leibniz, who tried to obtain it from innate representations, he derived it rather from the *possibility of experience* which is found *determined* in the mind *prior to all experience*. Of course, many among the more acute thinkers had already suspected that in the dispute about the origin of representations, and by implication about the source of human knowledge, the truth must lie midway between the opposing claims championed by those two great men. By putting together whatever truth there is in Locke's empiricism and in Leibniz's rationalism it had to be possible to erect a system that would rise above all the objections offered by Hume's skepticism, and satisfy its rigorous but fair requirements. But what even the sharpest thinkers could only *guess at*, but could not see clearly, this Kant actually provided in the *Critique of Pure Reason*. In this work he was // not satisfied with stating in general terms alone that the *possibility of experience* is the ultimate foundation (which is more like what Locke did as regards simple representations, or Leibniz for his principle of contradiction); instead he offered a criterion by which we can conclude *how, by which means,* and *to what extent,* this is so. He showed "*in what* the possibility of experience consists" through an exhaustive analysis of the *faculty of cognition*.[14] He did not utter the propitious thought that "the origin of representations is to be found neither in experience alone, nor just in the nature of the soul, but in the two

[56]

[57]

together,"[15] as one utters a generality. He did not simply announce, so to speak, that the ground of the coming to be of those representations that carry with them the character of necessity is to be sought in the possibility of experience as determined in the mind, but that for all other representations the ground of their coming to be is to be sought in actual experience; or that nothing can be *innate* save the determinate possibility of experience (i.e., the faculty to generate experience), but that nothing on the other hand can be drawn *from experience* save the material for the representations of objects that belong to the sensible world. He definitely identified, rather, *what* our representations owe to experience, and what to the soul. He exhaustively enumerated the number of the *original* representations that have their ground in the possibility of experience determined in the mind (i.,e., the *a priori* representations). In brief, he measured what is innate to the human spirit and accurately separated it from what is obtained from experience, while making visible the connection between the two.

[58]   //

The *Critique of Pure Reason* undercuts *dogmatic skepticism* by uncovering the arbitrariness of its foundation. That system stands or falls by the thesis, "Representations are originally nothing but impressions", which Hume assumed without proof. Kant was the first to call attention to the *essential* distinction between simple impression and representation that Hume ignored entirely. He showed that only the material of representations, or more precisely, of that specific kind of representations that belong to outer sense, can be made out of impressions given from the outside; in no way can every effect of the mind's activity be, or be taken to be, just an inner impression.

[59]   The *Critique* undercuts *empiricism* by uncovering the arbitrariness of its foundation. That system // stands or falls by the thesis: "Representations are derived exclusively from experience." Kant was the first to call attention to the *essential* distinction, overlooked by Locke, between *experience* understood as the joining together of perceived objects, and *impressions* or sensations which contain only the material of perceptions. The *connection* between objects cannot be sensed, it cannot be produced from sensations.[16] Inasmuch, therefore, as it must be *thought* to be determined (i.e., subject to immutable laws), it can only be so within the form of the faculty of cognition, independently of all experience.

The *Critique* undercuts *rationalism* by uncovering the arbitrariness of its foundation. That system stands or falls by the thesis: "Anything necessary and universal of which we can be conscious is grounded in innate representations," or as some more recent Leibnizians have stated it: ". . . is to be found in an innate system of eternal truths of reason." Kant was the first to call attention to the *essential* distinction, ignored by Leibniz, between the form of mere representation, which is

determined in the mind by // its disposition prior to all experience,   [60]
and actual representation; and to show that the immediate representation necessary to the *cognition of things outside us* (i.e., intuition) can
obtain its material only through external impression. The necessity
and universality grounded in the form of representation, therefore,
can apply to *objects* that are not just forms of representations, but
knowable, real things, only to the extent that that material is given to
the mind. Hence the reality of the necessary and universal characteristics
of knowable objects depends on experience and is restricted to its
domain. There cannot be any knowable object inside us save the
forms of representations determined in the mind; nor any outside us,
except objects that can be represented exclusively in sensible
representations (i.e., the appearances of the sensible world). Our
knowledge can thus extend no further *a priori* than those forms or
what follows from them, and *a posteriori*, no further than mere
experience.

Thus Hume, Locke, and Leibniz would find again, synthesized in
the system of the *Critique of Reason*, // the indisputable truth that   [61]
each had in mind when he laid the foundation of his own system.
Hume would find again the *impressions* which he regarded as
indispensable to the representation of genuine objects—though at times
he confused them with representations, and at other times with objects.
In the *Critique of Reason*, on the other hand, they are taken as the
representatives of objects, and in this way they are distinguished from
the objects as well as from the representations whose material they
constitute. And since they are declared to be indispensable to every
cognition—to any representation of an individual—they are in fact
elevated to the status of *objective element* of knowledge. Locke would
find again the *experience* which he had elevated into the source of *all*
representations only because of an unphilosophical confusion of objects
that can be cognized with objects of representation in general. According
to Kant, the reality of the representations of cognizable objects is
grounded upon it through the medium of impressions. Finally, Leibniz
would find the *innate* [element] on which the necessity and universality
of certain characteristics of objects is based. He confused the forms of
representations, which originally belong only to the subject of
representations, with the representations themselves. And as a result
he made that *innate* [element] consist of representations that were
already actual—such, moreover, as would have given us cognition of
objects as *things-in-themselves*. //   [62]

With Hume, Locke and Leibniz, philosophical reason had imposed
certain requirements upon itself which Kant met by demonstrating
that the foundation of philosophical knowledge lies in the *possibility
of experience*. Yet, however successful he was in this, it still cannot be

denied that his [newly] uncovered foundation fails to ground the *whole* of philosophical knowledge; on the contrary it can *only* ground ONE PART of it. In respect of its foundation this part is, to be sure, the most controversial; and with respect to its consequences, it is the most important. It is the part that Locke, Leibniz, and Hume had exclusively in mind, as did everybody else who was also engaged in the task of investigating the groundworks of philosophical knowledge. There has been a tendency, especially in modern times, to call it simply "philosophy", sometimes by exclusion, and sometimes in an eminent sense. But for all that it remains only one part—no more and no less—of the science which is entitled by right to that name. In short, the only part of philosophical knowledge that Kant grounded is that philosophical science properly called *metaphysics*. Not even Kant's explicit declaration that his *Critique of Pure Reason* is nothing else than *propaedeutic to metaphysics*[17] has effectively prevented followers who

[63]   are more faithful to the letter than to the spirit of the // master from taking it as constituting the *doctrine of the elements of philosophy*. A prejudice of this sort could not prevail among the friends of critical philosophy without stifling its *spirit* and trivializing its mighty aims.

The only problem that the *Critique of Reason* could resolve, and did in fact resolve, by appealing to the possibility of experience, is whether the *science of objects proper* [*eigentlicher Objekte*], that is to say, of objects [*Gengenstände*] that are distinguished in consciousness from all mere representations or the properties of representations, is possible or not. This problem concerns the possibility of *metaphysics* as a science; and this possibility could not be put to the test, and demonstrated, without the foundations of all *previous* metaphysics being tested at the same time, and the foundation of a *future* metaphysics being established. Hume, Locke and Leibniz in their *essays concerning the human understanding* had no other science than this in mind.[18] From Locke's simple representations, immediately drawn from experience, or from Leibniz's innate representations of the necessary and universal, we should be able to grasp the *possibility* of a science of objects proper (i.e., a real science)—or its *impossibility*, should the representations

[64]   turn out to be originally nothing but // impressions, as Hume would have it. By the *real truth* whose demonstrability they investigated in their works Leibniz, Locke, and Kant understood the agreement of mere representations with objects proper (i.e., objects that are distinct from representations) or what was once called METAPHYSICAL truth. Locke just took this agreement for granted in the case of his simple representations, without any proof. Leibniz made it out to be demonstrable, in the case of necessary and universal representations, through the principle of contradiction. Hume denied its demonstrability, on the ground that representations are nothing but impressions. Kant,

in contrast, restricted it to objects of possible experience, i.e., to such objects whose representations can be given a sensible material through outer impressions. Of course, to these objects there also belong, with necessity and universality, a number of characteristics founded on the possibility of experience as determined *a priori* in the mind. But since these characteristics are originally nothing but forms of representations, they owe their *objective reality*, i.e., their actual, // [65] not merely possible relation to objects other than representations, to the impression in some actual experience.[19]

Hence the *Critique of Pure Reason* proclaimed, and also demonstrated, that any metaphysics not meant to be the science of objects of possible experience is untenable, unfounded and contradictory . [And this applied to] the metaphysics of supra-sensible objects; to the *former ontology* inasmuch as, *qua* science of objects in general, it also included supra-sensible objects; to *rational psychology, cosmology* and *theology*. The *Critique* showed that if metaphysics is to be the science of knowable, real objects, it has to be metaphysics of *sensible nature*, i.e., the science of the necessary and universal characteristics of appearances, the sum-concept of which constitutes the *sensible world* or the *domain of experience*.

"*Metaphysical truth* can be demonstrated only in the case of objects of actual experience, i.e., objects knowable *a posteriori*; *real science* can only consist, *qua* philosophy, in the science of the characteristics of those *a posteriori objects* that can be cognized *a priori* // because [66] they are determined in the possibility of experience, and in this sense they are necessary and universal."[20] This is the *principal result* of the *Critique of Pure Reason*; it fulfills, and confirms, the true intention (1) of Hume's demand that "the representation of a real object must arise through sensation"; (2) of Locke's demand that "the reality of a representation be based on experience"; finally, (3) of Leibniz's demand that "necessity and universality must be based on something innate." At the same time, however, this result secures a *concept* of 'object proper' and of 'knowable object' of a kind that neither Locke nor Leibniz had in mind when defending their theses, nor Hume when challenging the foundation of real science. By 'knowable object' they understood, each and all of them, not just an object distinct from its mere representation, but the *thing-in-itself*. But inasmuch as the real object *can be cognized* at all, it can be referred to, according to *its form*, by a representation founded only in the mind; hence it can never be represented as *thing-in-itself*. This tiresome *thing-in-itself*, which is just as vehemently defended by phantasy as it is contested by reason, is introduced in the *Critique of Pure Reason* simply as something that *cannot be known*. And as long as it is taken to be REPRESENTABLE, // Kant's concept of an *object proper* will never be understood. Any [67] Humean will then maintain, of course, that it is absurd for the *Critique of Reason* to parade as the *science* of real objects what is in fact the science of the characteristics of mere appearances; and any Lockean will object to being offered the science of mere objects of experience as the science of things independent of experience; and any Leibnizian, finally, will refuse to treat the necessary and universal predicates that make up the content of a real science as the characteristics of mere objects of experience.

The *one single* science for which Kant has discovered and defined the foundation, and which he has therefore *fully established* as far as analysis goes, is metaphysics *qua* science of the objects of possible experience. He did not provide a foundation for science whose objects are beyond all possible experience, e.g., for a science of the substance of the soul, or of the cosmos, or of the divinity. On the contrary, he expressly showed that no such foundation is possible. And the one example that we have of a text-book of metaphysics written in [68]   accordance with the principles of the *Critique of Reason* supplies, // in lieu of those parts of metaphysics once called "Psychology", "Cosmology", and "Theology", an excerpt from the text of the *Critique* where the impossibility of metaphysics is demonstrated.[21]

It belongs to the groundwork of a science as the ultimate condition for its foundation and as sign that it has been completed, that its *first principle* should be discovered and expounded. The *Critique of Reason* found that the only tenable metaphysics is the science of the objects of possible experience, and for this it did establish a first principle in the proposition: "Every object stands under the necessary conditions of synthetic unity of the manifold of intuition in a possible experience,"[22] or what amounts to the same: "To every real object, insofar as it is to be knowable as such, belong the formal and material conditions of experience"[23] (i.e., the forms of intuition and of the concept that are determined in the faculty of cognition; and the material that is given through impression). This principle expresses nothing but the concept [69]   of an object of experience (of a knowable, authentic object). It // identifies the [one] characteristic which belongs necessarily and universally to all objects of experience, and is consequently the predicate of the proposition upon which the unity of all possible metaphysical cognitions of an object of experience depends. This is the proposition, in other words, to which metaphysics owes its systematic unity and its rank as philosophical science.

This proposition stands at the head of all the principles, theorems, and corollaries of the metaphysics of sensible nature. It grounds their demonstrability, and it defines the scope of the science (i.e., *the [element] common to its content*). Yet, like any other first principle, it *is not*, and *cannot be, demonstrated* in the science it grounds, or through it. Its meaning can be elucidated in the science only through its application;

it cannot be further developed or grounded without circularity. As the propaedeutic to this metaphysics, the *Critique of Reason* has grounded the meaning of this principle. It has done so by developing the concept of the possibility of experience, and by showing that the formal conditions of experience are grounded *a priori* in the faculty of cognition. (These conditions are: the forms of sensible representations, or space and time, and the forms of concepts, or the // categories.) [70] The fate of Kant's newly founded metaphysics depends, therefore, on this explication of how experience is made possible in the mind, i.e., of how the faculty of cognition is originally constituted. And although its principles, theorems and corollaries may well be universally valid, they can never become universally binding unless the foundation itself is secured with principles, theorems and corollaries that are universally binding. This is to say: Unless the propaedeutic to this metaphysics is itself raised to the status of the science of the faculty of cognition.[24].

This science, which Kant did not establish, would have to be distinguished from the *metaphysics* he did establish thus: whereas the latter is the science of the characteristics (determined *a priori*) of *objects proper*, the former would have to be the science of the characteristics (determined *a priori*) of *mere representations*. The metaphysics has as its object the objects of experience, i.e., what can be cognized *a posteriori* by being represented through the *a priori* forms of sensible representation and of the concepts; the other science would have for its object these very forms, but precisely as what is originally knowable *a priori*. Or again, one is the science of empirical nature inasmuch as this // can be known *a priori*; the other would be the science of the [71] empirical faculty of cognition, which is made up of sensibility and understanding.

Now, since *sensibility and understanding* exhaust the *empirical faculty of cognition*, whereas reason is its *pure faculty* (i.e., the faculty by which we recognize the forms of representations *qua* determined *a priori*), the science of sensibility and understanding, taken *together with* the science of reason, would be the science of the *entire faculty of cognition*.

This science of the *faculty of cognition* would have to be *preceded* by another that establishes its foundation. This other science too would be a science of sensibility, understanding and reason—not, however, inasmuch as these are identical with the faculty of cognition, but inasmuch as they stand in common at its foundation (and indeed, at the foundation of the *faculty of desire* as well). It would be the science of the *a priori* form of REPRESENTING through sensibility, understanding and reason; on this form depends the form of knowledge, as well as that of desire. In a word, it would be the science of the *entire faculty of representation as such*.

For this science, which I name general *Philosophy of the Elements* [*Elementarphilosophie*]²⁵ because it serves as the common foundation to both *theoretical* and *practical //* philosophy, the *Critique of Reason* has indeed provided *materials*, but never the idea, let alone the actual *foundation*. And if it is ever to be realized, *philosophical reason must press forward yet another step in its analysis past the point attained in the Critique of Reason. This is the final step that philosophical reason can take, proceeding analytically, on its way to higher principles; through it, and it alone, is the ultimate and proper foundation of* PHILOSOPHY *discovered*.

The object of this science is all that can be known *a priori* concerning the representations of sensibility, understanding and reason— and nothing else. Its object can consist, therefore, in nothing but the *forms* of these representations as determined in the faculty of the representation; the science must identify them and how that they are the *original being of the representations*, i.e., their forms or most essential characteristics, their nature *simply qua representations*. In this science alone can it be established, through a proof that is universally valid, and will eventually become universally binding, that *space* and *time*, the *twelve categories* and the *three //* forms *of ideas*, are *originally* nothing but the properties of *mere representations*. And on this proof rests the possibility of another *universally binding* proof by which the *science of the faculty of cognition* must show that the only objects that can be known, through sensibility and understanding are those of *experience*; that no others can be known through reason, save the *forms of representations* and whatever can be deduced or derived from them. The proof would also show, therefore, that the only objects that can be known *a posteriori* are in the form of sensible representation (*appearances*), and that those that can be known *a priori* are characteristics of appearances for forms of representations determined in the faculty of cognition; consequently, that *things-in-themselves* cannot be known either through sensibility and understanding, or through reason. The momentous upshot of the Critique, viz., *things-in-themselves cannot be* known rests on the proof of two propositions: "Nothing can be known *a priori* save the form of mere representation, and what is possible through it," and "The form of mere representation cannot be the form of things-in-themselves." These the *Critique* has demonstrated by means of a complete induction; but this can only satisfy those who approach what Kant says about the forms of sensible *//* intuitions, and about the concepts and ideas, without any misconception regarding the *form of representation in general*, and the *possibility* of *representing* the *thing-in-itself*. These are topics about which Kant himself does not say very much, or at any rate nothing determinate. The *science* of the faculty of cognition, strictly taken,

[72]

[73]

[74]

must be rigorously confined to *knowledge*; it presupposes that we have already become acquainted with the forms of representation as such in the science of the faculty of representation. This prior science alone is also capable of establishing the fundamental proposition, ["] *The form of representation as such cannot be the form of the thing-in-itself"*, which the science of the faculty of cognition requires for its scientific demonstration of the other proposition: "*A thing cannot be known in-itself.*"[26]

If the science of the faculty of cognition is to remedy the *confusion*, which has been the main pitfall of all previous philosophy, between the predicates of mere representations, that are determined *a priori*, and those of knowable objects that we derive from experience, it must proceed from the *concept of representation as such*, and exhaustively identify its essential characteristics; only then will it deserve its name.[27]

Of course, from the // concept of *representation in general*, *qua* generic   [75]
concept, we cannot derive the concept of *sensible representation*, or that of *concept* itself (*qua* representation of the understanding), or that of *idea* (*qua* representation of reason), with respect to their *specifying characteristics*. Yet, what these concepts *have in common* can only be cognized from the concept of 'representation', and can only be derived from the source from which that generic concept is *originally* obtained. It is what makes them *simply representations*, and it does not in any way depend on their specified properties. [For instance,] we cannot have knowledge through a sensible representation, a concept or an idea, of a thing as it is 'in-itself', *not because* the *specifying characteristics* of these representations make them unfit to yield such knowledge, but because *a thing* cannot be known *in-itself* through *any representation* simply *qua* representation.
[See my *Contributions to the Rectification of Misconceptions Hitherto Held by Philosophers*, Vol. I, pp. 269ff. (Jena: Mauke, 1790)].[28]

Precisely because the science of the faculty of representation must come first in order to ground the sciences of the faculties of cognition and desire—it is the propaedeutic, that is, not just to metaphysics, but // to all *philosophy* (theoretical as well as practical)—it cannot   [76]
derive the characteristics of the *concept of representation* from any *part of philosophy*. I know that critical philosophers have asserted that the concept of representation has been *sufficiently* determined in the *Critique of Pure Reason*, or that it can be derived from the concept of sensible representation, the concept of concept, and the concept of idea secured in it. In my view, however, this very claim demonstrates that they still lack a determinate concept of representation. The *Critique* only deals with the specifying characteristics of the various kinds of representations; the concept of representation *qua representation* can no more be derived from these specifications than the concept 'triangle' can be derived

from 'equal sides' and 'unequal sides', or the generic concept of 'humanity' from the *gender concepts* 'male' and 'female'. Even granted that the *Critique* were already the authentic *science of the faculty of cognition* (which is by no means the case), it would still not be possible to demonstrate the essential characteristics of the concept of representation from it, for the concept of 'cognition' presupposes that of 'representation'; and the form of cognition, although it cannot be [77]   derived from the // mere form of representing alone, essentially *depends* upon it nevertheless.

What has to stand at the *head* of the *Philosophy of the Elements* —and hence of all philosophical explanations and proofs—cannot itself be established through a proof drawn from any part of philosophy whatever, nor for that matter can any philosophy, past or future, prove it. In respect to its essential characteristics the concept of *representation* cannot be demonstrated, therefore, by the science of the faculty of representation. Those characteristics can, and must, be identified by it by means of an exhaustive analysis, but they cannot be produced by it. The analysis that the science performs on the concept presupposes that they are already joined, with determinacy and necessity. But this is to say: The concept of representation, which the science of the faculty of representation is to determine *analytically*, must have already been *synthetically* determined to this end. So determined—independently of all philosophizing, for the latter depends on this original determinateness for its correctness—the concept of representation can only be drawn from the CONSCIOUSNESS of [78]   an *actual fact* [*Tatsache*]. This fact alone, *qua* // *fact*, must *ground* the foundation of the Philosophy of the Elements—for otherwise the foundation cannot rest, without circularity, on any philosophically demonstrable proposition. It is not through any inference of reason that we know *that in consciousness representation is distinguished through the subject from both object and subject and is referred to both,*[29] but through simple *reflection* upon the actual fact of consciousness, that is, by ordering together [*Vergleichung*] what is present in it.

The concept of *representation, inasmuch as it lies at the foundation* of the proposition just stated, is *immediately* drawn from consciousness; as such it is entirely *simple* and incapable of analysis. Its source is an *actual fact* which is suited to yield the *last* possible foundation for all explanation precisely because, *qua fact*, it admits of no explanation but is self-explanatory. No definition of *representation* is therefore possible. The principle of consciousness, far from being a *definition*, qualifies rather as the *first principle* of all philosophy precisely because it presents a concept that does not allow definition; it is not itself the highest among possible definitions, yet it makes that highest definition [79]   possible in the first place.//

The concept of *representation* does not merely stand as a *simple concept*, at the ground of the principle of consciousness; it is also determined by what the principle expresses, viz., the *actual facts* of *consciousness*. And *inasmuch* as it is so determined, it constitutes (when expressed in words) the *definition of representation*. It is the *scientific concept* of representation, and the task of the theory of the faculty of representation is to exhaust its content. The original, unexplainable and simple concept of representation *precedes* consciousness; it stands at its ground. In contrast, the original but complex and explainable concept of the same *follows* from consciousness, and is determined by the facts that make up the latter—i.e., the *distinguishing* of the representation which is as such unexplainable from the object and subject, and its *being referred* to them—as well as through the *proposition* expressing these facts. The former concept can only be expressed by a word, "representation", for which no definition is possible; the original complex concept, on the contrary, can be expressed by the *definition* of precisely this word. One is dependent on the incomprehensible possibility of consciousness; the other, on its known possibility. One is presupposed by the principle of consciousness; the other presupposes it.[30]// [80]

To call the *principle of consciousness* a definition, one must have misunderstood it. In the state of philosophy to date this can perhaps very easily happen even to the most famous and practiced among philosophers. Of course the definition of representation is included in the principle—*inasmuch*, that is, as it can be *derived* from it, and from it alone. But it is no more possible for the principle to be itself this definition than for a ground ever to be both ground and consequence in the same respect. My first principle expresses, *qua principle of consciousness*, only the *actual fact* through which the concept of representation is determined; the *definition* of representation, instead, expresses nothing but this concept. The principle grounds the definition without being in turn grounded by another definition. Its ground is consciousness, and [more precisely], the fact in consciousness which it expresses.

Anyone who accuses me of *building upon mere definitions*, therefore, is misinterpreting the entire foundation on which my system rests, and hence my entire system as well; he is just passing judgement on something he has not understood. My foundation is *consciousness*; and while consciousness itself // is certainly not all that I offer as a [81] *scientific* foundation, what I do offer rests on nothing else but consciousness. I do not pull my *definition** of representation out of

---

* By *definition* I understand a methodical, indeed scientific explanation. The rule that any such explanation must specify for each concept its proximate genus and specific difference does not apply in the case of the *absolutely first* among all possible definitions because the concept that it exhibits, being the most generic one, cannot stand under any *genus*.

thin air, but I ground it upon a *principle which is determined through itself*. And since it is so determined in its entirety, it keeps the definition that is *determined through it* free of any *arbitrariness*. Thus it establishes the *first* definition about which it can be shown that it cannot contain any arbitrary characteristic at all. "Representation is that which is distinguished in consciousness by the subject from object and subject, and is referred to both". Precisely because the sense of this formula derives *solely* from the principle of consciousness, it excludes any characteristic not contained in that principle—hence, any characteristic (whether true or false) drawn discursively from

[82]   // some theorem or other, or again, any that would not have to be found just in consciousness. Of course, no verbal formula or literary device in the whole world can prevent *phantasy* from interpolating in the formulation of the definition of representation a meaning which is not determined by the principle of consciousness (which is the only source of genuine meaning for it). Phantasy *behaves arbitrarily*, being driven by whims and prejudices (especially by *those that tend to flatter*). And against *this* kind of arbitrariness either there is no remedy at all, or the remedy must be sought in *practical* philosophy.

I have called the principle of consciousness "*self-determined*". By self-determined principle I understand one whose meaning cannot be determined through any higher proposition. The principle of consciousness can indeed be unfolded *analytically* (elucidated) —but only on the basis of what is (*synthetically*) determined through it, i.e., of what follows from it and from it alone, and in respect to which it is therefore presupposed as already established. Not only does the definition of consciousness say nothing that would not be originally included in it; it also says nothing that could be understood without

[83]   presupposing what the principle expresses. // This is the self-explanatory fact of consciousness. it determines the principle immediately, and it is not open to further analysis, or to the possibility that it might be reduced to characteristics simpler than those indicated by the principle itself. It is *self*-determined in the sense that any possible explanation of the concepts that it exhibits is only possible through it; for its part, on the other hand, it does not allow of any explanation, and it needs none.

The principle of consciousness is determined *through itself in its entirety*; in this respect it stands apart from *any* other possible principle. I say "in its entirety", for we simply would not find in it any supposed characteristic except one that both can and must be determined *exclusively* through it. Neither its subject nor its predicate contain any characteristic which, so far as it is determinable, would not be determined solely through it. Even the *axioms* of mathematics are self-determined only as regards the one predicate that each attaches to its subject. The latter is not determined simply by that predicate, but contains characteristics definable independently of the axiom. And although in the case of tautological mathematical propositions, e.g., 'The circle is round', // the necessity of the judgement is made [84] apparent through intuition of the subject, any such proposition is still *self*-determined *independently of the proposition* — everyone can convince himself of this simply by reflecting on the individual characteristics of 'circle' as stated in any possible definition of it. One only needs to consider, for instance, the characteristic 'figure' which must appear in any of its definitions, and ask himself whether it is not capable of definition — of one, moreover, that cannot at all depend on the judgement, 'The circle is round'. Let anyone try, however, to do the same for any at all of the characteristics of the concepts exhibited in the principle of consciousness, and he will find that he is either totally unable to define it, or that he can do so only through the principle itself.

The *principle of contradiction* which, inasmuch as it has been accepted as absolutely first, has also been taken to be entirely *self* -determined, suffers from an ambiguity that can be removed only by appealing to the prior correct concept of // representation. This is so whether [85] the principle is stated in its older formulation or in Kant's.[31] The concept 'thing' present in it can only be determined through the concept 'thinkable'. But this presupposes 'representable' which is the common characteristic of 'thinkable', 'intuitable', and 'sensible', and hence cannot be determined through the concept 'thought'; the latter is only one *kind* of representing. Now, since the concept 'representable' depends on 'representation', and this depends (as regards its definition) on the principle of consciousness, it follows that the principle of contradiction can be fully determined only through the principle of consciousness. Premises which the theory of the faculty of representation must first develop are indispensable to the determination of its true meaning. Even then, since it is a statement about intelligibility, it can lay claim to the rank of first principle only in logic. To take it as supreme principle of philosophy is to confuse philosophy with logic, and to take it as principle of the *form of representing* is to mistake 'representing in general' for 'mere thinking'. Of course, the principle of consciousness is also subject *to it* — not, however, in the sense that is determined by it, but as a law which it is not allowed to contravene. The principle of contradiction cannot include any real ground of truth. And unless the principle of consciousness drew this ground not from it, but from the *consciousness* it expresses, i.e., *from itself*, its mere lack of contradiction // would make it no more true than the thousands [86] of other propositions which are non-contradictory, yet false just the same. Of course, the principle of consciousness would not be thought if it did not allow itself to be thought. But *on this justification* – i.e., because it can be thought, or for that matter, because it is actually being thought – its being thought still does not have a ground. It is not its logical truth but its real truth, not the possibility of thinking it but WHAT *is thought in it*, that makes the principle of consciousness the *fundamental principle* – not just a logical or formal principle, but a real or material one – of the science of the faculty of representation. And by being the principle of this science, which is the Philosophy of the Elements, it is also the *fundamental principle* of philosophy in general.

The definitions of *representation*, *object*, and *subject* that are directly derived from the principle of consciousness are no less thoroughly determined than the principle from which they derive all their characteristics. That of 'representation' comes first; but among all the explanatory principles that philosophers have hitherto laid down, the [87] three of them are the *first* to have a sense that is so thoroughly // determined as to make impossible the arbitrary inclusion of foreign characteristics in the concept being defined, or the exclusion of essential ones from it. For since the principle of consciousness only expresses the actual fact of consciousness, *as long as* it brings this fact to light simply through *reflection*, it is not open to misunderstandings caused by false reasoning. And the characteristics of consciousness which it makes known are absolutely *simple*; they do not consist of some aggregate into which a foreign characteristic could be interpolated, or from which something could be left out that properly belongs to it. Consequently, either they cannot be thought at all, or must be thought rightly. Hence, anyone who wants to derive the concept of representation, or more precisely, the *original* concept of representation, not from a metaphysical system of his own making which rests on some wrong concept of representation, but from its first and purest source, i.e., from consciousness (as we should expect to be the case, for obvious reasons, for the majority of professional philosophers and reputable writers of philosophy) – or again, anyone who does not *want* to declare the definition of representation either superfluous or impossible, or perhaps to derive it from indeterminate definitions in preference to the principle of consciousness (for, no doubt, even with philosophers much depends on what one *wants*) – anyone who is so inclined can [88] rest assured // that he has found an unfailing and exhaustive definition for the concept of representation.

If I were writing for popular philosophers, I would have to contend with the objection that here too *everything* DEPENDS *on the choice of terms, and that this choice is ultimately arbitrary*. These philosophers who garner their concepts only from *hearsay*, yet are accustomed to hear only with one ear, are all too eager to remind themselves that by *words* we have always meant, from time immemorial, *arbitrary signs of thought*. The fact that 'arbitrary' must mean, in this context, not 'dependent on free choice, but 'the contrary of natural' (a 'natural sign' is one determined by what is signifies) — this the popular philosopher is all the less likely to remember because he is conscious of the arbitrary attacks that he has allowed himself, in the name of free choice, upon the rights of linquistic usage. And this is a practice which, given the state of philosophy to date, has unfortunately been *common* not only among the popular philosophers. To a philosopher of independent mind the proposition, 'The choice of terms (in a principle or even in a correct definition) is *ultimately* arbitrary', can carry no meaning. For he knows that unless words have a meaning independent of any arbitrary choice, he would not understand either himself or anybody else. // He knows that when words are being [89] used arbitrarily, thought comes to an end. One of the first duties of every philosophical writer, therefore, is to oppose this practice [in others], and to abstain from it himself as rigorously as possible. Since he recognizes the importance and the proper place in philosophy of *principles* and *definitions*, he also knows that nowhere must he be as carefully on guard against the arbitrary choice of terms as in their case.

The definitions hitherto found in philosophy have been rightly faulted for *arbitrariness*. To my knowledge, however, no independent thinker has yet claimed that this arbitrariness is rooted in the nature of definitions, or that in *any definition* the choice of terms to be used is *ultimately arbitrary*. On the contrary, any such arbitrariness has always been decried wherever it was supposedly detected, and blamed for the misunderstandings in philosophy, as well as for the confused state of its concepts. And this is as it should be. But in my opinion *high-handed* deviation from ordinary usage, motivated // by some [90] subjective interest, is not the most important cause of these evils — not at least among disciplined thinkers. The most important cause has gone entirely unrecognized, and is to be sought rather in the lack of determinateness that has hitherto affected philosophical concepts. This vagueness cannot be remedied by mere fidelity to established usage, however unbending. More often than not, serious philosophers have done one another wrong in their mutual accusations of *arbitrariness* when defining words. The parties to these disputes knew that each had scrupulously attended to common usage. Their failure, in each case, lay neither in a lack of acquaintance with it, nor in a lack of good will towards it, but in the fact that the *meaning* of a word was still far from completely *determined*. The failure was due to some concept whose characteristics were inaccurately *put together*, and *analysis* could not make any more accurate. Either one characteristic too much or one too few had been included in one or more of the single concepts (the aggregates) that make up the *total concept*. And although two philosophers might still agree on the definition of a concept *as regards its formulation*, and might imagine because of their agreement over words that they were heeding common usage, their agreement was

[91]   often the consequence // of a misunderstanding about concepts. And the latter made itself felt soon enough (though its cause went unrecognized) the moment the question was raised concerning which single characteristics were included in the defined concept. For one disputant would have a concept in mind that included some superfluous characteristic; the other disputant would have a different concept that did not include that characteristic—but he might have left out an essential one instead. In every case, of course, the difference between concepts was disclosed by the different meanings with which the disputants employed one and the same word. But this difference, far from being the consequence of arbitrariness in the use of words, reflected rather the conviction on the part of the disputants that the word they were using only meant what each intended by his concept. Neither knew that the concept was still indefinite. And because of their conviction, each felt obliged to accuse his opponent of an arbitrary use of words. So if one claims that "in definitions the choice of terms is always arbitrary," one shows instantly that one has not given much thought to the nature of definitions, and to the conditions of their

[92]   validity, or not to have done so with much success.[32]//

In the situation of philosophy hitherto, the most important cause of the incorrectness of definitions has been the failure of philosophical reason to attain the ultimate and highest concept in its analytical advance, i.e., the most universal characteristic. Philosophy has had to leave this concept completely indefinite, along with the characteristic represented by it—and has had to use it like that. The fact is that the concept regarded until now as the *highest* has been that of 'thing', and its *most universal* characteristic, that of 'intelligibility'—for by 'thing' we have meant 'what can be thought' in general. But the vagueness and ambiguity to which this concept and the characteristics that it represents were subject—together with the consequences that have resulted in every part of philosophy—all this can hardly be a secret to anyone who has dealt with recent philosophy. And this infirmity of philosophy will endure, with all its consequences, as long as 'intelligibility' is held to be the highest and most universal characteristic, and the principle of contradiction by which we traditionally determine its concept, is regarded as the first principle of philosophy. In other words, it will endure as long as we do not realize that 'representing'

[93]   stands to 'thinking' as genus // to species; consequently, that 'capacity to be represented' expresses a higher characteristic than 'intelligibility'.

The concept of intelligibility will not be exhaustively analyzed, it will not be secured against superfluous or missing characteristics, as long as its generic characteristic, the 'ability to be represented', is left undeveloped, i.e., as long as *that* concept is still not *exhausted*.

The ultimate condition for that correctness of the *philosophical definitions* that depends on the complete definition of their sense is the thoroughgoing determinateness, i.e., the exhaustive unfolding, of the *highest* and *ultimate* characteristic. The *mathematical* concept is determined through intuition, through the immediate representation of its object; the *philosophical* concept is only defined through reasoning, and often only by way of a long series of inferences. In the case of mathematics, it is the intuited object that prevents the combination of improper characteristics; in the case of philosophy, there is only the accuracy of the single partial aggregates that come before the [final] all-inclusive combination, and which are each more or less made up in turn of other such aggregates. The accuracy of all possible philosophical definitions thus presupposes the accuracy of one that is supreme and ultimate—one whose characteristics do not allow of further // definition, but must be exhaustively determined through a self-determining principle. This is not to say that we could derive every other possible definition from it *alone* —with the result that its accuracy would be all that is required for the accuracy of the rest. The point is rather that, since the *most* universal characteristic necessarily pertains to every representable object, and hence must enter—not explicitly of course, but not on that account any the less necessarily—into any given definition, it determines the sense of such a definition from above; it has a decisive influence upon all the characteristics present in it, explicit as well as *implicit*. In a word, the accuracy of the highest characteristic does not *alone* determine that of the subordinate ones; but its *inaccuracy* makes their accuracy impossible.   [94]

Short of maintaining, therefore, that the so-called arbitrariness so far exhibited by philosophical definitions—their illegitimacy, their disputable accuracy, or worse still, their decided inaccuracy—is a failure of nature, an incurable sickness of the human spirit—short of maintaining this, I say, it would be unphilosophical indeed to look for the ground of the failure in the failure itself; or // to adduce the failure itself as an objection against the attempt to uncover and remove its real ground; or finally, to believe that by appealing to the so-called arbitrariness of philosophical definitions one can dispose of the importance and authority of the definiton of representation. On the contrary, this definition, being determined in its entirety through the principle of consciousness, is the first to be drawn out in all its characteristices. And since it defines the highest and most universal of all characteristics, i.e., the 'capacity to be represented', it should   [95] remove what has been until now the principal cause of that so-called arbitrariness of philosophical definitions. This cause has until now been unavoidable, because it was rooted in the situation of philosophy itself.

But did not Kant himself say: "The system of philosophy cannot in any way be based on definitions; these must come rather at the end than at the beginning of our enquiries?"[33] Indeed he did; but how often has he been quoted without being understood. Of course, defining *philosophy* is only possible if philosophy itself holds the determinate possibility for it—and it has this possibility only when it uncovers and sets forth its own foundation. This latter, precisely because it is [96] the foundation, cannot be the concept of philosophy itself. // I have never even dreamed, therefore, of giving my *new definition of philosophy* as groundwork of my philosophical system. What I set at the foundation of my philosophy is not a definition at all, but a fact [*Faktum*], the expression of which yields the one self-determined principle that is possible. And in virtue of this principle it also provides the first and highest definition from which philosophy in general, but in particular the Philosophy of the Elements, must proceed. *This* definition (or *any other* for that matter, for the legitimacy of *all* the rest depends on it) could certainly not have been put at the foundation of any previous philosophical system, not even at that of *critical* philosophy. Before the work of analysis could be undertaken on the *supreme* characteristic, it had first to be successfully carried out on those that are *subordinate* to it. Kant had first to discover the *distinguishing characteristics* of the several *species* of representation before the one *proper* to the *genus* could be discovered—which, while it cannot be produced out of the species, can also not be presumed *before* them. This discovery of the ultimate and authentic foundation of philosophy, as well as of the ground that determines the first in the series of all [97] possible definitions, // the one that legitimizes all the rest, could only *bring* the labour of analytical progression *to conclusion*, not *initiate* or even accompany it.

"But definitions are in general completely opposed to the *spirit* of critical philosophy. Kant did not draw his proofs from definitions; for the aim of the whole section of the *Critique of Pure Reason* on The Transcendental Deduction of the Pure Concepts of the Understanding is to show that nothing can be proven about objects from concepts (consequently, not from philosophical definitions either), but that a *third something* must intervene from which the possibility of applying concepts becomes apparent."[34] This is an important objection because it clearly brings to light the aversion against definitions in philosophy which the *Kantians* share with the *popular philosophers*, (who otherwise stand poles apart from them) and the real cause why neither party will hear of allowing any philosophical proof to originate from a definition at all. The cause, as I now hope to show straightaway, is this: The Kantians are slave to the *letter* of their master.

Kant's deduction of the categories undoubtedly shows that // [98] nothing can be learned about objects from mere concepts. But which objects are here at issue? Obviously not every object of a representation (anything that can be represented) but objects — i.e., objects that are different from representations or properties of representations, that are neither mere representations nor forms of representations but *real objects*. For the cognition of *these*, a sensible intuition is needed as well as a concept, and for the intuition a sensation. How can anyone claim then (unless he takes the term 'object' or 'counterpart of representation' [*Gegenstand*] in an entirely different meaning than Kant did here) that the deduction proves that nothing can be shown from concepts about objects in general, and consequently that nothing can be shown about the objects of transcendental philosophy either, i.e., about the objects of *a priori* representations, or the *forms* of representations as determined in the nature of the mind?[35] All that Kant has ever proven with respect to these objects, he has proven only from concepts — nor could he have proved it in any other way. Moreover, he did it with concepts which were incomplete and which were, as he admitted, incapable of strict definition but allowed only a kind of explanation which // he called "exposition".[36] [99]

And anyway it is not the case that the new science of the faculty of representation or the Philosophy of the Elements demonstrates *just* from *concepts*. The definitions it derives from its principles of consciousness do, of course, only lay down concepts; the third something that must intervene, however, before the possibility of justifying these concepts or the fact that they can be applied to *their* objects becomes apparent, is not thereby being forgotten at all. This third something is consciousness. and it is from the principles expressing consciousness that those definitions obtain their decisive point of determination. These principles are what Kant requires before granting to an explanation the name of "definition" proper.

"To define", we read on p. 755 of the *Critique of Pure Reason*, "as the word itself indicates, really only means to present the exhaustive, original concept of a thing within the limits of its concept."[37] ("Thing" is not [to be] understood, of course, as excluding any subject matter or person.) The conditions which this concept of definition stipulates are precisely those that are satisfied by the fundamental explanations of the Philosophy of the Elements and nowhere else can they be satisfied in philosophy *save in them*. The basic explanation of // [100] representation, 'It is what is distinguished in consciousness from object and subject and is referred to both', *exhaustively* presents the concept of representation. "*Exhaustiveness*", Kant says in a note to the cited text, "means here clarity and sufficiency of characteristics."[38] [But] the characteristics in the explanation are *clear*, for they are determined immediately through evident facts. They are *sufficient*, because through them representation can be distinguished from all that is not representation. The explanation, moreover, presents the concept of representation *within its limits*, for in keeping with what Kant also rightly demands in the same note, it contains no more characteristics than are required for the exhaustive conception of representation. Finally, it presents the concept *originally*, for the determination of the limits of the concept that occurs in it (as Kant likewise requires in the note) is not derived from another explanation; hence it "does not require proof or explanation; for if it did, that would disqualify it from standing at the head of all judgements concerning representations."[39]

[101]   I call the definition of representation the "*absolutely* fundamental explanation" of // the Philosophy of the Elements because it includes no characteristic that would either allow of explanation or need any. The definitions of 'sensible representation', 'concept', and 'idea' which will be established in the continuation of the NEW *Exposition of the Principal Moments of the Philosophy of the Elements*[40] that we began in my *Contributions* are true fundamental explanations—though they are not absolute ones. They are *fundamental explanations* because they draw the characteristic *proper* to their objects from particular kinds of consciousness, which are expressed in particular propositions about consciousness. But they are *absolute*, for they all include the common characteristic 'representation, and presuppose the *explanation* of it. *Only one absolutely fundamental explanation is possible in philosophy*, and as long as we do not have it or do not recognize it, what Kant says of all philosophical explanations on p. 756 applies indeed to them, viz., "I can never be certain that the clear representation of a given (but still confused) concept has been *exhaustively* effected unless I know that it is adequate to its object."[41] (I can know that it is adequate only when I am certain that my concept exhausts all that can be known about the object— that my concept is completely determined,

[102]   // through and through.) "But since the concept of an object may, as given," (and before I am assured of its thoroughgoing determinacy) "include many obscure representations, which we overlook in our analysis, although we are constantly making use of them in our application of the concept, the exhaustiveness of the analysis is always in doubt; and while repeated suitable examples might make it *probable*, they can never make it apodictically *certain*." This *probability*, which the Philosophy of the Elements simply cannot tolerate if it is ever to

realize philosophy as *science*, gives place to *apodictic certainty* in the science of the faculty of representation. In virtue of the principle of consciousness, the one absolutely fundamental explanation is determined through and through; and in it the original concept of representation is exhaustively drawn out in all its characteristics, none of which is further analyzable. Through it those other definitions which are fundamental but not absolutely so (since they are derived partly from it, and partly from particular principles of consciousness) are likewise elevated to the state of thoroughgoing determinateness, and are then in a position to yield the grounds for rigorously scientific proofs. // [103]

Kant's assertion on p. 759, "In philosophy we must not imitate mathematics by beginning with definitions, unless it be by way simply of experiment",[43] can only apply therefore to what has passed for philosophy so far, and even to the *critical* philosophy, but not to that philosophy for which the critical was only intended to *pave the way* — least of all to that part of it that constitutes the *science of the elements*. Kant's reason for his assertion vanishes in the *Philosophy of the Elements*. He says: "For since the definitions are analyses of given concepts, *these* antecede them even though they are in a confused state. Incomplete exposition precedes the complete, and as a consequence we can infer much, in advance, from a few characteristics derived from an incomplete exposition without having reached yet the complete exposition, that is, the definition."[44] But in the *Philosophy of the Elements* the fundamental explanation is already a complete exposition of its object (i.e., of representation) on its own, and hence the authentic *definition* of it. The principle of consciousness, which is all that precedes it, is neither a complete nor an incomplete exposition of the *concept* of representation. It is the exposition, rather, of the // immediate [104] expression of the self-explanatory *actual fact of consciousness* from which the fundamental explanation directly draws its exposition. Inferences drawn from the latter do not lead to a more complete exposition of *representation qua representation*, for the exposition has already been given as fully as possible in the fundamental explanation. And whatever is afterwards said in addition about the *material* and the *form* of representation, far from making the *original* concept — which, however, it is the exclusive function of the definition to give — more complete, can on the contrary avoid being misunderstood only because that concept is already fully established. What is said only elucidates the concept without enlarging it. Because it only paved the way for the Philosophy of the Elements without actually laying it down, *critical* philosophy could only premise its proofs and arguments with incomplete expositions. But the complete expositions of the Philosophy of the

Elements could never have been discovered if these very arguments drawn from the *Critique's* incomplete expositions had not *come first.* The work of the *critical philosophy* could be—and had to be—brought to *completion* only with the fundamental explanation of representation. With the establishment of that, however, philosophy ceases to be [105] // *critical*, and the *science of the foundation of the philosophy which is philosophy* WITHOUT SURNAMES [OHNE BEINAMEN] begins. This is the Philosophy of the Elements. It is the last on the road leading to science, yet the first on the side of science itself. For the Kantians, of course, this saying must be a hard and insurmountable stone of scandal; for they would not deserve the name they bear were they not convinced that everything must be left to rest just as Kant has laid it down, and that no other philosophy is possible save the one which *for them* is critical.

The definitions of 'sensible representation', 'concept', and 'idea, from which the sciences of sensibility, understanding and reason, respectively, must proceed, presuppose the definition of 'representation'. It is presupposed by the concept of each of them, as their generic trait together with the characteristics of the species, and apart from its determinacy, not one of them could ever be definitively explained. *In this sense*, they *must be derived* from the definition of 'representation'. [106] And we would be losing sight // of this crucial consideration completely if we wanted to claim that, *since* what is proper to the species of representation cannot be derived from what they have in common generically, the sciences founded on them can dispense with the definition of 'representation', as well as with the science of the *general faculty of representation.*[45]

The definitions of 'sensible representation', 'concept', and 'idea' must be determined for their respective sciences, in respect to their *particularity* which is not derivable from the definition of 'representation', through particular *principles of consciousness.* These express *particular kinds of consciousness. In respect to* what they have in common they are subordinated to the *principle of consciousness in general* (which expresses what is present in *every* consciousness); *in respect to* their *specific properties*, however, their evidence rests immediately on the *specific fact* that they signify. The proper, *original*, and simple (i.e., not further analyzable) characteristics of 'sensible representation', 'concept' and 'idea' are just as exhaustively given through these particular principles of consciousness as the characteristics of representation in general are given through [107] the universal // principle of consciousness in general. Together with them, therefore, the principle of consciousness constitutes the *complete foundation* of the entire science of the *faculty of representation*, i.e., of sensibility, understanding, and reason (inasmuch as these three are faculties of representations, and manifest themselves to be such in *cognition* as well as in *desire*). The particular sciences of the *faculty of cognition* and of *desire*[46] must lay down the particular doctrines of the elements for *theoretical* and *practical* philosophy just as the science of the faculty of representation as a whole must lay down the *doctorine of the elements for philosophy* in general. They all draw their definitions of cognition and desire, from which they proceed, from the same source, viz., from the consciousness in which cognition and desire are manifested. But they draw the form of cognition and desire (in so far as it depends on the form of representing) and their various forms (in so far as these depend on sensibility, understanding and reason) from the science of the faculty of representation. Thus consciousness constitutes, taken generically and according to its species, the *unique and complete foundation of the entire Philosophy of the Elements* — *general* as well as *particular*. //   [108]

I admit that in my *Essay towards a New Theory of the Human Faculty of Representation* I pointed this foundation out rather than presenting it exhaustively. I have tried to remedy this shortcoming in my *Contributions*, particularly with the essays on the *first principle*,[47] and on the *possibility of philosophy as science*.[48] So far I have yet to come across any reaction to them; even the critic who reviewed my first volume of *Contributions* in the *Allgemeine Literatur-Zeitung*[49] only mentions them in passing. In the same volume I have also made public the beginning of a *New Exposition of the Principal Moments of the Philosophy of the Elements* in which I have attempted a rigorously scientific derivation of the theory of the faculty of representation in general from the principle of consciousness and the fundamental definitions drawn from it. In the *continuation*, as I have already expressedly promised in the essay, "Discussions about the Theory . . . "[50], I shall elaborate the other parts of the Philosophy of the Elements stage by stage, just as I have already done for its fundamental doctrine. That is to say, I shall have to impart the theories of sensibility, understanding and reason simply *qua* faculties of representation — theories that will have to be derived from *particlar principles of consciousness yet to be exhibited* by me, and from the fundamental definitions of 'sensible representation', 'concept' and 'idea' // to   [109] be determined by these principles.[51] What am I to think therefore, of the conduct of the critic to whom I have just referred? In his review of the first volume of my *Contributions* he leaves untouched all the grounds [that establish] the indispensability, the possibility and the constitution of what I present as the foundation of the Philosophy of the Elements. Instead he objects to the particlar ways in which I ground my theories of sensibility, understanding, and reason, even though I myself have already promised a more illuminating exposition of this.

And all his objections originate, moreover, in misunderstandings which were certainly avoidable even on the basis of the exposition already given, but which he would have been expressly guarded against in the one that was to come.

I distinguish between *material* and *formal* foundation of the Philosophy of the Elements. The former is *consciousness as an actual fact*; the latter, the *principles of consciousness* and the *definitions* that are immediately derived from, and exhaustively defined by, them. From the *one* we draw the *content* of the Philosophy of the Elements, (and of the *simple* characteristics that make up the original material of the sciences of the faculty of representation, cognition and desire too);

[110]   // through the other we determine its *scientific form*, the thoroughgoing interconnection of its material, the unity under one principle of the manifold that makes up its content—in a word, its *systematic* character. And as matter and form, although different, are everywhere equally inseparable, so are they in the case of the foundation of the Philosophy of the Elements too. The *fact of consciousness* has always been with us, and so the matter for the foundation of this philosophy to come has been with us too. Only through the *principle* of consciousness, however, could the unused matter be elevated to the state of actual matter for the foundation. A block of marble comes likewise to be the material of an actual column only through the figure that it obtains at the hand of the artist. The *form* of *science in general* has *long* since been known in philosophy. We have known for a long time that it consists in *systematization*, and consequently that it has to be determined through *principles* which are all of them necessarily subordinated to a *first.* but since the principle that was hitherto officially held to be the first, i.e., the *principle of contradiction*, had no matter at all to offer for the foundation of the philosophy of the Elements, it also could not provide for it its true formal foundation. And indeed,

[111]   // in the future the principle of contradiction will no more be used as the foundation of the Philosophy of the Elements (and through the latter, of *philosophy in general*) than it has until now. The Leibnizian school assumed it as the *first principle of metaphysics*, and so used it; future philosophy will recognize it, and employ it, as the first *principle of logic* instead.

With respect to its matter, the criterion of the *foundation* of the Philosophy of the Elements is the immediate evidence of its *content* discoverable by mere reflection, independently of any reasoning— the unanalyzable nature of the concepts in which it is originally exhibited, or the *de facto* nature of its characteristics. With respect to its *form*, the criterion is its *rigorous systematization* — the thoroughgoing determinacy, based on principles, of its theorems and corollaries, and the subordination of all its principles under a *single* one. The criterion [by which we know that] in the foundation of this science the proper matter *has been joined* with the proper form is *the fact that the* FIRST PRINCIPLE of the Philosophy of the Elements *is self-determined*; the self-determinacy of the principle confers upon it its rank of the ABSOLUTELY FIRST among all possible principles, and upon the foundation expressed by it, the property of being ULTIMATE. //   [112]

Among the *dogmatic skeptics* only the *impossibility of any* foundation is discussed; among the *empiricists*, only a *material* foundation; and among the *rationalists* only a *formal* one. The *Kantians* for their part only speak of a foundation of *metaphysics*. But *I* am speaking of the foundation of the Philosophy of the Elements, and so (indirectly) of the foundation of *philosophy in general*.

In the simple representations drawn from experience, Locke gave us a *material foundation* of philosophy, or rather, he pointed to a foundation to which, since it would have consisted of concepts that are not further analyzable, the criterion of *material* foundation could certainly be applied too. The criterion of *formal* foundation is altogether lacking, however. It did not cross Locke's mind, or the mind of any of his disciples, to claim that it would be possible, by the systematic exposition of the simple representations drawn from experience, to go through them exhaustively; but still less did it occur to them that a reduction to systematic form was strictly indispensable for the simple representations if they were to constitute the foundation of philosphy.

Leibniz gave us a *formal* foundation in the principle of contradiction which he defined as the principle of all necessary and universal, //   [113] i.e., scientific, propositions; or rather, he pointed out a foundation which, SO FAR AS it was the *first principle*, would admit the criterion of formal foundation. The criterion of *material* foundation was altogether lacking to it, however. The *principle of contradiction* is false if we take it to express the most universal characteristic of a thing independent of its mere capacity to be thought—of the *thing-in-itself*, in other words. If the only characteristic that it expresses, however, is a thing's *capacity to be thought* — so far as it can be thought—then the principle falls short of the criterion of a material foundation. For the characteristic 'capable of being thought' is not simple but composed rather of one general trait, 'representation', and of another, 'thought', by which we mean a 'kind of representation'—it is composed of genus and species, in other words. The principle of contradiction does not get the perfect definitiveness of its sense through itself alone, but partly through the principle that perfectly defines the concept 'representation'. And if the principle of contradiction is determined by the latter, this shows that it has ceded to it the rank of first principle of philosophy, and has to content itself instead with that of first principle of logic. //   [114]

In the *possibility of experience* Kant laid down a foundation for the *metaphysics of sensible nature* which did satisfy the conditions of a material as well as formal foundation for *this science*, but not for philosophy in general and especially not for the Philosophy of the Elements. Metaphysics is not, and cannot be the Philosophy of the Elements, i.e., the science of the foundation of all philosophy, whether theoretical or practical. Its material foundation, therefore, cannot and ought not in any way to consist of simple characteristics which, since they are directly drawn from consciousness by simple reflection, carry immediate evidence with them. On the contrary, metaphysics can—indeed, it must—assume these characteristics from the Philosophy of the Elements. The Kantian foundation for the metaphysics of scientific nature, i.e., for the *science of knowable real objects*, consists of what Kant calls the *principles of pure understanding*; that is to say they are metaphysical laws of nature that are subordinate to the *first principle*: "*Every knowable object stands under the formal and material conditions of experience.*"[52] Because of its systematic and rigorously scientific form, this foundation satisfies the condition of a formal scientific foundation; and because

[115]   of the evidence that its principles have // for those who have understood their sense, it satisfies the condition of the material scientific foundation as well. For this evidence, however as well as for the *understanding* of the proper sense of the foundation that is indispensable to it, Kant's readers depend solely on the *Critique of Pure Reason* which is the preparatory science or "propaedeutics" for it [the foundation]. This much will have to be granted to me not only by impartial observers, but by anti-Kantians and Kantians alike— especially by the latter, for they declare this "propaedeutics" to be the only Philosophy of the Elements that is truly possible.

I am not speaking here about my great teacher, who never claimed anything of the sort. I am speaking about those among his pupils who misunderstand the title "Doctrine of the Elements" that he gives to one part of his *Critique*, and who make him say in it something which *he* never thought of, and never could have thought so. All he wanted and all that he could supply was a doctrine of the Elements. Of course, there would never have been any thought about this general doctrine if *he* had not [first] supplied the special one. But no matter how impossible that fundamental science of philosophy would have

[116]   been *without* Kant's propaedeutics to metaphysics, it was still // not realized *by* it—for it is, and must be, something essentially different from it, drawn from an entirely different source.

To claim that a propaedeutics to metaphysics can be, and can be called, the doctrine of the elements of philosophy in general can only make sense to one for whom *metaphysics* and *philosophy* are the *one thing*. But it can conly be conceded that Kant's propaedeutics is *preparatory* SCIENCE even for metaphysics if we take the word "science" in a broad and weak sense that ought not to be employed in philosophy at all, especially when one part of it is at issue. Whenever Kant speaks of philosophy as *science*, he demands *systematic form*,[54] i.e., the thoroughgoing unity of a manifold of cognitions under one principle. And wherever he outlines the plan for a science, e.g., the *metaphysics of sensible nature*, he does this by the exact specification of its systematic groundwork. How could he have overlooked this condition of science then, which *he* stipulates and abides by, if he had really intended in the *Critique* to deliver the *science* that leads to metaphysics—nay, even to the whole of philosophy, whether theoretical // or practical— [117] and not just a *preparatory work* for some such *future* science which the *Critique* itself, of course, cannot and may not be? But suppose that the *Critique of Pure Reason* already is authentic science: where are then the principles which, together with the one which is the highest, would make up its foundation?

As long as the *Kantians* cannot exhibit this foundation, they will assert in vain that the *Critique of Pure Reason* lays down even that part of the Philosophy of the Elements that consists in the *science of the faculty of cognition* —not to mention the Philosophy of the Elements in general, and least of all its fundamental doctrine, i.e., the science of faculty of representation. They can call the *Critique of Reason* "Philosophy of the Elements" with just the same intent and with the same right—but then, also with just the same result—as that opponent of Kant who recently called Leibniz's [*New*] *Essay* [*s*] *Concerning Human Understanding* a "critique of pure reason."[55]

The Philosophy of the Elements is the *scientific* source of the principles for all the parts of derived philosophy; the principles of theoretical and practical philosophy are its result—// it is the direct source of [118] the principles of pure philosophy, and indirectly (through that) the source of empirical principles.

Hence it must impart, not just to metaphysics but to logic as well, the principles that must stand at the head of it as science; consequently, it cannot obtain its thoroughgoing determinateness *from them*. The *Critique of Pure Reason* has indeed attached the common name of "logic" to the last two parts of *its* "Doctrine of the Elements", viz., the Transcendental Analytic and the Dialectic. But by the attribute "Transcendental" it has equally distinguished this "Logic" from logic *as such*, i.e., from *general* logic. As compared with this, transcendental logic is a kind of particular logic whose enquiries are restricted simply to the rules for the thought of certain objects (in this case, transcendental ones). Like every other particular logic, the transcendental logic presupposes *general* logic, or rather, *logic proper without surnames* — as the *Critique* itself quite unambiguously asserts. Hence the *Critique* cannot be Philosophy of the Elements if only for the reason that *general*

[119]   *logic* // must precede the transcendental logic, and therefore cannot be derived from it.[56]

To be sure, for a long time general logic has had many universally binding principles to its credit, as well as theorems and corollaries — but, they are in fact nothing of the sort. The meaning of many of its rules is ambiguous, for since it has hitherto lacked a recognized first principle (and has usurped it instead from metaphysics) it was bound to fall short of a perfect determinacy of meaning in the rest of its principles as well. It can offer no certainty, therefore, as to whether they are complete in number, or how they rank — or whether they are of the same order or stand subordinated each to the other. It owes its universally acknowledged reputation more to a number or rules universally binding in a logical practice (e.g., the rules of syllogistic inference) than to the determinateness and coherence of its content, or in other words, to its still undiscovered systematic nature. And even if we already possessed logic in a genuinely systematic form, still we would look in vain for the completely determined concept of *thought* in it. This is the concept from which it must proceed but which, precisely for this reason, it cannot provide. But so far nobody has

[120]   had the slightest inkling of this important fact. Either we // have maintained that "we must learn what representation, thought and knowledge mean from ourselves', i.e., that every man extracts these determinate concepts from himself without any danger of error, and hence we have gone on assuming without worry what the logic assumes, viz, perfect determinateness [of meaning], or we have fancied that we could exhaust the concept of thought within the logic itself, with a couple of explanations more in need of explaining than what they explain — thus taking it to be completely determined where in fact it is not. And so this indeterminate, ambiguous and vacillating concept of *thought*, which is nevertheless supposed to be the principal concept of the entire science, has been dragged in into every logic [text] so far produced, and with it have come scraps at first from metaphysics and later on from empirical psychology that do violence to whatever authentic logical content had already been discovered, while hindering the discovery of what was still missing. In this situation of the logic, it is not difficult to understand that there was little, if anything at all, that Kant could safely take over from the *general* logic into his *Transcendental* Logic. He could draw little that was profitable from the

[121]   previous texts concerning the characteristics of the concepts that he // needed as his *starting points*, i.e., those of *intuition, sensation, concept, judgement*, etc. (These are the concepts whose incomplete expositions he put at the base of his complete ones.) And indeed, he would not have had the right to presume that anything he assumed as estab-

lished regarding intuitions, concepts, or ideas, *qua representations*, had been established by logic, for no logic ever can possibly establish what he was assuming.

The authentic Philosophy of the Elements neither can nor may be founded in any way on logic. Only the science of the faculty of representation can determine the concept 'thought' through and through.

The name that the Kantians give to the *metaphysics of nature* fails to distinguish it sufficiently from the metaphysics of both sensible and supra-sensible nature.[57] They contrast the metaphysics of nature only with the metaphysics of morals, and restrict it to the objects that can be known, i.e., appearances. Now, the Philosophy of the Elements must lay down the principles not just for the *metaphysics of nature*, but for *general metaphysics* as well[58]—*qua* metaphysics of knowable objects [of course],[59] but no less *qua* metaphysics of those supra-sensible objects that are present only to thought, // yet are so with necessity.[60]   [122]
This task it must undertake in a part that grounds *theoretical philosophy,*[61] in the sciences of the sensible and the supra-sensible faculties of representation. In the one science it shows that all objects knowable *a posteriori* can only be *appearances*; in the other, that all the objects KNOWABLE *a priori, inasmuch* as they are knowable, can only be *forms of representations.* In the first science, it [takes those] characteristics of appearances that are original and, to the extent that they are knowable, entirely determined *a priori,* [and] establishes them in the forms of cognoscibility (i.e., in the combined forms of concepts and intuitions). In the second science, it [takes those] characteristics of the three supra-sensible objects, viz., of the 'absolute subject', the 'absolute cause', and the 'absolute community', [that are] original, and hence entirely determined *a priori,* [and] establishes them in the *three forms of the ideas* determined by the nature of reason. These are the objects that are inaccessible to sensibility and understanding, yet are necessarily represented by reason even though it too cannot know them. And the ideas in which the Philosophy of the Elements establishes their characteristics are those presupposed // by the particular sciences   [123]
of *higher metaphysics,* i.e., rational psychology, ontology, cosmology, and theology. Only through them is it possible to give a thoroughly determined account in these sciences of how their objects, although *incomprehensible,* must yet be *thought* in conformity with the original disposition of reason—partly, in the interests of the theoretical employment of reason in the study of the field of experience, and partly in the interests of its practical employment in moral affairs.

For the *kind* of *metaphysics* which would be a pure science both of sensible and supra-sensible nature—one that would deal with *objects proper* (i.e., the kind that are neither representations nor forms of representations) and which, together with logic would constitute pure *theoretical philosophy*, one as material and the other as formal philosophy— for metaphysical science of this sort, the *Critique of Pure Reason* has provided no plan, principles or concept. Its only interest was to enquire into the possibility of 'metaphysics' as *hitherto* understood, i.e., the science of objects that are *things-in-themselves*. And it showed that in this sense metaphysics is utterly impossible, for things proper, i.e., objects that are neither representations nor forms of representations, [124] can only be *known* through sensibility // and understanding *as appearances*, and not at all through reason. Consequently, if by metaphysics we understand the science of *knowable things* of this kind, i.e., such as are neither representations nor forms of representations, no other is possible save the metaphysics of (sensible) nature, or the science of those necessary and universal characteristics of *appearances* that are determined *a priori*.

I am convinced that the new meaning given to the work "metaphysics" in the architectonic of the *Critique of Pure Reason* is no more determinate than any previous meaning, and can no more be adhered to than any of them. It is said on p. 869 (second edition): "The system of the pure science of reason, i.e., the whole of philosophical cognition, true as well as *illusory*, arising out of reason and presented in systematic connection, is called *metaphysics*— even though *this* name may also be given to the *whole of pure philosophy, including* criticism, in order to comprehend the investigation of all that can ever be known *a priori*, and also the exposition of what constitutes a system of pure [125] philosophical cognitions of this kind—// in distinction, therefore, from every empirical as well as mathematical employment of reason."[62] Why should pure philosophy have any other name than "pure philosophy?" Why should it carry, although it is presented here as genus, the name of *one* of its *species*? And why should the propaedeutics to metaphysics be called "metaphysics" itself?[63] Moreover, what are we to understand by the "system of pure reason", the "science", to which the name metaphysics is here attributed in its *narrower* sense? Certainly not the *Critique of Reason* which Kant here distinguishes, as a part of pure philosophy, from the science to which the name "metaphysics" preeminently applies. But if we grant that the name of "system of pure reason", of "science", does not apply to the *Critique of Pure Reason*, then ought not a science of the faculty of representation, cognition and desire to be possible which would carry that name in its strictest sense, yet would not be metaphysics? And finally, in the words that follow the name of metaphysics in the text, "the whole of philosophical cognition, true as well as *illusory*," the object of metaphysics is more closely characterized, for by "true" cognition we can understand the object of the *metaphysics of sensible nature,* and by "illusory" cognition the metaphysics of the *supra-//* sensible. But then, there is discussion [126] in what follows of a metaphysics of the *practical* employment of reason, i.e,.of a *metaphysics of morals.* And this metaphysics, as the science of objects that are distinct from representations and their forms, cannot by any means be introduced under the above mentioned common science of sensible and supra-sensible objects. What has always been meant by these objects is *objects* that SUBSIST, and consequently objects that belong just to theoretical, not practical philosophy. It might indeed be advisable for the sake of determinacy in philosophical nomenclature, to usurp the name "metaphysics" and restrict it again, as it has been done from time immemorial, to the field of *theoretical philosophy.* and even within that field to designate by it merely that portion that embraces *material theoretical* philosophy.

Just as material theoretical philosophy (or metaphysics) cannot be reduced to that part of it called the "metaphysics of sensible nature", for which the *Critique* has laid down the system of principles, so too *practical philosophy* cannot be exhausted by the *moral theory* for which the *Critique of Practical Reason,* along with the // *Groundwork of a* [127] Metaphysics of Morals, have made ready the foundation. A science of the necessary and universal characteristics of the *empirical objects* of desires is just as possible as the science of the necessary and universal characteristics of *appearances.* These are objects that can be known *a posteriori,* and their science is made possible by what is determined *a priori* in the *lower* faculty of cognition (i.e., in the understanding and in the sensibility taken together). For our *empirical objects* of desire, on the other hand, a science is made possible throught the determinations brought to the *sensible faculty of desire* by the forms of *sensibility and understanding,* and of reason *operating empirically* (not *purely,* as in morality).[64] But this science is, of course, only possible because the two particular parts of the Philosophy of the Elements, the theoretical and the practical, or the sciences of the faculties of cognition and desire respectively, are subordinated to one common fundamental science. And since this is the science of the faculty of representation taken both in general, and as faculty of the sensible, intelligible and rational representations, it secures both the inferior and the superior faculties of cognition and desire, both for the empirical and for the pure faculties, their *common* principles—so far, of course, as these principles are determinable through the forms of representation. Without such a // UNIVERSAL *science of the elements,* which stands in [128] relation to the two *particular* ones (i.e., the theoretical and the *practical*) as their ultimate scientific foundation, there could not even be the thought of the systematic unity of the *whole* Philosophy of the Elements, still less that of *philosophy in general.*

I will put off showing that a rigorously systematic, PURE Philosophy of the Elements is indispensable to the groundwork of every part of *empirical* philosophy to another opportunity in the near future.[65] I shall then specifically discuss a *universal, empirical Philosophy of the Elements* which must exhibit the constitution, source and value of *empirical* principles, as well as their relation to the *pure* ones. Without such an empirical Philosophy of the Elements, which we would not be able to think of prior to the founding and completion of the *pure* one, all enquiries into *empirical psychology*, for instance, would still depend just as they have done so far, more on the lucky intuitions of some genius than on the secure guidance of philosophical reason acting according to principles; they would never succeed in establishing concepts that are both fundamental and thoroughly determined for

[129]   the powers and capacities of the *soul*. //

Nobody can be more convinced than I that concerning all the objects of these philosophical sciences, the most important lessons can be drawn from Kant's *Critique of Pure Reason* —from the critique of *theoretical* as well as *practical reason*. It is to these lessons that I owe the *possibility* as well as the *occasion* of my idea for the *Philosophy of the Elements*, and of *philosophy in general*. I only deny that the *Critique of Pure Reason* is itself the *Philosophy of the Elements*, or that the latter can be grounded upon principles and demonstrations laid down in it.

The *foundation* of the *Critique of Pure Reason* is neither *universal* enough (i.e., all-encompassing) nor *firm* enough to carry the *whole philosophical edifice* of philosophy. Not *universal* enough: for the critique of *theoretical* reason grounds only *metaphysics*, and indeed, only the metaphysics of *sensible nature*; and the critique of *practical* reason grounds only the *metaphysics of morals*. Not *firm* enough: for however *true* all that the *Critique presupposes* as *established* regarding its own groundwork may be, (or all that on which it actually erects its edifice) it is equally true that none of it HAS BEEN ESTABLISHED *as true*. The concepts of the *possibility of experience* and of the *nature* and *actuality* of *synthetic*

[130]   // *a priori judgements**, which are laid down in the *Critique* as the foundation of the edifice of Kantian doctrines, are assumed in this founding function without any proof. They are adduced in *incomplete expositions*, and without a thoroughgoing determination of their characteristics. And there was nothing else that could or should have been done. Of course, the essential characteristics of these important concepts are unfolded and demonstrated throughout the work, but only on the basis of grounds that *presuppose* the Kantian foundation of the *Critique* —hence the *reality* of the *concepts* at issue (or rather, the unproven assertions, the incomplete principles, in which those concepts are laid down as foundation) is *presupposed*. The foundation of the *Critique* can only be proven from the *Critique* itself through a

---

*See *Contributions*, vol. I, the essay "On the Relationship of the *Theory of the Faculty of Representation* to the *Critique of Pure Reason*".[66]

vicious circle. All those *Kantians* who have responded to the objections raised by Kant's opponents against the fundamental principles of the system by using Kant's own *theorems* and *corollaries*, or simply by repeating the principles themselves, have fallen into this circle. How often have the friends of critical // philosophy given us to under-   [131] stand, how often have they asserted or shown, that the *Critique of Pure Reason*, as presented in the reviews of it undertaken by Mr. Feder on behalf of the empiricists,[67] by Mr. Eberhard for the *rationalists*,[68] and by so many others, famous or not so famous, for the *syncretics*, has been entirely *misunderstood?* Yet, to my knowledge, no defender of Kant's philosophy has conceded, or even expressed as a mere conjecture, the view that there might be, and actually are, objections to the *Critique* that cannot be answered from the *Critique*; or that its *foundation* might need to be argued for and justified independently of anything that is already constructed on it (and hence independently of the entire *Critique*) if the same foundation and, with it, every principle aspect of the *Critique* itself are not to be (as they have been so far) misunderstood by the followers of older systems, and taken by them to be something unjustified and long since shown to be wrong. *Kantians* and *anti-Kantians* have been refuting one another on grounds that constantly presuppose as established what the opponent is challenging. And it is my conviction that on the whole the *Critique* has suffered more from the defence than from the attacks. //   [132]

The *future* Philosophy of the Elements must first establish what is assumed as established in the *Critique of Pure Reason* (which is only *preparatory* to it). It will develop what the other takes for granted in its undeveloped state; it will prove, what the other lays down as being in no need of proof; will found on complete expositions, what the other infers from incomplete ones. It will derive from principles as final as ever can be given, and from their exhaustive analysis, what the other has inferred from subaltern and (as regards their higher characteristics) still indeterminate principles. It will reduce systematically to *one* [base] what the other abstracts *rhapsodically* from *many*; and will exhibit *dogmatically* what the other *prepares for* critically. The Philosophy of the Elements is therefore *essentially* different from the *Critique of Pure Reason.* And the *philosophy* of which it is a part—in the sense that it is the *scientific foundation* on which the other parts rest—can no more be called CRITICAL than it can *empirical, rational, or skeptical. It is philosophy* WITHOUT SURNAMES. The insufficiency of *empiricism* brought about *rationalism*, and the insufficiency of the latter sustained the other in turn. *Humean skepticism* unveiled the insufficiency of both of these dogmatic systems, and thus occasioned *Kantian criticism.* The latter overturned *one-sided* dogmatism and   [133] dogmatic skepticism, but not in order to replace them just with *critique* (which is only the *means* to science, not *science* itself), but to salvage from the still usable ruins of the previous systems the *materials* for a *future edifice of doctrines constructed according to strict scientific norms.* The plan for this [new] system could NOT have been laid out WITHOUT the knowledge of these *materials* that was brought about by the *Critique* – but neither COULD it be simply abstracted FROM them, or established by critique alone.

Empiricism looked for the *foundation* of philosophy (i.e., the ultimate, and in this sense the only sufficient ground of *science*) in objective nature; in this last is presupposed, without proof, the source of *necessity* and *universality* indispensable to the thought of any science. Rationalism went one step further. Like empiricism, it indeed also assumed as an established truth that the *necessity* and *universality* of science are grounded in objective nature. It showed, however, that this presupposition is not sufficient to yield the foundation of science, for besides the necessity and universality founded in objects science [134] presupposes a subjective // necessity and universality that is present in consciousness. For since *impressions* can only justify individual and accidental [truths], this subjective necessity and universality can only be comprehended in terms of *innate representations.* In empiricism and rationalism, the two one-sidedly dogmatic systems, philosophical reason thus PRESUPPOSED *the agreement of representations with real objects* (i.e., objective truth). Locke and Leibniz, who were the final artificers of these two systems, had no inkling that not only was a proof of this agreement possible, but also indispensable to it and necessary. With David Hume, therefore, philosophical reason propelled itself yet another step forward, since he for the first time demanded this proof. That was how the crucial question by which philosophy *qua* science must either stand or fall came to utterance. From the *presupposition* that the representations of *real objects* consist of mere impressions, Hume inferred the impossibility of a proof for *objective truth* (its indemonstrability), and he went on to declare *all knowledge* to be the mere illusion of a reason mistaken about itself. Following upon Hume, the *Critique of Pure Reason* showed that his *presupposition* was unfounded and absurd, and undertook the *first attempt* at a demonstration of objective truth. [135] And since it derived this from the // *possibility of experience as determined in the mind,* for that very reason it *restricted* the proof exclusively to objects of possible experience. Whereas from the nature of *sensibility* and *understanding* it showed that those objects of our knowledge that are *real* and can be represented *as such* (are *knowable,* in other words) can only be *appearances,* from the nature of *reason* it showed that the reality of the objects that are representable through *pure* reason is incomprehensible, and utterly indemonstrable by means of *theoretical* reason. In this it proceeded from the *presupposition* of the reality of the concept of *experience*, which it understood *as the necessary combination of sensible perceptions*, and of the *presupposed actuality of synthetic a priori judgments*. Thus with the *Critique* philosophical reason took the *final step* towards the resolution of its great problem. But in doing so it had to start from the *presupposition* of something that was still in need of future proof. To undertake and to carry out, without a presupposition of this kind, the proof of what the *Critique* presupposed, and had to presuppose – this is the FIRST step in the direction of philosophical *science* proper, i.e., towards the display of the solution to the problem of philosophical reason, or again, towards the complete founding of the only possible edifice of doctrines in which future philosophy will consist. Just for this reason, however, The proof [thus undertaken] // cannot be carried out unless one [136] starts from a *fact* [*Faktum*] – a fact, moreover, that could be thought only in utterly simple concepts, not in concepts that need further analysis and demonstrations (such as, for instance, that of 'experience'). And it would have to be expressible in an entirely *self-determined* proposition. This proposition is the *principle of consciousness*. From it we can draw the *absolutely first* fundamental definition, i.e., the *first* complete exposition, or the definition of the *highest* among all possible philosophical concepts. (These are the concept of 'representation' and, dependent on it, that of 'representability' by which we think a characteristic as *universally* as it can ever be thought.) On this the science of the *faculty of representation* is finally founded. And among its rigorously demonstrated theorems and corollaries we shall find, established in perfect determinacy [of significance] through complete expositions, Kant's concepts of *experience*, of its *possibility*, and of the *a priori synthetic judgement*. Thus the principles of the *Critique* become the scientific *corollaries* of the Philosophy of the Elements.

How much I have achieved or failed to achieve in the *attempt* at such a Philosophy of the Elements that I first undertook with my // *Essay towards a Theory of the Faculty of Representation*, and then [137] again with the *first volume* of *Contributions*, and now in this present *essay* – an attempt to which I am pledged to enlist all my future leisure – this question I would indeed prefer not be left to my own judgment. For whenever I reflect on the reviews so far come to my notice, I am tempted to despair. However learned these reviews might be in other respects, I have learned from them nothing germane to *my purpose*. No one has understood either what I was aiming at, or the means that I proposed [to employ].

Whether this attempt of mine will endure until *the future generation of professional philosophers* for which it was especially intended, and how they will judge it – this I do not know. This much, however, I believe that I can predict with certainty: Twenty years hence it will no longer be so difficult to comprehend that without *universally binding first principles*, neither *logic* proper nor *metaphysics* (the metaphysics of sensible and supra-sensible objects), neither *moral* nor *natural* law, nor any other particular part of philosophy hitherto dubbed "science" can attain the rank, the stability and the advantage of authentic *sciences*; [138]   but that we cannot even think of // *such* first principles for the particular sciences of philosophy before the *Philosophy of the Elements*, which is the system of all philosophically pure principles, has been *firmly secured* as rigorous science on universally binding principles; that one among these (i.e., the absolutely first one) must be determined solely through itself, and must express the most universal fact of consciousness. Of course, *not every* occasion of past or future misunderstandings among independent philosophers will be removed by the discovery and recognition of such a principle—not if the occasion is rooted in the limitations of the human spirit. But at least the occasions will be removed forever which lay in the situation in which *philosophical reason* found itself before. For philosophical reason can only find rest in a *ground* which is *ultimate* in an *absolute* sense, and as long as it has still to attain to that ground as it makes its advance on the highway of analysis, it *must* still be *at odds* with itself in [the persons of] the independent thinkers who are its representatives.

Notes

1. Reinhold is not quite accurate. The problem is whether any 'alteration' in the object of experience is truly a case of 'coming to be' on the part of the object, and not just a modification in the subject's mental states. Hume had claimed that it is neither intuitively nor demonstrably certain that everything whose existence has a beginning should also have a cause. (*A Treatise of Human Nature*, ed. Selby Bigge, Oxford: at the Clarendon Press, 1967, pp. 72ff). And against this claim Kant had argued in his Second Analogy of Experience that, although the relation between events is indeed never the logical one between 'cause' and 'effect', unless we grant a like relation to obtain at least between *some* events, we would never be able to distinguish in experience between mere 'alterations' and cases of objective 'coming to be'. Of course, Hume could have answered back by pointing out that whether we can *in fact* make this distinction is precisely the point at issue. For Spinoza, whom Reinhold mentions in the following pages, since 'motion' is only a metaphor expressing *our* view of the infinitely small difference between finite modes, the latter cannot be said to be the effects of God (even though they exist in Him). But the same would have to apply, *mutatis mutandis*, to Leibniz's view of changes in monads—though not necessarily to the Leibnizians'

views on 'change'. As for Chr. August Crusius (1715-1775), he too had clearly distinguished between the logical relation of 'cause' to 'effect' and the real connection between events, even though he never drew from his distinction Hume's skeptical consequences. Cf. *Entwurf der notwendigen Vernunftwahrheiten* 33ff.,72 (Leipzig 1745; *Die Philosophischen Hauptwerke*, ed. Giorgio Tonelli, Hildesheim: Olms, 1964, Vol. II); also *Weg zur Gewissheit*, 260 (*Hauptwerke*, Vol. III).

2. Critique, A7-8, B10-11.

3. Ibid.

4. Ibid., A151, B191

5. Cf. note 1 above.

6. Probably Reinhold has in mind Eberhard's example of a synthetic judgement in metaphysics which he gives in *Philosophisches Magazin*, 1789 (I, 3), p. 325. For a note on Eberhard, see below, note 55.

7. *Allgemeingeltend*, which I have translated as "universally binding," has a special meaning for Reinhold. He distinguishes between the *de facto* truth of a concept or proposition, i.e., its 'universal validity' (*Allgemeingültigkeit*), and its effectiveness in commanding assent to the truth that it possesses, i.e., the fact that we cannot *not* accept it. Though distinct, these two aspects of a true concept or proposition are closely related. Thus Reinhold says that nothing should be introduced in the statement of the basic principles of science which is not only 'universally true', but also self-evident, i.e., 'universally binding'. Cf. *Theorie*, pp. 65-66. He also points out that a failure of a principle to command assent is indicative of a failure in intrinsic truth. *Theorie*, p. 120.

8. John Locke (1632-1704), *An Essay Concerning Human Understanding* (1690).

9. Gottfried Wilhelm Leibniz (1646-1716), *Nouveaux Essais sur l 'Entendement Humain* (*New Essays Concerning Human Understanding*). This essay was first published in 1765.

10. David Hume (1711-1776), *A Treatise of Human Nature* (1739); *An Enquiry Concerning Human Understanding* (1748).

11. Reading *"den"* in place of *"dem"*.

12. Ernst Plattner (1744-1818), *Philosophische Aphorismen*, Vol. I. Both the first edition (1776) and the second (1784) contain a "Refutation of Skepticism".

13. Thomas Reid (1710-1796), James Oswald (c. 1705-1793), James Beattie (1735-1803). For a detailed history of the reception of common sense philosophy in Germany, cf. Manfred Kuehn, *Scottish Common Sense in Germany, 1768-1800*. Ph.D. Thesis. McGill University, 1980.

14. Cr. *Critique*, A12-13, B26-27; A15-16, B29-30; ". . . the hitherto rarely attempted *dissection of the faculty of the understanding* itself . . ." A65, B90.

15. This is not a direct quotation from Kant. Cf. this passage in the first edition of the Critique that was dropped in the second: ". . . there are three original sources (capacities for faculties of the soul) which contain the conditions of the possibility of all experience . . ." A94.

16. Cf. *Critique*, B233: ". . . connection is not the work of mere sense and intuition . . ."

17. ". . . For reason is the faculty which supplies the principles of a priori knowledge. Pure reason is, therefore that which contains the principles whereby we know anything absolutely *a priori*. An organon of pure reason would be the sum-total of those principles . . . The exhaustive application of such an organon would give rise to a system of pure

reason. . . . [W]e can regard a science of the mere examination of pure reason, of its sources and limits, as the *propaedeutic* to the system of pure reason. As such, it should be called a critique, not a doctrine, of pure reason. . . . Such a critique is therefore a preparation, so far as may be possible, for an organon . . ." *Critique*, All-12, B25-26.

18. Cf. notes 8, 9 and 10.

19. There are echoes here from Bk. I, Ch. 3 of the *Critique*, "The ground of the Distinction of All Objects into Phenomena and Noumena." Cf. also, B165-166 (§27).

20. This is not a direct quotation from Kant.

21. The text-book that Reinhold is referring to is *Institutiones logicae et metaphsicae, scholae suae scripsit Joh. Aug. Ulrich*, Jena, 1785, but I have not been able to control the source. See Ulrich's letter to Kant dated April 21, 1785. *Briefwechsel*, Academy Edition, Vol. X, p. 378. Also, Reinhold to Kant, October 12, 1787, Vol. X, p. 476; Reinhold to Chr. Gottlob von Voight, Beginning of November, 1786, #35, *Korrespondenz*, R. Lauth, E. Heller, and K. Hiller eds, Stuttgart-Bad Cannstatt: Fr. Fromann, G. Holzboog & Verlag der Oesterreichischen Akademie der Wissenschaften, 1983m p. 151. Ulrich (1746-1813) was professor of philosophy at Jena.

22. *Critique*, A158, B197.

23. Reinhold is glossing.

24. What Reinhold says about the new science that he intends to establish must be read in conjunction with Ch. 3 of the Transcendental Doctrine of Method of the *Critique*, especially A841-847, B869-875. It is important to note that although in the *Critique* Kant tends to reduce "metaphysics" to the "metaphysics of nature" understood as the science of what we can know *a priori* about objects given to us *a posteriori*, he does not in *principle* identify the two. Under the general heading of "metaphysics" he includes the "metaphysics of morals" and the "metaphysics of nature", and under the latter he further includes (1) the science of possible objects in general (*ontologia*) and (2) the science of objects *given* to intuition (rational physiology). The use of reason in this second science can be either *immanent* or *transcendent*. In the first case, its objects are given in experience (i.e., to *sensible* intuition; this is the science which Kant normally calls "metaphysics of nature," *physica rationalis* and *psychologia rationalis*); in the second case, if its objects were ever given, they would have to be given to an intuition other than sensible. Kant has apparently in mind such objects as 'world', 'nature', 'finality', etc. (cosmology, and rational theology). Now the science that Reinhold wants to establish is one that would provide the foundation for "metaphysics" understood in *all* these senses. As described by Reinhold, this "science" would appear to Kant identical with what he calls "*psychologia rationalis*" and which he includes under "metaphysics of nature" as one of its parts. Cf. also note 17 above. See also the concluding pages of Reinhold's text (pp. 121ff.)

25. *Elementarphilosophie* is obviously an echo of Kant's *Elemen-tarlehre*. I have translated it "Philosophy of the Elements" following N.K. Smith's translation of *Elementarlehre* as "Doctrine of the Elements."

26. Cf. *Theorie*, Prop. XVII, pp. 244ff. Also, "Neue Darstellung der Hauptmomente der Elementarphilosophie," *Beiträge*, I, p. 185. See above, "The Facts of Consciousness," pp. 14-16. On the other hand, Reinhold pretends to *prove* the existence of the 'thing-in-itself'. His argument is based on the supposed presence in a representation of a material which, since it corresponds to an object *distinct* from the representation, cannot be

actually given without the object in question (i.e., the 'thing-in-itself') being also actual. Like all of Reinhold's arguments intended to establish Kant's supposed assumptions, this too turns out to be only a verbal game.

27. We see from this passage that Reinhold, though unwittingly, is giving a completely new direction to the *Critique*. Kant was not interested in the "predicates of mere representations" but in the predicates of possible objects as expressed, of course, in concepts. He was not interested, in other words, in mental operations as activities of the mind, but in their intentions. The *Critique* still remained a *logic*, even though of a *transcendental* type. Reinhold's new science will have to be a sort of "transcendental psychology," a phenomenology of the mind. See above, "The Facts of Consciousness." pp. 16-19.

28. "Neue Darstellung," *Beiträge* I.

29. This is the "principle of consciousness" on which Reinhold bases his Philosophy of the Elements. In *Theorie*, it is stated as follows: "We are all compelled by *consciousness* to agree that to every representation there pertains a representing subject and a *represented* object, and that *both* must be distinguished from the representation to which they pertain." Prop. 7, p. 200. In "Neue Darstellung," as follows: "Representation is distinguished in consciousness by the subject from the subject and object, and is referred to both." *Beiträge*, I, p. 265.

30. Reinhold is in fact saying that we have a *conceptual, yet preconscious,* apprehension of the facts of consciousness which determines our *conceptual* consciousness of them. After the *Aenesidemus* attack, he will change his position somewhat. The "principle of consciousness" is the representation of a fact which, originally, we only *feel*. See above, "The Facts of Consciousness," pp 25-6.

31. "The universal, though merely negative, condition of all our judgements in general . . . is that they be not self-contradictory . . ." *Critique*, A150, B189. "The proposition that no predicate contradictory of a thing can belong to it is entitled the principle of contradiction." Ibid., A151, B 190. Kant objects to the formulation, "It is impossible that something should *at one and the same time* both be and not be," because of the inclusion of a temporal reference. Ibid., A152, B191.

32. It is interesting to note that in the final stage of his career Reinhold shifted his interest to language, and to the problems that the use of words can generate in philosophical discussion. This turn to language is a typical empiricist move, and it is perhaps one more indication that Reinhold had never really departed from the spirit of popular philosophy. On Reinhold's final period, see H. J. Cloeren, "Philosophie als Sprachkritik bei K. L. Reinhold, Interpretative Bemerkungen zu seiner Spätphilosophie," *Kant-Studien* LXIII (1972), pp. 225-236.

33. This is only a paraphrase. Kant's text reads: ". . . For since the definitions are analyses of given concepts, they presuppose the prior presence of the concepts, although in a confused state; and the incomplete exposition must precede the complete. . . . In short, the definition in all its precision and clarity ought, in philosophy, to come rather at the end than at the beginning of our enquiries." *Critique*, A730-731, B758-759.

34. The reference is to *Critique*, A156-157, B195-196.

35. Here is again a clear indication of how far Reinhold has departed from Kant. Kant had applied the 'form-content' distinction only to concepts of objects of experience. Reinhold now applies it to *all* representations'. He has in principle removed, therefore,

Kant's sharp distinction between 'concepts of reflection' and 'concepts of experience', between 'transcendental' and 'real' objects. See above, "The Facts of Consciousness," pp.18-19.

36. Cf. *Critique*, A728, B756ff.

37. Ibid.

38. Ibid. "Here" is added by Reinhold.

39. Kant's text reads: ". . . and therfore does not require any proof; for if it did, that would disqualify the supposed explanation from standing at the head of all judgments regarding its object." Ibid., A728, B756, note.

40. The reference is to "Neue Darstellung." Note the special stress on "new".

41. The stress on "exhaustively" is Reinhold's.

42. *Critique*, A728-729, B756-757; stress on "certain" is Reinhold's.

43. The text is actually p. 758 of the second edition (A730).

44. Ibid. Stress on "these" is Reinhold's. There are other slight and insignificant variations.

45. i.e., Book II of *Theorie*.

46. i.e., Book III of *Theorie*. The Theory of the Faculty of Desire is given only in outline, pp. 560-579.

47. "Ueber das Bedürfniss, die Möglichkeit und die Eigenschaften eines allgemeingeltenden ersten Grundsatzes der Philosophie" ("On the Need, the Possibility and the Properties of a Universally Binding First Principle of Philosophy"), I, pp. 91-164.

48. "Ueber die Möglichkeit der Philosphie als strenge Wissenschaft" ("On the Possibility of Philosophy as Strict Science"), I, pp. 339-372.

49. Reinhold is obviously referring to an anonymous review that appeared in the issue no. 25 of 1791 (January 28), columns 201-214. this review occasioned the writing of *Foundation*. Cf. Pupi, *Reinhold*, p. 372. Pupi thinks that the author of the review was August Wilhelm Rehberg (1757-1836), statesman and political writer who tried to reconcile Spinozism with critical philosophy. A reply to the review was provided by J. B. Erhard and included in *Foundation* (pp. 139-182). Erhard (1766-1827), a medical doctor, wrote many essays in political philosophy.

50. "Erörterungen über den Versuch einer neuen Theorie des Vorstellungsvermögens" ("Discussions Concerning the Essay towards a New Theory of the Faculty of Representation"), *Beiträge*, I, pp. 373-404. Cf. p. 404.

51. Reinhold never fulfilled this promise.

52. This is not a formula of Kant.

53. Cf. note 17 above.

54. Cf. *Critique*, A832-833, B860-861; A645, B673ff. The systematic unity that Kant has in mind in these passages is the product of reason; it is based on the regulative employment of certain ideas, and it presupposes the knowledge already obtained by the understanding in certain areas of experience. From Kant's point of view, the systematic unity demanded by Reinhold would have to be the product of the understanding itself, for it would be based on principles that supposedly have *immanent*, not just *regulative*, employment.

55. Johann August Eberhard, ed., *Philosophisches Magazin*, Vol. I, No. 3 (1789), p.

289. The four numbers of Vol. I are mostly dedicated to an attack on Kant; Eberhard had founded the journal precisely in order to defend Leibnizian Philosophy. The attack was made in articles usually published anonymously. The reference is to an article entitled "Ueber das Gebiet des reinen Verstandes," pp. 263-289. The fourth article in the same issue, entitled "Ueber die Unterscheidung der Urteile in Analytische und Synthetische", pp. 307-343, was very likely written by Eberhard himself. Kant replied to it with *Ueber eine Entdeckung, nach der alle neue Kritik der reinen Vernunft durch eine ältere entberlich gemacht werden soll*, in 1790. (Academy Edition, Vol. VIII; English tr., Henry E. Allison, *The Kant-Eberhard Controversy*, Baltimore and London: The Johns Hopkins University Press, 1973). Reinhold reviewed the articles in the first volume of the *Magazin* in nos. 174, 175, 176 of the *Allgemeine Literatur-Zeitung (June 11, 12, 13, 1789) using material provided by Kant. Cf. the following letters: Reinhold to Kant, April 9, 1789, Briefwechsel (Academy Edition, Vol XX, pp. 17-18); Kant to Reinhold, May 12, 1789 and May 19, 1789 (pp. 33-48; English tr., pp. 136-150), Reinhold to Kant, June 14,1789, (57-60).*

56. For Kant 'transcendental logic' is not at all a species of 'general logic'. The latter is concerned with the rules that govern the operations of thought; 'transcendental logic' is concerned with the properties of the *objects* of thought instead. 'Transcendental logic' presupposes 'general logic' only in the sense that it obtains from it a 'clue' for the discovery of the categories; it does not presuppose it in any systematic sense. Cf. *Critique*, A69, B94: "[C]oncepts, as predicates of possible judgements, relate to some representation of a not *yet* determined object. . . . The functions of the understanding [i.e., the logical forms]. . . ."

57. Cf. note 24 above.

58. i.e., what Kant calls *ontologia*, *Critique*, A845, B873.

59. i.e., which Kant normally calls "metaphysics of nature".

60. i.e., "rational physiology", as Kant calls it in *Critique*, A845, B873.

61. But which Kant calls "metaphysics of nature" in *Critique*, A845, B873.

62. A841; stresses are all Reinhold's, except for "metaphysics." I have departed completely from the N.K. Smith's translation.

63. Cf. Ibid. Kant says: "The philosophy of pure reason is either *propaedeutic* (preparation) which investigates the faculty of reason . . . or is the system, etc."

64. Reinhold developed his "Outline of a Theory of the Faculty of Desire" with which he had concluded his *Theorie* (cf. above, note 46) in two places: in the second volume of his Kantian Letters which he published in 1792 (*Briefe über die Kantische Philosophie*, Vol. II, Leipzig; bei Georg Joachim Göschen; see especially Letter VI: "Versuch einer neuen Darstellung der Grundbegriffe und Grundsätze der Moral und Naturrechts," "Essay towards a New Exposition of the Fundamental Concepts and Principles of Morality and Natural Law," pp. 174-197; Letter VII: "Ueber den bisherigen verkannten Unterschied zwischen dem uneigennützigen und dem eigennützigen Triebe, and zwischen diesen beiden Trieben und dem Willen," "On the so far Ignored Distinction between the Interested and the Disinterested Inclinations, and between Both These Inclinations and the Will," pp. 220-261; and Letter VIII: "Erörterung des Begriffes von der Freiheit des Willens," "A Discussion of the Concept of Freedom of the Will," pp. 262-308), and in the second volume of his *Contributions* which he published in 1794 (see especially "Ueber das vollständige Fundament der Moral," "On the Complete Foundation of

Morality," pp. 206-294; in this treatise Reinhold presents his theory in 126 propositions). In his moral theory Reinhold tried to do for the several notions of 'will' which Kant, as he alleges, had left unexplained the same thing that he had done in his Theory of Representation for Kant's various notions of 'representation'. Reinhold's aim is to establish one fundamental concept of 'will and to derive all the others systematically from it. 'Will' is in general the faculty of desire, i.e., the source of a general inclination in us to realize the objects of our representations. This inclination assumes different forms according as it is determined in different instances by specifically different kinds of representations. If the representations come from the senses, then the inclination that they engender is 'interested', i.e., 'self-centered'; and it remains so even if it is further modified by the effect of theoretical reason which leads the will to abstain from an immediate satisfaction for the sake of some greater future one. If the representations come exclusively from reason, and if they have reason itself as their object, then the inclination that they engender is 'disinterested', i.e., its aim is the realization of the law simply for the sake of the law. Inasmuch as it determines the will in this way, reason is called 'practical'. Reinhold stresses that the 'disinterested' desires generated by practical reason are by no means opposed to the 'interested' ones generated by theoretical reason and by the senses. On the contrary , they are related to them as 'form' to 'matter'. It is possible, in other words, and even necessary as far as *actual* moral life goes, for an individual to seek his private pleasures, yet to do this while respecting the law for its own sake and conforming to it. This is a point on which Reinhold deliberately distantiates himself from Kant. At any rate, whether the will is determined by practical reason alone, or by the senses alone, or by senses in conjunction with theoretical reason, or by the three together, it still *does not act freely*. It is still functioning simply at the level of an inclination that is inherent in each and every faculty of the mind and which leads it to realize the whole range of objects available to it. But it is no more possible for a faculty *not* to seek its objects than it is for a body not to seek its natural place. (The analogy, incidentally, is not Reinhold's; the scholastic background of what he is saying, however, is obvious). It is possible to conceive of a man, in other words, who acts out of purely selfish motives, and equally so of another, who acts out of purely unselfish ones, without in each case having to assume more than a general, and essentially *amoral*, desire to realize certain possibilities inherent in man. According to Reinhold, morality proper begins only when the will, operating at yet another level, *freely* (*willkürlich*) commits itself to one pattern of conduct rather than to another for no other reason than simply in order to express itself as a power of self-determination. This free commitment does not, by itself, make the chosen conduct either right or wrong; conformity to the law or the lack of conformity to it is what determines this. Yet it adds to it precisely its *moral* quality; it is what makes a certain conduct the expression of personality.

His distinction between 'free will' and 'practical reason', his identification of 'free will' as the 'faculty of personality', and his reconciliation of 'interested' with 'disinterested' desires, constituted in Reinhold's view his great contribution to Kant's moral theory. In this case too, he declared himself to be simply grounding and clarifying doctrines supposedly already present in the masters's works. He only objected to Kant's theory because, as formulated by Kant himself, it tended to resolve man's conduct into a determinism of nature on the one hand, and a formalism of reason on the other, without ever explaining how individuality and freedom (*liberum arbitrium*) ever enter into it. As a matter of fact, Kant did recognize this shortcoming of his theory, and tried to remedy it in his *Religion Within the Limits of Reason Alone* (1793) (*Die Religion innerhalb der Grenzen der blossen Vernunft*, Academy Ed., Vol. VI; English tr. by Greene and Hudson, New York: Harper & Brothers, 1960). Yet, it must have been clear even to Reinhold that he was not just *completing* and *clarifying* Kant's doctrine with his proposed modifications, but changing it completely. He was actually reverting to a scholastic scheme of the 'will-reason' relationship. For Kant, after all, 'individuality' and *Willkür* had to remain limits of moral life which were indeed existentially important, but irrational all the same. 'Religion', not 'reason', could ultimately deal with them. Morality must be based as such only on the formalism of reason. For Kant, in other words, the only 'person' which is morally significant is a 'legal entity', This is precisely the point that Reinhold could not accept; *his* moral person had to be a real individual. It is clear here, more so than anywhere else, that Reinhold is operating at a completely different level of conceptualization and interests than Kant.

65. Reinhold never kept his promise. He was soon to declare himself for Fichte. See "The Facts of Consciousness," p. 9-10, 31.

66. "Ueber das Verhältniss der Theorie des Vorstellungsvermögens zur Kritik der reinen Vernunft," pp. 255-338.

67. Joh. Georg Heinrich Feder, *Ueber Raum und Kausalität, zur Prüfung der Kantischen Philosophie*, Göttingen: bei Joh. Chr. Dietrich, 1787.

68. Cf. above, note 55.

Aenesidemus
Or
Concerning the Foundations of The Philosophy of The Elements Issued by Prof. Reinhold in Jena Together with a Defence of Skepticism Against the Pretensions of The Critique of Reason

by G. E. Schulze

1792 [n.p.p.]

Nos et refellere sine pertinacia, et refelli sine iracundia parati sumus.

Cicero

[*Tusculanarum disputationum libri V*, 2.2.5: "We are ready to refute without obstinacy as well as to be refuted without passion."]

Translation and Notes by George di Giovanni

The following is the translation of an excerpt from Aenesidemus, oder über die
Fundamente der von dem Herrn Prof. Reinhold in Jena gelieferten Elementar-
Philosophie, nebst einer Verteidigung gegen die Anmaassungen der
Vernunftkritik, *which appeared anonymously, and without place of publication,
in 1792. Its author was Gottlob Ernst Schulze (1761-1833), a skeptic and professor
of philosophy at Helmstädt. The work is the earliest and best known reaction from
the side of skepticism against critical philosophy. It was directed especially against
the new form that Karl Leonhard Reinhold had just given to it in his "Philosophy
of the Elements" which he had presented to the public in three major works:* Versuch
einer Theorie des menschlichen Vorstellungsvermögen, *1789* (Essay Towards
a Theory of the Human Faculty of Cognition), Beiträge zur Berichtigung
bisherigen Missversändnisse der Philosophen, *Vol. I, 1790* (Contributions to
the Rectification of Misconceptions hitherto Held by Philosophers), *and* Ueber
das Fundament des philosophischen Wissens, *1791* (The Foundation of
Philosophical Knowledge). *Schulze's book professes to be a record of the
correspondence between two characters, Hermias and Aenesidemus, in the course
of which one of them (Aenesidemus) tries to dissuade the other from his newly
acquired faith in critical philosophy. Aenesidemus's main attack against the new
philosophy comes in a treatise that he appends to his second letter (the third in the
series). In it he cites verbatim thirty-six propositions from Reinhold's most recent
systematic presentation of his position, and he then subjects them to close scrutiny.
A special section of the treatise is dedicated to Kant's position, which Aenesidemus
recognizes not to be identical with Reinhold's. In a final letter, Aenesidemus also
attacks Kant's moral philosophy.*

    *The translated excerpts include Aenesidemus's criticism of Reinhold's fundamental
thesis, and also his criticism of Kant. The translation is from the original edition,
which is now also available in photo-mechanical reproduction in the series* Aetas
Kantiana (*Bruxelles: Culture et Civilization, 1969). It was re-published in 1911 by
the Kantgesellschaft (ed. Arthur Liebert, Berlin).*

"WHERE DO THE REPRESENTATIONS //that we possess origi-   [94]
nate, and how do they come to be in us?" This has been for a long
time one of the most important questions in philosophy. Common
opinion has rightly held that, since the representations in us are not
the objects [Sachen] themselves being represented, the connection
between our representations and the things outside us must be
established above all by a careful and sound answer to this question.
It is in this way that certitude must be sought regarding the reality of

the different components of our knowledge. Now, it is the thesis of critical philosophy that a large portion of the determinations and characteristics with which the representations of certain objects [*Gegenstände*] occur in us are to be grounded in the essence of our *faculty of representation*.[1] This claim combines the opposite explanations that Locke and Leïbniz gave for the origin of human representations,[2] and on its truth rest for the most part the soundness and the truth of what critical philosophy says regarding the limits and the determinations of the various branches of the human faculty of cognition. For a proper estimate, therefore, of the true value of critical philosophy, and of

[95]   the legitimacy // of the claims it makes for the apodictic evidence and infallibility of its results, we must give special consideration to the grounds and the principles from which, and in accordance to which, it establishes that there is in our knowledge something determined *a priori* by the mind, and that this something constitutes the form of the material given to our knowledge *a posteriori*.

    In this examination, however, we must also pay special attention to the demands of Humean skepticism. For it is not only a principal goal of the *Critique of Reason* to refute the Humean doubt in its assessment of the human faculty of cognition; but also the adherents to the critical system claim, indeed unanimously, that by deriving a certain part of human cognition from the faculty of representation this system has in fact conquered *all* of David Hume's doubts, once and for all. It has fully satisfied, even to the point of *superfluity*, all the legitimate demands made by that acute philosopher on the dogmatists—whether they had to do with the certainty of the principle of sufficient reason, or its use, or with the possibility of a transition from the representations in us to the being and to the positive and

[96]   negative components of the things that we presume outside us. // It is of great consequence, therefore, in adjudicating the value of the whole of critical philosophy, to press the question whether the *Critique of Reason* has done justice to the demands made by Hume; whether this *Critique*, which was occasioned by a protracted reflection on his doubt, as its great originator had admitted, has in fact resolved that doubt, and provided, with respect to the value and the origin of the different components of human cognition, a securely grounded system. A discussion of these questions, however, requires that we should draw a careful comparison between Hume's demands and Hume's problem on the one hand, and the principles of the critical system on the other, as well as the reasons by which the latter tries to establish that certain *a priori* forms are present in human cognition. To my knowledge, neither friend nor foe of this newest philosophy has so far engaged in such a comparison, even though the admission, on the part of its originator, that it was Hume's doubt that first interrupted

his dogmatic slumber and led him to the search for the principles of his system,[3] provided occasion enough for it.

In the search for the sources of the components of our knowledge, the Philosophy of the Elements[4] has followed a course of its own, and *appears* at any rate to have been led to their discovery by following an entirely different sign-post than // the one followed [97] by the *Critique of Pure Reason*. We shall also have to enquire, therefore, to which of these two sign-posts we can safely entrust ourselves, or with which the danger of being led astray is least great. Thus we shall not only have to examine the proofs by which the Philosophy of the Elements establishes that much of what is in a representation is determined by the mind, but also those advanced for the same purpose by the *Critique of Pure Reason*.

Now, paragraphs v-viii [of the Philosophy of the Elements] state the following preliminaries regarding the nature of the faculty of representation:[5]

(a) The faculty of representation is the cause and ground of the actual presence of representations;

(b) The faculty of representation is present prior to every representation, and is so in a determinate form;

(c) The faculty of representation differs from representation as cause from effect;

(d) The concept of the faculty of representation may be inferred only from its effect, i.e., the mere representation, and in order to obtain its *inner* characteristics, i.e., its determinate concept, one must develop exhaustively the concept of representation as such.

On the face of it, these propositions only concern the determination of the *concept* of the faculty of representation. But since they // [98] imply that by this concept we also think an objectively actual something which is the cause and condition of the actuality of representations, and is present prior to any of them, the question we must raise, before any other indeed, is this: by which means has the Philosophy of the Elements come to its extravagant cognition of the objective existence of this something, and with which argument does it justify it, granted that nothing at all is said about it in the principle of consciousness (for the latter, of course, is only meant to express actual facts)? Nowhere do we find, in the latest exposition of its principal tenets, a proof of the objective actuality of the faculty of representation. Mention of a proof only occurs in the *Theory of the Faculty of Representation* (p.190). And what is said there is this: "Representation is the only thing about whose actuality all philosophers agree. Indeed, if there is anything at all about which there is agreement in the philosophical world, it is representation. No idealist, no solipsist, no dogmatic skeptic, can deny its being. *Whoever grants a representation, however, must also grant a faculty of representation, i.e., that without which no representation can be thought.*[6] Considering how much in this newest philosophy depends on our being certain of the objective reality of the faculty of representation, a proof of this sort was hardly to be expected from a friend of critical philosophy which insists that *thought* is distinguished

[99]   from *being*. // Yet in the proof a conclusion is actually being drawn from the *constitution of representations and thoughts in us* to the constitution of objects [*Sachen*] in themselves, outside us. The proof really consists in the following argument: Any two things that cannot be *thought* apart from one another can also not *be* apart from one another; the being and actuality of representations cannot be *thought* apart from the being and actuality of a faculty of representation; hence a faculty of representation must also exist objectively, just as certainly as representation must also exist objectively, just as certainly as representations are present in us. Now, if this syllogism were right, and were it to prove anything at all, then Spinozism would be invulnerable to attack, as well as the Leibnizian system and idealism — in fact, the whole of dogmatism in all its diverse and contradictory claims about the thing-in-itself. We would then have, originating in theoretical reason, irrefutable proofs for the objective reality of monads, on the one hand, (for the being of what is complex cannot be thought apart from the being of its simple components) and, on the other, for the

[100]   objective simplicity and the personal // nature of the thinking subject in us (for this subject can only be thought as simple and as substance). Then theoretical reason would be capable of an apodictic proof for the objective existence of a world-creator (for the existence of the entire series of conditioned things cannot be thought without the existence of an original unconditioned cause). Then space and time would be something actual outside us, and would exist *realiter* (for the presence of bodies can be thought only in a given space, and that of alterations only in a given time). Then all that Kant has asserted, and believes to have demonstrated, about the inability of the understanding and of reason to discover by thought the nature of things-in-themselves — all this would be false and wrong-headed; we would instead possess a principle by which we can discover the nature of things as they are outside our representations.

"But," one will ask, "is the skeptic denying that there are in man sensibility, understanding, and reason? In his disputes with dogmatism he constantly appeals to grounds based on understanding and reason.How can he then deny or doubt either without contradicting himself?" No skeptic denies that there are in man intuitions, concepts,

[101]   or ideas, or that these are distinct from one another. // This is a matter of fact. Just as little does he deny that we possess the

representations of a sensibility, an understanding and a reason, which we take to be powers or faculties, respectively, of intuition, concepts and ideas, distinct from these; or, that in order to find more comprehensible the being of representations, we take these to be the effects of a faculty different from them. Whether or not, however, faculties of this sort have actual being outside our representations of them; whether or not the thought of something that ought to make intuitions, concepts and ideas possible in us in the first place is totally void of objective value; and where the representation of this something might originate — these are, according to skepticism, totally *undecided issues* that do not allow, on the basis of the principles that philosophy has so far had at its disposal, of a simple "yes" or "no" answer. Its claim is that these questions cannot be resolved before either of the following: (1) we have established on adequate grounds how far the employment of the real principle of sufficient reason extends — whether it may be applied to things as they are in-themselves or in the representations by which we refer to them; (2) we have established the connection between our representations and the objects outside them in accordance with some other undeniable principle, and also that this connection is knowable // to us. Whenever the skeptic makes use, therefore, of the words "reason" and "understanding", his only intention is to express himself in a way that is commonly understood. The astronomer can speak of the sun "rising or setting" in order to make himself understood, even though personally he is perhaps convinced that the sun does not move around the earth, but the other way around. The skeptic uses the words "sensibility", "understanding", "reason", "faculty of representation", and "faculty of cognition", in just the same way — to make himself understood by others and to refer, in keeping with accepted language practices, to certain distinctions in human representations. It is his conviction, however, that as philosophy and its principles now stand, the issue whether or not there is a true objective ground that differs from intuitions, concepts and ideas, or from any representation or cognition in man, yet has produced them all, still remains totally undecided.

    The Philosophy of the Elements, by deriving actual representations from a faculty which it takes to be something objectively actual, and by defining it as the cause of the representations,[7] contradicts its own principles as well as the results of the *Critique of Reason*. For according to the latter the employment of the categories // is to be restricted to empirical intuitions; knowledge can only be realized in us inasmuch as the categories are applied to objects of empirical intuition.[8] Hence the extension of the pure concepts of the understanding beyond our experiences to objects not immediately represented, but only thought, is totally inadmissible; nor could such an extension instruct us in the

[102]

[103]

least regarding the constitution of any object whatever. And in his *Theory of the Faculty of Representation*, Mr. Reinhold has not only not altered or otherwise defined the restrictions to the employment of the categories stipulated by the *Critique*; on the contrary, he wants to establish with even more precision than Kant that absolutely no other application of the categories is possible or conceivable than the one just mentioned.[9] It is, therefore, simply incomprehensible whence the Philosophy of the Elements obtains the right, in laying down its foundations, to apply the categories of *cause* and *actuality* to a supra-sensible object, viz., to a particular faculty of representations which is neither intuitable nor given to any experience. Yet, in presuming this right arbitrarily and counter to the results of its own speculations, it actually demonstrates—obviously by applying the real principle of

[104] sufficient // reason to things outside experience—that this principle can only be applied to objects of empirical intuitions and to these alone. But we shall have occasion later on,[10] when we come to examine the original and firmest arguments supporting Kant's system as laid down in the *Critique of Reason* itself, to speak at length of how real this contradiction is in its use of the concepts of *cause* and *effect* and

[105] related principles*//

Now, as regards the means which the Philosophy of the Elements prescribes and employs to obtain the characteristics of the faculty of representations, they are of no account. In fact, to try to derive the properties of that faculty from the properties of mere representation is altogether unproductive. For, from the constitution of an effect, it is never possible to infer with certainty the constitution of its cause or of the objective ground that supposedly had produced it, or the nature of this ground. Causes even require that they be thought as different from their effects; much can be present in them, therefore, (if there actually are any causes) that belongs to them as property, yet does

---

*Not the slightest indication is given in Paragraphs vi, vii, and viii of the Philosophy of the Elements that the faculty of representation is at issue only as a ground of actual representations that we *can think*, but not *know*.[11] Rather, everything said in these paragraphs leads to believe that their author, like most dogmatists, means by 'faculty of representation' something actual in an objective sense. It is to this claim, and to the grounds on which it rests, that the above comments are directed. But even if by the faculty of representation, from which the Philosophy of the Elements derives actual representations, we are to understand only an *ens rationis* (a possibility this, which from Paragraphs vi-viii we could only surmise), still, since the intention of this philosophy is to keep all quarrels from its domain and to put to rest all philosophical feuds, it would have to establish before all else (1) that we have no choice but to apply this *ens rationis*

[105] if we want to // comprehend the possibility of actual representations, and (2) that this *ens rationis* is fit and sufficient for the intended end. More about this in what follows.[12]

not occur in the effects at all and would never be manifested through them. This applies also to the effects. How can one possibly hope to discover, therefore, the characteristics of the faculty of representation, even if it were proved that any such faculty actually exists, by an extrapolation of the characteristics of representation? Would not this practice, moreover, consist in the transposition of the characteristics of a thing to something entirely different from it? The definition of the faculty of representation laid down in the Philosophy of the Elements // is in fact nothing more than a definition of the [106] characteristics of the very representation which is supposed to be the effect of the defined faculty, adorned however with the entirely empty title of *power* or *faculty*.[13] It has long since been understood that to appeal to some particular cause or faculty behind an alteration, or some other matter of fact, in order to explain it, as is commonly done, amounts to no more than a repetition of the phenomenon or actual fact whose properties we wanted to explain, with the addition of the word *power* or *faculty*. For instance, whenever we pull a rod out of the water, some drops remain suspended from it. Now, if one asks what causes this, the reply given may be that the rod has the faculty of attracting water. But does this answer make any more comprehensible the fact itself that drops stick to the rod? Does it determine what makes them stick? Whoever is untrained in reflection will no doubt find that answer satisfactory. Those accustomed, however, to reflect on the sense of words, and to distinguish empty from meaningful expressions, see quite well that wherever they are found, answers of the sort are nothing else but admissions of human ignorance regarding the ground of the given facts, or of the changes in // sen- [107] sible objects. This is exactly the case if we explain actual represen- tations by deriving them from an alleged faculty behind them. In doing this, the Philosophy of the Elements does not really make the presence of representations in us, nor their nature, any more comprehensible than they already are on their own. It arbitrarily assumes the being of a faculty of representation, and attributes to it as its property and mode of operation what, according to experience, ought to be found in representations instead. Moreover, the definition of the faculty of representation laid down in the Philosophy of the Elements could only make comprehensible those representations that "are referred to an object and subject and are distinguished from both", [14] if indeed it explained anything at all; for it is drawn only from this type of representations. It would not, however, establish the possibility of anything in us which, even without being referred to an object or subject and being distinguished from both, is nonetheless a representation and rightly deserves to be called so.[15]

Thus, although a great deal less is said, in Paragraphs vi-viii of the Philosophy of the Elements, regarding the nature of the faculty of representation, than the dogmatic schools once claimed to know, still,

[108]   even // the little that is said should not be assumed to be true, or professed to be such, without sufficient reasons. This is, however, precisely what the Philosophy of the Elements does. . . .'[16].

Has the Critique of Reason Really Refuted Hume's Skepticism?

[131]   The deduction of the necessary synthetic judgements from // the mind, and the determination of their connection to the cognition of empirical objects, provide the main support in the Kantian system for its specific doctrines and principles. If this deduction and determination were beyond doubt, and grounded on decisively certain principles, the system of critical philosophy would be unassailable. David Hume would then have been refuted once and for all, and his doubts as to whether the concepts of cause and effect can be applied to things would be groundless. The answer to the question posed in this section will above all depend, therefore, on our enquiring whether David Hume could have found Mr. Kant's proof that the necessary synthetic judgements must originate in mind, in the inner source of representations, and that they are the form of experiential cognition, sufficient and compelling; or, in general, whether Kant's deduction of these judgements from the essential determinations of the human mind, as well as his assessment of their value, are subject to well founded or reasonable objections.

Now, it is an undeniable conscious fact, and as such open to no doubt, that there are in human knowledge necessary synthetic judgements and that they are an indispensable component of it. It is

[132]   no less // indubitable that the necessity pertaining in these judgements to the subject-predicate combination can be derived neither from the occurrence of these judgments once in our mind, or even several times, nor from the agreement of a given number of experiences. That is to say, our having joined certain representations together once, or several times, does not produce the effect that we must, necessarily, so join them every time. The necessity that attaches to certain synthetic judgements in our knowledge cannot be made comprehensible to us on the basis of mere experience, or from our perception of the presence of such judgements in us.

Without prejudice to the undeniable truth of this, however, I maintain all the same that in fact the *Critique of Pure Reason* tries to refute Humean skepticisim by assuming as already unquestionably certain the very propositions against whose *legitimacy* Hume directed all his skeptical doubts. For the *Critique* claims that the original determinations of the human mind are the real ground or source of the necessary synthetic judgements found in our knowledge; but it does this by inferring, from the fact that we can only *think* of the faculty of representation as the ground of these judgements, that the mind must *be* their ground in *actual fact* too. With this claim, however, it has already *assumed as indisputably certain* [what Hume doubted, viz.,] (1) *that for anything present // in our knowledge there is also objectively* [133] *present a real ground and cause differing from it realiter; and, in general, that the principle of sufficient reason is valid not only for representation and their subjective combination, but also for things-[Sachen] in-themselves and in their objective interconnections; (2) that we are justified in inferring from the constitution of something as it is in our representations its objective constitution outside us.*

And to grasp the fairness of this judgement, one only has to compare impartially the highest principles on which the *Critique of Reason* grounds its new system of philosophy with what Hume subjected to doubt and declared to be uncertain. For if Hume is to be refuted, surely it can be done only by establishing the contrary of his assertions regarding the concepts and principles of causal connection from indisputably certain propositions; or alternatively, by showing contradictions or *non-sequiturs* in his assertions about the problematic nature of the use we make of our // representations of the relationship of cause to [134] effect. The *Critique of Reason* has done neither. On the contrary, it demonstrates all its claims regarding the difference in the sources of human cognitions precisely by the exclusive means of the very propositions which Hume held to be uncertain and deceptive. The fact that in these propositions the correctness of the combination of the subject and predicate can be questioned, and [hence] it is not in the least decided, makes the propositions useless for the purpose of establishing the foundation of a system of philosophy.

I can now hear many a follower of critical philosophy reply immediately: "This whole line of reasoning, or anything that might still be added to it, can only deceive somebody who has failed to understand the essential intention of the *Critique of Reason*. If we want to assess its merits in resolving Hume's doubt fairly, we must take the demands for certainty that he made on philosophers with respect to their metaphysical principles into account in their entirety, and not restrict ourselves to his doubts on the use of the concepts and principles of causality. Those demands have been masterfully and fully met by the *Critique in toto*, and as a result Hume's doubts on the employment of the principles of causality have been overcome as well. Hume's // skepticism takes its start from a single but [135] supremely important concept of theoretical reason, viz., the concept of the link between cause and effect (hence from the derivative concepts of power, operation, etc. as well). He demanded that reason, which pretended to have generated the concept in its womb, should give him an account of its right to think that something can be so constituted that, upon being posited, something else would also have to be posited necessarily—for this is precisely what the concept of cause and effect says. And he argued quite consequentially that reason is totally incapable of thinking any such combinations *a priori*, on the base of concepts. For the combination entails necessity, yet it is quite impossible to see how, just because something is, something else must also be necessarily—how the concept, therefore, of any such link between one thing and another could be introduced *a priori*. Hence he concluded that, as regards this concept, reason has completely deceived itself; that it has wrongly claimed the concept as its own child, and on the contrary, it is nothing else but a bastard of the imagination which, made pregnant by experience, has given birth to certain representations under the aegis of the law of association, but has substituted for the subjective necessity that springs from this law (i.e., custom) the kind of objective necessity that would spring from insight.[17] //

[136]

"Now, the *Critique of Reason* has first presented Hume's objection in general terms, showing that the concept of the cause-effect link is by no means the only one by which the understanding conceives links between things *a priori*. Then it has provided a complete deduction of all the concepts in question which shows that they do not originate from experience, but have arisen from pure understanding instead.

"That is to say, from the necessity and universality that attaches to those concepts and their respective principles, the *Critique of Reason* incontrovertibly proves that their cause is to be sought in the human mind; moreover, that since they are present in us as *a priori* cognitions, these concepts and principles cannot contain anything besides the forms of sensibility and of judgement which, in the representing subject, must come before any manifestation of its powers. However, that knowledge which is true *realiter* can only be attained if the *a priori* synthetic judgements and the concepts included in them are applied to objects of possible experience: this also the *Critique of Reason* demonstrates, as a particular thesis, from the inability of dogmatic philosophy to make good its claims to know things-in-themselves.

[137]

"Thus the Critique of Reason has completely refuted the skepticism of Hume. It shows // how we possess *a priori* synthetic knowledge, and how this knowledge can be legitimately applied to sensible perceptions. And in so doing, it has at the same time measured out the entire sphere of cognitions possible to man, and identified the sources of the components of all our insights."

Yet, however important as a *product of acumen* and *philosophical spirit* the explanation given in the *Critique of Reason* of how necessary principles are possible, it is nevertheless ineffective to prove, or in any way establish, anything against David Hume.

For it is obvious indeed that the author of the *Critique of Reason* arrives at his answer to the general problem, "How are necessary synthetic propositions possible in us?" simply by applying the principle of causality to certain judgements that occur in us after experience. He subsumes them under the concept 'effect of something', and in accordance with this subsumption he assumes, and declares, that the mind is their effective cause. And with this move he believes to have also definitively established the true function that these judgements have in our knowledge, and their value. For from the fact that these necessary synthetic judgements derive from the mind, in the inner source of representation, he concludes that they constitute only the // form [138] of experiential cognition, and that they only gain reference by being applied to empirical perception. He presupposes as established, therefore, that each segment of human knowledge has a real ground that causes it. Without this presupposition all that is said in the *Critique of Reason* concerning the origin of necessary synthetic judgements makes no sense at all. Thus the *Critique of Reason* gives its solution to that important problem of theoretical philosophy, "How are necessary synthetic judgements possible for us?", by presupposing that the questions: "Is the actual held together by the laws of causality?" and "Are there particular causes at the origin of our judgements and of their determinations?", have already been decided and agreed upon. Its search for the sources of the necessary synthetic propositions is guided precisely by this presupposition. Hume would therefore require its author to explain to him what right he had to apply the principle of causality in the groundwork of critical philosophy, and how he could presume, at the very outset of its construction into a system, that a circumstance such as the presence of synthetic necessary propositions in us is the effect of a cause different from them (be this cause what // you will.) Rightly could he say: "As long as the use [139] we may make of the concepts and principles of causality, or their status, is still uncertain and disputed; as long as the issue whether these concepts and principles are just something subjective, or whether they constitute objective predicates of actual things, is still open to doubt; so long as this is so, it is futile and pointless to want to enquire into the sources of the various parts of human knowledge, or to establish anything about them. For before we have the right to ask: "What are the sources and causes of our knowledge?", we must already have established that for every actual thing there exists a ground and a cause, and, specifically with respect to our knowledge, that all its determinations are the effect of particular causes."

Still, let us assume for the time being (1) that it is indubitably certain, *per se*, that anything actual is held together by causality *realiter*; (2) that the understanding is entitled to ask for the grounds of the origin and determination of our knowledge. And let us then enquire whether the argument by which the *Critique of Reason* establishes that the mind is the cause of the necessary synthetic judgements, and in virtue of which it rises from the knowledge that these judgements are in us to an insight into their cause and source, is correct and does prove

[140]   something, not just against // Hume, but in principle also. The argument runs as follows:

> Whatever can be *represented* by us as possible in just one way, the same *is* also possible in just that way; But the necessary synthetic judgements present in our knowledge can be represented by us *as possible* only if we take them to originate in the mind, from its mode of operation as determined *a priori*; Therefore, also the necessary synthetic judgements present in our knowledge can *actually have arisen* only in the mind, from its mode of operation as determined *a priori*.

From the fact, therefore, that we are incapable of representing to ourselves, or to think, how the necessary synthetic judgements found in our knowledge are possible, except by deriving them from the mind, the *Critique of Reason* proves that they must originate in it is actual fact too, or *realiter*. It thus infers the objective and real constitution of what is to be found outside our representations, from the constitution of the representations and thoughts present in us; or again, it proves that something must be constituted *realiter* in such and such a way because it cannot be thought otherwise. But it is precisely the validity of this kind of inference that Hume questioned. And he declared it to be a sophism because we know of no principle by which we can

[141]   determine to what extent // our representations and their characteristics agree with what is objective and its characteristics, or to what extent something present in our thoughts refers to anything outside them. This inference is also the foundation on which every dogmatism is grounded. Philosophy has made use of it from time immemorial to determine the objective nature of what lies outside our representations, or what is really true; by applying it thus, it has justified the contradictory results of all the systems of theoretical metaphysics. In short, in refuting Hume the *Critique of Reason* avails itself of an inference which, for him, was utterly deceptive and misleading. And to show that we men cannot know anything about the things-in-themselves, it employs a line of argument which could in fact lead us to the most important discoveries in that immeasurable

realm of things-in-themselves. Even less comprehensible, however, is how the *Critique of Reason* could avail itself of the same inference as it lays down the foundation of its system, considering how often and emphatically it urges on us the distinction existing between representations and the objective things [*Sachen*] that are supposed to be there independent of them. (With this distinction, of course, the inference necessarily loses whatever certainty it had and all power to convince.) And the *Critique of Reason* even justifies // one of [142] the most important parts of its system, the Transcendental Dialectic, above all by assuming that in spite of long-sanctioned practice, it will never be possible to infer, from the determinations that belong to our representations and thinking, those to be found outside us.[18]

And just as fallacious as the *major* of the syllogism by which the *Critique of Reason* proves that the necessary synthetic judgements spring from the mind and lie in us *a priori*, is its *minor*. It is simply not true that, in order to be thought as possible, these judgements *have* to be thought as present *a priori*, and as originating in the mind. Because the human understanding, at the present level of its culture, can represent to itself the possibility of something in just one way, it does not follow in principle, nor with any certitude whatever, that it will be able to think it in only that way at all times, even at some future age when it will have acquired greater maturity. And as a matter of fact, it is possible [even now] to explain how necessity and strict universal validity can be found in certain areas of our knowledge otherwise than it is in the *Critique of Reason*, and to think some ground other than the *Critique* has given to it for the necessity that attaches to certain synthetic judgements. It is possible to think, for instance, that all our knowledge has its origin in the efficacy // that objects [143] present *realiter* have on our mind; also, that the necessity encountered in certain of its areas is generated by the special manner in which external things occasion cognition in the mind by affecting it; that the necessary synthetic judgements, in other words, along with the representations included in them, originate not in the mind, but precisely in those objects which, according to critical philosophy, are to produce in us only accidental and reformable judgements.

That is to say, it is (a) incorrect to assume, as the *Critique of Reason* assumes, that the *consciousness of necessity* that accompanies certain synthetic propositions constitutes an *infallible* sign of its having originated *a priori* and in the mind. For instance, critical philosophy grants that the materials of all the sensations of outer sense do not originate in the mind but in things outside us. Yet, in spite of the empirical origin of these sensations, there is a consciousness of necessity bound up with them. For as long as a sensation is present in us, we *must* recognize it as being so present. We can indeed *think* its not having been there

or, while it is there, *think* its not having been there or, while it is there,
[144]   *think* some other occupying its place. But // we cannot actually
have this other sensation or blot out the first altogether; on the contrary,
we are conscious of its present existence as of something necessary.
In just the same way we must leave the order or combination of the
characteristics present in an actual sensation of external objects just
the way that it occurred at a specific time. It is *necessary* that we perceive
the branches of a seen tree in the order in which they are present to
the mind at some given moment. Here we have an actual case, therefore,
of objects outside us arousing in the mind by their influence on it a
consciousness of necessity, making it impossible to perceive something
otherwise than it is perceived.[19] There is of course a considerable
distinction between the necessity that accompanies actual external or
internal sensations, and the one that occurs with certain synthetic
judgements. For the first lasts only for a time, and occurs only under
certain circumstances, while the consciousness of the necessity to
combine a property with the subject in those judgements occurs each
and every time the judgements are present in us. But if it is not
impossible, in principle, for empirical objects to affect our mind in
[145]   such a way as to arouse in us, at least for some // time, a feeling
of necessity, then it is possible that they also produce in us cognitions
which, when combined, would be accompanied at all times by the
consciousness of necessity. At least one cannot say that the necessity
of a cognition is a sure and unerring sign of its origin *a priori*. (b) If
things-in-themselves were entirely unknown to us as the *Critique of
Reason* claims, we cannot know at all which determinations can be
produced in the mind because of their influence on it, and which
cannot. A thing that is entirely unknown to us is also unknown in
respect to all that it can or cannot bring about. How are we ever to
be certain, then—indeed, apodictically certain—that the external objects
of sensations, entirely unknown to us, cannot generate cognitions such
as would carry necessity? (c) Deriving what is necessary and universally
valid in our cognition from the mind does not make the presence of
such necessity in the least more comprehensible than deriving it from
objects outside us and from their mode of operation. For since we
know nothing of what the mind is in itself, as the *Critique of Reason*
[146]   also concedes, by // choosing one derivation over the other we
do nothing more than substitute one form of non-knowledge for another. After all, if the origin of the necessary synthetic judgements is
to be more comprehensible when traced to the mind rather than to
the objects outside us, we must be able to know at least *one* property
in the mind which objects lack that would indeed make the origin of
those judgements in the mind more comprehensible. But the *Critique
of Reason* has failed altogether to identify any such property in the mind.

"But Hume is indeed totally in agreement with the *Critique*," so it is said, "in this respect: that the concepts of cause and effect cannot have arisen from experience at all, for their relation to each other entails necessity. Moreover, in deriving these concepts from custom and from the laws of association of ideas which he laid down, he was attempting to discredit the dogmatism of contemporary philosophers, though he does not seem to have set much store by the attempt personally. How could we take what has just been said, therefore, as anything that Hume would have seen as an objection to the claims of the *Critique of Reason* about the origin of the necessity and universal validity of human cognition?" // Hume would undoubtedly have [147] disputed the correctness of the derivation from the mind of the necessary synthetic judgements by the *Critique of Reason*, for the derivation has not been demonstrated, nor could it be. Moreover, he does not at all claim in the same sense as the *Critique of Reason* does, that experience cannot instruct us about what is necessary. For he used this claim against those philosophers of his days who said: "Nature's constancy throughout its alterations irrefutably proves that there are powers that exist in the given objects and necessitate certain specific results, and that the ground and the source of our representation of the necessity that accrues to the reciprocal relation of cause and effect is to be found in the uniformity of several experiences." Against this Hume objected, rightly, that the constancy and uniformity in the succession of a number of alterations does not entail the necessity of those that follow; that it is possible to think this constancy and uniformity even though at some time, upon the positing of the alleged cause, the consequence fails to appear; hence, that experience does not really contain what those metaphysicians wanted to find // in [148] it all."*

The Critique of Reason, instead, while also allowing that *necessary* propositions belong to the totality of our cognition, denies that they can have originated in experience, i.e., in the influence of existing objects upon the mind. Whenever Hume says, therefore, "Experience does not teach that something is necessary, but only that it is constituted in such or such a way," he means by it: "The necessity that we expect in a series of alterations with respect to any succeeding term is in fact not there; consequently, since the concept of necessity is not a constituent part of perceptions that resemble one another, it cannot have arisen from them." Whenever the *Critique of Reason* says the same thing, however, it means, "The very objects that produce contingent knowledge in us by affecting the mind cannot have also given rise to that element in our cognition which is necessary and

---

*See *An Enquiry Concerning Human Understanding*, Section IV.[20]

universally valid." According to Hume, in other words, the issue is what, in fact, is to be found in experience; whereas according to the *Critique of Reason*, the issue is the origin of what is present in our [149]   cognition.** //

Moreover, the *Critique of Reason* has not shown that the a priori representations and judgements that we assume to be present in us are just forms of empirical cognitions, and that they have validity and meaning only with reference to empirical intuitions. It has not definitively established this any more than it has demonstrated that anything necessary and universally valid in our knowledge can only originate in the mind and in its mode of operation. In other words, the *Critique of Reason* has not *fathomed* the full power, nor the lack of it, of the human faculty of cognition. The arguments by which it [150]   establishes the value // of every *a priori* cognition are these:

A) There is only one way to *think and represent*, as *possible*, that intuitions and concepts which precede the actuality of an object refer to it. And that is by assuming that these intuitions and concepts contain, or are, nothing else but the *forms of the cognition* of an actual object that precede in my subjectivity the actual impressions with which I am affected by objects: Hence the *a priori* intuitions and concepts present in us contain or *actually* are nothing else but the forms of experiential cognition, and have meaning only if applied to empirical intuitions.

B) Dogmatic philosophy has not only been incapable so far of demonstrating its claims to knowledge of things-in-themselves; it has incurred contradictions, from time immemorial, in its determination of what a thing is supposed to be "in-itself": So it follows also that the human faculty of cognition must by nature and vocation be equally incapable of attaining knowledge of the "thing-in-itself".

Concerning the first of these two arguments, (a) it is once more

---

**The explanation by the *Critique of Reason* of the possibility of synthetic propositions is indisputably the strongest and most important // argument it has put forward for the independence of certain components of our representations from all experience, or from any impression by external objects on the mind. In our present examination of the most fundamental reasons in support of its results, therefore, we certainly have no need to engage in a criticism of the other, much weaker, reasons it puts forward in the Transcendental Aesthetics for the presence of a 'pure space' and a 'pure time'. For the priority of certain representations with respect to experience, they prove even less than the necessary synthetic judgements do; instead, as the opponents of critical philosophy have already often objected, they amount to false assumptions or incorrect deductions.[21]

being inferred in it that something *can be* only so *constituted — objectively and actually—//* as *we are capable of* representing it *to ourselves.* [151] The specific manner in which our representations are objective is determined in terms of how we can, and must, think about them. In other words, this argument deals with *objective being* starting from *subjective thought.* (b) We can quite easily think how the representations and concepts present in us *a priori* can refer to actual objects otherwise than *just* by providing for them the conditions and forms of knowledge. They could refer to the objective constitutions of things outside us by virtue of a *pre-established harmony* between them and the effects of our faculty of cognition.[22] Because of this harmony, the *a priori intuitions* and *concepts* which the mind must use in its operations would then represent to it something which does not have mere subjective validity in our mode of cognition, but would conform to the constitution of the thing-in-itself instead: they would [truly] make it present. There is certainly nothing absurd or unthinkable about the hypothesis of such a pre-established harmony between *a priori* representations and objective being. *Nature //* itself, since it was unable to arrange for [152] knowledge of all the properties of things outside man to reach him via the senses and sensations, may instead have arranged matters in such a way that man's *a priori* representations include what the objective properties of things-in-themselves would have imparted to him, if their influence on his mind had been possible. Who knows *nature-in-itself?* Who knows which purposes it had in mind for man and his knowledge? And who can determine by which means it has attained them? Surely, we would have to know at least one predicate of nature 'in-itself' that would preclude our ascribing to it anything of the sort. In fact, we can easily discover or invent still more such possibilities of how the *a priori* representations and judgements indispensable to the knowledge of a thing may refer to actual objects without being the form of their knowledge.

As for the second of the two arguments, careful examination reveals that it proves just as little as the first. For it does not necessarily follow, from the fact that human // reason has so far failed to accomplish [153] something in spite of all its trials and efforts, that it is incapable by nature of ever accomplishing, overall, something like it. The many errors of philosophical reason in the field of speculation should of course make us wary and fearful. And the audacity of these errors should make us wise enough not to venture into the boundless realm of the thing-in-itself without holding on to the hand of a reliable guide. But it does not necessarily follow just from the fact alone that this realm is yet to be discovered that it will not or cannot ever be so discovered. As regards the natural power or the impotence of the human faculty of cognition therefore, we are still in exactly the same uncertainty as of old. And since the attempt of the *Critique of Reason* to determine them has failed altogether, no free spirit would be justified in refraining from striving for some cognition of things-in-themselves.

But finally, in the case of the proposition, "The necessary synthetic judgements originate in the mind's *a priori* determined mode of operation," the same also holds: Either the *Critique of Reason* proves it by an employment of the principle of causality that conflicts with its own principles for the application of the categories, or it does not prove [154]   it in conformity with its own // principles at all. This entire objection hinges on our investigating what the *Critique of Reason* says the mind truly is—or the subject behind our representations, which is presumably the cause of the necessary synthetic judgements in our knowledge—and *to what extent* it says that the mind contains the ground of those judgements.

By 'mind', however, inasmuch as for critical philosophy it is supposed to be the source of whatever is necessary in our knowledge, we are to understand either a *thing-in-itself*, or a *noumenon*, or a *transcendental idea*.

Now, if the *Critique of Reason* means to say that the mind, *qua thing-in-itself*, is the source of the necessary synthetic judgements and of the representations that belong to them—that is to say, if it attributes to it the predicate 'cause of certain areas of our knowledge' by taking it in itself and on its own account, independently of the manner we represent it to ourselves, or *realiter* and objectively—then of course the *Critique of Reason* would be following the accepted mode of thought. [For it is commonly] assumed that the *real* existence of a thing presupposes as well the *real* existence of something else which is its ground, and that the original thing can be explained through the other only inasmuch as this other, too, is something that exists *realiter*. It is perhaps because of this [common assumption] that many followers [155]   of the critical // system understand by the subject of representations a real and objectively actual thing to which they attach, granted the presence in us of necessary representations and judgements, the *knowable* predicate 'cause'. Yet this derivation of the necessary synthetic judgements from a thing-in-itself clearly contradicts the whole spirit of critical philosophy. It presupposes a knowledge which, according to it, should be totally impossible to man. For its most important principle and its most important result is that the categories 'cause' and 'actuality' can only be applied to empirical intuition if their application is to have any sense or reference. Since we cannot intuit, however, the alleged subject of representations but can only immediately perceive the alterations of the inner sense, as the critical philosophy concedes, it follows that this subject cannot belong to the domain of objects knowable by us. In other words, according to the critical philosophy's own claims, we cannot attribute either knowable and real actuality to it. or knowable and real causality. Moreover, if we were to appeal to the thing-in-itself to make the presence in us of the necessary synthetic judgements comprehensible we would be annulling in this matter the explanatory function of the understanding and [thereby] abetting intellectual sloth. // But it is for precisely this [156] reason that the *Critique of Pure Reason* dismissed any explanation of the order and purposiveness of nature based on God's Being and God's Will as unemployable, and declared instead that even the wildest hypothesis, provided that it is a physical one, is more acceptable than the appeal to some transcendental 'thing' or some 'divine author' whom we assume just for the purpose.[23] The *Critique of Reason* would be betraying its own principles, therefore, if it were to derive the presence of necessary synthetic judgements in us from the mind *qua* a thing-in-itself. It would clearly be making up for the lack of natural explanatory causes by supposing supra-natural ones, and encouraging intellectual sloth in the search of comprehensible causes for the presence of those judgements. It would thus be even more in keeping with the spirit of critical philosophy to explain the existence in us of each necessary synthetic proposition by deriving it from the characteristics of the judgements and representations that have preceded it in us, than to posit the cause of this existence in a transcendental object that we do not know at all. Of course, in this way, we cannot really grasp how it is possible for necessary synthetic propositions to arise in us and to be found there. But no more comprehensible is how their cause could be a 'mind' about // which, as regards its objective qualities, we [157] understand nothing at all. As the *Critique of Reason* claims, moreover, we are in principle incapable of understanding how the existence of a thing must be connected with the existence of something else in order to be posited with necessity in the subsumption of perceptions under the concepts 'cause' and 'effect'. Hence, our inability to grasp how a necessary synthetic proposition is connected in our knowledge to the cognitions preceding it, or to derive from the latter the determinations we find in the proposition, cannot be taken as valid reason for objecting to the derivation itself. On the contrary, since this derivation rests on the empirical principles by which all experiences must be explained, it is the only one acceptable; it alone measures up to the spirit of philosophy. Should anyone still insist, however, that the whole series of representations and alterations in a man's given life-time requires a subject 'in-itself' in which the series exists, [I say] that nothing would thereby be proved against the reasonableness of deriving the necessary synthetic judgements in us from preceding proposition and representations. For the entire series // of [158] representations, as presumably found in my subjectivity, could be

124   G.E. Schulze

derived, complete with its determinations, from another preceding series, and this from yet another, and so on, according to the principles of experience, with no need at all to derive from the 'subject' itself anything present in my representations. In a word: To wish to explain certain properties of our cognitions from a transcendental being, or from a supra-natural subject and its mode of operation 'in-itself', of which we understand nothing at all, is just as unphilosophical and as much an encouragement to intellectual sloth as to explain the order and purposiveness of nature, not on natural grounds and according to natural laws, but by appeal to a transcendental author. And as little as this appeal can explain that order and purposiveness, just as little would the appeal to a like being explain the presence in us and [159]   the determinations of certain judgements.* //

If we suppose that the mind is the cause of what is necessary in our knowledge *qua noumenon* (as a merely intelligible object that can only be represented through the understanding which uses it to join in it, for lack of something else, the cognitions drawn from experience), then the *Critique of Reason* would be promoting an empty product of thought to source of a constituent component of our knowledge; but, [160]   as the *Critique* itself asserts, not only // do we not need it for an insight into what is actual for us, it is also completely unknown to us and hence we cannot ever know whether it is anything at all.[24] And the *Critique of Reason* would be applying the category 'cause' to it even though, according to the *Critique*, the categories can actually determine only objects given through sensibility, and have no sense at all when applied to *merely thought* objects. The derivation from the mind of the element of necessity in our cognition, on which the validity and truth of the most important among the results of critical philosophy rests, would thus be, in fact, only a formal thought exercise, totally devoid of truth. Hence, on the supposition that the mind is the ground of the necessary synthetic judgements, in accordance with the very

[159]   *To derive from the mind in this way, as from a thing-in-itself, the element of necessity in our knowledge contradicts the clearest and // most distinct explanations that Kant gives in the *Critique of Reason* regarding our knowledge of the representing subject. Even a superficial reading of the section dealing with the Paralogisms of Pure Reason would reveal this much. (This section, incidentally, is one of the most splendid in the *Critique of Reason*; each line exudes philosophical spirit.) In this case too, however, my intention has not been to test the derivation in the form in which Kant himself presented it for us, but only as understood by quite a few friends of his system, who still profess that the subject 'in-itself' is the cause of the forms of our representations, thus presuming a knowledge of the soul totally denied to man by the *Critique of Reason*. From this can be seen how unsuccessful Kant was in being understood even by those who hold his critical system to be the only true system of philosophy, and who are forever suggesting to its opponents that to understand the system correctly, and to hold it for the only true, indisputably certain philosophy, is one and the same thing.

teaching of the *Critique of Reason*, we would have to deny truth and certainty to anything derived from it.* //   [161]

We would be no less bound to deny any certainty or real truth to the *Critique of Reason*'s most important teaching if we were to attribute to the mind (the subject of representation) the ground of what is necessary in our knowledge only *qua transcendental idea*, and if the *Critique* were [in fact] to consider it as such a ground only in this sense. For even then, on its own principles and assertions regarding the function of ideas and the limits of our knowledge, [we still could not accept] its explanation of the origin of the necessary synthetic propositions in our knowledge. But to show how this is the case, we must state first of all what the *Critique of Reason* teaches concerning the nature, origin and function of transcendental ideas.

Reason is the faculty of drawing conclusions, or of cognizing the particular from the universal.[26] The *Critique of Reason* claims that it has not only a *logical* employment, but also a *real* one of *generating* concepts and // principles not borrowed either from the senses or   [162] the understanding.[27]

Now, in its logical employment reason strives to find, for the conditioned and dependent cognitions of the understanding, the *unconditional* from which they receive their highest possible unity and absolute completeness.[28]

This logical operation of reason also gives us secure information about its real employment, and about the principle on which it is based. This principle is expressed in the proposition, "If the conditioned is given, the entire series of its conditions is also given and objectively present; each of the conditions is subordinated to another, but the whole series is itself unconditioned."[29]

This proposition is necessary and synthetic; consequently it is *a priori*. But there is also no adequate empirical employment for it, and in this it is clearly set apart from all the principles of the understanding.

Just as the form of judgements, however, when transformed into a concept of the synthetic unity of intuitions, yields the pure concepts of the understanding, so the form of the syllogisms (i.e., the mediated inferences), when applied to the same unity under the rule of the categories, gives rise to certain *a priori* concepts. These must be called

---

*I have taken the word "noumenon" here in the sense most common in the *Critique of Reason*, and still not distinguished from 'idea of reason'. Many a friend of critical philosophy, however, understands by 'noumenon' the thing-in-itself—a practice to which Mr. Kant himself has given occasion by using the word "noumenon" on two or three occasions in its once accepted scholastic meaning. // (See *Prolegomena*, 101, 106, and   [161] *Critique of Pure Reason*, p. 423, note.)[25] This point deserves to be noted again only because it shows that one can be a follower of critical philosophy, yet not have duly *understood* either its premises or its conclusions.

"transcendental ideas" so as to be able to distinguish // them clearly   [16
from the categories.[30]

The highest of these ideas is the concept of the *absolutely unconditioned*.[31]

In order to discover the various ideas included in the highest concept of reason, we need only consider the different forms of the syllogism, for to each of these corresponds a particular idea. Thus there are three ideas immediately subsumed under the highest concept of reason, viz., (a) the idea of an absolute complete subject which is not, in turn, the predicate of another thing; (b) the idea of the absolute unity of the series of the conditions of appearance; (c) the idea of the absolute unity of the condition of all objects of thought in general.[32]

But just as with its concepts and principles the understanding refers merely to the unity of sensible perceptions, and unless it applied [them] to sensations it could not yield any objective insight at all, so with all its principles and ideas reason refers to the unity of the cognitions already attained by applying the understanding to sensible perceptions. Just as the categories, therefore, are particular forms of the thought of empirical objects, so in respect to the cognitions of the understanding [164]   the ideas of reason are particular *forms* // *of their unity* as determined by the nature of that faculty. Hence the ideas never extend to the objects of experience directly; their only function, rather, is to encompass the experiential cognitions attained through sensibility and understanding, and to produce in them the supreme unity and completeness which reason needs, but which is totally foreign to the understanding.[33]

Precisely because of their function, therefore, the ideas and principles of reason do not provide us with the knowledge of a transcendental object understood in the sense of something that exists outside our representations. Reason's intention is not at all to cognize through them objects that transcend experience; rather, it has only designed them in accordance with its essence, so that together they would bring unbounded unity and completeness to our experiential cognitions. This completeness is achieved through the completeness of principles. The employment of the ideas of reason is thus only regulative, that is, merely directed to an *a priori* unity which experiential knowledge needs in order to be perfect as far as reason is concerned.[34]

Yet the semblance of having objective validity outside human representations still clings to the principles and ideas of pure reason. And by a misunderstanding that nothing else but the *Critique of Reason* [165]   can remove, they were // always taken for something that extends our knowledge beyond the sphere of the sensible world, and makes us acquainted with things-in-themselves. In other words, they were thought to be cognitions of actually existing things, and how they only served to bring the cognitions of the understanding to completion escaped comprehension. What belongs to the disposition of our knowledge was confused with what belongs to the objective nature of things-in-themselves. And to this confusion we owe the origin and influence of the empty subtleties of rational psychology, transcendental cosmology and theology.[35]—

Now, in order to confirm our verdict, it is important that we examine whether, and to what extent, that which the *Critique of Reason* itself states regarding the misuse of ideas and the illusions to which this misuse gives rise, applies as well to the foundations of critical philosophy, particularly to its derivation of the necessary synthetic judgements from the subject behind the representing.

By the 'mind' which is alleged to be the source of what is necessary in our knowledge, we are to understand according to critical philosophy a transcendental idea. This is apparent from the most unequivocal statements of its most perceptive defenders. To my knowledge, indeed, nowhere in the *Critique of Pure Reason* has // Mr. Kant declared himself clearly and expressly on this matter. In the Introduction to the *Critique*,[36] in the Transcendental Aesthetics,[37] and in all the passages where representations and principles are presented as originating in the mind, he never indicates what this 'mind' truly is—this mind which, as he claims, we ought to think as the source of some of the components of our knowledge. He leaves his readers free to understand by it a 'thing-in-itself', a 'noumenon', or an 'idea'. Nor does the section that deals with the Paralogisms of Pure Reason offer any information on the subject, even though it certainly provided him with the opportunity of stating clearly in what sense the 'mind', or the 'representing ego', is to be considered the ground and source of what is necessary in our knowledge. It must not have occurred to him at all, in composing this section, that after reading it through we would naturally ask, "If the subject of our thoughts is *entirely* unknown to us, how can we know, and see, that it is in actual fact the source of some of the components of our knowledge?" // Moreover, reference is also made in this section to practical reason, said to be the only faculty through which we can attain an insight into the nature of the rational subject adequate to our true needs.[38] Speculative reason, instead, is denied all competence in this matter; it is unable to pass the least judgement concerning what the subject of representations might in fact be or not be. From a few passages in the Critique of Reason, and especially from the *Prolegomena* (§46)[39], we must nevertheless conclude that by 'subject of representations' (inasmuch, again, as this subject is presumed to be the source of what is necessary in our knowledge), the author of the critical philosophy wants us to understand nothing else but a merely transcendental idea. It is only in this sense, moreover, that he attributes the predicate of *logical* causality to it with respect to the necessary synthetic

[166]

[167]

judgements present in us. Mr. Reinhold, on the other hand, has expressed himself on this matter with particular distinctness and clarity in his *Theory of the Faculty of Representation* (see especially pp. 530ff.)[40] And according to his explanation, we may and can attribute to the representing subject the *thought* predicate 'ground of what is necessary and formal in our knowledge' only *qua* idea.

[168]   As regards, therefore, the explanation by the *Critique of Reason* of the origin and possibility of the necessary // synthetic propositions which it lays at the foundation of its new system of philosophy, we can justifiably say the following: (a) The explanation supplies an insight that goes beyond all experience; for we never experience how representations *arise* in us, but always only the fact that they have arisen and are in us; their mode of origin can only be thought and inferred. (b) The explanation enlists the help of a transcendental idea in order to make something about experience comprehensible, i.e., the presence of necessary synthetic judgements, and their functions. But the idea is in fact of no use to us in our empirical employment of the understanding, nor can it be confirmed or denied through experience. Yet it is indispensable to the aims of reason, for reason uses transcendental ideas in order to elevate the knowledge gathered by the understanding from experience to absolute unity and completeness, and thereby impress upon it a character suitable to its needs. (c) In the explanation, the understanding first leaps from something in experience directly to the absolute subject of the alterations of inner sense, and then it immediately descends from this subject back to that which belongs to experience, in order to determine its

[169]   possibility and its causes. // (d) Finally, the explanation applies the categories of the understanding to the object of an idea of reason, because it assumes that only in this way can we think the possibility of something belonging indisputably to experience.

The *Critique of Reason* has erected a new system of philosophy on its explanation of the origin of the necessary synthetic principles. We can entertain no further doubt, now that we have reviewed the essentials of that explanation, as to how much we have really gained through it in true insight into the actual origin of these principles, as well as into the actual limits of our knowledge. There is equally no doubt as to the value of the explanation by the *Critique's* own standards. For we can turn against it, against its grounds and the insights gained through them concerning the origin of an element of our representations, everything that the *Critique of Reason* says against the truth of the theses of rational psychology, cosmology and theology, and against the validity of the proofs that dogmatism has so far advanced on their behalf.*

[170]   For to hope, *first*, // that we would know more of an object than

what pertains to its possible experience, or to pretend that we can know a *thing* which is not the object of experience, ought indeed to be in principle *totally absurd* now that the *Critique of Reason* has so carefully investigated, as it claims, the human faculty of cognition. However, neither the *genesis* of the various components of man's cognition, nor the *mind* and its // mode of operation, are objects [171] of experience; neither is given to us in some single empirical intuition. According to the *Critique of Reason* itself, therefore, it is totally absurd to pretend that we shall ever gain insight into the actual origin of our knowledge, particularly its origin in the mind, or into its true mode of operation and what it contributes to actual knowledge. *Second,* according to the *Critique of Reason* the only function of all the transcendental ideas is to bring the knowledge that the understanding gleans from experience as near to perfect completion as possible.[44] These ideas impart to us no knowledge at all of anything that does not belong to experience, or is not really to be found there, provided, that is, that we do not misunderstand their function. Even by the *Critique's* own standards, it is therefore a misuse of the concepts of reason to apply the idea of 'absolute subject' to explain the origin of what is necessary in our knowledge. Moreover, again according to the *Critique of Reason*, this explanation too would have to be relinquished to the understanding whose proper function, however, does not include applying concepts to objects outside experience. In this respect too, therefore, to apply the ideas of reason to actual facts to make them comprehensible would constitute a misuse. Such ideas may // only be used to bestow absolute completeness on the know- [172] ledge of the understanding, and to use them otherwise is to remove and restrict the employment of the latter.*

And *third,* according to the *Critique of Reason*, the understanding is indeed only deceiving itself if it imagines that it has reached objectively

---

*To be quickly convinced // of this, we need only substitute for the principal con- [170] cepts found in the *Critique's* demonstrations of the *a priori* origin of certain representations those of the notorious arguments of rational psychology, cosmology, and theology. By this process we come up again with the same proofs on which these sciences were constructed, in all their details. Take for instance the proof that our 'thinking ego' is truly a subject. It runs as follows: "What can only be thought to exist exclusively as subject, exists only as subject. But we cannot think of our 'thinking ego' in any way except as an existing subject. *Ergo,* it also exists only as subject." To establish that certain concepts originate *a priori*, the *Critique of Reason* argues in just the same way: "What can only be thought to have arisen exclusively *a priori* has also, in fact, arisen only *a priori*. But what is necessary in our knowledge can only be thought to have arisen exclusively *a priori*. *Ergo,* etc.

** Reason itself does not require that we derive what is necessary in our knowledge from the subject of representations. If we were to suppose as established that representations, and *all* their determinations, originate in things outside us, our knowledge of the alterations of the inner sense would still not be complete without the idea of the 'absolute subject'; even then we could not dispense with this idea.

actual being through *thought*, and it infers the properties of being from the determinations that pertain to *thought*. Even by the standards of the *Critique*, therefore, it is only a deception originating in the understanding's lack of self-knowledge to believe that, since we can only think of the the mind as containing the ground of what is necessary in our knowledge, we have thereby discovered the proper and objective ground of this necessary element. In a word: All that counts against the reality of the insights promised by rational psychology, cosmology and theology, counts also against the truth of those promised by [the attempt to] explain the origin of the necessary and synthetic propositions from the subject of representation. This explanation, and all its proofs

[173] and foundations as laid down in the *Critique of Reason*, is //nothing but a sophism whose semblance of truth vanishes as soon as we have duly learned from the *Critique* itself the only true determinations of the concepts of understanding and reason.

And Hume's skepticism is supposed to have been annulled and exploded by this sophism? Surely we must have a very tenuous grasp of the problem raised by skepticism if we find anything of the sort even likely. The first thing that Hume would have retorted to [the attempt to] derive from the mind what is necessary in our knowledge, as the *Critique of Reason* has done, is at least this: The derivation belongs, on the basis of all its characteristics, to the chapter of the Dialectic of Pure Reason. The *Critique of Reason* should have expanded this chapter, especially the part dealing with paralogism, with [a consideration of] the claim that a part of our knowledge derives from the soul.

"But these objections," it is said, "do not in fact touch the *Critique of Reason* at all. For its only aim was to establish *how we have to think for us* [uns] the origin of what is necessary in our knowledge, in keeping with the natural dispositions of our understanding and reason. It did

[174] not in the least mean // to determine what this origin is in an objective, *actual* sense. The *Critique of Reason* does not promise, nor does it impart by this derivation, any knowledge of some transcendental object or other—either the mind 'in-itself', or anything supposedly present in it, and occurring there, prior to all experience. Since its derivation is determined by the essence of reason and understanding, the *Critique* only wants to prove that we cannot presume, on the basis of it, any knowledge of things-in-themselves, and that all our objectively real insights are to be confined to the sensible world. But of course, to us whatever accords with the essence of our reason and understanding is by that token also true."

To this we would have to retort, first of all, that we certainly cannot conclude from the *Critique of Reason* itself that its intention was no more than to establish *how we have to think for us* [uns] the origin of our various representations. For it does not attribute *merely logical truth*, to its statements on the subject, but above all *real truth*. And it declares these statements to be the most conclusive thing that philosophy could ever show — the sort of thing that we must not merely *think* as philosophy has determined, but which *is* in fact so *constituted* in itself, outside our representations. Moreover, it is the practice of transcendental psychology, cosmology and theology to prove their theses on the ground that [what] they [assert] can only be thought in the way they prescribe. But if the *Critique of Reason* had demonstrated the truth and // [175] certainty of its claims about the origin of the components of human knowledge, in a manner that satisfied the human understanding, simply by arguing that that origin *cannot be thought* in any other way than it alleges, then the theses of those other sciences would be sufficiently established as well. They would have as much of a claim to certainty and legitimacy as the *Critique of Reason* itself and all its results. In fact, as far as grounds are concerned, they would be on exactly the same footing as the *Critique*. And finally, if we suppose that *all* the grounds adduced by the *Critique of Reason* for the origin of the necessary synthetic propositions in the mind are *merely subjective*, that is, that they originate simply and solely in previously determined functions of our thought, then we can indeed ask: "What else could these grounds ever yield save a *semblance* [*of truth*] measured by the laws of our knowledge and answerable only to them? And this semblance is to lead us to a *true* insight into the conditions and circumstances of our entire Knowledge?"// [176]

Another general point to be considered here is: the moment we declare that the real principle of sufficient reason is merely subjective, and that it applies to the connection of our representations only in experience, we can no longer speak of *an actual ground* of the components of our cognition. Any enquiry about it becomes *meaningless*, for the principle would not signify anything that pertains to things as they are 'in-themselves' outside our representations. Before we can reasonably ask, "What is the genuinely 'real ground' and the cause of this or that constituent of the insights we possess?", we should establish beyond doubt: (1) that 'causality' is an objective predicate of actuality, and (2) that the components of our knowledge are causally joined to something in itself, or *realiter*. We cannot assume that 'causality' belongs only to our representations, or to our way of thinking, yet ask how in actuality our knowledge originates in something different from it, or ask for some true cause of it. As determined by the *Critique of Reason*, the function of the principle of causality thus undercuts all philosophizing about the where or how of the origin of our cognitions. All assertions on the matter, and every conclusion drawn from // [177] them, become empty subtleties, for once we accept that determination of the principle as our rule of thought, we could never ask, "Does anything actually exist which is the ground and cause of our representations?", but only, "How must the understanding join these together, in keeping with the pre-determined functions of its activity, in order to gather them as one experience?"

To all the opponents of critical philosophy, the greatest stone of scandal has been precisely the determination of the principle of causality as a merely subjective principle of the understanding. They cannot understand how anyone can say that what is necessary in our knowledge actually originates in the mind, and yet assume that the concepts 'cause' and 'effect' are mere modifications in the combination of our representations. For them, the cardinal proposition of critical philosophy, "The necessary synthetic judgements found in us are products of the faculty of our representing subject," makes no sense at all; for by the *Critique of Reason*'s own definition of the nature of the categories and of the ideas of reason, this proposition properly says no more than this: "On the strength of the subjective maxims of the understanding, we must view the necessary synthetic judgements present in us as products of a *form of the employment of the understanding* (of a faculty)

[178] // which accrues to a *form of the employment of reason* (to the subject of representations) as its characteristic."

But I believe I have said enough to decide the question, "Has the *Critique of Reason*, by deriving the element of necessity in our cognition from the mind, sufficiently refuted Hume's criticism?" At least I am not aware of anything that I might have overlooked in this condemnation of the fundamental grounds of critical philosophy that could have come to its aid in its battle against skepticism, or in the justification of the results of its own system. Nor did I come by my doubts about these grounds simply by leafing through the *Critique of Pure Reason* simply with the intention of finding fault with it. On the contrary, long after I had become acquainted with it, I still nourished the hope that by its instruction I would be guided to a final decision on whether or not knowledge of things-in-themselves is possible; and I hoped that I would be instructed about the true limits to the reality of our insights. But just as I saw this hope being realized, as I was going over the basic proofs of the system presented by the *Critique of*

[179] *Reason* in their simplest form, the doubts that I have just // been expounding about their truth began to press upon me. And the more that I reflected on the premises behind its results, the more illuminating and weighty the grounds of the doubts became for me. How I wish that the friends of critical philosophy might yet resolve them and put them to rest! But I have yet to come across even one of them who adverts to these doubts in his writings. Yet I would have thought that above all by facing up to Hume's demands, in their defence of critical

philosophy, would they have been truly worthy of that undoubtedly immortal and masterful work which is the *Critique of Reason*. As things now stand, the charge is not unfounded that its boast of victory over Hume's skepticism is unjustified and hence idle. And if the *Critique* has not won that victory, it has also failed to establish any claim to lasting validity. Sooner or later it will be robbed of its reputation at the hand of skepticism. Without fail it will be shaken at its foundation just as thoroughly as it once shook many an old dogmatic system whose founder fancied he had constructed for all eternity. Moreover, no deeper wound // could have been inflicted on philosophy in   [180] its present situation, than by Hume's attacks on the employment of the concepts and laws of causality. For since Locke and Leibniz, we have based every philosophy on a search for the origin of representations. And so we have been left, after his attacks, with no materials with which to build a system of philosophy. Until we have remedied this loss in full, therefore, we should not presume to say or decide anything about the origin of human knowledge. We must either show from universally valid and indisputable propositions that the principles and the categories of causality also hold for the origin of our representations, or we must establish on some other principle that there is a connection between our representations and something outside them. Before this is done, we ought not to think that whatever we say in philosophy about the reality of the components of man's knowledge, or about anything that might or might not exist outside the representations, amounts to more than a tissue of arbitrary opinions.

Notes

1. This is Reinhold's thesis, cf. *Foundation*, pp. 55ff, p. 71. Cf. *Critique*, B2.

2. *Foundation*, p. 56.

3. Kant, *Prolegomena*, Academy Ed., Vol. IV, p. 260, English tr., p. 8.

4. Cf. the introductory note to this text, above p. 105.

5. "Neue Darstellung," *Beiträge*, Vol. I, pp. 173-178. For a translation of Reinhold's propositions, see Maimon, *Letters of Philaletes to Aenesidemus*, pp. 159-203 below. For a translation of Props. I-V, see ibid., below, pp. 00-00.

6. *Theorie*, p. 190. Stresses are Aenesidemus's.

7. Cf. "Neue Darstellung," *Beiträge*, Vol. I, pp. 175-180.

8. *Critique*, B146-148.

9. Cf. *Theorie*, pp. 482-483 (Prop. LXXVI); also p. 244ff.

10. Pp. 131ff.

11. Cf. above, note 5.

12. Pp. 167-172.

13. "Neue Darstellung," *Beiträge*, Vol. I, pp. 177-178 (Props. VI-VII); cf. above, note 5.

14. The reference is to Reinhold's general definition of 'representation'. Cf. *Theorie*, p. 200; "Neue Darstellung," *Beiträge*, Vol. I, p. 168 (Prop. II: "Representation is what is distinguished by the subject in consciousness from both the object and the subject and referred to both.")

15. Cf. *Aenesidemus*, pp. 84-86. Aenesidemus argues against Reinhold that in intuition, which is also a kind of representation, there is no distinction between the representation and the object, ". . . for as long as the intuition lasts, there is no notice at all of an object distinct from it" (p. 85). See also Maimon, *Letters of Philaletes to Aenesidemus*, pp 318-320; Letter of Maimon to Kant, Sept. 20, 1791, *Briefwechsel*, Academy Ed., Vol. XI, p. 372; English tr., p. 176: "An intuition, in my opinion, is not related to anything other than itself. . . ."

16. Aenesidemus proceeds to give a brief exposition of Hume's skepticism (pp. 108-117), and of Kant's position regarding the origin and the value of "necessary synthetic judgements" (pp. 118-130).

17. Cf. Hume, *An Inquiry Concerning Human Understanding*, Sections IV-V.

18. Cf. *Critique*, A296-297, B353-354.

19. Beck's position on this score is not unlike Aenesidemus's. Cf. *Standpunkt*, p. 167, and above, "The Facts of Consciousness," p. 39.

20. Pp. 33-34.

21. Cf. J. G. H. Feder, *Ueber Raum und Causalität*, Haupstück I, *Ueber die letzen Gründe menschlicher Erkenntnis von Raum und von der Körperwelt*.

22. Kant considered this possibility, but dismissed it because "the necessity of the categories, which belong to their very conception would then have to be sacrificed." *Critique*, B168.

23. Ibid., A773, B801.

24. Ibid., B412.

25. Academy Ed., Vol. IV. pp. 312, 314; English tr., pp. 60-61; *Critique*, B423, note.

26. Ibid., A249-300, B356-357.

27. Ibid., A299, B355-356.

28. Ibid., A307, B364.

29. Ibid., "and made objectively present" is not in Kant's text.

30. Ibid., A321, B378.

31. Ibid., A326, B382.

32. Ibid., A334, B391.

33. Ibid., A643-644, B671-672.

34. Ibid.

35. Ibid., A334ff, B391ff.

36. Cf. ibid., B2: "For it may well be that even our empirical knowledge is made up of what we receive through impressions and what our own faculty of knowledge. . . . supplies from itself."

37. Ibid., A20, B34.

38. Ibid., B424-426.

39. Academy Ed., Vol. IV, p. 333; English tr., p. 81.

40. Theorie, p. 530: "The *subject* of the faculty of representation can be represented, *qua* subject, only by reason. . . ."

Aenesidemus,
or
Concerning the Foundations of the Philosophy of
the Elements issued by Prof. Reinhold in Jena,
together with a *Defence of Skepticism against*
the Pretensions of the Critique of Reason.
N.p.p. (1792), 445 pp. (in octavo).
[*Allgemeine Literatur-Zeitung,*
nos. 47, 48, 49; February 11 and 12, 1794]

by J. G. Fichte

Translation and notes by George di Giovanni

When Fichte's review of Aenesidemus appeared in 1794, its author had already been meditating for over two years on the possibility of philosophy as strict science. While he was convinced that philosophy could be built on a single self-evident principle, Schulze's book had equally convinced him that the task of thus systematizing it had yet to be accomplished. Reinhold's Philosophy of the Elements had shown itself particularly vulnerable to the skeptical attack, and in his review of Schulze's Aenesidemus, while attacking skepticism, Fichte also gives clear indications of his intent to go beyond Reinhold's principles. The following translation is from the text in the Gesamtausgabe, Vol. I, pp. 1-25. *The text is also to be found in the edition of the* Bayerischen Akademie der Wissenschaften *(eds. R. Lauth, H. Jacob; Stuttgart-Bad Cannstatt: Fromann Verlag, 1965, Vol. I. 2, pp. 32-67). It is also available in a French translation: P. Ph. Druet, "La recension de l'Enesidème par Fichte,"* Revue de Métaphsique et de Morale, LXXVIII (1973), pp. 363-384.

IT CANNOT BE DENIED that philosophical [*philosophierende*] reason owes every noticeable advance it has ever made to the observations of skepticisim upon the precariousness of the position where it has for the moment come to rest. This fact has been conceded by the great discoverer of its critical employment, precisely with reference to the latest remarkable progress made by it through this very employment.[1] Yet, because of the constant spectacle of the dissensions among the friends of the new philosophy that are continually increasing as they press forward in their enquiries, it must have become apparent even to the uninformed observer that reason has not, as yet, reached its great goal of making philosophy into a science, however close it may have come to it. But if this is the case, nothing was more desirable than that skepticism should crown its work by impelling reason to the sublime goal of its enquiries; or since there has long been an impression that the remaining stock of justified skeptical objections to philosophy have yet to be voiced with adequate clarity, nothing was more desirable than that skepticism should finally get a spokesman who would let nothing diminish their force, and would at the same time have the eloquence to present them clearly. To what extent the author of the present work is this desirable spokesman remains to be determined by a criticism of the work itself. //   [4]

In the person of this representative, skepticism naturally had to direct its weapons against Reinhold's Philosophy of the Elements in particular, and of course against the latest presentation of it in his *Contributions*,[2] for by the admission of most admirers of critical philosophy, this writer has either already completed the grounding of philosophy as science, or at least done more than anyone else to prepare for it. But for the sake of those who deny this, skepticism had also to turn its weapons against the most authoritative document of the new philosophy, the *Critique of Pure Reason* itself, if its attack was to be pressed to a decisive battle.[3]

The book is in the form of letters. Hermias, an enthusiastic admirer of critical philosophy, declares to Aenesidemus his complete conviction (founded especially upon Reinhold's Philosophy of the Elements) of the truth and universal validity of this philosophy. Aenesidemus, who is of a different mind, responds with an examination of it.

In order to meet Reinhold's well founded requirement, Aenesidemus lays down as the basis of his censure of the Philosophy of the Elements the following propositions, which he accepts as already agreed upon and valid[4]: 1. (Actual Fact): There are representations in us with certain characteristics, some of which differ while others agree. 2. (Rule of Judgement): The touchstone of all that is true is general logic, and every reasoning about matters of fact can lay claim to correctness only to the extent that it conforms to the laws of logic. At the head of each part of the investigation, the paragraphs of the Philosophy of the Elements under discussion are reproduced *verbatim* (just as Reinhold has presented them once more in his *Contributions*, Vol. I, pp. 165-254).[5]

Examination of Reinhold's principles regarding the function and the essential properties of a Philosophy of the Elements.

Aenesidemus concedes to begin with that philosophy has so far lacked a supreme, universally valid principle, and that it will be able to elevate itself to the rank of a science only upon the establishment of some such principle. Moreover, it also seems undeniable to him that this principle cannot be any other than the one which would secure and define the highest of all concepts, // the concept of representation and of what can be represented[6]. But, however close the agreement of the skeptic and the elemental-philosopher on these two points may be, it remains dubious in the eyes of this reviewer whether philosophy itself would benefit from their unanimity as regards the second point; it might turn out, some time in the future, that what can be justifiably said against the principle of consciousness as the *first* principle of philosophy as a whole will lead to the suspicion that there must be for the whole of philosophy (and not just for theoretical philosophy) yet a *higher* concept than that of representation.[7]

Against Reinhold's §1 (In consciousness, representation is distinguished by the subject from subject and object, and is referred to both)[8], Aenesidemus points out that (1) "this proposition is not an *absolutely first* proposition, for as a proposition and judgement it is subject to the highest rule of all judging, the principle of contradiction."[9]

[5]

If this reviewer correctly understands what Reinhold has said in reply to this objection already raised against him (*Foundation*, p. 85), and what Aenesidemus finds unsatisfactory, viz., "that the principle of consciousness is indeed *subject to* the principle of contradiction, not as to a first proposition by which it is *determined*, but as to a *law* which it may not *contradict*"[10]; then it follows that Reinhold denies to the principle of contradiction all *real* validity (as Kant also did, but only for merely theoretical philosophy)[11] and grants to it only *formal* and logical validity. And to this extent his reply is entirely correct. It comes down to the one he has already given often enough to the gratuitous critics of his Philosophy of the Elements, viz., that one cannot think *about* the laws of thought save *in conformity with* these laws; a reflection on the principle of consciousness is subject, with respect to its *form*, to the logical principle of contradiction just as any other possible reflection; its *matter*, however, is not determined by the logical principle. If Aenesidemus's objection is to have sense, he must be ascribing to the principle of contradiction (even though he has nowhere declared himself clearly on this point), a *real* validity in addition to its *formal* validity, i.e., he must assume, or conjecture, some actual fact about the mind which // grounds the principle [6] originally.

What this means is at once clear, for Aenesidemus points out that (2) "the principle of consciousness is not a proposition *completely determined through itself*. For according to Reinhold's own explanation, the concepts of subject and object are determined only by distinguishing them in representation, and by referring the representation to them. At least this *distinguishing* and *referring* must therefore be complete, and be so determined as not to allow for more than one meaning ["]."[12] But this is not the case, as Aenesidemus has sufficiently demonstrated, at least for this reviewer, by the enumeration of several possible meanings, and by citing the various expressions (also ambiguous) by which Reinhold surreptitiously tries to explain the concepts. Indeed, how could it be the case, for the very indeterminacy and indeterminability of these concepts point to a higher principle that is to be sought, to a real validity of the principle of identity and opposition; the concept of distinguishing and referring only allows of being determined by means of the concepts of identity and opposition.[13]

Finally, it is said that (3) "the principle of consciousness is neither a universally valid proposition, nor does it express a fact [*Factum*] which is not tied to some determinate experience, and to some definite reasoning."[14] Aenesidemus submits several manifestations of consciousness given in experience in which, in his opinion, the three parts required in any consciousness are supposedly not present. How far an objection of this sort, which is based on experience, is in general to be accepted, or how far it is legitimate to reject it—this will be further discussed later on.[15]

After a more complete examination of what such a principle cannot be, the question is raised of what, in fact, it might possibly be. Aenesidemus answers the question in this way: "It is (1) a synthetic proposition in which a predicate [that] is joined to the subject (consciousness) is not included in its concept but only added to it in experience."[16] As is generally known, Reinhold holds that his proposition is simply analytical.[17] We want to abstract here from the fact that Aenesidemus denies the universal validity of the proposition, and thus also assumes some form of consciousness // to which it does not apply.[18] It is possible to disclose an even deeper ground for the position of Aenesidemus with respect to the two different points of view from which the proposition can be considered. For suppose that no consciousness can be thought without these three parts; then these parts would certainly be contained in the concept of consciousness, and in regard of its logical validity the proposition specifying them would certainly be, as a reflective proposition, analytical. But obviously the performance of representing, the act of consciousness, is itself a synthesis all the same, for it differentiates and refers; indeed, it is the highest synthesis, and the ground of all other possible ones. And with this consideration there arises, then, the very real question, how is it ever possible to trace back all the performances of the mind to the one [act of] putting together? How is *synthesis* to be thought without the presupposition of *thesis* and *antithesis*?

The principle of consciousness is (2) "an abstract proposition expressing, according to Aenesidemus, what *some* manifestations of consciousness have in common or, according to Reinhold, what *all* of them share."[19] As is well known, the latter denies that this proposition is based on some abstraction.[20] Against those who would suppose that the proposition abstracts from the conditions of intuition, concepts, and ideas, it is quite easy to demonstrate that, far from the concept of mere representation having to be based on these, their very concept is made possible only through the distinction and the connection of several mere representations *as such*. It is possible to determine the concept of representation in general completely, without having to determine the concepts of intuition, concept and idea; but it is impossible to determine the latter completely without having determined the former. But if what is being said is not just that this proposition is not based on *this particular* abstraction, but on no abstraction *at all*, then it is possible (inasmuch as the proposition as the first principle stands at the apex of all philosophy) to prove the opposite. For if all that is to be discovered in the mind is a representing, and all representing is undeniably an *empirical* determination of the mind,

[7]

then it follows that the representing itself is given to consciousness with all its pure conditions only through representation of it, and hence // only *empirically*; and that all reflection upon consciousness [8] has empirical representations as object. Now, the object of every empirical representation is given determinately (in space, in time, etc.). The representation of representing in general, which is expressed by the principle of consciousness, however, necessarily abstracts from these empirical determinations of the given object. Accordingly, the principle of consciousness, which is placed at the apex of the whole of philosophy, is based on empirical self-observation and, as such, it undoubtedly expresses an abstraction. Admittedly, everyone who understands this proposition well enough, feels an inner resistance against attributing a merely empirical validity to it. It is not even possible to think its opposite. But this, too, hints that the proposition must be based on something more than a mere actual fact. This reviewer at any rate has convinced himself that the proposition is a theorem based upon another principle, but that it can be rigorously demonstrated *a priori* from that principle, and independently of all experience.[21] The first wrong presupposition which led to its being posited as the principle of all philosophy is that one must start from an actual fact.[22] To be sure, we must have a real principle, and not a merely formal one; but—if I may venture a claim which can be neither explained nor proven here—such a principle does not have to express a fact just as *content* [eine *Tatsache*, actual fact]; it can also express a fact as *performance* [eine *Tathandlung*, actual deed].[23] Now, inasmuch as Aenesidemus must hold this proposition to be empirical, one must of course go along with him in allowing experiences which supposedly contradict it. But if the same proposition is demonstrated from undeniable principles, and if the opposite is shown to be a contradiction, then all the supposed experiences which are alleged not to agree with it must be dismissed as unthinkable.

Examination of §§2-5, which determine the original concepts of representation, object, subject, and mere representation.[24]

Besides repeating what has just been discussed more than once, Aenesidemus submits against the [proposed] explanation of represen- tation that it is narrower than what it has to explain.[25] "For // if, [9] according to Reinhold's definition, that alone constitutes a representation which is distinguished by a subject from object and subject, and is referred to both; but if, according to Aenesidemus's presupposition, that alone can be distinguished which is already perceived, it follows that intuition (which is the first perception) is not representation. But it should be; indeed, according to Reinhold it is a representation; therefore, etc."[26] Reinhold will rightly deny to Aenesidemus the presupposition in the minor of his syllogism. The original object is not perceived at all, and cannot be perceived. Therefore, intuition can be referred, prior to all other perception, to an object, the *non-ego*, which is opposed to the subject ab origine; such *non-ego* in general is not *perceived*, but *posited ab origine*.[27]

Moreover, "that distinguishing and referring which is required for representation is itself a representing"[28] has rightly been denied by Reinhold. Both the distinguishing and the referring can become the object of a representation, and in the Philosophy of the Elements they do, in fact, become so. Originally, however, they are not an object, but only a mode of operation of the mind which must be thought as a means of producing a representation. But of course, it follows from this that representation is not the highest concept of all the performances conceivable in our mind.

Reinhold said in his remark to § 5: "Mere representation is present *immediately*; subject and object, however, are present only *through the mediation* of the connection of the one to the other in consciousness; for what is referred to both object and subject in consciousness must be present *prior* to the performances by which the referring occurs, not indeed temporally, but by nature, for nothing can be referred if there is nothing at hand that admits of being referred to."[29] Aenesidemus tries to demonstrate the invalidity of this proof by pretending to prove, conversely, that the object and subject occur immediately in consciousness, and that representation, by contrast, occurs mediately, "for nothing can be referred to something else, if this other to which it is referred is not at hand; therefore, etc."[30] And to be sure, subject and object must be thought before //representation, but not in consciousness as an empirical determination of the mind, which is all that Reinhold discusses. The absolute subject, the *ego*, is not given in an empirical intuition, but is posited through an intellectual one; and the absolute object, the *non-ego*, is what is posited in opposition to it.[31] In empirical consciousness, both occur in no other way than by a representation being referred to them. They are in it only mediately, *qua* representing, and *qua* represented. But the absolute subject, that which represents but is not represented; and the absolute object, a thing-in-itself independent of all representation — of these one will never become conscious as something empirically given. Reinhold could well have kept these elaborations to himself for some future occasion.

It appears to emerge from what has been said so far that all the objects of Aenesidemus are groundless in so far as they are to be taken as directed against the truth of the principle of consciousness *as such*, but that they are relevant to it as *first* principle of all philosophy and as a mere fact; thus the objections make a new justification necessary. It is worthy of notice, moreover, that as long as Aenesidemus

[10]

is true to his own two stated principles, he also stands on good grounds before his opponent, but that he forfeits these grounds as soon as he ceases to be true to those principles, as will soon become apparent. If his examination ended here, he could honourably lay claim to a contribution to philosophy, and would deserve the respect of all impartial, independent thinkers; but we shall see to what extent he can claim either as he proceeds with his investigation.

For §§ 6-8, which determine the original concept of the faculty of representation, lead our critic to an examination of the specific claim of critical philosophy, namely, that the ground of a large portion of the determinations of the objects of our representations is posited in the essence of our faculty of representation.[32] And this is where we gain a definite insight into the nature of Aenesidemian skepticism. This skepticism leans towards a very presumptuous dogmatism; to some extent, it even takes this dogmatic position as established // and granted, in spite of its own previously stated principles. Our skeptic first enumerates the assertions allegedly contained in those paragraphs: a) the faculty of representation is the ground of the actuality of representations; b) the faculty of representation[33] is present in some determinate form prior to all representation (What can this mean, and where does Reinhold say it?); c) the faculty of representation is different from the representations as every cause is from its effects; d) the concept of the faculty of representation can be derived only from its effects, and in order to get to its intrinsic characteristics one only has to develop carefully the concept of mere representation.[34] After this enumeration he brings up the question, how could the Philosophy of the Elements ever come to this extravagant awareness of the *objective existence* of such a thing as the faculty of representation. And he cannot get over his amazement at the inference drawn by Reinhold, a critical philosopher, viz., "whoever grants a representation grants by the same token a faculty of representation." (*Theory of the Faculty of Representation*, p. 190).[35] This reviewer, or anyone else with a penchant for being amazed, would not wonder any less at the skeptic for whom, only shortly before, nothing was established except that there are different representations in us, and who now, the moment the words "faculty of representation" hit his ear, cannot think by them anything but a 'thing' (Is it round or square?) that exists as thing-in-itself, *independent* of his *representing* it, and indeed as a thing *that represents*. As the reader will soon see, no injustice is done to our skeptic by this interpretation. The faculty of representation exists *for* the faculty of representation and *through* the faculty of representation. This is the necessary circle in which any finite understanding (and this means, any understanding we can think of) is locked. Whoever wants to escape from this circle does not understand himself, and

[11]

does not know what he wants. With this single principle, this reviewer spares himself the adducing of all further comments by Aenesidemus on this matter, for he clearly misunderstands Reinhold throughout, or misinterprets him, and reproves the Philosophy of the Elements for claims which he himself has imported into it from his own store.

[12]   Completely denying (by this misinterpretation) // that Reinhold has made any contribution to the tempering of the distinctive principle of critical philosophy, the examiner turns to those proofs which the originator of this philosophy has laid down himself for it in the *Critique of Pure Reason*.[36] This examination is prefaced by a brief exposition of Humean skepticism.[37] "Hume himself did not earnestly hold as true the proposition that all our representations of things derive from their impressions upon us, for he could not have done so without having already presupposed the validity of the law of causality (in virtue of which things would be the cause of those impressions in us) which he in fact disputes—thus he could not have held this without crass inconsistency. Rather, he proposed this principle merely hypothetically in the context of the Lockean system, which was at the time the prevailing philosophy among his countrymen, in order to contest the system on its own terms. Hume's own true system consists of the following propositions: (1) Whatever is to be cognized, must be represented; (2) Any cognition, to be real, must be in conformity with the things outside it; (3) There is no principle in virtue of which we could know anything about objects in so far as these are supposed to be something different from our representations, or something in itself; (4) Even the principle of causality is not usable for this purpose; nor is the principle of contradiction of any use in grounding the causality principle for the required determination."[38]

Since the question whether what is now being refuted is in fact Humean skepticism is of no consequence to anyone who holds that all skepticism stands refuted, this reviewer need not be concerned with the issue of whether or not the system expounded is in fact Hume's. It is skeptical enough, for it appears to be seeking something which it despairs of ever finding; and the question is whether such a system is refuted by Kant. Aenesidemus replies to this question in the negative, first, "for in the *Critique of Pure Reason*, from the fact that the disposition of our mind is all that we can *think* of as the ground of synthetic judgements, it is inferred that this mind must *be actually* and *in itself* the ground of these judgements; and thus precisely

[13]   the one manner of inference is being presupposed as valid // which Hume has contested."[39] And here is where this reviewer kindly asks the skeptic: (a) to explain to the public straightaway, quite clearly and distinctly, what it could ever mean to say, "A certain A, which is indeed itself a *thought*, is *in itself*—and *independent of our thinking*—

the ground on which we judge"; (b) to indicate where in Kant he has come across any such nonsense—"Kant says: The mind is the ground of indubitable synthetic forms of judgement. *That* those forms must have a ground is quite openly presupposed here; the validity of the law of causality, which is just the point at issue, is thus already presupposed, in that it is presupposed that those forms must have a *real* ground."[40] If it is merely said: *We* have of necessity to seek a ground for them and to posit it in our mind, and if nothing more is said as to how [we can do this], then the principle of ground is being used at first merely with respect to its logical validity. But since what is being grounded exists only as thought, the implication would have to be that the *logical* ground of a thought is at the same time the *real* or *existential* ground of it.

Secondly, Aenesidemus replies to the question [about skepticism] in the negative, on the ground that nowhere has Kant proven that it is possible to think *only* of our mind as the ground of synthetic judgements.[41] This assertion, were it possible to demonstrate its truth, would indeed be decisive against critical philosophy. But Aenesidemus has refuted nothing in what he has said except what nobody holds, and he demands only what nobody understands. He justifies his assertion in the following manner: (a) "From the fact that at present we might not be able to explain and to think of something otherwise than in a certain way, it does not at all follow that we shall never be able to think of it otherwise."[42] This is an objection, however, which would have its place against an empirical proof, but which is misplaced against a proof derived from *a priori* principles. If the principle of identity and contradiction is finally made the foundation of all philosophy, as it should be (a system for which, after all, Kant provided all the possible materials, although he himself had no intention of constructing it) let us hope // that nobody will then still maintain [14] that we may yet advance, in the future, to a stage of culture at which contradiction would be thought to be possible. Aenesidemus tries, (b) to show that it is in fact possible to think of some other origin of those forms of judgement; however, he does so in a way which clearly betrays the fact that Aenesidemus has still not understood the *Critique of Pure Reason*, in spite of his naïve assurance of having read it and even understood it.[43] "It is possible to think," he says, "that all our knowledge proceeds from the effect on our mind of objects present *realiter*, and that even the *necessity* which is found in certain areas of knowledge is generated in virtue of the special manner in which things affect us. It would thus be necessary for us, e.g., to think of a sensation as being present during the time in which it is present; and this necessity would come from outside, for the impression would come from outside."[44] An unhappier example could not have been chosen! It is necessary to think of the object of this sensation as *actual* (in opposition to *possible* and *necessary*), yet this immediate relation to our very faculty of representation is supposed to be outside us, independent of it! "It is necessary to perceive the branches of a seen tree in the order in which they are present to our mind at a specific time."[45] Yes indeed; by means of the perception of the individual parts of the branches in stable space, and of the necessary connection through the category of reciprocity. "If things-in-themselves were completely unknown to us, we would not even be able to know that they can*not* have produced in us certain determinations."[46] If things-in-themselves cannot produce in us, independently of our faculty of representation, *any* determination *at all*, we are indeed able to know that they have not produced determinations actually present in us. "Deriving what is necessary and universally valid in our cognition from the mind does not make the presence [*Dasein*] of such necessity in the least more comprehensible

[15]   than deriving it from the // manner in which objects outside us affect us."[47] What could 'presence' [*Dasein*] possibly mean here; or 'comprehensible'? Are we perhaps to seek a still higher ground for that necessity which is assumed as entirely grounded in our mind? Is the unconditional necessity discovered in our mind to be conditioned by it? To be derived from it? To be explained and comprehended through it? And where is this higher ground to be sought? *In* us, where we have reached absolute autonomy? Is *absolute* autonomy to be *grounded*? This is a contradiction. Or *outside* us? But simply, the question is of a *transition* from the outer to the inner, or the other way around. It is plainly the business of critical philosophy to show that we are not in need of a transition; that all that arises in our mind is to be completely explained and comprehended by the mind itself.[48] It does not occur to it to reply to a question which, according to it, transcends reason. Critical philosophy shows us the circle which we cannot overstep, but within it, it provides our entire knowledge with the strictest coherence.

"*The Critique of Pure Reason* has not proven, as it alleges, that the *a priori* representations and judgements, which supposedly are present *in us*, are mere forms of experiential cognitions, and that they can have validity and meaning only with reference to empirical intuitions. For it is indeed possible to think of still another manner of relating *a priori* concepts to things besides supposing them to be mere conditions and forms of our knowledge of them, viz., that they relate to things in virtue of a *pre-established* harmony, so that the *a priori* representations in man would contain the counterpart of the objective properties of things-in-themselves, if their influence on the mind were possible."[49] Even supposing that those *a priori* forms of judgements are unities of the kind that can be found in the manifold as such, it is still the case

that the harmony is the union in one of a diversity. Our *a priori*
representations, on the one side, and the objective constitution of
things-in-themselves, on the other, would still be two things that are
at least // numerically different. And would not some faculty of   [16]
representation, after all, be a third thing which is, on its own account,
neither the first nor the second, but should unite both within itself?
Now, our faculty of representation is no such third thing, as
Aenesidemus himself admits by his hypothesis. It would have to be,
therefore, a faculty different from ours. Any such faculty, however,
i.e., a faculty of representation which did not judge according to the
principle of identity and of contradiction, is quite unthinkable for us;
equally unthinkable, therefore, is that alleged harmony supposedly
found in it. Aenesidemus continues: "Yet, the hypothesis of such a
pre-established harmony between our representations and what is
objectively present certainly does not contain anything absurd."[50] Should
we believe him?

Aenesidemus then raises the question whether the mind is the ground
of *a priori* cognitions as thing-in-itself, or as noumenon, or as
transcendental idea.[51] It cannot be such a ground as thing-in-itself, as
he acknowledges quite correctly.[52] "According to Kant's own contentions,
the category of causality cannot be applied to a *noumenon*."[53] Nor can
the principle of real ground be applied to it, but only that of logical
ground. Logical ground, however, becomes real ground inasmuch as
the mind is *simply intelligence*. Inasmuch as the mind is the ultimate
ground of certain thought-forms, it is noumenon; inasmuch as these
are unconditionally necessary laws, the mind is a transcendental idea,
but one which is distinguished from all the rest in that we realize it
through intellectual intuition, through the *ego sum*, and indeed through
the 'I am simply because I am'.[54] All the claims of Aenesidemus against
this procedure are based merely on the fact that he wants the absolute
existence [*Existenz*] or autonomy of the *ego* to be valid *in itself* (just
how and for whom we do not know), whereas it should only hold *for
the ego itself*. It is *for* the *ego* that the *ego* is *what* it is, and is *why* it is.
Our knowledge cannot advance beyond this proposition.

But then, how does the critical system differ from the one which
was defined above as Humean? Simply in that the latter leaves open
the possibility that eventually one might still be able to go beyond
that limitation of the human spirit. The critical system demonstrates
instead the absolute impossibility // of any such advance, and shows   [17]
that the thought of a thing, which supposedly has existence [*Existenz*]
and certain constitutional characteristics *in itself* and independently of
any faculty of representation is a whim, a dream, a non-thought. And
to this extent the Humean system is skeptical and the critical one dogmatic, though it is dogmatic in a *negative* sense.

148   J.G. Fichte

Examination of §§ 9-14[55]

Aenesidemus believes that in Paragraph 9, which lays down the proposition that mere representation must consist of two distinct components,[56] Reinhold has argued from the following premise: Anything that refers to different objects must itself consist of different components. And, of course, it does not take him much effort, then, to invalidate the conclusion.[57] But in the premise which he attributes to Reinhold he neglects the condition, 'if and only if it is through this relation that the different objects are first to be distinguished'. It is clear on this condition, however, that if x is supposed to be $= A$ and $= B$, there has to be in x a $y = A$ and a $z = B$; and that the opposite would be contradictory. Aenesidemus's distinction (which is to be found here too) between the *logical* [*gedachter*] and *real* difference of those two components of mere representation does not deserve serious consideration. What sort of thing can mere representation ever be on its own account, independent of a faculty of representation? And how could the components of a mere representation ever differ except because they are distinguished by [the subject] that is representing them? Is Aenesidemus making this overly subtle distinction in earnest, or is he poking fun at the public?

The objections against the designation, in §§ 10 and 11,[58] of that which in representation belongs to the subject through the *form*, and that which belongs to the object through the *material*, appear more justified to this reviewer. Aenesidemus says that it would have been possible to turn this designation right around[59]; and this reviewer too has never been able to take these definitions, as they stand, as anything other than arbitrary nominal determinations. (If A and B are altogether unknown and indeterminate before x is referred to them, as the Philosophy of the Elements explicitly states, it follows that they first acquire the predicate 'they are mutually different' only through two different components found // in x (y and z). *How* they are different, however, can only be decided from the way in which y and z differ.) Now, if these definitions were used merely as arbitrary nominal determinations, and if nothing were derived from them, nothing could be said against them. But Aenesidemus points out (and with reason, as it seems to this reviewer) that, deep down, what is being based on the definitions is the conclusion that the material must be *given*, whereas the form must be *produced*.[60]

Finally, the censure moves on to what appears to it to be the original mistake of the Philosophy of the Elements and the ground of all its errors: "It is not the case that just one thing is referred in the representation to the subject, and another thing to the object; it is, rather, that *the whole* representation is referred to both, the subject and the object, but in a different way to each: to the subject, as any property to its subject; to the object, as any sign to what it designates.

[18]

Reinhold has overlooked this manner of referring, and for this reason believes that he can explain how the reference to two different things is possible only on the presupposition of two different components within representation itself."[61] The proposition is *per se* quite correct, except that this reviewer, instead of the terms used by Aenesidemus, would rather say, "The representation is referred to the object as effect to cause, and to the subject, as accident to substance." However, seeing that Reinhold ascribes to the subject the form of the *whole* representation, and to the object the *material*, and admits of no representation without both, it follows that the truth cannot really have remained entirely hidden from him, as Aenesidemus believes.[62] But, if subject and object are determined merely by the connection of the representation with them, and are previously entirely unknown, how does Aenesidemus then come to refer the representation to the object as *cause*, or, as he says, as *something designated*, unless there is something in it by means of which it manifests itself originally as *effect*, or as *sign*? And how does he come to refer it to the subject unless there is something distinct in it by means of which it manifests itself as *accident*, or *predicate*? //   [19]

With reference to § 13 which states that no object can be represented, *qua* thing-in-itself,[63] Aenesidemus declares the following: "It was originally implanted in us, by the disposition of our nature, to be at peace about our knowledge only when we have perfect insight into the relation and the agreement of our representations (and their characteristics) with a something, *however independent of them it may exist*."[64] And so we have here, at the basis of this new skepticism, quite clear and distinct, that old mischief about a thing-in-itself which was going on all the time until Kant. Kant and Reinhold (as it at least seems to this reviewer) have long declared themselves against it, though not loudly and emphatically enough. This mischief is at the origin of all the skeptical as well as the dogmatic objections raised against critical philosophy, but it is simply not implanted in human nature to think of a thing independently of *any* faculty of representation; on the contrary, it is absolutely impossible for it to do so. Kant has not traced the pure forms of intuition, space and time, to a single principle as he has done for the categories; nor could he have done so in accordance with his plan of merely paving the way for science.[65] After him therefore, the notion did indeed persist of a state of affairs which would be thinkable by some faculty of representation other than the human one, for in Kant the forms of intuition could pass for mere forms of the *human* faculty of representation. And he himself has given a certain authority to this notion through the often repeated distinction between things as they appear to us and things as they are in-themselves—a distinction, however, which was certainly intended to hold only provisionally, and for the general reader. Nobody, however, has ever thought, no matter how often one might so declaim, nor could one ever be brought to think Aenesidemus's thought of a thing which supposedly has reality and properties independently, not only of the human faculty of representation, but of each and every intelligence. *Along with the thing, one always thinks oneself as the intelligence striving to know it.* Hence even // immortal Leibniz, who saw a bit more than most of his followers, had to endow his thing-in-itself, or his monads, with the power of representation.[66] And the conclusion he drew would be indisputably right, if only it did not overstep the circle to which the human spirit is restricted but which Leibniz, who saw everything else, failed to notice. *The thing would have to be constituted in itself as it represents itself for itself.* This is the circle that Kant discovered. After Kant, Reinhold gained for himself the immortal merit of drawing the attention of philosophical reason to the fact that the whole of philosophy must be traced back to one single principle, and that one cannot discover the system of the permanent modes of operation of the human spirit prior to the discovery of its keystone. (Without Reinhold, philosophical reason would have gone on commenting on Kant, for a long time perhaps, without ever discovering the special character of his system, for that character cannot be found unless one makes one's own way to its discovery.) Should we ever discover in the future, by means of further back-tracking upon the way so gloriously opened up by Reinhold, that what is immediately certain, the *ego sum* holds only *for* the *ego*; that all *non-ego is* only for the *ego*; that this non-ego derives all the determinations of this *a priori* being only through its connection with an ego; that all these determinations, however, to the extent that their knowledge is possible *a priori*, become absolutely necessary only on the simple condition of the relation of a *non-ego* to an *ego* in general; it would then follow that a thing-in-itself contradicts itself, to the extent to which it is supposed to be a *non-ego* not opposed to any *ego*; and that the 'thing' is so constituted, actually and in-itself, as it would have to be thought by any conceivable intelligent *ego*, i.e., by any being who thinks according to the principle of identity and contradiction; that therefore whatever holds as logical truth for any intelligence which finite intelligences can think, is at the same time real truth, and that there is no truth other than it—Moreover, it would not occur to anyone to claim (as Aenesidemus often does) that critical philosophy is idealistic,[67] and that it explains everything as a *show*.[68] // i.e., it assumes that it is possible to think of an intelligence with no connection with something intelligible—Aenesidemus takes issue with the proof drawn up by Kant against idealism in the *Critique of Pure Reason*,[69] and shows (quite soundly, to be sure) that by means of *this* proof the Berkeleyan idealism (against which it is, as he believes,

[20]

[21]

directed) is not refuted.[70] He could have read in clear words on pp. 274ff of the *Critique of Pure Reason* that the proof is not at all directed against the dogmatic idealism of Berkeley, "which has already had its ground removed in the transcendental aesthetics,"[71] but against the problematic idealism of Descartes.[72] It is against this problematic idealism that the proof definitely demonstrates that the consciousness of the *thinking ego* admitted by Descartes himself is possible only on condition that a *non-ego be thought*.

Since this reviewer has demonstrated the inadmissibility of the ground upon which Aenesidemus's skepticism is built, he may, perhaps with some justification, spare himself the consideration of Aenesidemus's remaining objections against the theoretical part of critical philosophy in general, and especially against its presentation by Reinhold, in order to say something more against Aenesidemus's remarks against Kantian moral theology. "This moral theology infers from the fact that something is commanded the existence of the conditions under which alone the command can be fulfilled."[73] The objections that Aenesidemus raises against this inference are based on his lack of insight into the true distinction between theoretical and practical philosophy. These objections are implicit in the following syllogism: We cannot judge *that* it is commanded to us to do something or to forego doing something prior to it being established *whether* this doing or foregoing is *possible*; now, it is only possible to judge the possibility or impossibility of an action according to theoretical principles; the judgement, therefore, *that* something is commanded rests also on theoretical principles. What Kant derives only *from* the command must already be proven and settled *before* one can reasonably assume a command at all; // the [22] recognition of a command is far from being capable of justifying belief in the existence of the conditions of its fulfillment; on the contrary, the recognition can only occur after this belief [is established].[74] One can see that Aenesidemus is attacking the very foundation of Kantian moral theology, the primacy of practical reason over theoretical reason; but also that he has made this attack easy for himself. What we *do* or *forego* doing, what we really should make actual for sensation in the world of appearances — this must fall indeed under the laws of this world. But who is ever talking of *doing* or *foregoing*? The moral law is first directed, not to a physical force, as an efficient cause producing something outside itself, but to a supra-physical power of desire or endeavour, or whatever one wants to call it. That law should produce (in the first place) not actions, but only the constant striving after an action, even if such striving, impeded by the force of nature, were never *effective* (in the sensible world). For if, to present the stages of the inference in their most abstract form, the *ego* in intellectual intuition *is because* it is, and *is what* it is, it follows that to this extent it is *self-positing*, absolutely self-subsistent and independent. In empirical consciousness, however, the *ego*, as intelligence, *is* only with reference to something intelligible, and to this extent it has dependent existence. Now, this *ego*, which is thereby posited in opposition to itself, constitutes not *two*, but only *one* ego; and this is impossible on the required condition, for dependent and independent are contradictory. But since the *ego* cannot give up its characteristic of absolute self-subsistence, a striving thus arises to make the intelligible dependent upon itself and thus bring to unity the *ego* which represents the intelligible and the self-positing *ego*. And this is the meaning of the expression, *reason is practical*. In the pure *ego*, reason is not practical; neither is it practical in the *ego* as intelligence; it is practical only in so far as it strives to unite the two. This is not the place to show that these principles must also be at the basis of Kant's presentation, even though he has nowhere laid them down specifically; // nor to show how, through the representation of this striving (which is in itself supra-natural) of the intelligent *ego*, a practical philosophy emerges by going through in *descending* order the stages which one must *ascend* in theoretical philosophy[75]—That union, an *ego* which by means of its self-determination would at the same time determine every *non-ego* (the idea of Deity), is the final goal of this striving. When the goal of this striving is represented outside the self by the intelligent *ego*, it is a *faith* (faith in God). This striving cannot cease except with the attainment of the goal, i.e., the intelligence can assume no moment of its being as final in which this goal has not yet been attained (faith in eternal continuance). With respect to this idea too, however, nothing else is possible but a *faith*, i.e., the intelligence has as the object of its representation, not some empirical sensation, but only the necessary striving of the *ego*; and nothing else can ever become possible through all eternities. So far is this faith from being merely a *likely opinion*, however, that it shares with the immediately certain *ego sum* (at least according to the most sincere conviction of this reviewer) an equal degree of certainty, one which infinitely surpasses all objective certainty made possible mediately only through the intelligent ego.—To be sure, Aenesidemus wants an objective proof of the existence of God and of the immortality of the soul. What could he possibly have in mind? Could it be that objective certainity appears to him incomparably preferable to a certainty which is (only) subjective? The *ego sum* has itself only subjective certainty; and, inasmuch as we can think to ourselves the self-consciousness of God, God himself is for God subjectively.[76] And now, what we want is an objective being of immortality! (These are Aenesidemus's own words.)[77] If some entity looking at its being in time could say at one moment of its being, "*Now* I am eternal", it would *not* be eternal then—Thus, far from being true that practical reason must acknowledge the primacy of

[23]

theoretical reason, its whole existence is in fact grounded in the *conflict* of what, in us, // is self-determining with what is to be cognized [24] theoretically, and it would itself be annulled if this conflict were removed.

A second comment of Aenesidemus is also based on this total misunderstanding of the moral ground of faith, viz., that the form of inference in the moral proof differs in no way from the one in the cosmo-theological proof reflected by Kant, for in it too it is argued: Since a world is at hand, the only thinkable condition for its possibility must also be at hand. [78] — The essential difference of this proof from the moral-theological one is this, that the first is based merely on theoretical reason, while the second is based on a conflict of the *ego* in itself with the latter. In matters about which it is supposed to prove something, theoretical reason must still at least be at one with itself. Now, it comes indeed to unity within itself only in that it thinks to itself a *world* as an unconditional whole and hence a first cause of this world. But even in the thought of such a first cause, theoretical reason gets itself again into an insoluble conflict with itself, for any cause it might think to itself in accordance with its proper law must again have its own cause. Consequently, although the task of seeking a first cause remains, nevertheless no cause which has been found can ever be the first. Thus reason can never realize the idea of a first cause, and assume it as determined and discovered, without contradicting itself. And no proof which leads to a contradiction can be valid.

This reviewer has taken it as his duty to assess this work in somewhat greater detail [than usual], partly because it does include several good and pertinent remarks; partly because the author has complained in advance of unproven verdicts, of which it is hoped, he will not accuse this assessment; partly because it is said that it has in fact attracted attention here and there, and that many readers of it already consider the cause of critical philosophy to be lost; and in part, finally, in order to help certain people get free from the prejudiced belief that we have only // an inadequate appreciation of the objections to [25] Kantian philosophy, and that we prefer to relegate them to oblivion for lack of anything solid to say in answer to them. There is nothing that this reviewer could wish more ardently than that his assessment might convince a good many independent thinkers that in itself, or in its own inner substance, this philosophy still stands as steadfast as ever before; but that it is still in need of much work to bring its materials into a well integrated and unshakable whole. Would that they might be inspired by this conviction, each in his place and so far as in him lies, to contribute to this exalted goal.

Notes

1. The reference is to Kant's admission that David Hume awoke him from his "dogmatic slumber." *Prolegomena*, Academy Ed., Vol. IV, p. 260; English tr., p. 8.

2. "Neue Darstellung." *Beiträge*, Vol. I, pp. 165-254.

3. *Aenesidemus*, pp. 130-180 ("Has the Critique of Reason Really Refuted Hume's Skepticism?").

4. Ibid., p. 45.

5. "Neue Darstellung." *Beiträge*, Vol. I.

6. *Aenesidemus*, pp. 53-54.

7. This is the first hint in the Review that Fichte intends to ground Reinhold's Philosophy of the Elements on more fundamental principles, just as Reinhold had tried to do for Kant's Critique.

8. "Neue Darstellung," *Beiträge*, Vol. I, p. 167: "Representation is distinguished by the subject in consciousness from both the subject and object and referred to both."

9. *Aenesidemus*, p. 60.

10. *Fundament*, p. 85.

11. Cf. *Critique*, A151, B190.

12. *Aenesidemus*, pp. 63-65; not a quotation but only paraphrase.

13. Cf. *Grundlage der gesammten Wissenschaftslehre* (1794), *Gesamtausgabe* I, pp. 97-98 (§§8-10); pp. 102-103, 105. English tr., pp. 98-99, 102-103, 105.

14. *Aenesidemus*, pp. 70-71. In the original the sentence is stressed.

15. P. 8.

16. *Aenesidemus*, p. 75; not a quotation but only a paraphrase.

17. Cf. *Fundament*, p. 77.

18. Cf. note 16 above.

19. *Aenesidemus*, p. 75; not a quotation but only a paraphrase.

20. "Neue Darstellung," *Beiträge*, Vol. I, p. 168.

21. Cf. the "Deduction of Presentation [*Vorstellung*]" in the *Grundlage*, I, pp. 227-246. English tr., pp. 203-217.

22. "Neue Darstellung," *Beiträge*, Vol. I, p. 143; *Fundament*, p. 80.

23. Cf. *Grundlage*, I, p. 91; English tr. p. 93. *Tathandlung* is rendered in the English text with "Act." *Zweite Einleitung in die Wissenschaftslehre*, I, p. 463; English tr., p. 38.

24. "Neue Darstellung," *Beiträge*, Vol. I, pp. 168-173. For a translation of these propositions, see below, Maimon, *Letters of Philaletes to Aenesidemus*, pp. 00-00.

25. *Aenesidemus*, p. 84.

26. Ibid., pp. 85-86; not a quotation.

27. *Grundlage*, I, pp. 104-105 (§11), 128; English tr., pp. 104-105, 195.

28. *Aenesidemus*, p. 86; not a quotation.

29. "Neue Darstellung," *Beiträge*, Vol. I, pp. 174, 173. This is a *composite* paraphrase of two distinct passages.

30. *Aenesidemus*, p. 90: "For things [*nichts*] cannot be referred to each other [*auf einander*] unless there are things that allow to be referred to each other; hence the actual representation cannot be referred in consciousness to the subject and object unless these are already present simply as subject and object."

31. Cf. above, note 24.

32. "Neue Darstellung," *Beiträge*, Vol. I, pp. 175-180. For a translation of these propositions, see below, Maimon, *Letters of Philaletes to Aenesidemus*, pp. 00-00.

33. *Vorstellungsvermögen*: Fichte normally uses the abbreviation V.V.

34. *Aenesidemus*, p. 97.

35. Ibid., pp. 98-100. *Theorie*, p. 190. Fichte is paraphrasing the quotation in *Aenesidemus*.

36. *Aenesidemus*, pp. 118-130.

37. Ibid., pp. 108-117.

38. Ibid., pp. 120-121, note; not a quotation but only a paraphrase.

39. *Aenesidemus*, pp. 132-133; not a quotation but only a paraphrase.

40. Ibid.

41. Ibid., p. 142.

42. Ibid., not a quotation but only a paraphrase.

43. Ibid., p. 5.

44. Ibid., this is a composite quotation up to: "affect us"; it is an almost *verbatim* quotation from pp. 142-143; the rest is a paraphrase of a text in pp. 143-144.

45. Ibid., p. 144; some modifications.

46. Ibid., p. 145; only a paraphrase.

47. Ibid., some slight modifications.

48. This is certainly not true of *Kant's* Critical Philosophy. Kant does not reduce 'consciousness' to 'self-consciousness'. For this reason the distinction between 'thought' and 'sensation' is important for him, and the transition from purely *thought* objects to actually *given* ones is a real problem.

49. *Aenesidemus*, pp. 149, 151; not a quotation.

50. Ibid., p. 151; some modifications.

51. Ibid., p. 154.

52. Ibid., p. 155.

53. Ibid., pp. 159-160; not a quotation.

54. Cf. above, note 13.

55. "Neue Darstellung," *Beiträge*, Vol. I, pp. 180-187; Prop. IX: "Representation as such must consist of two distinct components which by their union and their distinction constitute the nature or the essence of the representation"; Prop. X: "That which refers in the representation as such to objects, and through which the representation refers to them, is called the *material* of the representation"; Prop. XI: "That which refers in the representation to the subject, and through which the representation refers to the subject, is called *form* of representation"; Prop. XII: "The *object* is called that which is *represented* insofar as the representation refers to it through its material; it is called the *thing-in-itself* insofar as it is thought as that to which ONLY the *material* of the representation belongs"; Prop. XIII: "No object is, *qua thing-in-itself*, representable"; Prop. XIV: "Confusing the represented object with the thing-in-itself or transferring the form of the representation from that which can be represented to that which cannot, is unavoidable as long as we have not discovered and recognized what belongs, in the objects that are, or can be, represented, to the faculty of cognition. . . ."

56. Cf. above, note 55.

57. *Aenesidemus*, pp. 187-188.

58. Cf. above, note 55.

59. *Aenesidemus*, p. 203.

60. Ibid., pp. 211-212.

61. Ibid., pp. 212-213; not a quotation.

62. Ibid., p. 218.

63. Cf. above, note 55.

64. *Aenesidemus*, p. 223; not a quotation.

65. Cf. *Critique*, All-12, B25-26. Of course, Kant explicitly resisted any reduction of the type Fichte is proposing. Cf. letter to J. S. Beck, July 3, 1792, *Briefwechsel*, Academy Ed., Vol. XI, p. 334; English tr., pp. 193-194.

66. *Monadologie*, §14.

67. *Aenesidemus*, p. 257.

68. Ibid., p. 267.

69. *Critique*, B274-279.

70. *Aenesidemus*, pp. 268-269.

71. *Critique*, B274; not an exact quotation.

72. Ibid., B275.

73. *Aenesidemus*, p. 427.

74. Ibid., pp. 430-432, note.

75. Cf. *Grundlage*, I, pp. 245-246., English tr. p. 217: "If the self reflects upon itself and thereby determines itself, the not-self is infinite and unbounded. If, on the other hand, the self reflects upon the not-self in general (upon the universe), and thereby determines it, it is itself infinite. In presentation, therefore, self and not-self are reciprocally related; if one is finite, the other is infinite, and *vice versa*. . . ." This is the theoretical standpoint. "If, at a still more elevated level of reflection, we reflect that the self is itself the absolute determinant and therefore also that which absolutely determines the foregoing reflection, on which the conflict depends, then the not-self in each case again becomes determined by the self. . ." This is the practical standpoint. Heath and

Lachs translate *ich* as 'self'.

76. Aenesidemus would have reason to be puzzled by what Fichte is saying. since we *cannot*, as Fichte would admit, "think to ourselves the consciousness of God", it follows that the only faith that can be as certain as the *ego sum* has to be, not at all a faith *in* God, but a faith in *our idea* of God—or for that matter, a faith in *any* idea required by us in order to express the supposed certainty of the *ego sum*. This is where 'philosophy' becomes 'ideology'.

77. *Aenesidemus*, p. 434.

78. Ibid., p. 436.

Solomon Maimon
*Essay Towards a New Logic or
Theory of Thought,
Together with
Letters of Philaletes
to Aenesidemus*
Berlin: at Ernst Felisch's, 1794

Audiatur et altera pars

[Let the other side be heard too]

Translation and Notes by George di Giovanni

Solomon Maimon's (1754 [53?] - 1800) writing career hardly spanned ten years. During this brief time, however, he managed to produce over ten books and innumerable essays, articles, and letters. His three major works are Versuch über die Transcendentalphilosophie *(Berlin, 1790)(Essay in Transcendental Philosophy), which Marcus Herz sent to Kant in manuscript form in 1789,* Versuch einer neuen Logik oder Theorie des Denkens *(Berlin, 1794, republished unchanged, 1798) (Essay Towards a New Logic or Theory of Thought), and* Kritische Untersuchungern über den menschlichen Geist oder das höhere Erkenntniss-und Willensvermögen *(Leipzig, 1797) (Critical Enquiries Concerning the Human Spirit or the Higher Faculty of Cogniton and Will). In* Essay Towards a New Logic, *the skepticism which was already implicit in this first book, but which came to the fore only during his controversy with Reinhold, is clearly stated. The* Letters of Philaletes to Aenesidemus, *excerpts from which are here translated, were appended to this book. The first letter is translated in part, the second, fifth, sixth, and seventh in toto. In the third and fourth that do not appear here, Philaletes continues his point by point criticism of Aenesidemus (and also of Reinhold) begun in the second. The translation is taken from the original edition which is now also available in photo-mechanical reproduction in an edition by the Wissenschaftliche Buchgesellschaft (Darmstadt, 1963), and in the* Gesammelte Werke, *ed. Valerio Verra (Hildesheim: Georg Olms, 1970), Vol. V. It was also republished by the Kantgesellschaft, ed. Bernhard Carl Engel, Berlin: Reuther & Reichard, 1912.*

First Letter

WHAT YOU PLAN to do in your work, worthy Sir,[1] is to define the relationship of *skeptical* philosophy to the *critical* more accurately than has hitherto been done; to declare that the legitimate *demands* made by the first have been [left] *unsatisfied* by the other; and finally, to award the victory to skeptical philosophy not only over the *dogmatic*, but also over the *critical*.

For some years I too have made *philosophy* my favorite study. I too have thrust myself into the battle between *dogmatic* and *critical* philosophy, and as everyone knows I have spoken up on behalf of the latter. Lately I have tried to speak equally in favour of *skepticism*, and to defend its hereditary prerogatives. It seems, therefore, that we are following exactly the same plan in our philosophical endeavours. From what follows, it will be clear, however, that the plan is common to us only in its bare outline. In spite of our general agreement, we are in fact so far from sharing one and the same concept of the two different *methods of philosophizing* in question, either *per se* or in their *relation to one another,* that I shall even champion against *you* the cause of the great *commander in chief of* [. the forces of] *critical philosophy* — the very Mr. Reinhold, that is, whom I have also had occasion to [299] attack (cf *Disputes in the Domain of // Philosophy; Philosophical Correspondence*).[2] Our *agreement* regarding the plan but *divergence* in its *execution* will serve, I hope, to elucidate the object of our common enquiry all the more and set it in clear light.

Your intention (p 20) is nothing less than to prove that "*skepticism is justified in vigorously challenging the [alleged] certainty and universality of the principles and premises on which critical philosophy rests.*"[3] Also (p. 24):

> In my view, skepticism reduces to the claim that *nothing in philosophy has been established from indisputably certain and universal principles regarding either the being or non-being of things-in-themselves and their properties, or the limits of man's faculties of cognition.*[4]

So it is only in the second half of this definition that you oppose skepticism to critical philosophy, for as far as the first is concerned [300] (i.e., ". . . nothing in philosophy has been // established from indisputably certain and universal principles. . . etc. . . . .") the *critical* philosophy is in complete agreement with your *skepticism.* Your *skepticism* only differs from it in that, as regards the *being or non-being of things-in-themselves and their properties, critical philosophy* not only holds that so far nothing certain has been established about them in accordance with universally valid principles, but also that *nothing can be so established* in principle. Your *skepticism,* although it appears on the surface to stand even more radically *opposed* to dogmatism than *critical* philosophy, is in fact much more in *sympathy* with it. Nowhere does it declare (as critical philosophy does) that the *questions posed by human reason concerning the being or non-being of things-in-themselves, their objectively real properties, and the limits of the faculties of cognition, are absolutely unanswerable*; it posits nothing definite at all on the question of what *reason can* achieve in the domain of *speculation,* or what it *will* perhaps achieve some day, etc.

My *skepticism,* on the contrary, far from saying anything in support of *dogmatism,* stands opposed to it even *more* so than *critical* philosophy does. It assumes as *fact of consciousness two kinds of cognition,* viz., [301] *knowledge a priori and a posteriori*; and it // finds the characteristic of *necessity* and *universal* validity in one, but not in the other. *A priori* knowledge is so either *absolutely* or *in a relative sense.* In the first case, it is the *form of the faculty of knowledge* with reference to an *object in general*; in the second, it is itself grounded *on some determinate kind of given objects* instead. In the first case, it refers either to an *object of* thought or to an *object of knowledge in general*; that is, it abstracts not only from all the *particular determinations* with which *an object is given* to thought, but also from the *a priori conditions* which allow an *object to be thought* in general under *particular determinations* (no matter which). In the second case, it abstracts only from the *particular determinations* but not from the *a priori conditions* that make these possible. *Skepticism* is occupied, above all, in seeking out these *conditions*, and their *systematic order*, so as to determine and secure the *limits of the faculty of cognition*. To this extent it marches in step behind the *critical* philosophy (except for a number of variations and improvements which it feels justified in adopting in the process).

But now we come to the point where the two part company. *Critical* philosophy accepts the *actual* thinking of *objects* in accordance with *conditions* grounded in the faculty of cognition *a // priori* as a *fact* [302] of consciousness, and only shows in which way they are *conditions*. *Skepticism* puts that same *fact* in doubt, and seeks to establish that on this question the *witness of common sense* is not valid, since it rests on an *illusion* that can be accounted for in terms of psychological laws. Moreover, *skepticism* declares certain representations, which the *critical* philosophy — in order not to break away from the dogmatic philosophy completely — assumes to be ideas of reason that are grounded in its nature, to be grounded only in the nature of the *imagination*.

We shall have to discuss this in greater detail in the following letters. Of course, the propositions [which you take to be] valid beyond doubt (p. 45), and on which you ground your censure of the Philosophy of the Elements, both can and must be granted in any case. Only the second one requires a qualification. [You say]: "*General logic is the touchstone of all truth.*"[5] Right you are! But this holds only for every *formal* truth.

You say, further (p. 46, Note),
> Whenever the skeptics have cast doubt on the certainty of the syllogistic art, their intention was in fact only to doubt whether this art could help us attain to a cognition of things-in-themselves.[6]

I do not know which kind // of skeptics you have in mind here. [303] The truth of the syllogistic art rests on the principle of contradiction; a reasonable skeptic, therefore, will not doubt it even as regards *things-in-themselves*, since that principle applies to *objects in general*, and hence also to *things-in-themselves*. On the other hand, the syllogistic art cannot help us attain to any objectively real knowledge, not only in respect to things-in-themselves, but also in respect to *appearances*. Thus there is no doubt about this, in any case.

So much for the general plan of your critique. In the following letters I shall go through it after you step by step, commenting *in extenso* upon the details, as well as upon the conclusions to be drawn from them.

Philaletes

Second Letter

You cite from the *Philosophy of the Elements* the following propositions: "§1. In consciousness the representation is distinguished by the subject from the subject and the object, and is referred to both."[7] All that this proposition expresses *immediately* is the original fact of consciousness; // it expresses the concepts of representation, object and subject, only *mediately*, i.e., inasmuch as they are determined by that fact.

[304]

Prior to consciousness there is no concept of representation, object and subject; these concepts are made possible, for the first time, only through the consciousness in which, and through which, they are originally distinguished from, and related to, each other. The original characteristics with which these three components occur in consciousness cannot, inasmuch as they are original, be obtained through abstraction from any object whatever. *Qua* components of consciousness, therefore, their characteristics spring immediately from consciousness itself, without any abstraction. And to this extent they do not presuppose any reasoning, but precede all philosophy.

The principle of consciousness does not presuppose, therefore, any philosophically determined concept of representation, of subject and object. On the contrary, these concepts are first determined and laid down in it through it. They can only be expressed in the first place by the propositions that obtain their sense from the principle of consciousness—propositions that are completely contained in it and immediately derived from it.[8] //

[305]

Regarding this *principle of consciousness* that is laid down at the foundation of the *Philosophy of the Elements*, you remark, first:

> that it is not (as Mr. Reinhold requested that it should be) an *absolutely first proposition*, neither subordinated in any respect to some other proposition, nor determined through that other in any way at all. *Qua* proposition and *qua* judgment, it is subordinated to the highest rule of all judging, which is the principle of contradiction, i.e., the principle stipulating that nothing supposed capable of being thought may contain contradictory characteristics. In respect to its form and the combination of its subject and predicate, the principle of consciousness is determined through this other principle.[9]

This comment of yours strikes me as not a little strange. The *principle of consciousness* is indeed *dependent* on the *principle of contradiction* as a condition *sine qua non*. But is it *determined* by it? Not at all! A proposition is *determined* by another if the latter, since it applies to *objects generally* (or at least to those of higher order), contains the ground why the other must apply to certain *given objects* (of a lower order). For instance, the proposition: "Two rectilinear triangles equal in two sides and in the included angle must also be equal in respect to their third side," must be determined by the principle: // "Between two given points, [306] one straight line, and one alone, can be drawn." In this case the first proposition defines a relation between *given objects* (two triangles equal in certain stipulated parts) which, though not fully *determined* through the principle, is nonetheless *grounded* in it.

Let us now see how matters stand with the *principle of contradiction* and that of *consciousness*. The *principle of contradiction* holds universally of all the *objects of thought* as their *conditio sine qua non*; it also holds, therefore, of the characteristics combined in the *principle of consciousness*. But does it follow that these characteristics are thereby actually being thought as so combined? [No.] In virtue of the principle of contradiction these characteristics are only *capable* of being thought as combined (since they do not contradict one another). In the above example, for instance, "Two triangles, etc.," the proposition is fully determined by the *principle of contradiction* with the help of other synthetic propositions. The *principle of consciousness*, on the other hand, is the first principle of all synthetic propositions; it cannot, therefore, be determined by other synthetic propositions in combination with the principle of contradiction. Mr. Reinhold's intention in his *Philosophy of the Elements* was not to provide a *general logic* (which he assumed) but the *foundations* for a *critique of the faculty of cognition*. And at the foundation of that // he laid the *principle of consciousness* which must serve as the [307] ground for every synthetic proposition not just as a *condition sine qua non*, but as the *real ground* of the possibility of a synthesis in general.

You say, further (p. 61):

> But, as Prof. Reinhold quite rightly explains (*Contributions*, p. 115), to derive other propositions from a principle means nothing else but to derive from it the necessity of the combination of the representations found in them. And since it cannot be denied that in the principle of consciousness the combination of subject and predicate is determined through the principle of contradiction, it follows that the former principle is subordinated to the latter. But since this is so, the principle of consciousness must be determined through the principle of contradiction according to its form, etc.[10]

Here, most worthy sir, you confuse again '*being determined by a proposition*' with '*being dependent on a proposition*'. According to their *form*, all propositions are determined by the *principle of contradiction*, i.e., they are only allowed to have a *form* that conforms to this *principle*. But just for this reason, since *all* propositions are determined by it according to their *form*, *none* of them is determined by it in a way that differentiates it from all the others. The mere *form* 'a is b' ('a

[308] does not // contradict b') can determine just the *possibility*, not the *necessity*, of the bond uniting subject and predicate in the principle of consciousness; in other words, it can determine the principle *qua postulate*, but not *qua axiom*.

In a note on p. 62 we read: "Since the principle of contradiction is the supreme law of thought, it no more stands under the principle of consciousness than a genus stands under its species, or a species under its individual."[11]

But according to Mr. Reinhold, it is exactly the other way around: The *principle of consciousness*, since it relates to all the *functions of consciousness* (thinking, representing, etc.) is the highest genus to which the *principle of contradiction*, since it relates simply to thought, must be subordinated. For instance, the simple representation that I have of the colour red (of the material contained in it) is already cognized [by me], *qua* given representation, through the *principle of consciousness* without [my] having first to test it against the *principle of contradiction*; in fact, since the representation does not contain anything *manifold*, no such testing would in this case even be possible.

And again we read: "In *The Foundation of Philosophical Knowledge*, p. 85, Mr. Reinhold says indeed: 'Of course the principle of consciousness is subordinated to that of contradiction – not, however, in the sense that it is determined by it, but as a law which it is not

[309] allowed to // contravene'. "However," you say, "I would have thought, first, that what stands under a law in the sense that it was not permitted to contravene it, is also determined by this law and by its formula as a principle."[12]

This objection I consider to be justified, for every *principle* is at the same time a *law of thought*. In Mr. Reinhold's position, I would have expressed myself this way: The *principle of consciousness* is subordinated to the *principle of contradiction* inasmuch as it ought not to contravene this supreme principle of *general logic*. But it is not *determined* by it (in respect to its content).

Then you go on to say:

> And in the second place, if to be subordinated to a law and not to be allowed to contravene it does not mean exactly the same as to stand under a first principle, and be determined by it, then the principle of consciousness too, which the Philosophy of the Elements claims to express the law of representing, is not a principle by which other propositions are determined – still less the ultimate principle of all principles in

philosophy. It is only a law, rather, which propositions in philosophy ought not to contravene.[13]

I shall pass over the question of how the *principle of consciousness* is a fundamental proposition in philosophy through which other propositions are determined. I venture to assert with confidence, however, // that the *principle of determinability* laid down in this [310] work is a principle of all *objectively real* thought, and consequently of *philosophy* as a whole too.[14] All the propositions of philosophy can be derived from it, and be determined by it. For all *real* thought is distinguished from that which is *formal* as well as from that which is *arbitrary* by the fact that, whereas formal thought is a mere *form* without an *object*, and arbitrary thought is an *object* given to thought without determinate *form*, *real* thought (i.e., thought cognized in accordance with the *principle of determinability*) contains instead a given *object* as well as a *form* determined through this object. For instance, 'quadrilateral virtue' is just an *arbitrary* thought; 'virtue' and 'quadrilateral' have, as *objects of consciousness*, reality *in themselves* apart from their being thought or combined in a unity of consciousness. That they are so thought or combined, in other words, has no ground; it is merely *arbitrary*. But, of course, the relationship between cause and effect, e.g., 'If a is given, b must also be given', is not an *arbitrary* thought, since cause and effect are not to be found in consciousness apart from each other. They must be thought, therefore, as bound together, As long as no *object* is subordinated to them, however, their being thought or combined in a unity of consciousness is a merely *formal* // thought, [311] not a *real* one. For the relationship between the two is only thought of as *possible*, in virtue of the *negative* criterion which is the *form* of the thinking of an object in general (because cause and effect do not contradict each other); it is not *cognized*, however, through any *positive* criterion in objectively real objects. The thought of a triangle, on the contrary, i.e., 'a space enclosed by three lines', is a *real* one, for 'space' is being thought here as *something standing on its own* (substance) and the determination 'three lines' as *inhering* in it (accident). It is not here a question of thinking *objects in general* in a *possible* relationship of substance and accident, but of cognizing the relationship between *given objects* as *actual*. For since 'space' can be an object of consciousness also in itself, apart from the determination 'three lines', but not 'three lines' apart from it, the thought 'triangle' is as little *formal* as it is *arbitrary*. It is not formal, because it does not refer to an *object in general*, but to a *determinate object* (the triangle); and not arbitrary, because without space being thought or determined through 'three lines', the latter could not be *object of consciousness* (as in fact it is).

Here, therefore, you have a *principle of the whole of philosophy* (of real thought) which not only may not be contradicted by any proposition [312] // that refers to real objects (no proposition can refer to real objects if its subject and object are not in the relationship of determinability), but through which other propositions referring to given objects are determined *qua* propositions.

For instance, if the proposition, 'A line can be black', is given to me, I declare it to be just arbitrary, since 'line' and 'black' are not in the *relation of determinacy*. For 'line' is an *a priori* determination of space for thought, whereas 'black' is an *empirical* determination of sensible intuitions, so 'line' and 'black' can be found in consciousness one without the other. Hence their combination in a unity of consciousness is *arbitrary*, and without any ground.

If on the other hand what is given to me is the proposition, 'A corporeal figure of ten planes can be regular', I do not simply say that it is *arbitrary*, for 'planes' do indeed stand to 'space' as *determination to determinable*, and apart from 'space' they cannot occur in consciousness. From the *construction* of this object, however (i.e., of a regular decahedron) it results that, although the thought of this object does not contain any *contradiction* and hence is not *impossible*, and although between subject and predicate there obtains the relationship of determinacy, and hence the thought is not *arbitrary*, yet, the *object* [313] being thought through it is // *impossible*. The thought is thus *formal*, it cannot refer to any *real* object; and the like.

You say (p. 63):

> But secondly, the principle of consciousness as expressed in the Philosophy of the Elements is very far from being a *proposition determined entirely by itself* — i.e., the kind of proposition that can only be thought correctly if it can be thought at all, a proposition that could be accurately understood simply by reflexion on the meaning of the words in which it is laid down; or whose concepts would not allow of being combined with either too many or too few characteristics, etc.[15]

You show that the concepts of subject, object and the double way in which they are connected are highly precarious and indeterminate. The expression, '*The matter of the representations refers to the object*', should equally mean, according to Mr. Reinhold's own explanation, 'takes its place', 'is commensurate with it', 'is to be attributed to it', 'depends on it', 'is determined and given through it', 'corresponds and conforms to it', 'can claim some affinity with it', So too the expression, 'The form of representation refers to the subject', is elucidated by him with the following locutions: 'the form of representation belongs to the subject', 'is its effect', 'is added by it to the matter of representation', 'can claim some affinity with it', In this [314] I fully agree // with you. I have already repeatedly shown (in Volume IX of the *Science of the Animating Principles of Experience*

[Erfahrungsseelenkunde], no. 3;[16] in *Quarrels in the Domain of Philosophy, Philosophical Correspondence*)[17] not only how precarious and indeterminate this explanation is, but also that those locutions have been carried over *into philosophy* from ordinary usage without *any critical scrutiny*, and as a result the illusion they harbour gains *philosophical sanction*, as it were. In what follows, however, I shall have occasion to explain my views about this matter in greater detail.

You say:

> Thirdly and finally, the principle of consciousness is neither a universally accepted proposition, nor does it express a fact that is not bound to some determinate experience or some specific reasoning but which would on the contrary accompany every possible experience and every thought of which we are conscious. For in the first place, because of its ambiguity (it can in fact mean something different for anybody) this proposition cannot be universally accepted (by all philosophers). And in the second place, it is not even universally valid (for every kind of consciousness).[18]

Here too I agree with you. I have already shown in the writings just referred to that the *principle of consciousness* does not hold for the *original* consciousness, but only for the one determined by it, i.e., the one produced through the *reproductive* imagination, // as I shall soon elaborate.[19]   [315]

You remark further that the *principle of consciousness* is, in the first place, a *synthetic proposition* the predicate of which states something about the subject (consciousness) not already thought in it as a characteristic or component. But its real truth is grounded on just those experiences according to which a representation, an object, a subject, and the connection we establish between the representation and these two, belong to many utterances of consciousness. The principle therefore cannot have the *universality* and *necessity* required of a *principle*.[20]

But to this Mr. Reinhold would retort: The *principle of consciousness* is indeed a *synthetic* proposition, but one in which the subject cannot be thought in a determinate way without the predicate. Without the concepts 'subject', 'object', 'representation', and of the connection established between 'representation' on the one side and 'subject' and 'object' on the other, consciousness can be *thought in general*, but not *determinedly cognized* as the highest condition of all its functions (representing, thinking, etc.). The principle does indeed express a *fact*, but one which is determinate *per se*, and does not depend on any contingent *experience*; in this respect it is in no worse a position that the *principle of contradiction* which // also expresses a *fact*   [316] of consciousness.

You say further (p. 76):

Secondly, the principle of consciousness is an abstract proposition and indicates what certain expressions of consciousness (according to the author of the Philosophy of the Elements all of them) have in common. It cannot lay claim, therefore, to any higher degree of certainty than accrues to it because of its extension, etc.[21]

To this too Mr. Reinhold would answer: I claim that the *principle of consciousness* no more *abstracts* from *certain* expressions of consciousness than it does from *any* of them (how could it, after all?); it is produced not through *abstraction* but through *reflection*. And his answer would not be without right, for as I have already remarked in this work, *abstraction* succeeds only on condition that [the object] upon which it is performed is not completely abolished by it. This is the case with all the characteristics of *empirical* objects whose *linkage* is not cognized as necessary and whose *separation* is therefore known to be possible. What enters into the thought of something as the *condition* of its *possibility*, on the other hand, cannot be *abstracted* from it but can only be determined in the thing through *reflection*. According to Mr. Reinhold the *principle of consciousness* holds of *every* expression of consciousness, not because our // perception shows that *it is* [in fact] *to be found* in all of them, but because it *must be found* in them as their condition.

[317]

The Original Concept of Representation

§II.Representation is what is distinguished in consciousness by the subject both from the object and the subject and referred to both.[22]

The Original Concept of the Object

§III.The object is what is distinguished in consciousness by the subject both from the subject and the representation, and to which the representation that is distinguished from the subject is referred.[23]

The Original Concept of the Subject

§IV.The subject is what is distinguished in consciousness from the representation and from the object by the subject itself, and to which the representation distinguished from the object is referred.[24]

The Original Concept of Mere Representation

§V.Mere representation is what lets itself be referred in consciousness to object and subject, and is distinguished from both.[25]

About these definitions you remark (p. 84):
The definition of the essential characteristics of *representation* laid down

by the Philosophy of the Elements is undeniably narrower than the *definendum*. And just as the principle of consciousness does not give all that is actually to be found in consciousness, so this definition // of representation on which that entire philosophy rests—all its arguments about the origin of the components of representations and the nature of their faculties— does not determine the characteristics that in fact occur in every representation. On the contrary, it merely determines the concept of a particular kind of representation, and of a particular way in which the mind represents something to itself. For if a representation is made up only of something distinguished from, and referred to, the object and the subject by the mind; if it is certain, moreover, that only something perceived can be distinguished from, and referred to, something else by the mind (for the operation of distinguishing and referring can occur only if there is something there that can be referred to, and distinguished from, something else; and where there is nothing at hand that can be distinguished, 'distinguishing' cannot be thought of at all), then it follows that 'intuition' is not a species of the genus 'representation' because the concept of 'genus' is not applicable to it at all. In intuition, of course, there is no distinguishing of object from representation; for as long as it lasts, absolutely no // notice is taken of an object different from the intuition. But since intuition is a species of representation, as Mr. Reinhold asserts in all of his writings too, it follows etc.[26]

[318]

[319]

I am overjoyed to find, worthy sir, that you fully agree with me about something I have long been urging (in the writings mentioned above)[27] against Mr. Reinhold. I have already shown that according to its common meaning 'representation' is nothing else but 'partial presentation'. It only occurs, therefore, if the object has first been *made* entirely *present* (perceived); only afterwards does the imagination—in accordance with its function—reproduce it in part and refer its copy back to the original by means of the faculty of memory, i.e., it *represents* the original. The *original* sensible perception (i.e., not the one reproduced through the imagination) does not represent anything besides itself—and this means that in fact it does not represent anything at all. If we nevertheless refer every original perception to something (outside consciousness) in the manner of a *representation* (and it cannot be denied that this is in fact what we do), this happens because of an illusion of the imagination. Accustomed as it is to refer its *reproduction* to *objects* or to their original perceptions, // the imagination ends up by referring even the original *perceptions* to something outside consciousness.

[320]

It is easy to explain, however, how such an astute thinker as Mr. Reinhold could have overlooked this. Mr. Reinhold found his concept of *representation* in the *Wolffian-Leibnizian philosophy* in which every *perception*, even an original one, is called "*representation* of something." But he did not notice that in that philosophy the practice is of course justified, because according to it every *perception* refers to a *thing-in-itself*. As as *critical philosopher*, however, Mr. Reinhold had no right to permit this transition beyond the cognitive faculty—precisely because of the reference to *thing-in-itself*. For what could it mean? *Reference, relation*, and the like, are *modes of combination; combination*, however, always presupposes that there is something *to be combined* and a *ground of combination* in consciousness. Why this *fact* did not stand in Mr. Reinhold's way is easily explicable as an *illusion* of the imagination according to psychological laws, as we have already shown.

[321] The universality of this concept of representation (that every modification of consciousness is referred to something, *qua* representation) completely annuls the // concept, for it is exposed to a question like that of the *Indian* who, upon being told that the world rests on a pair of *elephants* and the *elephants* on a large *turtle*, innocently went on to ask: ". . . and *what does the turtle finally rest upon?*"

The Original Concept of the Faculty of Representation

§VI. The faculty of representation is that through which the mere representation is possible, i.e., that in consciousness which lets itself be referred to object and subject but which is distinguished from both; it must be present in the cause of representation, i.e., in what contains the ground of the actuality of a representation, prior to any representation[28]

§VII. Just as 'sensible representation', 'concept', and 'idea' have in common the name "representation" (which designates, under the predicate 'representation' generally what they have in common) so 'sensibility', 'understanding' and 'reason' are called, *qua* faculties of sensible representations, concepts and ideas, [respectively], "faculties of representation", and what is common to all of them is called "the faculty of representation in general."[29]

§VIII. The faculty of representation in general cannot of course be located outside the power to represent, and outside sensibility, understanding

[322] and reason. Yet its // concept cannot be derived from the power, but only from its effect, viz., the mere representation—indeed, only from the concept of representation as determined through the principle of consciousness.[30]

Here you comment (pp. 94-96) that

For a proper estimate of the true value of *critical philosophy*, and of the legitimacy of the claims it makes for the *apodictic evidence* and infallibility of its results, we must examine above all the grounds and principles from which, and in accordance to which, it establishes that there is in our knowledge something determined *a priori* by the mind, and that this something constitutes the *form* of the material given to our knowledge *a posteriori*.

In this examination, however, we must also pay special attention to the requirements of *Humean skepticism* . . . — whether *critical philosophy* has done justice to these requirements, as it claims, and has removed the skepticism by the roots, etc.[31]

What we must determine first of all is what we are to understand by *critical philosophy* and by *Humean skepticism*. Just about all the *Kantians*, except Mr. Reinhold, hold that Kant's *Critique of Pure Reason* and its *conclusions* is the only *critical philosophy* possible, and they dare not deviate from it by a hair's breadth. Even if they now want to be called *critical philosophers*, rather than *Kantians*, // this is simply in order to shake off the *embarrassing image of being just parrots*, and to give the impression of having accomplished something on their own. But *parrots* is what these so-called *critical philosophers* are, just the same, as closer investigation reveals. [323]

Mr. Reinhold, animated by an unusual *philosophical spirit*, and equipped with all the *talents* necessary for the task, could no longer bear this *slavery*. In his view, Kant's *Critique of Pure Reason* is not the *only one possible* critique, nor is it even the *best* of its kind. And without denying its value, but granting to it on the contrary all due praise, he dared to reproach it modestly all the same for many an *imperfection and lacuna*, and to open up a *new road to critical philosophy* for himself.

For reasons that I have already stated on various occasions, and shall state again in what follows, I am unable to follow the same *path*, but consider myself obliged to stand here as an *opponent* of Mr. Reinhold. Nonetheless, I agree with him on these capital points: (1) A *critique of the faculty of cognition* must precede *all cognition*; (2) Kant's *Critique* is not the *only one possible*, and is not even the *best* of its kind. //

I diverge from him, on the other hand, on the following points: (1) I declare that his *expectations* regarding *critical philosophy* are in general *exaggerated*; (2) I declare that the *fact* on which he grounds his *principle of consciousness* and his *explanations* of *representation*, *object*, etc., is an *illusion* of the imagination, and in doing so I undercut his foundations; (3) but I have made available a *supreme principle of all objectively real thought*, viz., the *principle of determinability*, which I have presented in this work, and have established as the ground of the whole of *pure philosophy* — a principle which, if it is ever understood, will, I hope, withstand every scrutiny. [324]

However, the very concept of *skeptical philosophy*, as understood by the ancient and by the modern philosophers, is highly ambiguous and indeterminate. It will be shown in what follows that my own concept of *skepticism* does not concur with yours.

Kant and his followers claim that they have undermined the *Humean* skepticism at the roots with their *critical philosophy*; and perhaps according to the concept they have constructed of it this is quite true. At this point, however, I shall refrain from considering all ambiguous concepts of that sort; instead I shall put forward, as precisely as I can, [325] my own concept of a *reasonable skepticism*, and the // method that I have followed in grounding it. It will become an easy matter then to define its relation to the *critical philosophy*.

My *skepticism* sets the solution to the following seven questions at the foundation of my *critical philosophy*:

First Question:	Do we have *a priori pure cognition* (concepts and principles) that refers to an *object of thought* in general?
Answer:	Yes.
Second Question:	Do we have *a priori pure cogniton* that refers to an *object of a priori cognition*?
Answer:	Yes.
Third Question:	Do we have *a priori pure cognition* that refers to an *object of a posteriori cognition*?
Answer:	No.
Fourth Question:	With what right can we *employ* the *a priori* pure cognition that refers to *objects of a priori cognition*?
Answer:	In accordance with the *principle of determinability*.
Fifth Question:	Do we *actually* employ it with respect to these objects?
Answer:	Yes.
Sixth Question:	*Why* must we *employ* it?
Answer:	Because otherwise we could not have any *object* of cognition (such as we do in fact have). //
Seventh Question:	With what *right*, and *why*, can we employ, and must we employ, *a priori pure cognition* in respect to *objects of a posteriori* cognition (granted that in fact we do so employ it)?
Answer:	With just the same *right* and on just the same *ground* as we *can* and *must* employ it in respect to *objects of a priori* cognition.

[326] appears next to the Seventh Question row.

Let me now elaborate on what I mean:

The first question we must raise in this enquiry is *whether* we have *pure cognitions*, i.e., *concepts, principles* and *postulates*, which, being *conditions of the thought of an object in general*, refer *absolutely a priori* (i.e., *before the determination of the object*) to every *given object* (whether *a priori* or *a posteriori*). This question is answered in the *affirmative*; the demonstration of the answer is provided for us by *general logic* which lays down in strictly a *a priori* fashion, as *postulates for the possibility of the thought of an object in general*, the *principle of* contradiction and the *forms of thought*. In fact, the answer to this question, or the proposition: "We have pure cognitions, etc." belongs to *general logic*; in our *Critique of the Faculty of Cognition*[32] we simply presuppose it as a *theorem*.

The second question is: "Do we have pure cognitions that refer to an *object of* //*a priori* *cognition* absolutely *a priori*?" This question presupposes the *fact* that we have *objects of cogniton* — which means for us: objects that are *determined outside thought* (i.e., in intuition) — and in addition we have objects that can be determined by thought; the question is only whether we have pure concepts and principles that refer to them *absolutely a priori* (before the determinations of these objects). This question is answered likewise in the *affirmative*; and the demonstration of the answer is given by *pure mathematics*.

[327]

We have already shown in this work that a *real*[33] object is possible only because the *manifold* held together in it is cognized in the *relation of determinability*, i.e., one of its components is cognized as *subject* and the other as *predicate*, and not the other way around. The first component is the one which is *determinable*, and can be object of consciousness by itself; the other is the *determination* of the first, and can be object of consciousness only in combination with it, not by itself. Without this *criterion*, thought can only be *formal* or quite *arbitrary*, not *real*. Thus the *objects of mathematics* presuppose the *pure concepts* of 'determinable' and 'determination', and the *principles of determinability*; these refer to mathematical *objects* strictly *a priori* (before any determinate cognition of them). //

[328]

The third question is whether we have *pure cognitions* that refer to *empirical objects* strictly *a priori*. Kant's *Critique of Pure Reason* answers this question in the affirmative. Instead of proofs, however, it brings only common *practice* in evidence as a matter of *fact*. We say, for instance, that fire warms the stone, i.e., that fire is the *cause* of the *warming up* of the stone, or the like, and in the same way we look for *its cause* in every appearance. We presuppose, therefore, the *concept of cause* and the *principle*: "Every appearance must have a cause."

Our *Critique of the Faculty of Cognition*, however, replies to this question with a "no," for it shows that the alleged *fact* rests on an *illusion* of the imagination. Of course the pure *concepts* and *principles* are *a priori*.[34] But their only meaning is one they acquire in their *real employment*. And they have no such employment save in respect to *a priori objects*. According to our *critique*, for instance, *substance* does not mean something that would endure *existing in itself* while the *accident* changes, or *accident* something that cannot exist *in itself* but only as the *accident of substance*; rather, *substance* is something which is *in itself* an *object of consciousness*, whereas *accident* is something that cannot in itself be an object of the sort, but in combination with substance,

[329]   etc. // This [claim] constitutes the entire *foundation of our skepticism*.[35]

The fourth question is how can we employ these pure concepts and principles, even in respect to *objects given a priori, absolutely a priori*. For since they refer quite generally to *indeterminate objects of cognition* simply as a possibility, we have no *ground* for actually employing them in respect to determinate objects. What right do we have, for instance, in the case of 'straight line', to think that the concept of line in general is the *subject*, and that of *straightness* is the predicate, and not the other way around? Indeed, what right do we have to think that these concepts stand at all in the relation of (real) *subject* and *predicate*, and thereby to determine '*straight line*' as a *real object*? Why not also think 'line' and 'sweetness' in the same relation, and thus determine the concept 'sweet line' as a *real* object? The answer is that the right is given to us by the *principle of determinability*. We think certain concepts in a certain *logical relation* because we recognize that they are in the *real relation* in respect to consciousness in general that we presuppose as the criterion for the use of the *logical* relation. 'Line' is determined in thought as the *subject* and 'being straight' as the *predicate* because 'line' can be an *object of consciousness* even *by itself*, whereas 'rectilinearity' can be so as the *determination* of 'line',

[330]   not *by itself*. // 'Line' and 'sweetness', on the other hand, are *independent* of each other in respect to consciousness. Hence, their being thought together in the relation of *subject* and *predicate* is merely *arbitrary*, it is without a *real ground*.

Since these concepts and principles refer to *all* objects of cognition, they are *necessary* to cognition, and we must employ them in respect to objects of cognition in general. Hence the fifth question is: Why *must* we use them? And the answer: Because we could not otherwise have any *real object* of thought (as we in fact have); for as I have already shown in this work, only thinking that is determined through the criterion of being thought [das gedachte *Kriterion*] can determine a *real* object.

The sixth and seventh questions concern the *employment* of *pure cognitions* in respect to *empirical objects*. Since I do not admit this *employment as fact*, yet I do not for this reason deny its *possibility*, I can only raise these questions hypothetically (Kant's critique, since it presupposes the fact, raises the questions without qualification, and answers them accordingly): On the presupposition of the *fact*, viz.,

[331]   that we employ // *pure cognitions in respect to empirical objects, how can we, and why must we*, so employ them? The answer coincides with that to the previous question: Because I do not attribute reality to any *thought empirical object* unless I cognize it to be in the *relationship of determinacy*, just like *a priori real objects*, or at least I *suppose* it to be in this relationship.[36]

What kind of *skepticism* the ancients had in mind, or Hume in modern times, I do not know. Boasting apart, however, you have a *skepticism* here, and a *Critique of the Faculty of Cognition* closely connected with it, which are certainly not inferior to the *Critique of Pure Reason* as far as *thoroughness* goes.

Whether critical philosophy has undermined D. Hume's skepticism at the roots, we shall see in what follows. It certainly will not undermine the *skepticism* that I have just outlined here.

You say (p. 97): "What has been said provisorily in §§VI-VIII [of the Philosophy of the Elements] regarding the nature of the faculty of representation, . . . etc."[37]

I shall not venture to make glosses on Mr. Reinhold in order to defend him against your objections. A critical philosopher as exact as Mr. Reinhold is should of course have refrained from metaphysical utterances of this kind. He ought simply to have unpacked all that // is contained in 'representation', or what must be posited prior [334] to it as the condition of its possibility, without worrying in the least about the cause, power, etc., which make it actual. Enquiries of this sort belong to metaphysics, and the possiblility and limits of metaphysics are only to be established through a critique of the faculty of cognition. So I shall simply comment as follows: (1) Mr. Reinhold's definition of 'faculty in general', upon which his definition of the faculty of representation is based (§VI), is incorrect. The faculty of representation is [said to be] that which makes mere representation possible; thus 'faculty' is in general the ground of the possibility of a thing. This not only goes against every accepted linguistic practice in philosophy; it has no meaning at all. According to the accepted philosophical terminology, 'faculty' is not the ground of the possibility of a thing, but the ground of its actuality; 'power' is what contains this ground. 'Ground of possibility' signifies the universal (the determinable) without which the particular (the determinate) cannot occur in consciousness. For instance, the representation of space is the ground or the condition of the possibility of a triangle. The two stand to each other, therefore, in a relation of reciprocity. 'Space' can be thought as 'triangle'; 'triangle. for its part, must be thought in 'space'. Here, however, the // [335] word "faculty" cannot be used. We cannot say, "Space has the faculty of being triangular," but only that "It can be triangular," for "faculty" always refers to something that is brought about through an operation of the subject. Not space, therefore, but the subject that represents it has the faculty of determining it as 'triangle'.

Since according to critical philosophy, however, the subject of representations is merely a formal concept for us, it can no more be called "power of representation" than "faculty of representation"; both equally presuppose a real object and a real relation (that of causality).

If by 'faculty of representation', however, Mr. Reinhold does not understand the real ground of the actuality of representations (their cause) but simply what is common to all actual representations (just as, for instance, by 'power of attraction' we do not understand a cause of the attraction, but just the universal mode or the laws according to which it occurs), then "faculty of representation" is not in fact distinguished at all from mere 'representation' (which is the [element] common to all representations). After defining 'representation', therefore, he should have ignored the 'faculty of representation' altogether (for it does not add anything new). //

(end of Second Letter)

* * * * *

Fifth Letter

To a thinker who is interested not as much in the *results* of a science as in the variety of *routes* that *the human spirit* follows in its march toward perfection, the fate of the new *critical philosophy*, the way it originated, its first reception, its progress, and the obstacles that have stood in its way, will appear extraordinary indeed. Even the design of a *critical philosophy* is impressive — worthy of its author. It does not try [386] to determine // the *objects of cognition* directly, but the *faculty* itself, and through that the objects to which the latter refers. But because of the *retreat* that reason finds so hard, and the complete *surrender* of cognitions which it believed to be already securely in its possession, it could expect only a cold reception to begin with. But the *critical philosophy* did not relent in its demands upon *dogmatic* philosophy, and finally it began slowly to attract attention. People divided into parties. One party tried to fortify itself within its ancient holding, while the other tried also to make its claims acceptable. In spite of the great crowd that made gestures of being active in the fight, however, an observer would have noticed that it was only the leaders of the two parties who were actually engaged in a duel. For the most part, both the dogmatists and the critical philosophers do nothing but *jurare in verba magistri*; in almost all of the textbooks, the *compendia*, the journals, etc., that daily flood the literary world, there is neither more nor less to be seen than Baumgarten's *Metaphysics*[38] and Kant's *Critique of Pure Reason*, without the least alteration. And after all the effort and expense we still find no more gold in the crucible than we put in it to begin with. There are independent thinkers however — though they are but few — for whom nothing is as insulting as this *slavery of the mind*; and they are not only trying to draw those remarkable theories [387] from their springs, but // are even tracking down the *sources of* the *springs*, following them through their *deeps* and *shallows* along the many *turnings* and *windings* imposed on them by the accident of circumstances. Just those independent thinkers who are convinced by the *Critique of Pure Reason* that a critique of that kind is indispensable for the grounding and securing of universally valid principles of knowledge, [now] find that the one provided by the originator of the idea of critique is not the *only one possible* — nor is it even the *best that is possible*. They differ, however, [as to the reason why.] For one of them, the principles upon which the *Critique of Pure Reason* rests are not sufficiently *abstract* and *universal* to be the principles of our entire knowledge; for the other, the opposite is true, i.e., those principles, precisely because of their broad *universality*, are too *indeterminate* to establish anything about our *real knowledge*.

This difference in the outlook of independent thinkers should not strike anyone as strange. Even among *mathematicians* there have been always some who were intent on demonstrating the propositions accepted as *axioms* in geometry, and thus *decreasing* their number, whereas others insist on *increasing* them. Both have good reason for their // demands. The first insist on the greatest possible *unity* [388] and on the *absolute necessity of the principles* of the science. The others prefer instead to relax this requirement, which does not contribute anything to the *extension* [of the science] but only to its *grounding* and *systematic order*, in order to satisfy another much more important requirement. Hence they prefer to accept as an *axiom* a proposition which, although evident enough in itself, cannot be demonstrated from the accepted axioms (such as, for instance, the postulate of parallels), instead of being obliged to reject it altogether because of its indemonstrability.

Precisely this difference in outlook is what has set me at variance with that most worthy and astute philosopher, Prof. Reinhold whom I esteem so highly. Both of us recognize the *necessity* of a *critique of the faculty of cognition*; both of us value Kant's *Critique of Pure Reason* as a masterpiece of its kind that is secured against any objection coming from *dogmatic* philosophy. But there is this difference between us: Prof. Reinhold, endowed as he is with much philosophical perspicacity, and inclined as he is toward *abstractions*, considers *philosophy* to be a self-grounding science, isolated from all the rest. *Philosophy* is for him the science of what is determined simply through the *faculty of cognition*. // For a *philosophy* to be possible as a science grounded [389] on necessary and universally valid principles, nothing more is necessary than to bring together into a *system*, through reflection and in accordance with principles, what announces itself in consciousness as the condition of cognition generally. This, indeed, is what the *Critique of Pure Reason* has done; but Mr. Reinhold believes that it has not gone far enough.

In his opinion it should have reached much further back and should have uncovered a *highest principle* to which all the others are subordinated. This is what he believes he has done in his *Theory of the Faculty of Cogniton* where he lays down his *principle of consciousness* as such a highest principle.

Whereas I, on the contrary, am far from reproaching Kant's *Critique* for the lack of a *highest principle,* for as I shall show later any such *highest principle can* not only *be dispensed with,* but is also intrinsically *impossible.* My claim is that *philosophy* is the science of the possibility of a science in general, i.e., of the possibility of a system of cognitons in general. The principle of each and every science, i.e., whatever is determined in itself *prior* to the science, and *independently* of it, and through which everything in the science is determined, must be different [390] from the principles of any other // science, just as the object of each and every science must be different from the object of any other. The higher the principles, however, the more universal and indeterminate they must be in respect to the science in which they serve as principles. Thus far we know of no absolutely highest principle, no principle determined only through itself. The principle of contradiction is indeed an absolutely first principle, but simply as *conditio sine qua non,* and it is only relevant to the thought of an entirely indeterminate object in general, not to the cognition through thought of determinate objects. Mr. Reinhold's principle of consciousness appears to be a transcendental first principle only because Mr. Reinhold defines its subject (consciousness) more narrowly than he should have done for the use he puts it to. The defects and lacunae that he believes he has discovered in the Kantian critique rest either on unjustified demands, or on demands to which, if they are justified, he does far less justice in his *Theory of the Faculty of Representation* than Kant did in his *Critique of Reason* (as can easily be shown).

In his essay (*Contributions to the Rectification of Misconceptions hitherto held by Philosophers*) "On the relationship of the *Theory of the Faculty* [391] *of Representation* to the *Critique of Pure Reason*"[40] // he identifies the defects and the lacunae that the *Critique* has left behind, but which his *Theory* has corrected or remedied. He does this with such perspicacity, and such a display of thoroughness, that one is bound to marvel at his skill in the matter. But how far are his claims justified or unjustified? This is what we shall now test:

On page 273 he says:

> Not only has the *Critique of Reason* not laid down any first principle for the whole of philosophy, nor for the science of the faculty of representation; it has none for the theory of the faculty of cognition in general either, none for the particular theories of the particular faculties of cognition,

none for the theory of sensibility, understanding, and reason. The proposition which it offers as *supreme* in the System of the Principles of Pure Understanding (p. 193, new edition), 'Every object stands under the conditions of the synthetic unity of the manifold in a possible intuition', is only the principle for the employment of the understanding in experience, i.e., the supreme law of experience inasmuch as the latter is possible through sensibility and understanding. And, so as not to be misunderstood, or even just in order to be provable, it presupposes the right theory of sensibility, understanding, and the faculty of representation.[41]// [392]

So the *Critique of Reason* has not laid down any *first principle for the whole of philosophy*! But I know of no other *principle* except the principle of contradiction that can be called the *first principle of all philosophy* (at least as *conditio sine qua non*). And the *Critique of Reason* was certainly not the first to establish *this*; for it presupposes it as already granted. If by the *first principle*, however, Mr. Reinhold understands not just the *conditio sine qua non*, but a *constitutive principle* (one that determines the object), I do not see why he will not accept the one adduced, 'Every object stands . . . .' What advantage would his own *principle of consciousness* have over it?

"But," says Mr. Reinhold, "this proposition is only the fundamental law of the employment of the understanding in experience, the supreme law of experience, etc."[42]

Why just "of experience"? On the contrary it is the law of all *real thought* in general, and even a *a priori objects* (those of mathematics) must be determined, *qua real objects*, in accordance with it. // [393]

The *Critique of Reason* has not laid down, moreover, any supreme principle for the *science of the faculty of representation* because, unlike Mr. Reinhold, the author of the *Critique* does not hold *representation* to be the most universal function or the *faculty of representation* the most universal faculty. *Representing* already presupposes the *thought* of an object to be represented. I do not comprehend how Mr. Reinhold can claim that the *Critique of Reason* has not laid down any supreme principle for the *faculty of cognition* in general, or any for the particular theories of the particular faculties of cognition, etc. Of course the *forms of sensibility* laid down in the *Critique of Reason* are principles of *sensibility*; the *forms of thought* are principles of *understanding qua faculty of thought*; the *categories* are principles of the faculty of cognition (in a narrow sense), etc. But [it is said] these are not first principles! Why not? What other principles are they derived from? As I have already remarked, the *principle of consciousness* presupposes *representation* — and this presupposes the *thought* of an *object* of which it is the *representation*, and consequently it also presupposes the *principles of thought*.

Page 276:

[394]   It (the *Critique of Reason*) has not at all explored the question // of what
a priori and *a posteriori* cognitions have in common, or the question of
how cognition in general differs from representation in general, or which
kinds of representations go to make up cognition generally, etc., for this
fell outside its aim, etc.[43]

But of course the *Critique* has explored the question of what *a
priori* and *a posteriori* cognitions have in common, and it has found
the common element to be the above mentioned principle of all real
thought, viz., *the synthetic unity of the manifold in a possible intuition.*
Cognition in general is distinguished from *representation in general* by
the fact that *qua characteristic representation* can also refer to an *arbitrary
thought* — *cognition* always refers instead to a *real thought.* I have a
representation of a two-sided figure (I represent the figure through the
determination of two sides) but no *cognition* of it, for a two-sided
figure cannot be given *qua real object*, and the like.

Page 279:

The proofs for the priority of the forms of intuitions based on the necessity
and universality of *mathematical propositions* are of course admirable, but
they only convince those who already have a determinate concept of
[395]   intuition, who concede the absolute necessity of those propositions, //
and who do not declare the whole necessity of mathematics to be hypothetical, as even a few mathematicians do.[44]

I would like to know who these "few mathematicians" are. Of course
applied mathematics is *hypothetical.* If a planet moves in an ellipse, the
rotation periods are always proportionate to the surface segments (as
determined by the *radius vector*), and the like. But how *pure mathematics*
could be hypothetical is to me incomprehensible. Just because I can
say, instead of 'The sum of the angles of a triangle equals two right
angles', 'If a figure is a triangle, the sum etc.', the proposition does
not genuinely become *hypothetical.*

The priority of the forms of representations is not demonstrated in the
Theory of the Faculty of Representation from their necessity; rather, the
necessity is demonstrated from the priority and the latter from the
possibility of consciousness.[45]

The priority of the principle of consciousness itself, however, must
finally be demonstrated from the necessity by which if manifests itself
as principle.

Page 281:

[396]   The concepts of *representation, sensible perception,* // *objects, connection*
and *necessity* are clearly necessary components of the Kantian concept of

experience, and require that its sense be developed and defined. But the concept is one that *simply cannot be extracted from the Critique of Reason*, for since it is the basis of the Kantian system, it cannot either be constructed on it or defined in its terms without circularity.[46]

But in this respect all principles are the same! The *axioms of mathematics* similarly manifest themselves in consciousness as *first principles* that cannot be derived from others. The *principle of consciousness only expresses what is common* to all principles. With respect to the *particular* to which these refer, however, they are not thereby derived from it or demonstrated through it. A proposition is derived from one or several other propositions only if it is *identical* with the one or the several others in all respects, or if they yield for it the *sufficient* ground—not, however, if they are *insufficient* ground or just a condition in general. *Space* is a ground or a condition of the possibility of *all the objects of mathematics*; yet, no mathematical // proposition can be [397] demonstrated just from the representation of space and its characteristics.

The concept of *experience* is not, of course, drawn in the first place from an already completed *Critique of Reason*, but rather, when properly developed, it is laid down at the foundation of the *Critique*. But the same applies to the *principle of consciousness*: it is not drawn from the *Theory of the Faculty of Representation*, but is laid down at the foundation of it. Even if the principle in general were right, therefore, it would not have any advantage over the Kantian principle in this respect.

> There cannot therefore be any *a priori* synthetic judgement for anyone who denies that experience is as it is conceptualized [in the *Critique*]. He must concede that the necessary and universal judgements have to be synthetic if experience is to be thinkable according to Kant's concept of it. But the moment that he disputes this concept, he is left without any ground for holding those judgements to be synthetic.[47]

But Kant has laid at the foundation of his system not *actual experience*, but only *its possibility*; I do not see how anyone could deny the *concept of experience* whose possibility he assumes as his foundation.[48] The *dogmatist* and the *skeptic* must of course grant the *concept of experience* as Kant defines it—the only difference being that for the dogmatist the *actual employment* of the concept // (which employment he [398] accepts as a fact of consciousness) is grounded in the *things-in-themselves*, whereas for the skeptic any such *intended employment* would be an illusion. The *concept* as such, however, is conceded by all sides.
Page 288:

> But has not Kant opened up another way of demonstrating the presence of *a priori* synthetic judgements—indeed, that it does so independently

actually contains such judgements—indeed, that it does so independently of all experience? Of course, etc. But etc.[49]

On this issue, I have already declared myself.[50] That pure *mathematics* can be supposed to be a hypothetical science makes no sense to me. Pages 296-297:

> According to my own deepest conviction, the proofs through which the *Critique of Reason* demon strates the *necessity* of the representation of time are true and exhaustive; but they are not at all immune from misunderstandings in the way they are presented by it . . . etc. An opponent of critical philosophy will grant this much, viz., that the representation of space is necessary for the representation of the externality of objects, but he will go on to claim that its possibility is only established in the mind by those very external objects which could not be represented as outside of, but next to, one another without its possibility thus being mentally determined. He will indeed concede that the // representation of space etc., is a necessary condition of the representation of the externality of things, but only provided that it has its *ground* in the *things-in-themselves*—somewhat as in the case of gold where its representation must necessarilly *precede* the representation of its pliability, through [some] impression.[51]

[399]

If an opponent of the *critical philosophy* concedes that the representation of *space* is necessary to the representation of the *externality* of objects, what else will still be left to him to allege against it? That the possibility of the representation of space is first established in the mind (how ambiguous) by just these objects outside us? but what does this mean? It is not the *possibility* of the representation of space but its *necessity* that is being determined in the mind through the representation of objects as external to one another; without that necessary representation, these objects could not be represented *qua* outside one another.[52] Likewise it is not the *possibility of the categories*, but their *necessity*, that is being determined through the concept 'objects of possible experience'. An opponent of critical philosophy cannot produce anything against it on this score, therefore.

[400]

Kant too grants that the actual representation of *empirical space* is only // determined through the *objects*. But how can the representation of space that announces itself in consciousness as the *condition* for the representation of the externality of things, and refers to external objects in general, be compared to the representation of *pliability* in the case of *gold*?
Pages 299 and 300:

> It is shown etc., so it is claimed in the *Critique of Pure Reason* that space and time are *representations*, and more precisely, since they each refer only to a simple object, they are *intuitions*. The *Theory of the Faculty of*

Representation shows that space and time [cannot] *in any way be understood* as representations, etc.[53]

Why space and time cannot *in any way be understood as representations*, I do not see. Everything that refers to an object as its characteristic is a representation of it. Space and time are necessary characteristics of sensible objects determined *a priori*; they are not only *representations* in general, therefore, but even necessary ones.

Page 301:

Since space and time cannot in any sense be called representations etc., it is simply impossible that mere ideality, properly understood, should attach to them . . . etc.[54]

It is exactly the other way around! No ideality can accrue to space and time for the reason that they are *necessary representations* of sensible objects, i.e., // they constitute that in virtue of which the latter are   [401] not [just] *sensations in us*, but *objects outside us*.[55]

On page 305, Mr. Reinhold finds great difficulty with Kant's deduction of the categories, and believes that he has found the ground of this difficulty (among other reasons) also in the fact "that in this whole discussion the concept of *consciousness* has remained *altogether undefined*; what is here understood by consciousness in general is not given at all, nor is what distinguishes it from mere representation, nor how it relates *qua* genus to its species either, etc."[56]

It is pointless, however, to ask for a *determinate concept* of consciousness in *general*. *Consciousness* is *the most universal generic concept* in the faculty of cognition. It cannot be defined therefore through any *higher generic concept* but must remain by nature *indeterminate*. Indeed, it was precisely because Mr. Reinhold tried to define something that does not allow of being defined at all, that he introduced determinations into the *concept* of *consciousness in general* that do not belong there. But when this concept goes, then the entire *theory* based on it falls with it.

Page 307:

In my opinion the principle of the synthetic unity of apperception is not being rightly expressed if nothing else // is asserted than that every   [402] manifold of intuition is subject to the conditions of the original synthetic unity, since every manifold of any representation whatever – including that of *sensation* and *concept* – must be subject to these conditions.[57]

What is this supposed to mean? It is the manifold of the *concept* and of *sensation* that is subject to the conditions of the original synthetic unity. An *empirical* concept or one given *a priori* in some mode or other is subject to them, not *qua concept*, but *qua intuition*. A *transcendental* concept does not contain any *manifold*, but refers simply to the *manifold of intuition*.[58] But if by 'transcendental concepts' Mr. Reinhold also means those which, simply *qua* concepts, already stand to one another in a relation of reciprocity, as for instance 'cause and effect', 'substance and accident', and the like, then these are not only subject to the conditions of the *synthetic unity*, but to those of the unity that I have called *analytic-synthetic*.[59] 'Cause and effect', are not indeed *identical*; in the principle referring to them, therefore, viz., 'Each and every cause has an effect', or its converse, their combination is only a synthesis. yet *cause* (simply *qua concept*) must be defined through 'what has an effect' (and the converse also applies), and to [403] this extent—since its // *subject* has no *meaning* without the *predicate* —the principle is *analytical*.

The manifold of *sensation*, however, is never comprehended in a synthetic unity, for otherwise sensation would not be just *sensation* (of an inner state of the subject) but *intuition* (of an object). Kant's principle refers no more to mere *concepts* than to *sensations*, but rather to real objects.

All the other defects and lacunae that Mr. Reinhold claims to have noted in the *Critique of Reason*, but to have corrected in his *Theory of the Faculty of Representation*, are in no way more justified than the one that I have presented here. I shall not dwell on them any longer, therefore, since I could not do so without repeating myself.

(end of Fifth Letter)

*   *   *   *   *

Sixth Letter

My intention in the previous letter was to show that the lacunae, defects and imperfections that Mr. Reinhold believes he has found in the *Critique of Pure Reason* and rectified in his *Theory of the Faculty of Representation* have no foundation in reality. What I now want to do is to display for your examination, and that of every independent thinker, the lacunae, the defects and imperfections that I have found [404] in it, and the way in which I have tried to rectify them in // my *Critique of the Faculty of Cognition*.

I. The *Critique of Reason* has shown the transition from logic to transcendental philosophy, from formal to real thought. But it has not shown how logic itself attained the dignity of a systematic science based on universally valid principles.

The *Critique of Reason* presupposes *logic* as a science long since perfected;

it is a science which has not had to take a step *backward* since Aristotle, but which has also been unable so far to take one *forward*. Its *axioms* (the principle of contradiction and identity) are *necessary* and *universally valid*. Its *postulates* (the forms of possible thought) are both *self*-grounded and grounded *negatively* in the *axioms* (they do not contradict them); and they are so determined, by simple reflection on thought in general, that they cannot be subject to any increase or decrease, or essential improvement. Its *theorems* are derived *from the axioms* and *in accordance* with them. Having made this assumption, the *Critique of Reason* investigates the possibility of *real* thought, i.e., of attributing *forms* which with reference to an *object // in general* are merely *possible*,   [405] to *objects given outside thought* in a *determinate way*. As regards objects determined *a priori* (i.e., those of mathematics), it finds the ground of their *possibility* in their *possible presentation a priori* (i.e., in the fact that it is only possible to present them through forms determined by thought, or in other words, they can be constructed); as regards *empirical objects*, it finds the ground in the *possibility of experience* in general. (The distinction between these two modes of explanation should be noted at once here. The reason for instance why I affirm, universally and apodictically, that the *predicate* 'three angles' belongs to the *subject* 'three-sided figure' is that I cannot construct such a three-sided figure otherwise than with three angles. The reason, however, why I think 'fire' (say) to be the cause of 'a stone warming up' is not that 'fire' and 'the warmth of a stone' can only be presented in this relationship, *qua these determinate objects*, but it is that only in this relationship *experience* is possible with reference to *objects in general*.) It shows that the forms of thought are employed in respect to *determinate objects of experience* only *qua* conditions of the *possibility of experience in general*, etc. //   [406]

I have shown, however, that the *logical forms* have no meaning at all when abstracted from their *transcendental meaning*. I demand of any philosopher to give me, for instance, the determinate meaning of *logical affirmation* and *negation* in abstraction from their corresponding *transcendental concepts 'reality'* and *'negation'*. Under 'affirmation' I can envisage in thought nothing but the kind of relationship between *subject* and *predicate* that determines a *real* objective *thought* (though not always a real object); under 'negation', on the other hand, the kind of relation through which any *real* objective *thought* is removed, and what is left over is only a subjective *thought* of the relation. I think, for instance, a 'right-angled triangle', in other words, I affirm of 'triangle' that it can be 'rectangular'; 'triangle' is thereby determined as a *real* object, i.e., a *reality* is brought forth. [Again] I think 'triangle' as having 'three angles', or I affirm that it must have 'three angles'. In this case a *new property* of it grounded in the object is determined thereby— not indeed a *new object*, but a *reality* just the same. And even in those cases where the *subject* does not have any *reality* in itself, and hence it is not possible through the attribution of a *predicate* to determine a property any more than the *object* (for a nothingness

[407] cannot have any // property), thought can nevertheless have a *reality* grounded in the *object* being thought as a reality; take, for instance, 'a regular decagon is regular': 'regular decagon' is of course impossible *qua object*, but since it is still thought as possible, the thought of it as 'regular' has of course objective reality in conformity to the *law of contradiction*, even though a *real object* is not thereby being determined, any more than a *property* of it.

In contrast, I deny that 'triangle' has 'four angles'; I give notice thereby that 'triangular' and 'quadrangular' stand in such a relation that they reciprocally annul each other, and that I cannot think them in an *objective* unity of consciousness, but only in a *subjective* one (the identity of self-consciousness); and that if they are thought in an *objective* unity, the result is a *negation*.

Thus relative and logical *reality* and *negation* (affirmation and denial) presuppose the *transcendental* and *absolute* categories; otherwise they would not have any meaning at all—and the same also holds for all the other forms. *Logic*, therefore, far from being the premise of

[408] *transcendental philosophy*, must have it as its premise instead. //

The *Critique of Reason* inverts this order. under the excuse of dealing with pure *logic*, separated even from *transcendental philosophy*, it accepts the *logical forms* as if they could not be improved upon—it assumes them just as their original author abstracted them haphazardly from the *practical use* for which they were intended, even though without a previous *critique* they cannot be either correctly *determined* or *complete in number*, and cannot have either a *meaning* or a *ground*. This is what it then puts at the foundation of a *Transcendental Philosophy*.

You can easily be persuaded of the validity of the objection I am raising against the *Critique of Reason* by the way in which it uses the *logical forms* as guides in the search for the *categories*. This is a point which I now want to submit to your scrutiny, as briefly as I can.

First the *Critique of Reason* divides the forms of judgements under four principal headings—quantity, quality, relation, and modality—each of which in turn includes under itself three forms. This much I presuppose as known. I note, however,

(1) that the forms of *quantity* are not *essential* to the *original* judgements (those not derived in the first instance from others); for such judgements

[409] have in fact no *quantity* at all. Only those have *quantity* // which seem to be *original*, but which are in fact the *conclusions* of *abbreviated syllogisms*. What else, for instance, is the ground of this universal analytic judgement: 'every ab is a' ('Every man, or every animal which is determined by its humanity is animal') save the fact that I immediately

see, in the first place, 'a' to be contained in 'ab', and then again, 'ab' in *every* 'ab' ('abc', 'abd', 'abe', etc.)? I am here combining two *original* analytical judgements that have no quantity, but from them I immediately derive the judgement given as universal. In the universal synthetic judgement, 'every a is b' (e.g., 'Every three-sided figure has three angles'), I combine the synthetic judgement 'a is b' ('three-sided figure is triangular') which is without *quantity* with the analytical one, 'every a is a' ('Every three-sided figure is three-sided'), and the same holds of every supposed *original* judgement; considered as simple judgements they have no *quantity*.

(2) According to their *quality* judgements are divided into affirmative, negative and infinite. These last, however, do not in fact constitute a particular class of judgements according to the meaning and the value hitherto attributed to them. 'a is not b' is a negative judgement; 'a is not-b' is an infinite one, but it is assumed to be equivalent to the other. Thus these two forms of judgements // are distinct from one another simply in the *way they designate*, not essentially. [410]

(3) According to *relation* judgements are divided into categorical, hypothetical and disjunctive. Hypothetical judgements, however, do not have a meaning, or a use, different from that of categorical judgements. It is within my discretion to call every judgement worthy of the name either categorical or hypothetical just as I please. For instance, instead of the categorical judgement: 'The sum of the angles of a triangle equals two right angles', I can posit the following hypothetical one: 'If a figure is triangular, the sum of its angles equals two right angles', and similarly in other cases. In other words, we have arrived at the form of the hypothetical judgement simply on the basis of its intended *employment in experience* — which employment, however, is not conceded by the *skeptic* who declares it rather to be just an *illusion*. But the *Critique of Reason* happens to put a lot of weight on this form. In this way it runs into an obvious *circle* — for it takes a form, whose origin the *logic* is unable to account for, and which without prior *critique* is lifted from its supposed *use in experience*, and puts it back at the foundation of precisely this *use*.[60]

(4) According to *modality* judgements are divided into apodictic, problematic and assertoric. // Apodictic are (a) all the *analytical* judgements, and (b) the *synthetic* ones determined with necessity through *construction*. By 'problematic', therefore, we can only mean those judgements in which the combination of subject and predicate is determined either as *positively* possible or at least, on the basis of a construction, as *negatively* so (not impossible). But what can 'assertoric judgements' possibly refer to? Logicians will offer me the example: 'Alexander is the son of Philip', Well and good. What does this proposition mean, however? If it means: 'Philip is the *actual cause* of [411]

Alexander', or 'Philip must *come first*, and Alexander necessarily *follow him*', then this judgement is not just assertoric, but apodictic. If it means, on the other hand: 'According to our perception Philip came first and Alexander followed', then this is in fact just *a perception* —hence no *judgement* at all.

Not only has the *Critique of Reason* omitted, therefore, the most important part [of a critique], the least dispensable in the delineation of the full extent of the understanding—viz., the study of the origin and extent of its forms, and of their true meaning; it has also imported [412] *mistakes //* that have crept into the *use* of these forms into *logic*, as part of their very determination.

II. With respect to the questions concerning our synthetic cognition, the *Critique of Reason* is incomplete.

The *Critique* proceeds as follows: I. It discusses the distinction between *analytic* and *synthetic* judgements, against which I have nothing to object. II. It lays down as an undoubted *fact of consciousness* that all the theoretical sciences (mathematics, science of nature) contain *a priori synthetic* judgements. III. It raises the general question: "*How are a priori synthetic judgements possible?*" And it answers these questions in its own way.

By the *a priori synthetic* judgements of Mathematics, Kant does not understand judgements that refer to *an object in general*, and consequently must apply *a priori* to every *determinate object* (as is the case with the first principle of the analytical judgements, the principle of contradiction). In fact *mathematics* does not contain judgements of this sort, for all the judgements that belong to it *qua* mathematics refer to determinate objects. By the synthetic judgments of mathematics [413] // he means, rather, those that refer to determinate objects of pure mathematics, and consequently must apply *a priori* to all the *empirical* objects that are to be subsumed under them. His answer to the question: "How are *a priori* synthetic judgements in general possible?" is "Through construction," i.e., we must attribute to the subjects of these judgements (i.e., the objects of mathematics) the predicates determined through them because apart from such predicates the subjects could not be presented as *real objects*. Hence what is explained as a consequence of the necessity intrinsic to the judgements with reference to the *pure* objects of mathematics, is just the *a priori* universality of the same judgements with reference to the *empirical objects* to be subsumed under him—but not the *necessity* itself.

Does not the way we explain the possibility of *a priori* synthetic judgements differ *toto coelo* from the way we explain that of *a priori* analytic judgements? To the question: "Why am I not permitted to attribute to this or that *determinate object* any predicate that would contradict its concept?" the answer is" "Because I am not allowed to attribute to any *object in general* predicates that would contradict its concept." Thus I immediately derive the *particular* proposition from the *universal* principle—which principle I think without reference to any *real* object, i.e., simply by means of signs that refer to an *object of thought in general.* On the other hand, to the question: "Why do I think that a // regular figure delimited by three or more lines is possible, but not one delimited by two?" the answer is not: "Because I cannot think any *object in general* otherwise," or even "Because I cannot think any *real object in general* otherwise," but rather: "Because I cannot think *this* object otherwise." *Before* answering the particular question therefore: "*How are synthetic judgements possible in mathematics?*", and even before answering: "*how are a priori synthetic judgements in general possible?*" the *Critique of Reason* should have first answered the other question: "*How are synthetic judgements possible simply qua judgements, without reference to the empirical objects to be subsumed under them, with respect to which they are a priori?*" I comprehend perfectly well how the mathematical proposition that I have adduced on the assumption of its *intrinsic necessity* with reference to an *object of pure mathematics,* must apply to *every* empirical *object* that is to be subsumed under it. But how am I to comprehend this *necessity* in itself from some universal *principle*? With reference to the *empirical objects* that are to be subsumed under it, a proposition of this sort would indeed be intrinsically *a priori*. But as long as its *necessity* is not explainable from some universal *principle*, are we to compare it with an *a posteriori* proposition? I think this *determinate object* in this determinate fashion. But // why? Because the objects cannot be otherwise presented in *construction*.

It is clear from the answer to the question: "*How are synthetic a priori judgements possible in the science of nature?*" that the question itself has a meaning just as different from that of "*How are analytical judgements possible?*" as from "*How are a priori synthetic judgements possible in mathematics?*" The meaning of the former [of these two last questions] amounts to this: "How can we predicate *a priori* something necessary of any determinate object, *prior* to the knowledge of its particular determinations?" To which the answer is: "*Prior* to the knowledge of its particular determinations, we must predicate of any determinate object whatever we must predicate of an *object in general*." The latter question means: "How can we predicate of *determinate objects,* with *necessity,* as being first determined not through these *determinate objects* but through the *form of cognition* with respect to an *object in general,* predicates that are only given through *those very objects?*" To which the answer is: "Through *construction*." And as we have already indicated, this answer is admittedly unsatisfactory.[61]

[414]

[415]

On the other hand, the question: "*How are a priori synthetic judgements possible in the science of nature?*" does not like the former mean: "How

[416]   can we // predicate anything with necessity of every *empirical object?*" (for in fact we do not indifferently predicate anything synthetically of every *empirical object*). Nor does it mean: "How can we predicate of *determinate objects* anything synthetic *a priori?*" as the other question does (for to answer, "[on the base of the] *possibility of experience,*" would not be satisfactory, because no *empirical objects* to which the *a priori* synthetic judgements would refer are determined by that answer).[62] It means rather: "*On what ground* do we refer *synthetic judgements, a priori*, to *empirical objects* in general, without specifying to which?" And to this question the answer is: "We do this on the ground of the *possibility of experience*, for *empirical objects* can be *objects of possible experience* only through these judgements."[63] When I judge that 'a is the cause of b', I do not think the given *objects* 'a' and 'b' in the relation of cause and effect because I must think not just these, but all objects in general, in this way. This is in fact not the case, for I do not think 'a' and 'c' in that relation. Nor is the relation first given to me *through* the objects at issue, for otherwise I would not be able to predicate it of them in a *necessary* fashion. I can do this, rather, because only on the assumption that the relation holds in all cases between

[417]   empirical // objects can the objects make *experience* possible.

I do not find any contradiction in supposing a 'figure' to be 'bilinear'. Nor can I determine *a priori* that no such figure can be constructed, but first I must attempt to construct it, and in doing this I see that the construction is impossible. On the other hand, when I think 'fire' (say) to be the cause of 'warmth', I do so not because to suppose otherwise would involve a contradiction, nor because 'fire' and 'warmth' are immediately perceived by me in the stated relation (perception cannot yield any necessity based on it). The reason is rather because, apart from that relation, I would have the merely contingent *perception* of the succession of warmth upon fire, not however an *experience* of it in accordance with universal laws.

The *Critique of Reason*, in other words, lumps together questions of entirely different meaning, and expresses them in one single form. The answer it gives, therefore, necessarily fails to satisfy some of them taken individually.

III. The *Critique of Reason* has not provided any criterion of real thought.

[418]   //The *Critique of Reason* establishes *real* thought or *cognition* on the base of a *manifold* that is given in intuition in general to the *unity* of form. It does not give any a priori *criterion*, however, by which to recognize whether a given *manifold* can be thought in a *unity of form*

at all, still less, in which unity. Not every given *manifold* lends itself *in principle* to being thought in some *objective unity* or other. 'Regular figure' and 'three (or more) lines' can be thought [together] under the form of *affirmation* (as possible); 'figure' and 'two lines', under the form of *negation* (as impossible). On the other hand, 'figure' and 'virtue' can no more be thought [together] in the form of *affirmation* than in that of *negation*. We can no more say: 'A figure is virtuous' than 'It is not virtuous', In the manifold given to thought, therefore, we must exhibit an *a priori criterion* by which we can recognize not only whether *the manifold in question* can *in principle* be thought in some *objective unity* or other, but also in *which unity* it can be thought.

The reason, however, why the *Critique of Reason* has not sought to exhibit any such *criterion* for *real thought*—indeed, has not even // suspected that it is indispensable—lies simply in the fact that it has utterly separated *general logic* from *transcendental philosophy*; it has considered the former as *standing on its own*, and has placed it at the foundation of the latter. And yet, *logic* itself must be subjected, as I have already shown, to a *Critique of the Faculty of Cognition* if its *forms* are to have *meaning* and any *employment* at all. How this is so will have to be established in yet greater detail in the following. [419]

IV. The *Critique of Reason* has raised the question *quid juris*, i.e., "What right do we have to employ, with respect to empirical objects, concepts and judgements that are pure and *a priori*?" And it has answered it by showing that we must employ these concepts and judgements as conditions of the possibility of experience in general. There still remains the question *quid facti*, however, that is, whether in fact we do so use them with respect to empirical objects. Their employment cannot be taken as an undoubted fact of consciousness, for this consciousness might rest on an illusion to be explained on psychological grounds.

There still remains the further question: "Since these *concepts* and *propositions* have their reality simply as conditions of the *possibility of experience* in general, how can they refer to *determinate* // objects of experience?" From the fact that *objects* must be thought *in general* in the relationship, for instance, of cause and effect if an *experience* is to be at all possible, it still cannot be explained why (e.g.) 'fire' and 'warmth' in particular must stand in this relationship. [420]

To this the *Critique of Reason* answers of course: "That this is so is immediately determined by the *faculty of judgement*." Judgement, however, as I see it, can only consist in the comparison of an *object* with a *rule* in virtue of which it comes to be *determined* —not in its comparison with a *rule* that [only] establishes the possibility of an *object of experience* in general. If I judge, e.g., 'this plate is round', I am of course comparing 'the plate' with the *rule*, thought *a priori*, in virtue of which 'round figure' is determined as object and thus becomes, through this comparison, a *characteristic* of 'plate'. The relationship of *causality*, on the contrary, is not a characteristic of the particular *empirical objects* to which it is referred, but simply the *condition* of the possibility of an experience of, or of the necessary link between, empirical objects in general.

[421]   *To judge* is not the function of a *particular faculty*, but simply // a *decision* [*ein Urtheil* regarding the *identity of the characteristics* of the *object* with certain determinate *concepts*. This kind of identity simply cannot occur in the *judgements of experience*.

> V. The *Critique of Reason* has not sufficiently discussed the representations necessary with respect to sensible objects, i.e., time and space.

It has shown that time and space are not *empirical* representations (characteristics of empirical objects). Hence they must be *forms of sensibility* determined *a priori* in the mind. That they are *original* forms, however, is not thereby proven, for they could be the *product* of a *function of the faculty of cognition*, yet be *taken* as *original* because of an *illusion* of the imagination. And if it is possible to show, according to known laws of psychology, how this could have come about, to *explain* them as originating in some *ground* is much more in keeping with scientific practice than to *assume* them as *original*, as an *indolent philosophy* would do.

And it so happens that space and time can be *a priori forms or conditions* [only] *of the sensible perception of a difference between empirical* [422]   *objects*. // They *originally* refer, therefore, merely to objects which are represented as *different* through *intrinsic characteristics* —not to any that would not admit of *differentiation*. Originally, for instance, a river made up of like parts is not represented in space. This only happens by referring its parts to the adjacent unlike parts of the objects on the bank. Through an *illusion of the imagination*, however, we are led to believe that the river is to be represented *in itself* in space, and the like. Since we become accustomed early enough to such references, so it is no wonder if we believe ourselves unable to dispense with the representation of space. The same can also be shown with regard to time.[64]

> VI. The *Critique of Reason* has obtained its whole doctrine of the ideas surreptitiously, for it derives them from the nature of reason whereas they originate in fact, as it is easy to show, from the nature of the imagination.

The *Critique of Reason* deduces the *ideas* from the *forms of reason*. It defines *reason* as the *faculty of principles*. According to it *reason* presses for *totality in the employment of the understanding* (which is restricted merely to experience). Thus *ideas //* are the representations of [423] this *totality* taken in its various moments. But this whole doctrine is surreptitious. It is not *reason* but the *imagination* that presses for *totality in the employment of the understanding. Reason* is not the *faculty of principles* but the *faculty to judge indirectly according to principles*, just as it has been defined traditionally. How large the series of the judgements to be combined may be is not determined by the nature of reason, and neither is the *absolute necessity of their principles.* "To deduce" means no more than to infer (from principles assumed hypothetically). *Reason* determines just the *form*; the *reality* of the *principles* themselves (their material truth) is determined through *sensibility* and *understanding* instead.

To extend empirical representations *beyond the limits of experience*, and to represent *absolutely* what is *restricted* by *conditions of experience* is on the contrary a *function of the productive* (poetic) *imagination. Ideal fictions* that cannot be met in *any experience* are of this type. Our desire for *totality* of cognition is grounded in the desire for the supreme *// perfection.* The *representation* of this *totality* in the form of *object*, [424] however, goes against the very desire [for it] — it is a function of our *limitation.*

Everything, therefore, that the *Critique of Reason* wants to ground on the so-called *ideas of reason* (religion, morality) is grounded in fact on our innate *desire for the supreme perfection.* But this desire is not a *formal principle of reason*, something that *belongs specifically* to it. but is *common* rather to all faculties.

What *religion* and *morality* might gain or lose by interpreting *ideas* in the *Critique's* way or in mine, or whether in this respect both ways are perhaps equivalent — this is not to be discussed here. From what has been said you can see how the *Critique of Reason* tries to enrich *logic* and *transcendental philosophy* at the expense of *psychology*, and how the entire *foundation* of my skepticism hinges on the discovery that the procedure upon which both *dogmatism* and *criticism* depend is illegitimate. // [425]

(end of Sixth Letter)
* * * * *

Seventh Letter

"Well!" I can just hear you exclaim, "You are not willing to grant me that *skepticism* consists, among other things, also in the claim that *reason* cannot determine anything regarding the *limits of our knowledge*; you hold rather that reason can indeed, after due *critique*, determine these *limits*, and must determine them *prior* to the *employment* of cognition. You consider my skeptical objections against the *Kantian Critique* unfounded, but grant for the most part my objections against Mr. Reinhold's *Foundational Doctrine*, and find so many defects and omissions, and such substantial ones, even in the *Critique of Reason* that you believe yourself to be justified in pursuing a *Critique of the Faculty of Cognition* of your own, so as to assign *limits* to *skepticism* just as to *dogmatism*. And how do you start? Which *principles* do you lay down as the foundation of your critique? Which *limits of human cognition* do you intend to establish as insuperable? and which *conclusions* that defy doubt will you bring forth?[''']

[426] To do justice to these questions is the aim of this letter. Since I have dealt in detail with the whole matter in // the present work, I shall be satisfied now with a brief survey.

In my *Logic* I proceed from the assertion that *general logic* must indeed be separated from *transcendental logic*, and yet must be dealt with with the latter constantly in view. The *fundamental propositions* of logic and its *forms* presuppose *transcendental principles*, without which they have no meaning at all. No other meaning can be given them, in other words, than that which is determined by these *transcendental principles*.

Accordingly the *object of logic* is an X which is *not* indeed *determined* by inner characteristics, but is *determinable* through the *conditions of the thought of a real object* in general. It is not the X of an *algebraic equation* for which we can only substitute a quantity determinable through the *conditions of the problem*.

This being premised, I move on to determine the *principles* and *forms* of logic. The principles are those of *contradiction* and, immediately derived from it, of *identity*. The *principle of contradiction* presupposes
[427] a *thought* // *object*, i.e., the combination of a manifold in a unity of consciousness. Contradiction only occurs immediately between *opposed forms*. 'a contradicts not-a' does not logically have any meaning at all. To have a meaning, it must be taken as saying: 'a is necessary' or 'a is actual' or 'a is possible' contradicts 'a is not necessary' or 'a is not actual' or 'a is not possible', or also: 'a is b' contradicts 'a is not b', i.e., it must say that the combination according to a *given form* contradicts the combination (with reference to just the same product of combination) according to an *opposing form*. In contrast, what does not contain a combination according to some form cannot be thought as incurring contradiction with itself.

I proceed now to determine the forms in conformity with their division in the *Critique of Reason*.
I. I note that the *forms of quantity*, i.e., universality, particularity and

individuality, are not employed at all in the *original* judgements (those not derived from others), but only in judgements which are *produced by way of inferences* but are taken by mistake to be *original*, because the inferences are abbreviated. I have already made this point in the preceding letter, and have expanded on it with examples; in order to avoid repetitions I only need to refer to it.[65] //   [428]

II. The *forms of quality*: affirmation, denial and indeterminacy (infinity), do indeed have a ground. 'Affirmation' means a *real combination* of *subject* and *predicate* according to the *principle of determinacy* which we shall have to define later on. 'Negation' means a *separation* grounded on a previously thought *combination* of the subject and a predicate *opposed* to the one being given. 'Infinity' means a merely *subjective* combination (based on the identity of the subject) in virtue of which the possibility of an objective combination as well as separation is denied.

III. According to *relation* judgements are divided into categorical, hypothetical and disjunctive. I note, however, that the *hypothetical form* is not a *particular form of judgements*, but rather the *general form* of *inferences*. For instance, the judgement, 'If a is b, a is c' ('If a triangle is equilateral, it is also equiangular'), is equivalent to this other: 'Every a which is b, is c' ('An equilateral triangle is equiangular'); it is distinguishable from it only according to outer form or *expression*.

The most *general form of inference* (the one of the first figure to which all the rest can be reduced) is: 'If a is b and c is a, c is also b'. In other words, we have here the genuinely *hypothetical* // *form*.   [429] An inference is therefore a *hypothetical judgement*, the *antecedent* of which is *composed* of two judgements having a term in common, while the *consequent* is the *conclusion*.

IV. According to *modality*, judgements are divided into apodictic, assertoric and problematic. But since for reasons that I shall have to declare later on I cast doubts on the *empirical employment* of the understanding, I cannot accept assertoric judgements. As for *mathematics*, in which the genuinely objective judgements are to be found, it only admits apodictic and problematic judgements, not assertoric ones at all.

So far logic has lacked, moreover, the *systematic unity* required of every science. People have been more concerned with the *external form* of its components than with their *intrinsic essence*.

The common practice has been to divide logic into the *three* so-called *operations of the understanding* – the doctrine of *concepts*, *judgments* and *inferences*; its parts have been *arranged one after the other in an orderly way*, but not *grasped* in one another.

I have sought to remedy this defect. I show that according to their essence the *three* so-called *operations of the understanding* constitute

[430]   one and the same // *operation of thought*, and stand distinct from one another only in a certain respect. For each of the three parts, therefore, I show how it can be *reduced* to the others. So much for *general logic*.

    As for my *Critique of the Faculty of Cognition*, I first lay down as its foundation a *fact of consciousness*: "We have *synthetic, necessary and universal judgements* that refer *a priori* to determinate *objects*." Then I raise the question: "Since these judgements are *determined* in the first place by *their objects*, how can they refer to them *a priori*?" For instance, I cannot know *prior to the construction* between two points of a straight line that this line is the shortest between them. Just as little could I know, *prior to actual experience*, that the rays of the sun melt ice. In both instances I would only be able to say: "*This is how it is* in my *perception*," but not: "This is how *it must be*. Every straight line that I shall construct in the future will be the shortest one between two points; every time I shall perceive the rays of the sun at the appropriate direction and distance from ice, I shall also perceive the latter melting away." The situation is quite other with *analytical* judgements; since their principle (the principle of contradiction) refers to an *indeterminate*

[431]   // *object in general*, they are not just determined through *determinate* objects.

    The task, therefore, is to find *a synthetic principle* (a first proposition) *that refers to an object in general just as the first analytical principle does, and from which all synthetic judgements referring to determinate objects can be derived.*

    The *Critique of Reason* responds to the question thus: with respect to the synthetic judgements of *mathematics*, the principle is the *possibility of a construction*, and with respect to synthetic *judgements of experience*, it is *the possibility of experience in general*. But see how uneven this answer turns out to be The *possibility of a construction* is, to be sure, *a principle* to which we can reduce all the propositions of *mathematics*. I think 'straight line' as 'the shortest between two points' because only a thought that one be *constructed* has *reality*. And it is not possible to construct 'straight line' except as 'the shortest [between two points]'. Therefore, etc.

    From the *principle*, however, 'Everything that happens, happens according to the laws of *causality*', how can I derive the proposition, 'The rays of the sun necessarily melt ice?' This is *determined through*

[432]   *given objects*. From // the principle it only follows that the *objects of experience* must be thought *in general* as standing to each other in *causal connection* — not, however, that precisely *these objects* must be so related.[66]

    In my opinion, therefore, the answer to the question just raised comes down to this: We only know of synthetic judgements that refer to *objects of a possible experience in general*; we know nothing, however, of synthetic judgements that refer to *determinate objects of actual experience*. *On the assumption* made by the *dogmatists*, the fact that we nevertheless believe that we have such judgements rests on [factors] external to the faculty of cognition. According to *Hume's explanation of the fact*, as developed philosophically by me, it rests on something merely *subjective* (custom), i.e., I put into doubt the *fact* that, with reference to *any determinate object* of experience, we have synthetic (objectively necessary) judgements. For whereas we have no insight into how it is *possible* that we have these judgements [as objectively necessary], we use their *possibility* based on psychological laws, but merely as *subjective* combinations.[67] Now I come to the most important point in my *Critique of the Faculty of Cognition* — the determination, that is, of an *a priori criterion* of real thought.

I have already noted in my previous letter that the *Critique of Reason* puts at the basis of all real thought some *presentation* which is *indeed possible* // *a priori* (a possible construction, a possible experience); [433] it has not given us, however, any characteristic by which we can know *a priori* whether a given object can be presented or not.[68] Whether the manifold we think in a unity of consciousness can be presented as object or not, therefore, cannot be established *a priori* simply with respect to its empirical employment — but it is not knowable in itself. E.g.: I know that 'triangle' is possible only through the actual construction of a triangle. Now, this construction is indeed *a priori* with respect to the empirical employment we have yet to make of it, i.e., I already know even before I find an empirical object marked out in experience in triangular form that some such object is possible. But I first cognize the possibility of 'triangle' as such only through the actual construction of it.

In order to find the required criterion, I had to examine more accurately than had hitherto been done the nature of real thought, and what distinguishes the latter from merely formal as well as from arbitrary thought. I found that there are three relationships in which the manifold bound together by thought can stand with respect to consciousness.// [434]

(1) Subject and predicate can be so related to consciousness in general that neither could be its object without the other. All relative concepts are of this type, such as 'cause' and 'effect', that define one another reciprocally; 'cause' cannot be determined by thought, *qua* concept, without 'effect', and 'effect' not without 'cause'. 'Cause' is 'what produces an effect', and 'effect' is 'what is produced through the cause'. The proposition expressing the combination of 'cause' and 'effect' is therefore an analytic-synthetic one.

'Cause' and 'effect' are not one in the sense of being identical, yet they cannot be determined in thought separately. This proposition is merely formal, however; it expresses a possible relation between objects, themselves indeterminate.

(2) They can also stand in such a relation that each of them without the other (outside the combination) is an object of consciousness. All arbitrary combinations—e.g., 'a stone that attracts gold', and the like—are of this type. Subject and predicate can each occur in consciousness without the other; their being thought in a unity of consciousness does not have, therefore, any objectively real ground, but is something merely arbitrary. In formal thought we have a determinate unity but [435] no manifold. In // arbitrary thought it is the reverse; we find a determinate manifold but no unity. Neither, therefore, can determine any real object.

(3) Subject and predicate can be so related to each other that the object [Objekt] can still be an object [Gegenstand] of consciousness without the predicate, but not vice-versa. All real objects that are determined *a priori* are of this type—such as those of mathematics, e.g., 'straight line', 'right angle', and the like. 'Straightness' cannot be found in consciousness without something that is 'straight', or 'right-angularity' without something that is 'right'. On the other hand, this 'something' (a 'line' or an 'angle') is a determinate object of consciousness even without 'straightness' or 'right-angularity'.

I lay down, therefore, the following principle as criterion of objectively real thought:

The given manifold must be internally so related that the subject can also be an object of consciousness in general by itself, without the predicate, but not the predicate without the subject.

With this criterion I have been able to fix the true reference of the judgements, usually called 'infinite' in logic, with which we would otherwise only make believe to be referring to something. (What we [normally] do with these judgements is to suppose that we have sufficiently determined them, and distinguished them from the negative [436] ones, simply by shoving the 'not' from the copula to the predicate).//

In my opinion, infinite judgements are negative judgements—but they are not grounded on the fact that there is already a predicate that is opposed to the given one included in the subject (as it is the case with the judgement properly called 'negative'), but on the fact that neither the [given] predicate nor its opposite can yield a possible *real* determination, for either can occur in consciousness quite apart from the other. 'A circle is not rectangular' is a negative proposition; 'rectangularity' is opposed to the determination already contained in 'circle'. On the other hand, this proposition: 'A circle is not sweet' is an infinite one, for 'sweet' is no more a possible determination of 'circle' than 'sour'. Philosophers must therefore forego the desire to undertake combinations of all sorts with concepts, apart from this touchstone (on the pretext that the concepts do not contradict one another) and to attribute to them objective reality. Of course they talk of arbitrary concepts, but they never stop to define what the arbitrariness consists in. The upshot is that, since in empirical objects the subject-predicate relationship required for the determination of a real object is not perceived, all these objects can [indeed] be thought on the assumption of the relationship, but they cannot be cognized as such (since the relationship is not seen).//   [437]

The *Critique of Reason* has distinguished cognition from mere thought only one-sidedly; [according to it,] that is, mere thought is just a form that refers, without any given content, to an indeterminate object in general. In a sense, this is correct. I find, however, still another mode of mere thinking which is precisely the opposite of the one just stated, namely thinking a given material as object through a simply logical form of cognition (i.e., through the thought-relationship that is required for objective reality).

'Gold', as 'something yellow' and (so far as we know) as 'the heaviest metal', is accordingly just as little a real object as 'green and the heaviest metal'. But since in space and time we find bound together the characteristics of 'gold', but not those of this [green] metal, we think ourselves justified in presupposing the thought-of relationship in 'gold', but not in the metal, even though we cannot see it [there]—and hence justified in thinking 'gold', to be a real object. This gloss [on the *Critique*] seems to me to be well founded in itself as well as extremely useful for the science. But others might think otherwise!

I am skeptical, therefore, about the empirical employment of the categories on two grounds: In the first place, because of the possibility (previously referred to) of explaining this alleged employment subjectively, as Hume does; and further, because with respect to empirical objects we lack the ground required for the employment of the categories, that is, insight into // the relationship of determinacy   [438] (the fact that the subject can be an object of consciousness as the determinable term in itself, the predicate on the other hand cannot be so in itself but only as a determination of the subject).

In my opinion, therefore, the categories are designed not for empirical employment, but only for employment in the determination *a priori* of the objects of mathematics;[69] this is how I have also presented them in this book.

Here, then, you have a sketchy outline of my entire skeptical system which I lay before you, before every independent thinker, for examination.

I remain, with all the respect due to an independent thinker like yourself,

Your
Philaletes

Notes

1. Philaletes is addressing himself to Aenesidemus.

2. *Philosophischer Briefwechsel, nebst einem demselben vorangeschickten Manifest* was one of the works included in *Streifereien im Gebiete der Philosophie*, Berlin: by Wilhelm Wieweg, 1793, *Gesammelte Werke*, Vol. III, pp. 199-266. The *Briefwechsel* is the record of an actual, and not always friendly, exchange of letters between Maimon and Reinhold. Maimon published the letters without Reinhold's permission. Cf. Pupi, *Reinhold*, pp. 511-523.

3. *Aenesidemus*, p. 20.

4. Ibid., p. 24.

5. Ibid., p. 145. the other proposition states that there are representations in us, and that we find in them characteristics in virtue of which we can distinguish them and also relate them together.

6. Ibid., p. 46, note.

7. "Neue Darstellung," *Beiträge*, Vol. I, p. 167; *Aenesidemus*, p. 58.

8. Maimon has summarized Reinhold's comments following his first proposition. "Neue Darstellung," *Beiträge*, Vol. I, pp. 167-168.

9. *Aenesidemus*, p. 60; slight variations in punctuation; stresses dropped.

10. Ibid., p. 61; slight variations in punctuation; stresses dropped. The reference to Reinhold is in "Ueber das Bedürfniss, die Möglichkeit und die Eigenschaften eines Allgemeingeltenden ersten Grundsatzes," in *Beiträge*, Vol. I, pp. 91-164.

11. *Aenesidemus*, p. 62, note.

12. Ibid., pp. 62-63, note; slight variations in punctuation; stresses dropped. The reference to Reinhold is in *Fundament*, p. 85.

13. *Aenesidemus*, p. 63, note; slight variations in punctuation.

14. Maimon will repeatedly refer to this principle. As stated in *Versuch einer neuen Logik*, it reads as follows:

"The first principle of every genuinely real object is one that I call the *principle of determinability*. It divides in turn into two other principles: (1) Given a proposition, with respect to the *subject* in general: Every subject must be a possible object of consciousness not only *qua* subject but also in itself; (2) Given a proposition, with respect to the *predicate* in general: Every predicate must be a possible object of consciousness not in itself but *qua* predicate (in combination with the subject). Whatever does not conform to these principles can only be a merely *formal* thought, or an altogether *arbitrary* one—not, however, a *real* one." p. 20.

15. *Aenesidemus*, pp. 63-64.

16. "Einleitung zur neuen Revision des Magazins zur Erfahrungssee-lenkunde," *Magazin zur Erhahrungsseelenkunde*, IX, 3 (1792) cf. pp. 9ff; *Gesammelte Werke*, Vol. III, pp. 470ff.

17. *Philosophischer Briefwechsel*, pp. 226-228, notes; pp. 231-234, notes.

18. *Aenesidemus*, pp. 70-71; an exact quotation (which stresses dropped) only up to "of which we are conscious." From that point on, Maimon is only rendering the sense of *Aenesidemus*.

19. Cf. above, notes 16 and 17.

20. *Aenesidemus*, pp. 75-76.

21. Ibid., p. 76; an exact quotation (which stresses dropped) only up to "have in common."

22. "Neue Darstellung," *Beiträge*, Vol. II, p. 168.

23. Ibid., p. 170.

24. Ibid., p. 171.

25. Ibid., p. 173.

26. *Aenesidemus*, pp. 84-85; slight variations in punctuations, stresses dropped.

27. Cf. above, notes 16 and 17.

28. "Neue Darstellung," *Beiträge*, Vol. I, p. 175.

29. Ibid., p. 176.

30. Ibid., p. 178.

31. *Aenesidemus*, pp. 94-95; the exact quotation ends with "Humean skepticism"; stresses are Maimon's.

32. The "Kritik des Erkenntnisvermögens" constitutes Part B of *Versuch einer neuen Logik*.

33. 'Real [*reell*] object' must be understood throughout in the way that Maimon now defines, i.e., as conforming to the principle of determinability. 'Real' means 'adequate' in this context; it is contrasted with 'formal' or 'arbitrary', and it is definitively *not* to be connected with 'existence' in any ordinary meaning of this word.

34. *Versuch einer neuen Logik*, pp. 119-126, 168-169.

35. This is the crucial point that Maimon makes against Kant, and never tires of repeating. It is actually a very strong one, and it was to be raised again by Kant's critics after Maimon over and over again. Kant can be accused of arguing circularly. On the one hand, he uses his categories of relation in order to determine what counts as a genuine 'event'; but on the other, he justifies the use of the same categories on the ground that, apart from them, we would not be able to identify a genuine 'event', And the question whether there ever occurs in experience an 'event' *as Kant defines it* is thus begged. Maimon's point is that *in fact* we do not *perceive* in experience the kind of order which we *think* by means of Kant's categories. What we perceive is rather a certain tendency among appearances to congregate in predictable patterns.

36. But this does not mean that we *perceive* it in that relationship. The whole point of Kant's transcendental deduction, on the other hand, is to establish that objects must be *given in perception* in the way they are thought through the categories.

37. Here Maimon reproduces exactly, omitting only a few lines from pp. 97-98 and some of Schulze's stresses, pp. 97-99 of *Aenesidemus*. A translation of these pages can be found above, pp. 107-8. As usual, in the last few lines of the quotation Maimon departs from the text, but gives a summary of what follows.

38. Alexander Gottlieb Baumgarten (1714-1762), *Metaphysica*, Halle, 1739.

40. "Ueber das Verhältniss der Theorie des Vorstellungsvermögens zur Kritik der reinen Vernunft," *Beiträge*, Vol. I, pp. 255-338.

41. Ibid., p. 273f; "provable" is stressed in Reinhold's text; the exact reference for the *Critique* is A158-B197.

42. Cf. ibid.

43. Ibid., p. 276; slight variations.

44. Ibid., p. 279; in Reinhold's text, this whole passage is in parenthesis.

45. Ibid., p. 279.

46. Ibid., p. 281.

47. Ibid., p. 287; stresses dropped. Notice that this is in essence the objection that Aenesidemus raised against Kant.

48. Maimon is defending Kant by conceding the skeptic's case against him. If *all* that Kant has done is to unfold *a* concept of possible experience, Hume's account of how experiences supposedly occur *in fact* remains unchallenged.

49. "Ueber das Verhältniss," *Beiträge*, Vol. I, p. 288.

50. P. 338.

51. "Ueber das Verhältniss," *Beiträge*, Vol. I, pp. 296-297; slight variations in punctuation.

52. For Maimon, however, the actual presentation of objects in this way can occur only in the imagination, not in perception; hence his skepticism.

53. "Ueber das Verhältniss," *Beiträge*, I, pp. 299-300; slight variations in punctuation and in the stresses.

54. Ibid., p. 301; stresses dropped.

55. Maimon and Reinhold are saying two quite different things. Maimon is interpreting Kant along strictly phenomenalistic lines. Space and time are not ideal in the sense that they allow us to distinguish between 'inner' and 'outer' experience without ever having to transcend the limits of subjectivity. They constitute the 'real' counterpart of concepts and ideas *within* consciousness itself. Reinhold is pushing Kant, on the other hand, towards a more realistic position. Space is indeed a subjective form; as such, however, it necessitates the subject's reference of its sensible content to a term outside consciousness. "This form present in the mind is precisely that *through which* the mind refers itself . . . prior to all representation to things outside it. . . ." (*Theorie*, p. 396). Hence Reinhold objects to critical philosophy being called, strictly speaking, *idealism*. Cf. "Ueber das Verhältniss," *Beiträge*, Vol. I, pp. 301-302.

56. Ibid., p. 305; some variations.

57. Ibid., pp. 306-307.

58. This is the point where Reinhold has diverged most radically from Kant. Cf. above, "The Facts of Consciousness," pp. 17-19.

59. *Versuch einer neuen Logik*, p. 124.

60. Cf. above, note 35.

61. Because this answer would be too particular if given to the question stated in a generalized form; it only applies to the objects of mathematics.

62. Because this answer would be too universal. Maimon's point is well taken; Kant cannot establish that the 'cause-effect' relationship in fact applies to experience without exhibiting it in some actual case, i.e., without further specifying the principle. Cf. the Seventh Letter, pp. 431-432.

63. But then we are only determining the *concept* of experience in general—not anything actually occurring in experience. Cf. the Seventh Letter, pp. 431-432.

64. Maimon is denying what Kant took for granted, viz., that "the synthesis which

takes place in [space and time] has objective validity." Cf. *Critique*, A89, B121-122.

65. Pp. 408-409.

66. Cf. above, notes 62, 63.

67. Maimon's text reads: ". . . weil wir die *Möglichkeit*, wie wir sie haben konnten, nicht einsehen, da ihre *Möglichkeit*, bloss als *subjektive Verbindungen* allerdings, nach psychologischen Gesetzen eingesehen wird."

68. P. 417-419.

69. This does not mean that for Maimon 'cause-effect' applies to the objects of mathematics; it means, rather, that 'cause -effect' is not strictly speaking a category of objective thought in general ('real thought', as Maimon calls it), but only of 'empirical thought.' (*Versuch einer neuen Logik*, p. 144). Empirical thought, however, never establishes *a priori* anything about particular, actual objects. This is the upshot of Maimon's skepticism.

*Explanatory Abstract of the Critical Writings
of Prof.* Kant, Prepared in Consultation with
the Same,
by Jakob Sigismund Beck
Volume Three,
which presents *The Standpoint from which
Critical Philosophy is to be Judged.*

Riga: at Johann Friedrich Hartknoch's, 1796.

Translation and Notes by George di Giovanni

Jakob Sigismund Beck (1761-1840) is the only one among the self-styled disciples of Kant represented in this volume who did not pretend to be re-building the critical philosophy on a new foundation, but who simply tried to expound it as it was. Beck's only aim was to present it from the proper "standpoint", so as to avoid giving rise to the misunderstandings to which Kant himself had left himself open. (Hence the name Standpunktslehre— "Doctrine of the Standpoint" —with which his philosophy came to be known). And yet, in spite of his professed aim, Beck ended up bringing to Kant's thought innovations which were just as radical, and certainly much more philosophically interesting, than any that either Reinhold, Maimon or Fichte ever contributed.

The most extensive and best known of Beck's expositions was published in three volumes under the title of Erläuternder Auszug aus den Kritischen Schriften des Hernn Prof. Kant auf Anraten desselben (Explanatory Abstract of the Critical Writings of Prof. Kant, prepared in Consultation with the Same): Erster Band, welcher die Kritik der Spekulativen und praktischen Vernunft enthält (First Volume, which contains the Critique of Speculative and Practical Reason) (Riga: Hartknoch, 1793); Zweiter Band, welcher die Kritik der Urteilskraft und die metaphysischen Anfangsgründe der Naturwissenschaft enthält (Second Volume, which contains the Critique of Judgement and the Metaphysical Foundations of Natural Science) (Riga: Hartknoch, 1794); Dritter Band, welcher den Standpunkt darstellt, aus welchem die Kritische Philosophie zu beurteilen ist: Einzig Möglicher Standpunkt, aus welchem die Kritische Philsophie beurteilt werden muss (Third Volume, which presents the Standpoint from which Critical Philosophy is to be judged: Only Possible Standpoint from which Critical Philosophy must be judged) (Riga: Hartknoch, 1796). Another exposition, Grundriss der Kritischen Philosophie (Halle: Renger, 1796) was translated into English by J. Richardson, and published anonymously under the title of The Principles of Critical Philosophy (London, Edinburgh and Hamburg, 1797). The following excerpt is taken from the third volume of the Explanatory Abstract. It should be read in conjunction with the Kant-Beck correspondence, substantial parts of which are included in the Arnulf Zweig's translation of Kant's Letters (Philosophical Correspondence, 1759-99, Chicago: The University Press, 1967). The translation is taken from the original edition which is now also available in photo-mechanical reproduction (Brussels: Culture et Civilisation, 1968).

SECTION I

The Difficulties of Penetrating to the Spirit of The Critique

§2

The Concept of a Bond Between the Representation and its Object, in so far as this Concept Itself has no Object, is the Source of all Errors of Speculative Philosophy.

WHAT COULD BE stranger than to assert that there is fixed in our mind, whenever our faculty of cognition is active, a certain concept, and that all of our representations present something to us only so far as we operate with this concept, but that it is itself quite empty, and has no object at all? Yet this is how things stand with the concept of the connection of our representations to objects. For the statement: 'To my representation there corresponds an object', or 'The representation is objectively valid', it seems that the sense of these equivalent expressions is only being brought out by this. The more I ponder, however, on this . supposed agreement between our representations and objects, the more I find that even the [literal] sense of what I am saying is a source of embarrassment. For I ask what on earth can it mean to say that my representation agrees with its object, yet, that the two are entirely different from each other. What is being said, after all, is that they too are somehow combined; but I only have to ask what this combination consists in, // in order to see that I do not know where to get the required concept. Where are we going to posit this bond between the representation and its object? To say that the object affects me, and thereby produces the representations, amounts to saying nothing. For we must have previously answered the question about a link joining the representation with its object if the representation of a 'causing object' is to be objectively valid. It also does not help to call this [alleged] correspondence between representations and their objects a 'designation'. For what does it mean to say that representations are the signs of objects? To assume in respect of representations a relation corresponding to one that obtains between objects is senseless. We must conclude, [therefore,] that the

[9]

concept of a bond uniting the representation and its object has no object; it is an entirely empty concept.

It cannot be denied, therefore, that the idealist's move to deny any such bond is philosophically sound. Dogmatic philosophers assert the bond, but are unable to indicate in any way [where to find] it. Anyone who has the notion that he can refute idealism fails to notice its point of truth. The issue does not depend here on whether we analyze the concept of representation in a certain way; it cannot be enough to say, in answer to the question, that the very concept of representation entails that it represents an object. For // since the representation [10] of an object is still not the object itself, it still remains an open question what the bond between the representation and its object might possibly be. Hence Berkeley has every right to deny the existence of things in space, for to deny these and to deny the agreement of representations with their objects is one and the same.[1] It is fair to say, therefore, that dogmatic idealism is far more consequent than the merely problematic variety.[2] When it is properly viewed, the issue does not really admit of doubt. Any [supposed] bond uniting representations with their objects is something entirely imaginary; the concept of any such bond has absolutely no object. For before I can say that the representation of an object has an object (that an object corresponds to it) I am of necessity obliged to indicate the object of the concept of the bond uniting representations with their objects. The idealist is inconsistent only if he gives the 'I am' out to be certain beyond doubt. For since the 'I am' too resolves itself into an agreement between the representation of me and me *qua* subject, the question of what the bond uniting the two might be still persists with all its weight.[3]

I wish that for once we could at least get the right feeling about how compelling idealism is.[4] For the first step in comprehending the spirit of critical // philosophy is an honest disclosure of its force, of [11] how irrefutable it is from the point of view of dogmatic philosophy, as what follows will show. The question that is argued back and forth nowadays is whether it is things-in-themselves we know, or their appearance. With all due respect to the merit of those worthy men who have decided the question in this way or that, I must confess all the same that I have seldom found an exposition of genuinely critical idealism [among them]. I cannot right now run ahead of what I shall develop only later. I shall only mention by way of anticipation that dogmatism and idealism both fall equally short of the critical standpoint in pronouncing judgement upon the relation of the object to the faculty of cognition. The idealism of the Berkeley type has every right to deny that there is a bond which unites representations with objects because any such bond is in fact a nothing. It stands on common ground with dogmatism, therefore, in that it aims at the knowledge of things-in-themselves, just as the latter does, and it does not have the slightest notion of a knowledge of objects *qua* appearances either. For before reason can be brought to the point where it will be able, on its own, to understand itself entirely—the point where it can be of a piece with itself—before this can happen, the profound investigation of the *Critique* into the *original* representing must have already come to pass. The real reason behind every attempt [to found] a science of the supra-sensible has always been, from time immemorial, our failure to raise ourselves above discursive representing, or to see that such a [mode of] representing is only derivative, and must be grounded in an original representing. In other words, the attempts were due to our constant failure, prior to the appearance of the *Critique*, to get to [12] Transcendental // Philosophy. There is not the least transcendental motive behind the investigations of a Locke or Leibniz—make no mistake about it. As long as we have yet to turn our eye to the original representing, and still expect to find the source of all cognitions in merely derivative, discursive representing, we shall be induced to believe that we know things-in-themselves by our very manner of thinking. There is no doubt about this—I only beg the reader to have patience with me until I can lead him further into the subject. In other words, as long as we have not yet attained the standpoint of a Transcendental Philosophy (i.e., the standpoint of the synthetic, objective unity of consciousness) we shall never fathom the paradox [*Gegensatz*] of saying that we know things only inasmuch as they appear to us. It is quite natural to press this assertion from the *Critique* so far as to make it into an assertion of Berkeleyan idealism—in other words, to press it into meaning that all of our cognition is nothing but mere dreaming. For how else, after all, are we to understand the *Critique*'s own statement that the objects of our cognition are not things-in-themselves but mere representations? But this is not the place to unravel the concept of appearance for the reader. To interpret this concept is the same as to disclose the original representing, and in my view, it is necessary first of all simply to suggest this operation to the reader by making him aware of the confusion that necessarily arises from the omission of a [13] transcendental meditation. //

This much, however, the reader will have noticed: We have been able to say that the concept of a bond uniting representation and object is empty only inasmuch as the concept at issue is discursive and is not grounded upon an original one; or (to put it in another way) the concept is empty inasmuch as the thing-in-itself is being represented in it. Berkeley, however, had no other view of the question but this; and on this view, the claim that there is no unifying bond between a representation and its object is completely irrefutable. But we must not think that just because we find a refutation of Berkeley's idealism in the *Critique*,[5] its intention is to establish the contrary position—i.e., that between the representation and its object there is in fact a point where they are joined together—in keeping with the concept of the bond uniting them which Berkeley shares with dogmatism. A bond of this sort is simply not an object. The *Critique* has procured [for us] the highest principle of philosophy and of the entire employment of the understanding. This highest principle consists in the synthetic objective unity of consciousness. Anyone who has fully grasped its sense, therefore, will now have to comprehend that between the representation and its object there is indeed a bond— provided, however, that by 'representation' we do not mean one which is only discursively determined in respect to its object, i.e., without any reference to the original representing. The bond is to be found, rather, in this original representing itself; it constitutes in fact the synthetic unity of the *Critique's* principle. //   [14]

Our intention in this paragraph was merely to indicate the source of the errors found in every philosophy which, not being transcendental, goes the way of speculation. The source of the error is precisely that, because the philosophy lacks a transcendental standpoint, it ignores the original representing completely; and hence it tries to find the connection of our representations to objects, or rather, the bond uniting the two, in discursive thinking. And for us too—as long as we have not mastered this transcendental standpoint ourselves—all the claims of critical philosophy will inevitably remain unintelligible. We may, of course, accustom ourselves to the language of the *Critique*; but if we have not attained to its standpoint a scale will still cover our eyes, so that, even though we walk in the light of day, we still shall not be able to see the objects surrounding us. In a word, whether we admit it or not, the critical philosophy will still look to us just like all the other systems that went before it—as if, like them, it were piling empty claim on empty claim, and waiting all the time for another system which will finally retire it to its proper place, albeit only in the history of man's unsuccessful efforts. This [unintelligibility] is what we now undertake to show. Our intention, that is, is to make visible the full extent of the unintelligibility—the contradictions—that must appear to mar the *Critique* to anyone who has not reached the standpoint from which alone it is to be judged.

SECTION II

The Transcendentality Of Our Knowledge As The True Standpoint From Which The Critique Of Pure Reason Must Be Judged

§1

The Highest Principle of Philosophy is the Postulate to Represent Originally

By priciple we understand 'a cognition that grounds certain other cognitions'. If a proposition of this kind still needs to be derived from other cognitions to pass as truth, it is not then 'self-grounded', or 'highest principle' in an unqualified sense. What we require, that is, from a principle of philosophy which is the highest without qualifications is that it should not be in need of being derived from other truths. There are philosophers nowadays whose aim is to discover this highest principle. It cannot, however, have escaped the attention of anyone who has found their efforts worthy of notice that, however commendable their project, these men are all misguided nevertheless. [121] For surely, if the proposition at issue is // a combination of some concepts or others, we must still be able to give an account for it because of its very complexity. One species of philosophers puts the principle of contradiction at the head of philosophy.[6] I think that I can state this principle without arousing any dispute with the formula: 'An object cannot be represented through mutually contradictory determinations'. Now, it is certainly possible to raise a question about the ground of this proposition, for anyone who would want to deny this would be saying no more than that the principle is evident to anyone simply by reflection on the concepts joined in it; but by the very fact that he appeals to such a reflection (whatever it might consist in) he shows that the principle of contradiction has a still higher one above it, in which its certainty is grounded. To be assured of what we are claiming, one only has to look attentively at the concepts contained in the proposition. For the meaning of the expression "object," which appears quite comprehensible to every student of philosophy is a source of embarrassment to any man who has begun to philosophize independently. Moreover, to state that no object can be represented by mutually contradictory determinations is to assume that an object can be represented by attaching to it certain determinations. Professor

Reinhold's *Theory of the Faculty of Representation* [on the other hand] gives as highest principle of philosophy the principle of consciousness which it defines with the formula: "Consciousness is the being referred // of representation to object and subject, and it cannot be separated [122] from any representation."[7] One only needs to take a look, however, at the concept 'being referred' to be assured of its indeterminacy. As regards 'representation', the *Theory* says that it relates to its object through its matter because the latter is produced by it.[8] But is this all that 'being referred' is supposed to mean? And what is the meaning of 'being produced' anyway?

We only have to take note of the way each philosophical school defends the proposition which it passes off as the highest principle of philosophy, to discover by ourselves the clue that will actually lead us to it. "I am completely of one mind with the author of the Philosophy of the Elements," so the eminent author of *Aenesidemus* says, "that philosophy has hitherto lacked a universally accepted highest principle that would ground, either directly or indirectly, all its other propositions. I also agree with him that philosophy can lay claim to the honour of being a science only after the discovery and the exhibition of such a principle."[9] There is no need to worry, therefore, that anyone will find fault with the project of seeking a supreme principle of philosophy. I claim, however, that the answer that is usually given to anyone who questions the proposition which is being paraded as supreme points, in fact, to the one which is truly so. For what is required // of the [123] object of any such proposition is that it be represented, since its certainty ought to derive simply from this representing. But if this is so, there must be a great many principles of this same kind, none of which we would thus be authorized to call 'highest' in an unqualified sense. All the axioms of geometry would certainly be of this sort. For the geometer, too, whenever he says, for instance, "Space can be extended in three directions", is simply stipulating an obligation on our part to represent only space to ourselves. And what does the principle of contradiction or of consciousness[10] possibly have over an axiom of geometry? Is it perhaps that the subject of these principles are higher concepts? To this we answer that in the principle of consciousness 'consciousness' is just as much a particular concept about which the principle states something as 'space' is in the axiom of geometry just mentioned; and in the principle of contradiction the particular object is the representation in respect to which the principle states that its parts must not be mutually exclusive.

If we now find, however, that any proposition which we hold without qualification to be the highest principle in philosophy is grounded in a certain original representing, nothing could be more appropriate to the facts of the case, it seems to me, than to make this very representing

[124] the subject matter of the highest principle. But here we are faced with the responsibility of // introducing the reader as carefully as possible, right at the beginning of our enquiry, to the full sense of what we mean. And I believe that this sense can hardly be missed if we pay attention to the way the geometer begins his science. He initiates it with the postulate: 'Represent space to yourself'. He does not say this or that about his object (i.e., space): he does not say that it is the form of external intuition, nor that it is the order of things as they exist together. On the contrary he requires from his pupil that he represent to himself space—this he must be able to do on his own. The geometer too, therefore, aims at an *original* representing of space in which every derived representation must be grounded; and in fact, any such representation must also be derived exclusively from this representing. In this way too the postulate, 'Represent to yourself an object originally', is the highest principle—not so much of philosophy (if by the latter we still want to mean a particular science) but rather of the entire employment of the understanding.

Before everything else we must note that the highest principle of philosophy must not have any other form whatever than that of a postulate. Its sense actually consists in our 'willingness' [*Anmutung*] to transpose [*versetzen*] ourselves into the very original mode of representing. Hence the principle says absolutely nothing, yet it is the ground of all possible statements. And that status does not depend on the meaning of 'object', or 'originally', or 'representing something to oneself', all of which are previously derived representations (concepts) which without exception presuppose original representing. To the question, "What does it mean to represent something to oneself?"

[125] // I give no answer, for the right answer is the original representing itself. I can do no more than indicate to the reader the mode of operation in which he has to involve himself on his own in order to capture the spirit of the postulate. And here he must indeed note that if he does justice to what the geometer requires of him, he will reject altogether any description or statement of what space presumably is. He will test any such statement against his original representation of space, and will have to find it either confirmed by it or contradicted. He must admit that the original representation of space is the source of any which is derived.

So that the reader not grasp here at the wrong thing but clearly understand what we mean, let him suppose that he finds himself transposed to a region (say, some other planet) where things are shown to him that have never occurred to him before. In a situation of this sort, he would only occupy himself with his original representing, for he would still lack concepts under which he could grasp these objects, and thus represent them to himself in derived representations. He would represent to himself the book that he is reading in an original manner—not inasmuch as he already recognizes it as 'book', but inasmuch as he takes it for the determinate object that it is, i.e., he exercises an operation of representation that antecedes any indication of what the object grasped is.

Accordingly, when we give the postulate: // 'To represent an object originally to oneself', as supreme principle of all philosophy, we are combining with this a claim which on closer inspection turns out to be the prior one. We are claiming that all philosophy must be grounded on 'actual fact' [*Tatsache*]. I have no doubt, that this proposition will go against the habit of thought of many philosophers. For these gentlemen have in mind certain cognitions stamped with the name "*a priori*", and these they suppose not *to rest on* facts at all but to be certain even before they are instantiated by facts. They grant, of course, that the cognition of being in possession of these *a priori* cognitions rests on actual facts; the cognitions themselves, however, are taken to be independent of all facts. As examples they offer us the axioms of geometry. What is especially astonishing in this respect is that they hold these truths of geometry to be *a priori* cognitions, yet they have been claiming ever since the appearance of the *Critique of Pure Reason* that it is possible to explain their *a priori* nature; the *Critique*, so they say, has fully done this. On the face of it this claim can only mean that the axioms in question are being regarded as derived propositions whose certainty rests on the ground of explanation that is alleged for them; but then they lose the force of axioms. In fact, the geometer rejects any ground of explanation. He holds fast to the original representation of the object, and from it he draws the proposition which he calls an "axiom". [Now, I realize that] if someone were to test the geometer's statements with a compass // and protractor, he would be led to the belief in their correctness on the strength of a fact. And since this avenue of certainty does not lead, of course, to the universality of the propositions of geometry, it appears that about authentic geometric knowledge we cannot validly say that it rests on actual facts. But our aim is to lead the reader into the problem progressively, just so far as it is possible for the moment. Although we still cannot present to him with all due clarity the real meaning of the *Critique's* principle that space and time are pure intuitions, or what the *Critique* truly means when it claims that the possibility of all synthetic propositions contained in geometry are only explicable in terms of this principle, still the possibility of these propositions should become clear to him from what we have said. In this way he will penetrate to the sense of the *Critique* sooner perhaps than he becomes fully acquainted with its language.

In order to be understood, we shall expound our thought using an

[126]

[127]

axiom of geometry as example. Whenever the geometer says: "Two straight lines cannot form a space limited on all sides", the question arises as to what the certainty of this proposition is based on. The proposition is not analytical; and since it is universal, no actual fact (as 'fact' is usually understood) can establish it, for a fact verifies only singular propositions. The stock answer of critical philosophers is that the proposition has apodictic certainty because the intuition which we found it upon is *a priori*; merely empirical intuitions are the source

[128]   // of particular propositions. I am quite sure that those who answer in this way do not understand themselves. For since this geometer does not attend to any ground of explanation, but simply attaches certainty to his operation as geometer, the answer must lie [rather] in this very operation. And that is nothing other than original representing. He represents to himself a right angle *originally*, and from this operation he derives the representation of *this* object as a surface not enclosed on all sides. By opening the sides of the angle, he then lets it attain every possible magnitude; and this operation is now the original representing by which he represents to himself a sphere of objects. From this original representation that encompasses a sphere he also draws the derived representation that *these* objects are collectively a non-enclosed plane. This reduction of a derived representation to an original representing is the essence of the proof typical of geometry. A theorem in this science is distinguished from an axiom because in the latter the representation of the object is immediately grounded in an original representing; in contrast the representation of an object expressed by a theorem is grounded in one or more previously derived representations. The reader will find supporting evidence for this if he takes any theorem of geometry, and investigates the way it is proved—how the proof, that is, derives representations from previously

[129]   derived representations, and grounds the whole derivation in an // original form of representing. In this way he will not make the mistake of thinking that geometry needs for its stability an insight into the philosophical proposition: 'The representation of space, indeed space itself, is a pure intuition'. The thread of our study will eventually lead us to insight into the nature of mathematics, and into the Kantian definition of it as a science [generated] by the construction of objects; so we want to abstain now from any further investigation of the way that we represent originally in mathematics.

Our intention in this paragraph has only been to make the reader aware of original representing. This aim will be attained only on the condition that the reader actually transposes himself into this original representing. Of course the investigation of this original mode of representing still lies ahead of us. But how shall we ground the investigation? Not from a derivation of conclusions from certain other propositions, but through the original mode of representing itself — and anyone who wants to pass judgement upon it must transpose himself into it. Representations taken from the original representing are derived representations which, inasmuch as through them a sphere of objects is represented, can serve as principles of further derivations. This derived mode of representation is the discursive. Opposed to it stands the original mode, and every derived mode must be reducible to it if it // is to deserve the name of a cognition of which it can [130] be said, not just that an object is being represented through it (this applies to every representation), but that it also *has* an object.

A representation *has* an object — this is just the point which we have so strongly stressed in the previous section because no philosophy has, as yet, come to terms with it.[11] It comes down to the question "What joins together my representation of an object with this object?" Might it be that the advantage an original representing has over any other is that in respect to it this crucial question cannot be raised?

We are only at the beginning of our investigation. But we already have cause to beg our reader to be on guard lest the discursive mode of representing interfere with the original one, for he would then spoil our whole plan. What follows will duly confirm that this remark has its proper place here: there can never be any question of an 'original representation', but only of an 'original representing', for what we want to signify by this expression is truly the act by which we generate for ourselves the representation of an object, and not the representation which we already have of it and through which we think it. The question, i.e., "What joins the representation of an object with its object?", can appear to have meaning and to be very crucial only to somebody who fails to // take to heart the original [131] mode of representing.

§2

What Does 'Transcendental Philosophy' Mean, and in What Does Its Distinction from 'General Pure Logic' Consist?

To characterize the science that we call philosophy adequately might well turn out not to be an easy matter. This much, however, is clear: We cannot define it by borrowing any of its characteristics from its object, for philosophy would then have to encompass all possible cognitions; and if we try to define it by its 'form', we are up against a term whose true meaning is still hard to come by. The critical system calls philosophy "a science on the base of concepts," and mathematics a "science through construction of concepts."[12] It will be a long time, however, before the full sense of this definition can be absorbed. For the distinction that it draws will not go over well with anyone if representation of the singular is called "intuition" and that of the universal is called "concept," and if by "constructing a concept" we mean no more than taking the singular from the universal and representing it to ourselves. Least of all will it satisfy anyone who has come face to face with the issue of the nature of the bond linking representation to its object on which every system has hitherto come [132]   to grief. For all the fame of // geometric evidence, the universal representations of geometry still cannot have real validity if this validity is denied to the representations of singulars.[13]

But even if we were to set the question of what philosophy is as science aside for the moment, the answer to the question, "What is it to philosophize?" would come by itself all the same. To philosophize, we say, means 'to derive cognitions from their principles.' But what is it that secures any derivation? It is the original representing which is incapable of being questioned further. About someone who appropriates the system of this or that man, we can only say that he has learned a philosophy, not that he philosophizes. Philosophizing is an original and spontaneous state of mind, and this is nothing other than original representing. A philosophy will always be something merely learned as long as somebody else has discovered its principles, and we only repeat after him the inferences that he has drawn. This way of acting will be void of philosophical spirit precisely as long as original representing is missing from it. To come upon an inference on one's own — this is to philosophize; and it can happen even if somebody else leads us to it. But if the man whose system we are making our own did not philosophize himself, or if we fail to take hold of his way of thinking and to represent originally what our great mentor presented to us, we are then left with the merely derivative retailing of representations, playing with hypotheses and thoughts. [133]   This happens because we miss the // point that can be only be got hold of originally. *The Critique of Pure Reason* teaches that the categories make experience possible, and in this lies the justification for their being applied to objects. Now, anyone who halts at the literal meaning of this statement and does not open his mind's eye to represent this process of making experience possible to himself originally, but accepts it as something well founded, behaves far more unphilosophically than somebody else who (to speak now the language of the *Critique*)[14] transforms the regulative employment of the ideas of reason into a constitutive one. And in order to become conscious of what is illegitimate in an exposition that could indeed long impede our discovery of the true sense of the *Critique*, we only have to set it on the same footing as some other hypothesis in which we posit something in order to explain a fact. Then you will have to note that we have good reasons to be perplexed by what the *Critique* is saying, because of the nature of the facts for which the ground of explanation it proposes (i.e., the categories) is intended, as well as because of the ground itself. What the *Critique* says requires original representing.

General pure logic is the science of thought. To think however is to represent something to oneself through a concept. The reader will detect more easily the true sense of the original representing if he turns his attention to the mode of representation which, since we represent objects to ourselves through concepts, is not original. Let us try to help him in this. //

[134]

When I think an object, a point of reference is given to which my representing subject stands in relation through an operation which, for lack of a better expression, we shall designate as *attribution* [*Beilegung*].[15] For we attach determinations to that point, and [this operation,] this attribution, is what we have in mind whenever we say that we have a concept of the object. We fail to see what 'thinking' is if we say, as we usually do, that it is 'combining representations together'; and there is every reason why we should attend to our failure. I say, 'The air is pure', in this judgement I am no doubt thinking— but I am not doing so, because I combine together the representations 'air' and 'pure', but because I have in mind a point of reference which I secure by attributing to it the determination 'pure air'. For this same reason we are able to represent something to ourselves even through empty concepts too. Suppose, for instance, that I think of a matter that exists only in virtue of its extension. This concept has no object; yet I have in mind a point of reference to which I stand in relation through the operation of attributing. We might want to say that of an object of this sort we have no concept at all; and in saying this we might be suggesting something quite right. But at the moment, we are still not sufficiently prepared to grasp the full sense of what we would be saying. We think objects also through negative concepts, for in actual negation, too, we have in mind a point of reference and an attribution. The concept of 'the most real being', for instance, is only negative, for we cannot declare any single reality // that could pertain to it. Of objects of this kind it is also right to say that "we do not have a concept of them at all"; but the meaning of this expression will become clear to us only later on. Our present aim does not extend further than to direct attention towards the essential property of thought. It is an operation of attributing by which we fix for ourselves a point of reference; only after this operation, and because of it, we say of that point that "we have a concept of it." A real confusion reigns among philosophers in this matter; this would not be the case, however, if they had paid more attention to the most

[135]

important point of the *Critique of Pure Reason*—the one that makes it truly critical philosophy—the point, that is, of *original* representing. (By 'critical philosophy' we mean the employment of reason in as much as it is secured to some point of support that can be held onto, i.e., that *can be understood*.)

General logic is not concerned with how we arrive at the concept we have of various objects. That we represent objects to ourselves through concepts is a fact for it; and on this fact it erects as the universal condition of thought the principle of contradiction which declares: "No object can be thought through mutually cancelling determinations". This is what thought itself makes known; and since thought is an actual fact, it is not for general logic to look further into what justifies [136]   it. // We must admit, of course, that appealing to an actual fact does not have the effect of inhibiting all further enquiry. But what else can our investigation devolve on, after we have recognized a fact, except the analysis of 'actual fact' itself? There are gentlemen [nowadays] who are busy constructing a philosophy of the elements through which they believe they are erecting under the *Critique* a foundation that its great author allegedly neglected to provide, at least in any developed form.[16] These worthy gentlemen, as will be shown, miss the true goal of this *Critique*. They are victims of an illusion which to me is remarkable, considering that these same gentlemen claim to be pursuing a very sound objective. They want to bring the philosophical arguments of critical philosophy back to the level of actual fact. But as it is, the fact from which all philosophy ought to originate is, according to one of them, the principle of contradiction[18]; according to another, the principle of consciousness[19]; according to yet a third, the principle of animation[20]; for a fourth, the principle of determinability[21]; for a fifth, the principle of selfhood[22]; etc. Who knows how many more of these actual facts from which the spring of philosophy is to gush there may be. These gentlemen, who are so sedulous in their interest in the progress of philosophy, and for this worthy of our respect, fail to notice nevertheless that before we adduce a principle as actual fact, we must analyze what 'actual fact' is first of all. But what 'actual fact' is, is precisely the object of the *Critique's* deduction of the categories, even though (as we now remark provisionally) with this deduction it was not undertaking the [137]   analysis of a concept. //

The object of pure general logic is thought; This is its actual fact: We have concepts by means of which we represent objects to ourselves. But it is one thing to analyze the concept of this fact, and quite another to analyze the actual fact itself. General logic merely does the first. It expounds the concept of a concept; it deals with concepts in general according to their range and content. It deals with their clarity; with how they are recognized, or with the operation by which an object is thought as subsumed under a certain concept, i.e., with judgements; and finally, with conclusions or with how a judgement is derived from another. This whole undertaking is throughout only analysis of the concept of a fact, not analysis of the 'actual fact' as such.

Let us now grasp, however, the idea of a science that strives to represent this actual fact *qua* fact. This science will not aim at definitions, or the unfolding of concepts; or at drawing up lists of determinations which we attribute to objects when we think of them; for in all of this the actual fact of thinking is not taken into consideration at all. Its aim will be rather to present the *original generation* of concepts. *Original representing* will be the object of this science. This in fact is *transcendental philosophy*. No philosopher before *Kant* ever attained to its idea, so it seems to me; and even now that this great man has so successfully realized it, experience is teaching us // how difficult it is to capture   [138] the true spirit of just what the *Critique* means by 'transcendental'. For this issue is not truly settled by the word "fact", or by appeal to the actual facts of consciousness.

The subject that we are now broaching is of the greatest importance. To give a sense of this importance—in a preliminary way still—I ask everyone accustomed to being candid with himself whether he has not indeed learned a lot from the writings of the most famous philosophers, both ancient and modern. Whoever in addition knows what it is to understand something, through the use that he has made of his understanding, will agree with me when I say that, undeniably, the mistake made in every age has been to overlook *what is understandable* and to strive [instead] only after the conceptualizable. This is precisely the point that makes critical philosophy worthy of its name. For its whole purpose is to analyze the employment itself of the understanding, to bring to view what is in itself understandable and to separate it from that which by its nature subsists in itself as something unintelligible [*seiner Natur nach in sich selbst bestehenden Unverständlichen*].[23] Its purpose is thus to trace the point to which we must attach every thought process, every merely conceptual procedure, if it is to count as philosophical activity. In declaring that the *Critique* has attained this purpose in full, we only profess something which we deeply believe. We maintain, however, that the method it has hit upon is mainly responsible for the fact that the goal itself has been widely misunderstood, even by those who revere the *Critique*. It leads the reader to that announced point, // (the very topmost point of the em-   [139] ployment of the understanding) only gradually. We now want to reverse this method, and strive to put the reader at the point *rightaway*. The moment he is there, he will behold the *Critique* in the full light of day

§3

The Objective Synthetic Unity of Consciousness is the Highest Summit of all Employment of the Understanding

We believe that what we have so far achieved in our investigation is the insight that the highest principle of all the employment of the understanding is a postulate, namely the postulate of original representing. The distinction between a postulate and a proposition seems to me to be very important. For a proposition is in each instance the representation of a thing through a concept. But now, it is an unavoidable need of our understanding to ensure that its concepts have a firm standing, for only so far as they have that, do they belong [so to speak] to its household. It is only on that basis that any train of thought enjoys the dignity of being understandable, and in the absence of this standing, anyone who deals with mere concepts does not even understand himself. We can very aptly call transcendental philosophy, therefore, an art of knowing oneself, and we can consider our postulate the principle of all intelligibility.

[140]   Our intention now is to turn immediately to the analysis of original representing, without further delaying the // reader with preparatory remarks. The task of preparation has been masterfully completed by the *Critique*, and there is little more left for us to do other than to direct his attention to the essential point.

Original representing consists in the categories. These are nothing else but modes of representation. Accordingly, we have no intention of viewing them here as concepts of objects at all; if we did that they would be on the same footing as any other concept. Thus, whether I say 'This body is solid or liquid', or 'It is a substance or cause', it would still be same as asking about the combination of the representation with the object. From this point of view, we completely miss that aspect of the categories in virtue of which they impart intelligibility and form (*Haltung*) to all our concepts. We shall now consider the categories in the order in which the *Critique* presents them, but precisely as modes of original representation.

The category of quantity is the original synthesis ('putting together') of the homogeneous that proceeds from the parts to the whole; it is space itself.[24]

The reader must transpose himself into this original mode of representation by himself, since our principle is a *postulate* and not a representation through concepts. Definitions — in this case what 'synthesis', 'originally', 'homogeneous', 'parts and whole' are — are therefore out of the question. We are here in the position of the geometer who does not define what 'space' is, nor does he presuppose // that we have obtained its concept somewhere else, but *postulates* [141] rather the original representing of it.

At this point, however, we must emphasize that there really is no original representing 'of an object', but simply an original representing. For whenever we have the representation of an object, it is already every time a concept, that is, it is already always the attribution of certain determinations by means of which we fix for ourselves a point of reference. Thus far, we have on occasion used the expression "representing of an object" quite deliberately, simply because we were not yet able, right at the beginning, to introduce the reader to the full sense of the postulate.

Accordingly, space itself is original representing, namely, the original synthesis of the homogeneous. Before this synthesis there is no space; we generate it, rather, in the synthesis. Space or this synthesis is pure *intuiting* itself. The *Critique* calls it a pure intuition; I believe that I am expressing myself much more in conformity to the sense of our postulate, however, if I call this category an "intuiting".

The representation of space is quite different from this original representing, for it is already concept. To have the concept of a straight line is something else than drawing it (or synthesizing it originally). I also have the concept of supplementary angles, but in that case there is no original representing. // [142]

Of course we can characterize this synthesis some more. It consists, for instance, in the transition by consciousness from one thing to another; and it is possible only in virtue of an identical self-consciousness. For our purposes, however, no observation is more important than this: we must analyze original representing, and not a concept. The reader must transpose himself to it by himself. Thus, whenever we call the operation a combination of the manifold into the unity of consciousness, we must be on guard not to allow a concept of it to distract us from the real point on which everything depends. We generate space in the original synthesis. [You will ask:] "But where does this combination lie? [I answer:] "Not in an object; *we* do the original putting together, and prior to this connection there is nothing that is connected".[25]

Different from this original synthesis is another operation which is combined with it in the original representing. I call it *original recognition.* The *Critique* gives it the name of "transcendental schematism of the categories" [instead]. Since everything still depends here too on original representing, and not on a concept of some thing or other, we shall now endeavor to lead the reader to this activity. // [143]

Consider a house. Let the reader now abstract from the fact that through the concept 'house' he is already representing the object to himself, and let him attend to nothing save the operation of the original representing in virtue of which he come to the concept of this determinate object in the first place.

Here he is synthesizing originally, that is, he generates space for himself; and as we have said space itself is this synthesis. In this original representing, however, time arises for me. The original securing of time (the determining of it) is the original recognition, and by fixating it thus I fix the original synthesis, and obtain thereby the concept of a determinate shape of time.[26]

The Critique calls the faculty of original recognition, "the transcendental faculty of judgement", just as it calls the faculty of original synthesis "transcendental understanding". These denominations are based on the meaning of the words "understanding" and "faculty of judgement" established in general pure logic. This science treats concepts as actual facts, as we said above. It does not concern itself with the 'actual fact' itself, with the original generation of a concept, but deals with concepts, rather, already in their capacity qua concepts. It does not ascribe to the understanding an original synthesis but the joining of concepts to one concept. And just as this activity of joining, which is a mere by-product of the original synthesis, falls apart from the synthesis, so the recognition of the latter is of this double kind too. Derivative recognition is the function of the faculty of judgement, 'This object is a house', the activity is recognition in a merely derivative sense; the object that I establish for the concept 'house' is one that I also represent to myself through a concept already; in brief, the recognition is a subsumption. But original recognition is the transcendental determination of time—the function of the faculty of judgement that we have just considered with reference to the category of quantity.

Thus, together with original recognition, original synthesis generates the objective unity of consciousness which is synthetic originally, i.e., it generates the original concept of an object, or again, not a concept that represents an object through this or that characteristic, but simply the concept of it as such. In the example above, through the original synthesis of the homogeneous and the original fixating of the time that arises for me in the course of the synthesis, I generated the determinate concept of this object, of this determinate figure.[27] The fact that the object belongs in the range of the concept 'house' has nothing to do with these functions. The Critique calls the property of a concept by which it represents certain characteristics in one and the same object "the analytical unity of consciousness". By "the originally synthetic unity of the consciousness of the concept" it designates instead the concept's aptitude to represent. The entire validity

of a // concept lies in this property. The analytical unity of each [145]
and every concept must be reducible to it if the concept is to have
meaning, that is, if we want to understand ourselves in our concepts.[28]

The category of *reality* is the original synthesis of the homogeneous,
a synthesis that proceeds from whole to parts.[29] Here too everything
depends solely on the original representing into which the reader
must transpose himself and not on any definition by which we would
still only represent the analytical unity of certain concepts to ourselves.
Our postulate, on the contrary, postulates the original synthetic unity,
that is, the original representing itself.

Accordingly, just as we have previously viewed the category 'quantity'
not as the concept of a thing, but as an original representing through
which we first arrive at a concept, so now the category 'reality' (the
objectively real) [*Sachheit*] is also not a concept to us, but an original
mode of representation. In it I synthesize my sensibility; and in this
synthesis, which proceeds however from whole to parts (whereas in
the former case consciousness of the parts preceded that of the whole),
I generate time. The determining of this time, through which the
synthesis itself is fixated, is the original recognition. In this original
representing the original synthetic unity of consciousness is generated,
i.e., the unity of the concept through which I think the reality of a
thing.

The body that I touch withstands my hand's incursion into the
space that it occupies. // If I reduce the analytical unity of this [146]
concept to its original synthetic unity, I find that the latter consists in
the fixing of the synthesis of my sensibility. And just as through this
original determination of time I obtain in the category of reality the
concept of determinate degree (intensive quantity) through precisely
the same determination of time. This synthesis is called "empirical".
The *Critique* also gives to it the name "empirical intuition", but I
believe that we stay nearer to its sense if we call it an empirical
"intuiting", for it is nothing else but one of the original modes of
representation.

Here too, therefore, just as in the case of the preceding category,
we find the objective validity of a concept in the analysis of the original
representing (i.e., of the original synthesis and the original recognition).
In this lies the true solution to the apparently important question
about the combining of representations with their objects. For as we
have pointed out several times, this question is in fact directed at
nothing. The statement, 'This question is not directed at anything'
means something quite different from 'This question is unanswerable'.
The latter applies whenever a question actually has an object; it has
meaning, therefore, because it actually aims at something. It is
unanswerable, however, because the object it is enquiring about is so

[147]   constituted as to be inaccessible to our cognition. // An example of this kind of question is the one regarding the constitution of the matter at the centre of the earth. For some sort of matter is surely there; but since to examine it as it truly is surpasses our means, the question is unanswerable. The true sense of the proposition, 'This question is not directed at anything', will gradually emerge for the reader from the analysis of original representing. For it will become clear to him step by step, that the entire sense and meaning of our concepts rests on the original representing; original representing *constitutes* all meaning. All *understanding* consists in this original representing. Right now we only wish to make the reader aware of this important point. The full force of the claim will become more apparent to him in the course of the analysis.

The whole employment of the understanding, all dealings with mere concepts (that is, whenever we represent the reality of a thing to us through concepts, i.e., the analytical unity of the concept) must rest on the originally synthetic unity of consciousness generated in the original representing of this category of 'reality'. And we can indeed see that this basis for the intelligibility of the concept is quite different from a mere analysis of it. Suppose, for instance, that we think 'the most real of all beings'. Our first inclination is to assume that in this
[148]   concept we understand ourselves as well; for we // are well acquainted, after all, with the realities of things (or so we think), and to obtain this concept no more is needed than to join together the most perfect reality of every kind in one single subject. But if we try to reduce the analytical unity of this concept to the originally synthetic unity, we realize that original representing will never be able to lead us to a 'great reality'. So we did not really understand ourselves in the concept.

The *Critique* says that our understanding is not intuitive but discursive.[30] It seems to me that what its great author meant by this statement is still not very well understood. I hold further, that it will forever remain hidden from anyone who does not take note that the highest principle of the employment of the understanding is the postulate or original representing, or that this postulate requires that we should transpose ourselves into the original representing itself. This is quite another thing than representing the postulate to ourselves in concepts. The meaning of that proposition of the *Critique* is this: Our understanding is so constituted that in every case it represents objects to itself through concepts, that is, in an analytical unity and not in the originally synthetic unity of consciousness. For whenever we represent objects to ourselves, we always have a concept of the things [represented]; that is to say, we fix a point of reference by the attribution of certain determinations. We thereby attach an object to certain characteristics.[31] In the original representing we do not strictly speaking represent any object to ourselves. [Instead,] the understanding generates // through it the originally synthetic objective unity which [149] constitutes, of course, the entire meaning of a concept. But in order for the object to be represented, this meaning must first pass over into an analytical unity, i.e., a concept.[32] It is totally wrong-headed, and also contrary to the intent of the *Critique*, to interpret it to mean that the reality of things are a manifold given *prior to* the original synthesis and recognition. On this view we let ourselves loose in a play of mere concepts—in an arbitrary domain in which we do not understand ourselves, where there is no end to the questions and answers we have to contend with. And with their reputation of being very philosophical, these finally lead, one and all, to the death of genuine philosophy (I should say rather of genuine 'philosophizing'). For if space is something given *before* the original representing, then the question arises what it could be; and thus we are led to take if for an existing non-thing. And just in the same way arises the question of what 'reality' itself [*Sachheit*] is—that is, by failing to notice the original representing of the category. I think that questions of this sort are bound to cause embarrassment to anyone who thinks seriously about them, for no matter how hard he tries, he can never find a bond between the representation and the object here.

We do not know things as they are in themselves, but only their appearances. This capital proposition of the *Critique* has the same sense, and one and the same meaning, as our postulate of original representing. It is this meaning that constitutes the meaning of all our concepts, i.e., that first and foremost imparts to them all that there is in them to be understood. // This proposition says nothing more [150] or less than that the understanding does the original combining and that we err therefore if we assume this combination in the things. Just as the postulate of original synthesis is the soul of the entire employment of the understanding and of everything that is intelligible, so the illusion that this combination lies in things (in other words, the alleged knowledge of things-in-themselves) is the source of all the aberrations of speculation. If we consider space to be something independent of the original synthesis, then we can no longer know what joins our representation of space with this presumed thing or non-thing. We cannot know this because space is precisely the original representing, i.e, the essence of knowledge, and we have thereby placed ourselves beyond the pale of all knowledge. [The truth about space] is not so much that there is a 'knowledge' of it as that there is rather a 'knowledge that is *space*'. As regards the category of reality, too, we recklessly commit ourselves to a darkness in which we lose hold of ourselves (i.e., in which we cannot understand ourselves) whenever we treat it as the concept of a thing rather than as original representing, and when we fail to transpose ourselves into this representing. I hope that the exposition of the categories of relation and modality will complete the introduction of the reader to the original mode of representation.

[151]   The category of substantiality is the original positing of something permanent, in respect to which time // itself is first represented. Here, as before, we must above all take note that everything depends, not on representing substance and accident through concepts, but solely on representing this category originally.

In this category, too, the original representing consists of an original synthesis and its original recognition. This synthesis is the original synthesis of my sensations. We must take care, however, to keep our attention fixed on the original representing, and not to allow it to slide off through concepts into representations. For to the extent that we allow ourselves to ask what substance or accident are, i.e., to look for concepts by which we can represent them to ourselves, to that extent we also lapse from the spirit of the postulate of original representing. Original recognition is precisely the operation [of representing originally]; in it the subject is posited as the permanent substratum, and time is represented in the subject [an ihm] by referring its various stages back to it.

I see a piece of wood. Here I am abstracting entirely from the fact that the object is subsumed under the concept 'wood', but direct my attention solely to the original representing by which the wood is *object* for me. In so doing I discover [three things:] *First*, an original synthesis of the homogeneous proceeding from parts to whole, i.e., space. In this synthesis time arises for me; and in the original recognition, as time is being determined, the synthesis too acquires determinacy. I

[152]   obtain thereby a determinate figure. // *Secondly*, an original synthesis of the homogeneous that proceeds from whole to parts and constitutes reality, i.e., or the filling of space. This is the synthesis of sensation, and it is *determined* through the original recognition by which a determinate *degree* is represented. *Thirdly*, I lay down 'something' (i.e., the permanent real) as the foundation of this original synthesis and then refer its predicates to it; it is just this, the predicates, that are obtained in the original positing. In the original recognition I determine time by positing this substratum as *something permanent*. First I represent time to myself in relation to the substratum, and then I represent the same substrate with reference to its states at different times.

What probably complicates the whole mode of representation of the *Critique*, and has certainly done a lot to inhibit insight into the true spirit of its deduction of the categories, is the disposition of our understanding. The latter cannot represent its object to itself save through concepts, and it is just for this reason that we cannot present the original representing to the reader except through concepts. For the same reason, so that the understanding's constitution shall not hinder him further from catching a glimpse of the nature of its employment, we are constantly and urgently reminding him that the highest principle of this entire employment is the *postulate*, 'Represent originally'. The reader will gather from this that we do not intend by it a principle needed for some conclusion—a principle // that would be laid down, that is, merely for the sake of representing things through concepts—but that our intention here is to analyze in a true sense the employment of the understanding. The more the reader penetrates into the true sense of our postulate, the better he will realize that there are no questions to be answered here regarding the correct constitution of the subject and its predicates—in other words, no question about the concepts we have to make of them. For concepts of this sort rest solely on the original positing, and are grounded on it. In the words of the *Critique* this means: The analytical unity of consciousness (in the concept) presupposes an original synthetic unity (in the original representing); or again: Analysis is only possible after a synthesis.[34] It is totally wrong-headed to interpret these statements to refer to analytical or synthetic judgements in which *concepts* are being combined with one another. It is not a question of the linkage of *concepts* here, but rather of an original putting together which make all concepts possible in the first place. Whenever we reverse the order of things and tarry with mere concepts, whereas our attention ought to be directed to the original representing, we lose ourselves in a labyrinth where we shall never find our way ourselves again. Then we have to contend with skepticism and idealism—with an endless stream of questions and answers which fantasy can quickly dress up to look like a system, even though their essential character is an inherent unintelligibility. //

[153]

[154]

The category of causality consists in an original positing that fixes the original synthesis of my sensations *qua* successive.[35] Here too the original representing divides into the two operations of original synthesis and original recognition. The first consists in the linking together of my sensations, and is further determined in the original recognition by the fixing of the time in accordance to which the sequence of the synthesis is fixated.

A stone falls from the roof. In the original synthesis I combine the two states of the stone—as it is found at one time on the roof, at another lying on the ground. Now, in the original recognition this synthesis obtains a determinacy; it is fixed. That is to say, what comes before and what comes after is fixed through this original time determination; and this happens with the original positing of a something through which the transition of the substance from one of its states to another is determined. In the present example I synthesize originally both the state of the stone on the roof and its state on the ground, (this synthesis, incidentally, is the objective combination of states that it is upon the original positing of a permanent reality; apart from this original recognition, it is merely a synthesis of sensations) and in the original recognition I then posit something (i.e., a cause) through which the time order of these states becomes fixed. //

[155]

The moment the reader takes his eye off of the original representing, and lingers with the concepts (by means of which alone, to be sure, we can make this original representing itself present to him) he forfeits every possibility of ever achieving conviction and insight into the nature of this category. Its essence always consists in the generation of the originally synthetic and objective unity of consciousness, which will always be different from the analytical unity of the mere concept.

Perception consists in the simple original synthesis, and in the original synthetic unity of consciousness generated through it. Hence the *Critique* calls this unity merely *subjective*. We distinguish it from the *objective* unity of consciousness. The synthetic unity attains to this dignity of objectivity in virtue of the original recognition whereby perception passes over into experience. For instance, the unity [obtained] in the categories of quantity and reality through the mere synthesis of the homogeneous is *subjective*: I only obtain a perception in it. But in experience the perception passes over into the original recognition, in which that synthesis is fixated, as in an original determination of time. In other words, what I obtain is the original recognition of the object, objective unity. The same applies to the category of relation; there, too, perception must be distinguished from experience. [For instance,] the perception that consists in the original but subjective // synthesis precedes the experience of the stone falling from the roof. This experience comes to be from the perception [only] in the original recognition.

[156]

I am quite ready to believe that it may be more difficult to grasp the original modes of these categories of relation than it was earlier to grasp those of quantity and quality. And the reason for this is very instructive. In order that the reader may not run into difficulties in the course of the discussion, I want to remove one that must have just occurred to him. For the categories of relation just expounded concern the existence [*Dasein*] of things, and it would seem that to posit this existence as a whole in the original synthesis and recognition of the understanding, as we have just done, is a typically idealistic move.

If I am asked how I come by the representation of the object that I see in front of me, I answer that it affects me. The object that I see or touch produces a sensation in me through the medium of light or because of its impenetrability. In spite of this, however, I shall still go on to say that the understanding is responsible for the original synthesis in the generation of the original and objective unity. It is *I* who posits something permanent in this original representing, and who represents time itself with respect to it. It is *I* who posits something (a cause) that gives temporal determination to the change in my subjective condition, viz., at one moment I was without this representation, but I had it at another. There is nothing contradictory in all this. We only have to // bear in mind that the transcendental statement, 'The understanding posits a something originally', is what first of all gives sense and meaning to the empirical statement, 'The object affects me'. For the first statement is the concept of the original representing itself in which all the meaning of our concepts has to be grounded. Indeed, the concept I have of my understanding as a faculty in me, even the concept of my *ego*, receives its sense and meaning in the first instance from this original positing. [157]

The whole spirit of critical idealism depends on this mode of representation which is expressed in the postulate of the original representing. This idealism maintains that in original representing it is the understanding itself that synthesizes and brings about whatever combination we put into things. It differs *toto coelo* from the idealism of Berkeley. The latter can be characterized as follows: It disavows any combination between the representation and its object, but it does not do it on the ground that any such combination would in itself be nothing—on the ground that I would not understand itself in it, or because it could not establish an understandable concept [for it]. The importance that the quest for a combination of this sort has for the idealist, as well as for the skeptic, reveals how much they both fail to recognize that it is in fact only a mirage. The idealist ends up denying its possibility; the skeptic makes it a practice instead (all too often successfully) to look like a philosopher by casting doubts upon it. In either case, however, it does not occur to them to uncover the sense of the question they are asking. To do so they would have to analyze 'the understandable' in its categories, as something that stands on its own, // i.e., they would have to analyze the employment itself of the understanding. Whether they are denying that combination, therefore, or just doubting it, they still assume that it is possible to ask questions about it—just as it is possible to ask whether the moon has inhabitants or not, in which case one of the two alternatives would have to be right even though it is admitted that it is beyond our power to establish which. Regarding the question whether things outside us affect us, and through their affections attest to their existence, it so happens that one side derives sensations from causes other than the things-in-themselves (in which common sense assumes them [158] to have their origin) while the other side discovers that the validity of the law of causality itself is open to doubt. It does not occur to either side, however, that in the intelligible shape in which they state their question, it includes the further question of a bond connecting the 'representation of my *ego*' with this *ego* itself, and that if there is anything dubious about that general question, it would have to apply also to this more particular one. For both parties take for granted that each of us is closest to himself, and that everyone is immediately convinced of his own existence through the immediately actual fact of his own consciousness. And this is proof enough that neither side has penetrated to the spirit of what 'original fact' means, nor have they taken original representing itself seriously. Critical idealism, on the contrary, is entirely in agreement with common sense. Just like common sense it declares that the objects affect us and generate sensations in us. But it secures the rightful claims of common sense by deriving the original representing done in the category of causality from the very employment of the understanding, and by exhibiting this representing as the original synthesis of the states of a permanent substratum, and as an original recognition through which, in being fixated, the synthesis becomes object. This analysis is an analysis of the very employment of the understanding, not of a concept. At the end of it, it becomes clear to anyone who has penetrated to the nature of our postulate that the question of a link between representation and object has been robbed of all meaning, and that it has no more intrinsic importance than the question whether the Holy Spirit proceeds from the Father and the Son or only from the Father alone. Both questions have been completely robbed of intelligibility. This kind of idealism is expressed in the *Critique* by the proposition that we do not know things as they are 'in-themselves', but as they appear to us. Appearances are the objects of cognition that affect us, and produce sensations in us. No thought is to be given in this connection to things-in-themselves; and anyone who construes the *Critique's* assertion that objects affect us to mean 'things-in-themselves' proves thereby that he has not attained to the standpoint from which this *Critique* is to be judged.

Before we proceed any further, we wish to introduce a comment here that may help lead the reader to the sense of our postulate in general, but above all to the sense of the categories of relation. Anyone [160] who has never really engaged // in speculative studies must have often indulged his natural inclination to speculate all the same, and he must have wondered about the substance or permanent substratum that stands at the foundation of outer appearances, or also about the 'how' of causality, i.e., *how* a cause has its effect. By this 'substance' and this 'how' of causality, many—I am sure—have meant the 'thing-in-itself' of the *Critique*. But since other passages in it appear to them to be saying the contrary, they believe they have discovered instances of the *Critique* contradicting itself. This line of interpretation is all too natural if one stays by the words of the *Critique*, and fails to make transcendental philosophy and the spirit of the *Critique* part of one's thought habits. What are questions of that kind really after? They aim at an intuition into the permanent substratum [of outer appearance], into the 'how' of causality; but since no such intuition can be had, one is inclined to suppose that the thing-in-itself hides from view. In fact, what we have lost sight of—through our own fault—is original representing; for that reason we fail to understand ourselves in what we seek, and as a result we do not even know what we really want. As we have been indicating, the categories are the original modes of representation. But the original synthesis of the homogeneous, i.e., the generation of space—in a word, intuition, or as we prefer to say intuiting or space itself—is another original mode of representation, distinct from the // original positing of a permanent substratum   [161] in respect to which we initially represent time to ourselves; it also differs from the original positing by which we fixate the synthesis of the alterations in the determinations of the substratum. This way of looking at things is for the understanding a source of scandal, because it does not abstain from operating with mere concepts, and it does not pay attention to the original representing upon which these concepts must in fact be grounded. For our part we shall not leave this paragraph before we are reassured that we have done everything necessary for the understanding of the Kantian deduction. We are in the same awkward position here that the *Critique* found itself in when deducing the categories. That is to say, we are trying to make the understanding itself understandable. Also the geometer finds himself in the same position in respect to his object. And the source of the awkwardness is still the same: We cannot ever represent the original representing to ourselves except through concepts, yet we expect the reader to transpose himself into this original representing. Let the reader be mindful of this imposition that we are putting upon him. Whenever he considers a matter that fills space, it is space itself that he is generating for himself; he is executing the original synthesis of the homogeneous which he fixates originally through transcendental temporal determination, thus obtaining a determinate figure. In the category of reality he further synthesizes his own sensibility, in virtue of which 'body' is given to him, and through the original temporal determination of this synthesis he obtains a determinate degree, i.e., the // real   [162] that fills space. There is a third and fourth mode of original representation that coincide with these two, but which must be distinguished from them all the same. Under the determinations of quantity and quality the understanding introduces a permanent substrate, and with respect to the substrate it represents these determinations to itself; with respect to their change, it represents time. The concept, on the other hand, through which we think that an object is given to us in sensation resolves itself into the original representing of the category of causality through which we originally fixate the change of the determinations in us. These two categories, i.e., 'permanent substrate' and 'causality', are categories of existence [*Existenz*]. Existence is therefore an original representing. To anyone who deals only in concepts this assertion must sound like the height of idealism. Let it be noted, however, that our concepts first obtain their sense and meaning in this original representing; that in them, therefore, we delimit for ourselves the area of truth where we first have our objects. This area thus delimited is the domain of experience; and it is in experience that questions about whether certain objects *are* or *are not* can for the first time be asked. It is by this limitation that we make the distinction between truth and imagination possible. This distinction is made on a empirical basis; the judgement, for instance, that the moon appears to be largest when it is near the setting is valid empirically. This distinguishing of the basis upon which certain questions are raised, and the observation that they belong to [163]   the empirical domain and that // they can only be answered empirically, is very important. For instance, if we are asked why it is that in the original representing the representation produced happens to be just so and not otherwise, so that we obtain through it the determinate representation of *such* a quantity, *such* a shape, *such* a determinate reality, etc., even though it is the understanding that performs the original synthesis, we shall answer in unison with common sense (since we are on its turf) that our determinate representation conforms to its determinate object. For instance, that the representation of the table that I can see in front of me differs from the representation of the chair which is equally in front of me is due to the fact that the first object is a table and the second is a chair, and that the two affect me in different ways. Were we referring here to the existence of things-in-themselves and have we attributed causality to them? Not at all. For our assertion is empirically correct; and if we trace it back along with the law of causality in general, to the origin of the meaning of this law in the category ['cause'], we discover that there the understanding is performing the original synthesis and the original positing, and that it will go on doing so. This is as much to say that those objects—the table and the chair—are appearances rather than things-in-themselves. All the meaning of our concepts starts in this original representing; either question regarding the cause of our determinate representations has no meaning at all, therefore, or it has [164]   meaning only where there is meaning, i.e., in the empirical domain. //

The category of reciprocal action is an original representing in which the synthesis of my sensations is originally fixed as an arbitrary one. This fixating is an original recognition (temporal determination) through which the experience of simultaneity is obtained.[36]

I see a house. In this original representing (in the course of which I attend solely to the generation of objective unity) the understanding synthesizes originally the states of the manifold parts, that is, of the substances that fill space. (This synthesis is objective, since it occurs on the basis of the previous original positing of reality that fills space.) The unity of consciousness thereby produced, however, is still only subjective; and to this extent representation is mere perception. But just as the understanding synthesizes originally, so the faculty of judgement schematized originally — that is, it effects an original temporal determination by positing substances as each determining the states of the other.

This is the analysis of the original representing in experience of the simultaneous being of things; in the same way category of causality constituted the original representing in experience of change in a thing. Here too, just as in the categories that came before, everything hangs on our attaining to the sense of our postulate. The latter has meaning only with reference to the original representing itself — exactly the contrary of what happens in representation through concepts. The intention of the postulate, in other words, is to exhibit // actual facts, not to appeal to them. This is precisely the point that was overlooked in the past — as far as I can see — and this failure led to the mistake of searching for first principles in philosophy. Certain propositions were called first principles; and in order to authenticate them, appeal was made to facts. The next step should have been to penetrate to the sense of actual fact as such; then it would have been discovered that what is contained in the principle of the original synthesis of the category as it stands in the *Critique of Pure Reason* is not so much the highest principle of all philosophy as the highest principle of every employment of the understanding. [165]

Possibility consists in the reduction of the mere concept, through which an object is thought, to the original representing in the categories of quantity, quality and relation. The reduction itself consists, therefore, in the original synthesis through which the concept is traced to the original representing, and in the original representing that determines the synthesis.[37]

I ask whether it is possible that the moon has inhabitants. The [earth's] planet falls here under all the categories. Similarly the animated beings that I am now positing on its distant surface in perfect conformity to the original mode of representation are objects of experience. The same applies, however, to the 'moon without inhabitants' also; it falls under the same original modes of representation just as much. Original recognition consists in thus fixating [in both ways, with and without inhabitants] the reduction of my concept ['moon'] to the original mode of representation. In the same way, if I am told that the heavens

[166]   // do not rotate around the earth in twenty-four hours, but that it is the earth that rotates in this period of time upon its axis, I quickly realize that the concept of 'axial rotation', when reduced to the original mode of representation, provides for every perception the same object as when I take the heavens to be in motion and the earth at rest. Thus both motions [that of the earth and that of the heavens] are possible.

Actuality is the original representing upon which the concept of object directly follows.[38] Here the original synthesis consists in the very categories of quantity, quality, and relation – not in a reduction to their original representing. The original recognition is likewise none other than the recognition in these categories.

The body that fills space is actual (it exists), for I obtain its concept from the original representing itself.

Necessity is the original positing of an object represented simply through a concept (not in the original representing). The objective unity that the understanding generates in the original synthesis upon which this category rests is in fact entirely other than the objective unity of the object that we think as 'necessary'. In contrast [to that synthesis,] this object is represented simply in a concept, as we have just said. Yet the positing of it, i.e., recognition, is original just the same.[39]

If an event exists, so does its cause. In the experience of the event,

[167]   however, which cause it is, is not thought – // i.e., there does not occur any original synthesis concerning it, even though the object must of course stand within the range of the original synthesis. 'The sky that at first was serene is now gloomy'. Independently of the original synthesis, I go on to posit a cause for this event.

Possibility, actuality and necessity have to do not with things, but solely with our faculty of cognition. 'They are': only this applies to things. For instance, I hear that an event has occurred, and at first I judge that it is a possible object. On closer investigation I become convinced that it is actual. Nothing, however, occurs in the object in the meantime. It existed when I held it to be (quite correctly) possible, and it still exists now that I think of it as actual, or again, I might discover with the help of a protractor that the three angles in an empirical triangle are equal to two right angles; this property thus belongs to the triangle in actuality. Suppose, however, that as a geometer I originally posit the same property on the basis of the concept of triangle alone; I then judge that the three angles of the triangle standing in front of me are equal to two right angles necessarily. [In other words,] the field of possible objects is not larger than the field of the actual, and the latter is in turn not exceeded by the area of the necessary. //   [168]

General Remark Concerning This Deduction of the Categories

We could not express the nature of the categories more determinedly than by saying that the understanding itself is synthesizing in them, and that unless the understanding itself first introduces into objects the synthetic unity thought in the categories, we should never find it there. Admittedly, this interpretation will appear to many to be a pronouncement of extreme idealism; but in fact it diverges so radically from idealistic thought that it is its exact contrary. In our exposition we have been trying to direct the reader's attention to the difference. But since the issue is of the greatest importance, we want to sum up the main points still, and retrieve others that we have purposedly left out in order to keep our attention fixed on the main point. Our deduction is what the great founder of the critical philosophy truly intended; it is the spirit of his philosophy, and the soul of all philosophizing. But this we shall establish only later, with illustrations from the *Critique of Pure Reason*, in a section especially dedicated to it.[40]

First of all then, let the reader attend to the special nature of our supreme principle of philosophy. We have said that it is strictly speaking the principle of all *employment of the understanding*; and let the reader pay careful attention to the fact that this characteristic is what distinguishes it // from every other proposition given as supreme   [169] principle. Our principle is a postulate. But a postulate is not a hypothesis, as the reader can very well see for himself after this discussion. There are very well known philosophers nowadays who find it necessary to found philosophies "of the elements", and they assure us with great urgency that without their Philosophy of the Elements the *Critique of Pure Reason* could not even be understood; only from their supreme principle does it obtain the required stability.[41] But what they all give us for principles are propositions, i.e., concepts of such things as 'consciousness', 'representation', 'animation', etc.; and to accredit these propositions, they appeal to actual facts. What other conclusion can we draw than that 'fact' itself must yield a still higher principle? The 'fact', however, is the employment of the understanding itself; it is precisely the principle that the *Critique* lays down as the highest — not in the role of highest proposition in an argument, in order to be able to derive from it other propositions contained in it, but as the original representing itself to which every concept must be reduced if it is to have any sense at all. The alleged first principles of those philosophers would be a lot less extolled, but more meaningful, if their discoverers had taken the meaning of 'actual fact' more to heart, i.e., what their principles refer to, viz., the original synthesis and the original recognition in the categories — in brief, the very employment of the understanding which the *Critique* has so admirably analyzed for us. //

[170]

Furthermore, let the reader be willing to pay careful attention to the concept of space that we have given. Space is precisely the synthesis of a manifold of homogeneous parts. Although we represent the original mode of representation constantly through concepts, we must never forget, all the same, that we only attain to the spirit of the categories in the original mode of representation, and that the categories are all summed up in the postulate: 'Represent originally'. Hence, concerning the particular issue of the original mode of representation that we call space, we must bear in mind the confusions mentioned in the previous section (and their source as we indicated it there).[42] They arise because we hold space to be a particular object of which we have a representation. Thus we feel obliged to look for a bond between it as it is in itself and its concept — but we can never find it, precisely because we do not really understand ourselves in the matter of what we are looking for. We must agree, therefore, that it is not *prior* to the synthesis, but *in* it, that space is a 'manifold of homogeneous parts' — a reminder that anyone will find to the point who got the point of our postulate. That this exegesis is [in conformity with] the intention of the *Critique* as set out in the Transcendental Aesthetics — of this we cannot be more firmly convinced; and we are just as convinced of the correctness of our whole exposition. Later on, however, we shall consider the method [of exposition] adopted by the *Critique*

[171] more closely, and it will be shown // that it is precisely this method that is to blame for the widespread failure to understand the *Critique*.[43] At this point I can only make the following provisional comments.

The *Critique* deals first with space, then with time, and calls them both pure intuitions. It considers them completely apart from the categories and their deduction. Now, since the *Critique* speaks of space as an intuition, rather than of an intuition of space, it should have alerted its readers to the truly transcendental point it was making. Experience has taught us, however, that it is very difficult to find the right way of transposing oneself into the original representing which really constitutes the transcendental element of cognition. Our natural inclination is to hold that space is, on the contrary, something *of which* we have an intuition; and on this view intuition itself is done away with. Since the representation of space is a concept, we find ourselves caught in a maze of unsoluble difficulties touching both us and the *Critique*. For what is intuition? And what could it mean to subsume intuition under the pure concept of the understanding? The true spirit of critical idealism will remain hidden to us as long as we are unable to unite transcendentally for ourselves all that the *Critique* separates for reason of method—in brief, as long as we have not got into the habit of viewing what we do from the transcendental standpoint of the original synthetic objective unity of consciousness. //   [172]

To make this idealism more comprehensible, and to do all that is in our power to prevent its being confused with the idealism of Berkeley, we shall now ask both the critical and the material idealist to state where the cause of the representations that we have of objects outside us is to be posited. To this question the two parties will respond with contrary answers, and this is proof that they are operating at a completely different level of thought. According to the system of criticism external objects affect us. They are the causes of our sensations, and exist just as assuredly as the subject of the representations in us undergoes change when these are altered. We live in a real world—not in an imaginary one. It is indeed possible to ask whether, under certain circumstances, we are being deceived and are mistaking appearance for truth; the question would fall, however, within the domain of truth, where it is possible to find criteria for distinguishing between truth and error. The transcendental insight that in the categories the understanding is synthesizing originally does not in the least contradict this claim. Indeed, the understanding originally posits a permanent substratum, and it first represents time to itself in respect to it; it also originally posits a something, in virtue of which change in the permanent substratum obtains its temporal determinations. The concept of cause only gets its meaning precisely from this original representing. Where else would even the concept of our understanding, *qua* faculty, derive its sense and meaning from, save from this original representing? This is what constitutes // all sense and meaning; it   [173] is self-subsisting intelligibility [das in sich bestehende Verständliche]. The material idealist, on the contrary, is not concerned about the meaning of his concepts. He imagines that in them he understands himself quite well—which is not the case at all. Thus he insists on the question, "What joins together our representation of an external object with the object itself?"—a question which to him seems to come up again even on the assumption that the object is the cause of the representation, for then too we would still have to ask, "What joins together my representation of a cause-object with the causing thing itself?" The question derives its apparent importance simply from the complete unintelligibility of the concept of causality here employed. The moment speculation turns exclusively to the understanding in an effort to make just its concept intelligible, it has to fall back on the assurance that common sense has about the reality of its cognitions.

But if we take one step beyond this original representing, everything is ruined again. I say that if we ask why we happen to have just the modes of original representing that we have, and not some others, our question is in fact directed at nothing. And the reason for this is that it aims beyond the limit of the domain of intelligibility; hence it lands where there is nothing to be understood. Yet the question has an air of respectability about it that inhibits the right interpretation of the categories as original modes of representation. What it really [174] aims at is the cognition of // things-in-themselves, for it represents the original modes of representing with the very concept by which we represent to ourselves the subjective ways [of representing] objects, through 'smell' or 'rays of light' [for instance]. Since the pleasantness or unpleasantness of smell, or the colours do not pertain to the objects in themselves, but are only ways in which we are subjectively affected by them, the same is also assumed to be the case as regards the categories, i.e., magnitude, substantiality, causality, etc., do not to pertain to objects, but are predicates that accrue to them only inasmuch as they stand related to our subjectivity, I can say in all honesty that none of this makes any sense to me. I can, however, comprehend, the cause of this nonsense (and so will anyone else who has even a modicum of honesty). It is this: We forfeit all intelligibility when we float in concepts, and even proclaim the clear intention of abandoning original representing completely. Our exposition of the categories does not make this mistake, for we collect them all together into one *postulate*. In so doing, we signify precisely the fact that outside the original representing they are empty, and we do not understand ourselves in them. We shall show later why the *Critique of Pure Reason* gives one to understand that it considers the categories to be subjective modes of representation, and regards objects as existing as things-in-themselves. Another question that has the air of being very profound but is in [175] fact directed at nothing is // why the table of categories should be complete. 'Division' is the concept of the complete enumeration of the objects that are thought through a certain concept. Now, inasmuch as this concept is assumed to have a ground and to enjoy sense and meaning, we should be able to reduce it to an original representing and to derive from that the limits of its extension. If we want to have a ground, therefore, in virtue of which we can determine whether the number of the categories is complete, we are in fact looking for an original representing which includes the original representing itself. But in my opinion this is all just a play, a stringing together of concepts that in fact cancels them all out.

Finally we must note that the locution, "a way of handling concepts that ends up cancelling them", is one that we have already used on several occasions, and that it is time that we pin down its sense. We mean by it a way of acting that consists in investigating concepts without having first bothered to secure their sense, i.e., without reducing them to the original representing. This happens, for instance, every time somebody decides to think of matter as consisting of simple, ultimate parts. He does then obtain a concept indeed—in the sense, that is, that he is representing an object to himself through the attribution of certain determinations. But he does not have an intelligible concept because (as he will have to realize) he cannot reduce it to an original presenting. // [176]

§4

The Distinction Between a Priori and a Posteriori Cognitions;
Concerning Analytical and Synthetic Judgements

There is nothing about which philosophers seem to agree so much as the distinction between *a priori* and *a posteriori* cognitions. There have to be *a priori* and *a posteriori* concepts, and the same goes for the corresponding judgements. For my part, no matter how universal this consensus may be, I remain convinced that on this issue we do not understand one another—and more often than not, even least understand ourselves. Let me remind the reader of what I have already said in the preceding section about this confusion. Our task now must be to unfold the true sense of the two expressions *"a priori"* and *"a posteriori"*; this will be possible, of course, only on condition that we are already in the habit of looking at the original representing in the categories as the source of the meaning and intelligibility of each and every concept.

Before all else, therefore, we ask: What does the *Critique* mean when it calls the categories "pure concepts of the understanding", "*a priori* concepts?

If we insist on treating the categories as concepts, we end up losing the distinction between *a priori* and *a posteriori* completely. For as concepts, they are the thoughts of certain determinations that we attribute to objects in order to represent them to ourselves; but it is all // the same whether we represent an object through one [177] determination or another—whether through 'red', 'solid', 'liquid', or 'quantity, 'reality', 'substance', etc. It is meaningless, moreover, to give sensation as the [distinguishing] mark between the two kinds of representation, i.e., to consider *a priori* any concept free of it, but 'empirical' any that contains some. For sensation itself is never a concept;

ultimately, therefore, we can with equal right say that the categories (which we display as pure concepts) contain just as much sensation as the empirical concepts do. Say what we will, to use sensation as the distinguishing mark between the two really amounts to saying ultimately that the categories are innate concepts. But this would be the essence of absurdity; it would be no better than to appeal to a *qualitas occulta*. We would in effect be saying that we have concepts of objects but we do not know where they came from.

If on the contrary we represent the categories as we have done, i.e., as the summit of the entire employment of the understanding, every trace of unintelligibility disappears. Considered in this way, we find in them the understanding and its full compass of intelligibility. In dealing with mere concepts we were all too often troubled by our inability to find anywhere among them the stable bearing we were looking for. We found it the moment we got a clear sight of the original representing in the categories, and learned how to reduce [178] concepts to the original // synthesis and recognition. The most crucial point, however, will always be that, just because they are original modes of representation, the categories constitute the employment of the understanding and all that has intelligibility. In their role as mere concepts, this propitious aspect of theirs is completely lost sight of. Take for instance the category 'quantity'; in it the understanding synthesizes the homogeneous originally, and fixates its synthesis—this is its employment. On the other hand, if it is through the concept 'quantity' that I think an object, I am no further ahead than if I think of it as something 'red'. In this *thinking* the *thing* (the object) is already present in the background, so to speak; in this respect all thought is quite the same; it always presupposes objective unity. In the language of the *Critique* this unity found in a mere concept is called analytical. Whatever validity it has, however, whatever intelligibility it has within itself, it can only have borrowed from the original representing, that is, (again in the words of the *Critique*) it must presuppose an original synthetic unity of consciousness obtained in the *original* representing of the categories. The categories, therefore, are called *pure concepts of the understanding* in view of their particular lineage, i.e., because the original representing that constitutes the entire employment of the understanding is the foundation of their analytical unity. In empirical concepts, on the other hand, the analytical unity rests upon an original synthetic unity—a unity carried out in the original representing of a [179] category. For instance, the // concept 'substance' is a pure concept of the understanding, for the objective unity that I think in it (i.e., the object that I represent to myself by the attribution of substantiality) is grounded in the original representing of the category (i.e., in the original positing of a permanent substratum with respect to which time can first be represented). But the concept of a permanent *quantum* of matter that abides unaltered throughout all its alterations (e.g., by its weight matter always shows itself to be the same quantity) is an empirical concept, because it rests on a synthetic unity generated through the previous original representing of the category 'substantiality'. It is only because of a certain subreption that we happen to regard the categories as concepts; this illusion, if not recognized, gives rise to the supposed knowledge of the thing-in-itself. The illusion consists in taking the objective unity in the concept to be independent of the determination through which we represent it to ourselves. And it is up to transcendental meditation to make us aware of the fact that this objective unity is generated through the original representing in the category. This, and no other, is the insight to which the *Critique* is alluding when it says that we know things as they appear to us.

If we have been fortunate enough to introduce the reader into Transcendental Philosophy—as has surely been the case if the reader has grasped that by the supreme principle of the entire employment of the understanding we mean a *postulate*—then it will be easy to convince him of the true essence of critical // philosophy, and of [180] its great value. So far as I know, three systems are nowadays identified by name and every new brood is forced under the wing of one of them. Every speculative philosopher, that is to say, must belong either to the family of the dogmatists, or of the skeptics, or of the critics. For our part, we must confess that we have endeavoured in vain to single out firm characteristics by which these systems are to be distinguished. It is closer to the truth to say that every philosophy should be at once dogmatic, skeptic, and critical. It is dogmatic because of the established truths it possesses; skeptic, because of its free admission of harbouring uncertainties; and critical, because it has let enquiry precede all its declarations. It is not our intention, however, to detract from the universal validity of the meaning that these designations have in common usage. Kant's philosophy has been called critical since it first made its appearance; our duty is to uncover the aspect which makes it truly so, i.e., the property that defines it as such, and in this way supply an appropriate meaning for those general designations.

The *Critique of Pure Reason* took issue with the speculative claims made about objects not found anywhere in experience. In this respect, of course, it was following a well established practice. The *Critique*, however, truly did not allow itself to be implicated in speculation; it refrained from spinning out more concepts; instead // it deemed [181] it necessary to look behind concepts for the point from which they have their support and intelligibility before trying to enrich itself with cognitions in this way. That is why it is a critical philosophy. We must of course admit that we shall know what philosophy is *as such* only

after we have made our acquaintance with the categories as the original modes of representation to which we must reduce the meaning of every concept. For philosophizing is the art of bestowing intelligibility on concepts by leading them to it. It differs from a mere conceptual game precisely in this; strictly speaking, therefore, the descriptive title "critical" is redundant when applied to philosophy. It was the *Critique of Pure Reason* that first founded this art of the intelligible. It did it by analyzing the employment of the understanding in its categories, and by measuring both the alleged results of speculation and the objections raised against them against the standard set by this employment. As it turned out, neither side stood up to the scrutiny. For anyone who has made the sense of the [Kantian] 'category' his own, this means that both the results and the objections were empty concepts, or that they lacked objects. The *Critique* deals with the speculative philosopher quite differently than had been done before. He is one who claims that matter is made up of either finite or infinite parts; that our spirit's substance is either simple and indestructible or the contrary; that either there is a God or there is none. The *Critique*, now, conducts itself critically towards him precisely by refusing to engage him in speculation, i.e., it refuses to lose itself along with him among mere concepts.
[182]   // Its intent is rather to secure the sense and meaning of the opponent's concepts, and thus to lead them back to the categories—to the original representing. Numberless vocal admirers of the *Critique* have missed this truth about it—and so do those who think that there must be a supreme principle of philosophy, which the *Critique* has neglected to establish, even though the demonstrative force of all its assertions are dependent on it.

Now that we have made explicit the sense in which our philosophy is truly critical, the reader will guess by himself what we take the essence of dogmatic philosophy to be. This essence lies in its habit of floating in mere concepts, regardless what its claims happen to be. It follows, therefore, that the dogmatist is the only speculative philosopher in the strict sense. And he betrays his habit of thought whether he is dealing with objects that fall within experience or with objects that transcend it. Even what he has to say about the objects of experience is metaphysical rather than physical; it is in truth speculation. For instance, he does not bother to ask for the determinate causes of natural events; he is interested, rather, in the 'ground of the ground'. His research is directed to the grounding of the grounded. But since he does not know how to give direction to his concepts—since his habit is to treat the categories, which are in fact the point of support
[183]   of those concepts and their source of intelligibility, as // if they were just over-blown concepts—all his searching turns out to be just a floating among them. After what we have just said about dogmatism,

however, it should be apparent that the many philosophers nowadays who revere the title of skeptic, and would gladly be counted as skeptics, are in fact true dogmatists. And this they are at all times, even when they are witholding assent to certain propositions, as long as in so doing they rest their case on mere speculation—as long as they pursue their opponent on his own high-flown regions, and even try to give him battle there using local weapons. As our definition of dogmatism implies, the only true skeptic is one who notes the ambiguity, the impermanence and total lack of intelligibility of speculation, but since he does not know what to do about it, he entirely suspends his judgements. I dare say that the number of those who have stood by this negative attitude of thought has at all times been very small indeed.

After this digression we return to the announced theme of the paragraph. We have endeavoured to give the true distinction between *a priori* and empirical concepts. The categories are *a priori* only when we view them in the guise of concepts. We then think an analytic unity in them; in other words, we furnish the objective unity with a conceptual determination. (What happens is that in the concept we attribute something to the object, and in this attribution we represent the object to ourselves.) This analytic unity, however, is not at all independent of the objective unity, as it seems to be to those who // treat the categories just as concepts. It lies, rather, in the original [184] operation of representing through which the objective unity is generated. In other words, rightly viewed the conceptual determination here at issue is the original representing through which each and every synthetic objective unity of consciousness comes about. Of course, the analytic unity of empirical concepts originates in a synthetic one. But in their case the prior synthetic unity is not the original representing itself, as it is with pure concepts; it is rather only a product of it. We are reverting to this point once more because we fear that the reader might suspect that we are just playing with concepts, in spite of our zeal against false philosophizing of that sort. Only after we have carefully analyzed the actual fact of consciousness, i.e., the original representing, do we dare with great circumspection, to appeal to it in order to establish the reality of our concepts. But now, in what respect do the concepts of the causality of a thing and of the fluidity of an object differ? Both are concepts; the analytic unity of consciousness consists in the attribution of a determination (causality or fluidity). The validity of both rests on an original representing which gives to them meaning and intelligibility. At the ground of the concept of causality, however, there lies the original representing itself; at the ground of the concept of fluidity, on the other hand, an original synthetic unity generated through the original representing. We shall now // go on to clarify [185] both the distinction between analytic and synthetic judgements, and between *a priori* and empirical judgements. This will cast further light on the explanation just given.

I begin by remarking that adducing criteria of universality and necessity to distinguish *a priori* from *a posteriori* judgements does not exhaust the matter at all. The *Critique* already speaks of the distinction in the introduction in order to direct the reader's attention to its concern. But the important question that it raises there is: "How are *a priori* synthetic judgements possible?"[44] And the answer it gives as the result of its investigation is presented through the concept of the possibility of experience. I claim, therefore, that the sense of the answer is not available to anyone who has not transposed himself into the original representing—anyone who has not made himself familiar with the objective synthetic unity of consciousness, or has not taken onto himself the sense of our postulate. It will also be evident at once that the digression in which we defined the difference between critical, dogmatic and skeptical philosophy above, is very germane to our purpose.

Judgement consists in recognizing that an object stands under a concept, that is in the representation of an object through a concept. The ground of it is the object therefore, i.e., the objective synthetic unity of consciousness. The understanding generates this unity in its categories. Out of this unity we then lift certain characteristics which [186] we refer to a // determinate point by attributing them to it. In so doing we fix the point for ourselves, and thereby represent the object. This is what the transition from the original synthetic unity of the category to the analytical unity of the concept (where the objects are thought by us through their characteristics) consist in, or the transition from representing an object originally to thinking it. This is the true nature of judgement in general, and we must be very clear about it if we want to understand the distinction between analytic and synthetic judgements.

The statement of the determinations which the understanding transfers from the original synthetic unity into the analytic one of the concept is an analytical judgement. These determinations are the characteristics which the understanding relies on in order to represent a thing to itself and to fixate its objective unity. But once this objective unity has, through those characteristics, acquired a stable analytical form, [i.e., once] they constitute it, we have a basis on which still other characteristics can be laid. Any further operation therefore, i.e., any other attribution or removal of further characteristics has the analytical unity of the concept as it unalterable foundation. Synthetic judgements are precisely those by which we represent an object to ourselves through still other characteristics than those that constitute this analytic unity. But we must stress here that the synthesis in a synthetic judgement is not at all the same as the original synthesis of

the category that we have already discussed. // The joining done [187]
in synthetic judgements is a synthesis of *concepts*, which must in any
case presuppose a prior original one if it is to have any sense or meaning.
We should now try to help the reader with an example.

I see a tree. Now, in this seeing the understanding is synthesizing
originally, and its synthesis will be fixated by the transcendental
determination of time (i.e., the original recognition). The objective
synthetic unity of consciousness is generated through this original
representing. In it, however, I still do not represent an object to myself;
rather, for this to happen, the understanding lifts certain characteristics
out of its original synthesis, and by attributing them [back to it] it
fixates it. The objective unity thus fixated is what the *Critique* calls
"the analytical unity of consciousness". The original representing has
thereby passed over into a thinking. The objective unity is fixed through
characteristics as 'a figure of *this* kind', '*this* reality', etc.: these
characteristics constitute the analytic unity, and the listing of them is
the analytical judgement. Once the analytical unity has been secured,
the understanding can join other characteristics onto it, or separate
them from it once more yet, without disturbing it. For instance, the
understanding thinks of the tree which now is covered with leaves as
it will be stripped of them in autumn, etc. This representation of the
object through characteristics that are in fact alien to its analytical
unity is what constitutes a synthetic judgement. The synthesis of the
latter, however, is merely derivative, // and is not to be confused [188]
with the original synthesis of the categories. It is a combination of
mere concepts, whose analytical unity always presupposes an originally
synthetic one.[45]

We are finally in a position to present clearly the distinction between
a priori and *a posteriori* synthetic judgements. A synthetic judgement
is empirical if the joining of concepts in it rests on a synthetic unity;
on the other hand, it is a pure judgement, or a judgement *a priori*, if
the joining of the concepts thought through it rests on the original
representing itself. Thus, in the case of the tree in the example above,
if I think that after some time it will be stripped of leaves, or that
sometime earlier it was stripped, this judgement is synthetic *a posteriori*.
For the joining of these concepts, i.e., the combination of a new
characteristic to the already secured analytical unity, rests on the
synthetic one in which the exfoliated tree appears as object to me
even though the characteristic in question (the 'exfoliation') has not
been taken up in the analytical unity. But if I judge that some given
fact must have a cause, this judgement is then synthetic *a priori*. For
in this case, if I look for the meaning of the concepts, I find it not in a
synthetic unity generated through the original representing, but in
the original representing itself.

It is from the attention given to this original representing that the demonstrations given by the *Critique* in its synthetic determination [Urteil] of the transcendental // faculty of judgement draw their force. The synthesis of its concepts is based on that representing, and the failure to pay attention to it is what made all demonstrations of concepts prior to the *Critique* a mere special pleading. For the common practice has been to abandon oneself to speculation, and thus to restrict all enquiry just to concepts. (I am referring to those cases, of course, where a search for demonstrations was still held necessary, and the propositions at issue were not just taken to be innate truths) Since people have failed to give prior attention to the *nervus probandi* of the *Critique's* demonstration, i.e., the original representing, it has come to pass that its intention has been missed even by countless of its admirers. These people stop short at the concept of the possibility of experience, and believe that they can establish the truth of the *Critique's* propositions through clarification and analysis of this one concept. In making this assumption, however, they part company with the *Critique;* then they lose themselves in speculations in which they always get back from their concepts just what they have chosen to put into them. We shall now present the true nature of the link connecting the concepts in the propositions of the *Critique;* to this end we shall consider them one by one.

The *Critique* makes clear this nature when it says: In the principle itself we shall avail ourselves of the category; in the execution, however, we shall replace it with the schema.[46] With this it expresses precisely what we said before, viz., that the propositions are, *qua* propositions, the statement of a link between concepts; that their synthesis is not original therefore, but that it rests rather on an original representing.
. . .

[189]

Notes

1. George Berkeley (1685-1753), *A Treatise Concerning the Principles of Human Knowledge* (1710, 2nd ed. 1734), Part I, cf §9 ff; *The Theory of Vision Vindicated and Explained* (1733) §51.

2 I.e., Descartes's type.

3. Cf. *Critique*, B276-277

4. Fichte thought that Beck's philosophy was the best introduction to his own idealism. Cf.; *Erste Einleitung, Gesammtausgabe*, I, 444, note 3; English tr., p. 24. Beck, for his part, thought that Fichte's idea of the Science of Knowledge was a jest. Cf. *Grundlage, Gesammtausgabe*, I, 89; English tr., pp. 91-92. Cf. also Letter of Beck to Kant, June 24, 1797, *Briefwechsel*, Academy Ed., Vol XII, p. 174. English tr., p. 234.

5. *Critique*, B274-275

6. This group includes the rationalists, but also a skeptic like Schulze. Cf. *Aenesidemus*, p. 45.

7. *Theorie*, p. 321.

8. Ibid., p. 257.

9. *Aenesidemus*, pp. 53-54.

10. This is Reinhold's principle.

11. Pp. 8 ff.

12. Cf. *Critique*, A724, B752.

13. This is an echo from Bishop Berkeley; cf. *Principles of Human Knowledge*, Part I, §5.

14. Cf. Ibid., p. A644, B672.

15. It is interesting to note that Kant asked Beck to make clear what *Beilegung* meant by giving the term in Latin also. Letter to J. S. Beck, July 1, 1794, *Briefwechsel*, Academy Ed., Vol XI, p. 496. English tr., p. 216. To my knowledge, Beck never did so. Zweig in his translation of Beck's letters to Kant renders *ursprüngliche Beilegung* as "original activity." Cf. p. 214. But see also p. 30.

16. The reference is not just to Reinhold, but to all those constructing elementary (i.e., basic) philosophy (*Elementar-Philosophie*).

18. Cf. note 6 above.

19. Reinhold.

20. Beck is probably referring to Maimon. Cf. Maimon's "Ueber die Welt-Seele, Entelechia Universi," published in the *Journal für Aufklärung*, VIII (1789), pp. 99-122 (cited by Pupi, *Reinhold*, p. 142). Cf. also, Kuntze, *Die Philosophie Solomon Maimons*, p. 287. But, as Pupi points out, Maimon's 'panpsychism' is a reflection of the romantic revival of Spinoza and Leibniz that was already well in progress at that time. Beck might just as well be referring to Herder, therefore; or to the neo-Spinozism in general.

21. Maimon.

22. Fichte.

23. For a clarification of what Beck means, cf. pp. 146-147.

24. Cf. *Critique*, A142, B182, and note 26 below where the text is cited. Note that for Beck the category 'quantity', which is for Kant a pure concept, *is* the "pure image of all magnitudes (*quantorum*) for outer sense". i.e., space. This identification of category with image is definitely not a Kantian move.

25. Although Beck *seems* to be simply repeating passages from Kant's letters to him, he is in fact modifying Kant's position radically. Kant says, for instance: "The synthesizing itself is not given; on the contrary, it must be done by us; we must *synthesize* if we are to represent anything as *synthesized* (even space and time). . . ." (To Beck, July 1, 1794). This sounds like Beck. Yet for Kant, although the synthesizing must be done *according* to the categories (which are the concepts of an object in general), the final synthesis cannot be simply their product. For as Kant equally reminds Beck in his letter, "Knowledge is the representation through *concepts* of a *given* object as such . . . ." Hence, "for knowledge, two sorts of representation are required: (1) intuition, by means of which an object is given, and (2) conception, by means of which an object is thought. . . ." But although "combination cannot be given . . . . but has to be made", and hence

"must rest on the pure spontaneity of the understanding in concepts of objects in general", since "concepts to which no corresponding objects could be given . . . would not even be concepts . . . , just for that reason a manifold must be given a priori for those a priori concepts" (To Beck, January 20, 1792). Or again, "the form [of sensibility] must be a priori, but it is not *thought* (for only the synthesizing as activity is a product of thought); it must rather be *given* in us (space and time) and must therefore be a *single* representation and not a concept . . ." (To Beck, July 3, 1792). In other words, the distinction between thought on the one hand, and space and time on the other, is for Kant irreducible, because the sense in which an object is said to be simply *given* in us, or its presence to imply *receptivity* on our part, is irreducible ("Perhaps at the outset you can avoid defining 'sensibility' in terms of 'receptivity'. . . [But that a sensible appearance] constitutes only the manner in which the subject is affected by representation . . .is already implied by its being merely the determination of the subject." To Beck, January 20, 1792). For the above references, cf. *Briefwechsel*, Academy Ed. Vol. XI, p. 496 (English tr. p. 216), pp. 302-33 (English tr. p. 184), p. 334 (English tr., p.193), p. 302 (English tr., pp. 183-184).

26. Cf. *Critique*, A142, B182: "The pure image of all magnitudes (*quantorum*) for outer sense in space; that of all the objects of the senses in general is time. But the pure *schema* of magnitude (*quantitatis*), as a concept of the understanding is *number*, a representation which comprises the successive addition of homogeneous units." Beck has reduced Kant's 'quantity' to what Kant calls the "pure image of all magnitudes" (cf. note 24 above) on the one hand, and the schema 'number' on the other. The category, in other words, is both the original intuiting and the original recognition of the object constituted in that intuiting. Synthesis of recognition and the generation of time are identified by Beck. This is again not a Kantian move. For Kant the category 'quantity' does not refer, *qua* pure thought, to either space or time. The connection with these is first established only in the *schema*, through the activity of the imagination, i.e., in that "transcendental function of the imagination" that mediates between pure thought and sensibility. On Beck's view, there cannot be any problem of mediation, and the fact that it *does* arise for Kant indicates that his categories are indeed what Beck calls "derived concepts." Although Kant dismisses the question of how the categories apply to the 'thing-in-itself,' he is still faced by the analogous, and just as intractable problem, of how they apply to sensibility.

27. Cf. what Kant says about the *schemata*: "The schemata of the pure concepts of understanding are thus the true and sole conditions under which these concepts obtain relation to objects and so possess *significance*" (A146, B185-186). One can well understand why Beck could identify 'categorial' and 'spatio-temporal' unity and still think that he was merely expounding Kant. On the strength of what Kant himself says about how pure concepts acquire *significance*, the supposed pure categories in virtue of which we can also think of, but not know, transcendent objects, can only be *derivative* or *discursive* concepts. They should not appear at all at the beginning of the Transcendental Analytic. On the other hand, one can also understand how Beck might have appeared to Kant to be delving into that "art" of the imagination which is "concealed in the depths of the human soul, whose real modes of activity nature is hardly likely ever to allow us to discover, and to have open to our gaze" (A141, B180-181).

28. *Critique*, B131-134, especially B133.

29. Cf. *Critique*, A143, B182-183.

30. Cf. *Critique*, B135, B144-145.

31. Cf. p. 134. *Beilegung* is 'conceptualization', i.e., it presupposes the prior activity of synthesis in original representation and of recognization in the temporal determination of that synthesis. See also below, pp. 186-187. In his letters to Kant, however, Beck seems to use *ursprüngliche Beilegung* to mean the original synthesis *and* the original recognition. Cf. note 15 above. Also, Beck to Kant, June 17, 1794, Academy Ed., Vol. XI, p. 490, English tr., p. 214.

32. The implication, of course, is that meaning is present in the original intuitive presentation of an object even before it is expressed in a concept, i.e., that "intuitions" are not after all "blind."

33. Cf. *Critique*, A143, B183: "The schema of substance is the permanence of the real in time . . ." etc.

34. Cf. above, note 28.

35. Cf. *Critique*, A144-B183.

36. Cf. Ibid.

37. Cf. Ibid., A144, B184. The implication seems to be that 'self-awareness' begins only with the synthesis of possibility.

38. Cf. Ibid., A145, B184; but the connection to Kant's text is here very tenuous. The categories as Kant understands them, viz., as the concepts of an object in general are 'fixated' only with the synthesis of 'actuality'. This seems to be the implication here.

39. Cf. Ibid.; again, the connection with Kant's text is very tenuous.

40. I.e., in Section IV.

41. Cf. above, notes 16-22.

42. Section I, §6, pp. 36-45.

43. I.e., in Section IV.

44. *Critique*, B 19.

45. Cf. above, note 31.

46. *Critique*, A181-B224.

PART

II

The Critical Philosophy
and the Critical Journal of
Schelling and Hegel

Skepticism, Dogmatism and Speculation in the Critical Journal
H. S. Harris

1. The "Idea" of philosophical criticism.

THE CRITICAL JOURNAL of *Philosophy* (from which four essays are here translated) was Schelling's brainchild. He proposed to Tübingen publisher J. F. Cotta in June 1800 that he should edit a philosophical journal for them. At that time he was hoping that Fichte would collaborate with him. But through his concern with the philosophy of nature Schelling had now begun to emerge publicly as the original thinker, which he always felt himself to be (even when he was writing the early essays which appear to us, as they did to their first audience, to be directly derivative from Fichte's *Science of Knowledge*).[1] The reading of the *System of Transcendental Idealism* made Fichte for the first time sharply aware of this; and he insisted that they should clarify their differences before they embarked on a new venture together.[2]

Schelling answered promptly, but their correspondence languished for some month after this. It was at this very time, (November 1800) that the unknown Hegel was writing to Schelling for advice on how to emerge from the obscurity of his life as a house-tutor in Frankfurt and begin to make an academic career for himself. With Schelling's encouragement he came to Jena; and while Fichte himself was meditating on the difference between himself and Schelling, Hegel was writing the essay in which that "difference" would be defined and discussed publicly for the first time.[3]

By the time Hegel's *Difference* essay was at the printers Schelling had received Fichte's negative decision about participation in the new *Journal*. He must have asked Hegel to be a collaborator already — since the Preface of the *Difference* essay promises the publication of further critical discussions in the near future. But it was only now (in August 1801) that Hegel became one of the editors.

Hegel's first task was to write the introductory essay. It was natural for everyone to assume when the *Journal* appeared, that this official manifesto of the new idealism was the work of Schelling. Certainly Schelling revised it. He seems to have thought of it as his, and spoke of it almost as if it was his own; so there can be no doubt that the two editors had discussions in which Schelling did most of the talking. The "main idea" of the Identity Philosophy — which Hegel expresses in his review of Krug as "to put God back again at the peak of philosophy, absolutely prior to all else as the one and only ground of everything, the unique *principium essendi* and *cognoscendi*" (100)[4] — was certainly Schelling's. The one "Idea of Philosophy" spoken of in the introductory essary is a revival of the Christian Platonic ideal of the *philosophia perennis*. Through his philosophy of nature Schelling gave to it a distinctively Spinozist emphasis. But there is no doubt that he (whom his Jena students called "Plato") believed as fervently as Hegel that the true "speculative" tradition of western philosophy must be rescued from the limbo to which Kant consigned *all* previous metaphysics in the "Dialectic of Pure Reason".[5]

But this belief that "in God we live and move and have our being" expresses a consensus in which both Hegel and Hölderlin had always shared. It probably goes back to the ideal of the Hen *kai Pan* at Tübingen ten years earlier. With it goes the view that every true proponent of the "Idea of Philosophy" can recognize his genuine predecessors intuitively. Hegel expresses this confidence in the *Difference* essay, and pours scorn on Reinhold's view of the prior history of philosophy as an exercise-ground. But even there the inadequacy of this doctrine of intuitive recognition was patent, since it was undeniable that Fichte had no appreciation of the true speculative tradition to which he supposedly belonged.[6] The *philosophia perennis* clearly needed a better theory of philosophical criticism. This is what the introductory essay provides; and from the way that the concept of "recognition" is developed in it, we can be reasonably certain that it is Hegel's theory rather than Schelling's.

At the very least, an adequate critical theory of the *philosophia perennis* must provide two things: a constructive way of articulating the relation of the (apparently) conflicting versions of the one true philosophy; and a way of distinguishing between genuine versions of the true philosophy, and those false pretenders that are always laying claim to her throne.

The introduction to the *Critical Journal* structures both problems in terms of the concept of "recognition". Between the (apparently) conflicting versions of true philosophy there can and ought to be a relation of *equal* recognition. So here the task of the philosophical critic is to raise the consciousness of his dogmatic opponents to the equal (or critical) awareness that he himself has of their shared 'identity'. Since it is actually the cultured *public* whose consciousness must be raised, we can define the office of the critic as that of making other students of philosophy see that an apparent disagreement is not real, or that what is properly affirmed on both sides is harmonious; and that what seems to be denied is not, or at any rate should not, be denied.

It is the application of the concept of recognition between "philosophy" and "unphilosophy" that is, to my mind, distinctively

Hegelian. For it is here that the conception of an *unequal* recognition (or of the "struggle for recognition" is born. The two parties in this relationship do not agree about *what philosophy is*. The only way in which they can be 'reconciled' is for one of them to submit; and in principle, of course, it is the false pretender that must give itself up, and enter upon the process of *Bildung* to learn the error of its ways. I find it hard to believe that Schelling had any significant part in formulating the relation of the Identity Philosophy to the rival contemporary schools in just this way. So I am inclined to suspect that although Schelling may have added some sentences and remodelled others, it was he whose "thoughts" were made into the instrument of Hegel's critical programme in this opening essay. Hegel's critical theory is not yet fully developed. One cannot say that it provides answers to the two problems that I have identified as crucial for the overcoming of Kant's dialectical picture of the history of speculative thought. But that is because the theory itself points towards an *ostensive* solution. The theory can only be developed by application. The seeming hopelessness of the quest for speculative truth is overcome by the quest itself. *Solvitur ambulando* — it is solved as we go. Thus the experience of putting his critical theory into practice (as he did in both directions in the *Critical Journal*) was of vital importance to Hegel's eventual ability to give a far more adequate theoretical statement of his critical theory, and his critical method, than he gives us here.

It must be admitted also, however, that Hegel's application of the theory in the *Critical Journal* suffers from a serious weakness. Only the great dead whom Kant had consigned to perdition are apt to receive full and unstinting recognition. Thus Spinoza is defended in *Faith and Knowledge*, and Leibniz in the Schulze review. Living thinkers receive a more ambivalent critical treatment. In the *Difference* essay Kant's achievement is more positively evaluated than it is in the introduction to the *Critical Journal*; and there is the same contrast between the presentation of Fichte in the *Difference* essay and the way he is treated in *Faith and Knowledge*.

In both cases the reason is easy to grasp. It is Kant's conception of the history of philosophy — his claim that the ceaseless squabbling of the old "dogmatic" schools sprang from the inherent impossibility of the enterprise in which they were engaged — that Hegel is fighting against in the introductory essay. His most appreciative account of Kant's work is actually to be found in *Faith and Knowledge*, where Kant comes off much better than either Jacobi or Fichte. (The student of this present volume will find it worth while to compare Beck's interpretation of Kant with the reconstruction of Kant's philosophy that Hegel offers there).[7] Fichte, on the other hand, had declined from the speculative heights of the *Science of Knowledge* of 1794 to the shallows of the *Vocation of Man* (1800). From the standpoint of 'speculation' (which begins from God as "the unique *principium essendi* and *cognoscendi*") he had fallen back almost to the crudest form of the standpoint of finite consciousness for which "the one self-certifying certainty (*das an sich und einzig Gewisse*) is that there exists a thinking subject, a Reason affected with finitude".[8]

Precisely in Kant's doctrine of the transcendental unity of apperception Schelling and Hegel saw the bridge by which "the fixed standpoint which the all-powerful culture of our time has established for philosophy" could be left behind. This fixed standpoint was "that of a Reason affected by sensibility" in such a way that "philosophy cannot aim at the cognition of God, but only at what is called the cognition of men". For the true speculative tradition on the other hand "man is . . . a glowing spark of eternal beauty, or a spiritual focus of the universe".[9] This intuition of humanity can still be recognized in Kant, Jacobi and Fichte—which is why Hegel chooses them to display "the reflective philosophy of subjectivity in the complete range of its forms" (in *Faith and Knowledge*). But the fact that he means (in a qualified way) to do them honor becomes apparent only when we compare his treatment of them with the way that he deals with lesser men like Krug and Schulze (who accept the "standpoint of consciousness" in its most fixedly finite form).

So it cannot be denied that the critical standpoint of the "Ideal of Philosophy" was too *absolute*. It was like Yahweh "in whose sight shall no man *living* be justified". Jacobi wrote to Friedrich Bouterwek in March 1802 that his close friend and associate Friedrich Köppen had announced to him "the appearance of the first issue of a new *Critical Journal* edited by Schelling and by a Mr. Hegel who is quite unknown to me, in which almighty wrath is to prevail."[10] When Jacobi came under the lash himself he was admirably good tempered about it; but at this distance of time, when the "quite unknown Mr. Hegel" has triumphed over all of these more prominent contemporaries, it is very easy to be misled. At the end of my introduction to the *Difference* essay I took the view that the challenge of Reinhold and Bardili's "reduction of philosophy to logic" was less important to Hegel than the sting of Krug's demand for a "deduction of his pen". In the light of Hegel's treatment of Reinhold in the *Difference* essay that verdict seemed to be the only possible (though I was careful to point out that it did not reflect a just appreciation of Reinhold's historic significance).[11] But I was not mindful at that moment of the appreciation of Reinhold's place in the evolution of idealism which Hegel himself gives in a few lines of the Krug essay itself (110-11) I can only conclude now, very tentatively, that the possible influence of Reinhold on the evolution of Hegel's logic deserves serious study.

Kant's critical philosophy overthrew not only the dogmatic pretensions of the rationalism that began from God, but also the dogmatic empiricism of Locke's "way of ideas". When we put all of Hegel's critical verdicts together, and study them both in their context and in relation with one another, we begin to appreciate how sensitive he was to the variety of *unfixed* forms that the "standpoint of consciousness" assumed among the more intelligent disciples of the sage of Königsberg. It is not surprising that after a few years he himself moved from the fixed standpoint of "speculation", and set himself to write the ideal history of the "experience of consciousness" as it climbs the ladder to that standpoint. *Faith and Knowledge* offered a systematic analysis of how the Kantian revolution had failed and the "fixed standpoint of the all-powerful culture of our time" had triumphed. But Hegel's earlier analysis of the types of skepticism in his review of Schulze, though it was less systematically performed and presented, had already identified the means by which the "standpoint of consciousness" can become effectively self-transcending. That is why the Schulze review is so important in the story of Hegel's intellectual evolution.

2. The "latest skepticism"

The view that the quest for wisdom demonstrates its own hopelessness is philosophical *skepticism*. Thus when Kant applied his critical theory to the historical record to explain why the supposed "Queen of the Sciences" has never made any progress towards being a "science" (either like mathematics or like physics) by showing that the speculative enterprise is unachievable in principle, he was a skeptic. On August 27, 1801 – i.e., shortly after, or shortly before, the "Introduction" for the *Critical Journal* was drafted – Hegel defended twelve theses at a formal *Disputation* through which he won the right to give lectures. Among them there are three that are relevant to Kant's "skepticism". The sixth defined speculative philosophy thus: "An Idea is a synthesis of the infinite and the finite, and all philosophy is in Ideas." The seventh drew a conclusion about the Kantian philosophy: "The critical philosophy lacks Ideas, and is an imperfect form of skepticism." The only puzzle here, is to know why the Kantian skepticism is imperfect; for the "dialectic of Pure Reason" appears to be a conclusive demonstration that we do, indeed, "lack Ideas" (as defined in Thesis VI). The reason is given, at least by implication, in the next thesis: "The matter of the postulate of Reason, which the critical philosophy displays, destroys philosophy itself, and is the principle of Spinozism."[12] Just how Hegel demonstrated this eighth thesis we do not need to inquire, for the reference to "Spinozism" as a badge of shame is certainly not sincere. What is interesting is the condemnation of the postulational use of pure Reason.[13] It is surely because of Kant's willingness, in the interest of practical Reason, to employ the Idea of God as a necessary postulate, that his skepticism is said to be "imperfect". Except for the loophole which the "antinomies of pure Reason" provide for a postulational access to the noumenal realm, the skepticism of the *Critique of Pure Reason* is about as perfect as any philosophical skepticism could be. Hegel's eighth thesis, however he proposed to demonstrate it, was clearly calculated to block that one loophole.[14]

As compared with Kant, the official proponent of the "latest skepticism" G. E. Schulze, the self-styled reincarnation of Aenesidemus, is not a *philosophical* skeptic at all. He is ready enough to appeal to the dismal record of speculative controversy, but he does not properly understand what the critical philosophy has done either for the conceptual defense of empirical science, or for the conceptual attack on speculative philosophy. (His one virtue, which Hegel like Fichte before him, passes over in silence, is to have recognized the point at which the critical philosophy becomes uncritical — viz., about the actual unity of the cognitive self.)

For Schulze it is enough to be skeptical about the possibility of philosophy in a commonsensical way. His philosophical skepticism does not touch any of the dogmatic certainties of the "healthy human understanding" of his time. Similarly, Krug, on the other side, is commonsensical in a critical framework — and one of the most amusing, as well as illuminating, aspects of Hegel's essay on Krug is that it makes us see how strange "common sense" looks when the philosophy which it must "take" (as its conceptual cloak) is Kant's. G. E. Moore would hardly recognize Krug's theory as "common sense". But then, for my part, I cannot see much common sense in *Principia Ethica* either. Schulze's common sense is probably sounder than either — because it does not "take philosophy" at all.

It is evident enough that, in Hegel's view, Schulze's "skepticism" is only a form of "unphilosophy"; and Hegel's critical attack upon it is only a foil for his attempt to rehabilitate ancient skepticism as a vitally important moment of the *philosophia perennis*. But when we see Hegel defending Leibniz against the jibes of Schulze, we should not forget that the real critic of Leibniz was Kant, and that Leibniz was the paradigm of that dogmatic slumber from which Hume aroused him. The "latest skepticism" does not make a very good showing in Hegel's essay. Schulze ranks below Sextus, and probably even below Cicero on Hegel's critical ladder. Sextus, in turn, ranks below the Academics Arcesilaus and Carneades; and the true fountainhead of philosophical skepticism is Plato's *Parmenides* (and hence the Eleatic tradition). But in spite of appearances, Hegel is no *laudator temporis acti*. He does indeed believe that philosophical truth is the "oldest of old things";[15] but unlike most other adherents of the perennial tradition, he did not think that the oldest was necessarily the best. In his view, the fortunes of skepticism go up and down with those of speculation. But the potential of both of them increases with historical experience. The oldest skepticism was what sparked, in Plato, the greatest achievement of ancient speculation. After Plato, both skepticism and philosophy went downhill. But since Descartes and Luther a rebirth has been in progress. I cannot remember any Hegelian references to Montaigne, and it is certain that Hegel had no deep philosophical appreciation of Hume; but his occasional, very sensitive, allusions to Pascal show that he was conscious of the importance of the negative moment in this rebirth.[16] And in Kant, the skeptical tradition had brought forth a representative greater even than Arcesilaus and Carneades, one who was inferior to Plato himself, only because Plato had, for his part, transcended skepticism altogether. Just as Plato integrated the skeptical impulse of Zeno into a great speculative vision, so the new speculative synthesis must integrate the impulse of the *Critique of Pure Reason*. Otherwise just as Carneades declined into the shallows of Cicero, so the Kantian river would disappear into the marshy bog of Krug and Schulze.

3. The "ancient" skepticism (a): Pyrrho.

What then are we to say about Hegel's revaluation of the ancient skepticism? In certain respects it is not historically accurate; but since Hegel is concerned about skepticism as a permanently necessary moment in the dialectic of speculative thought, we might think that the historical inaccuracies do not matter very much. Hegel himself would probably have said this, at the time that he wrote the essay. He certainly knew, for example, that the Eleatic skeptical inspiration of Plato's *Parmenides* had no demonstrable historical connection with the Pyrrhonian tradition; and it is quite evident that this does not matter to his thesis that the *Parmenides* is a "perfect and self-sustaining document and system of genuine skepticism" [19] at all. At the time that he wrote the essay, the actual temporal connection of the skeptical schools in the history of ancient speculation was *not* important to him. At that moment, the question about skepticism was for Hegel the very concrete, and actual problem of the relation between critical philosophy (Kant) and speculative philosophy (Schelling and himself). And this problem (concrete and actual as it was) was a strictly conceptual one; the solution was provided by Hegel's theory of "logic" as a critical introduction, or preamble to speculative "metaphysics". But after his partnership with Schelling broke up, Hegel abandoned the intuitive standpoint of the Identity Philosophy, and adopted the "standpoint of consciousness" (i.e., of Kant, Reinhold and Fichte) as the necessary starting point of philosophical inquiry; and finally the overcoming of this standpoint became, in the *Phenomenology*, the necessary critical preamble to proper (i.e., metaphysical) logic. That the *Phenomenology* still contains, or exemplifies, a critical logic is undeniable; but it is equally undeniable that it contains the analysis of a historical process of thought and culture that extends (at least) from the Stoics to Kant; and since the dialectical interaction of the Stoics and Skeptics is where the movement from "self-consciousness" to "Reason" begins, we can fairly say that Hegel's earlier attempt to construct the history of ancient skepticism was the falling stone that started an avalanche in his intellectual development. So the question as to how far his analysis is historically defensible turns out to be more important than it seems at first sight. It is more important than it appeared even to the living author of the essay.

The history of ancient skepticism is itself a very appropriate topic for the skeptical attitude. That is to say that there are very many questions in it about which suspense of judgement is arguably the most rational attitude. That may be why, except for Zeller, no Hegelians (that I know of) have attempted to deal with it since Hegel himself. I cannot myself claim to be competent to deal with it authoritatively. But this is, in a way, an advantage, since it means that I must depend on modern studies that are not biased (as I cannot help being biased) in a Hegelian direction. The bird's eye view that I shall now attempt to give is not as skeptical as it ought to be perhaps; but it is founded on the work of students who are themselves more skeptical than Hegelian; and it reflects a concern on my own part that is far more empirical or "doxographic" than Hegel's was.

There are, as I see it, *four* moments that need to be distinguished in the "school tradition" of Greek skepticism. The school itself—which I take to have been founded by the *historical* Aenesidemus—is only the last moment of the four; and its relation to any or all of the others is quite uncertain—though that will not inhibit me in offering plausible hypotheses about continuity (or the lack of it) between them. The significant earlier moments are: first, Pyrrho himself; second, Arcesilaus (or the "Middle" Academy); and third, Carneades (or the "New Academy). That there are some continuities between the second and the third moments cannot be seriously doubted; but what they are, and whether there are *any* connections between the first moment and the second, or the first and the fourth, or the third and the fourth, is debatable. (I shall say what I think, and the reader will see that my views have been influenced by Hegel's. But he will also know from the beginning where the principal hypotheses in my account are.)

The worst difficulty can be stated in a sentence. Not one of the first three "moments" in this tradition wrote a book; and in all three cases it is as clear as anything can be under the circumstances that this was a matter of conscious and deliberate policy.[17] The recording of "opinions" conflicted with the maintenance of a skeptical attitude toward them. But the nature of the perceived conflict varies (probably) in the three cases.

The founder of the tradition (or at least its patron saint) Pyrrho of Elis was born about 360 B.C. The biographical tradition (which seems to have early and reliable sources) asserts that he travelled to India with Alexander's army in the company of the atomist Anaxarchus, and that he was influenced on his travels by the Magi and the Gymnosophists. It seems probable therefore that his skeptical distrust of sense experience was rooted in the critical theory of Democritus. But unlike the atomists he did not take it to be the task of Reason to develop a hypothesis that could reconcile and account for the immense variety of the "unreal" sense-world that we are trapped in.[18] All that we can do is to recognize that that world is illusory and strive to ignore it. Since Pyrrho lived to be nearly ninety this policy of "having no opinions" about the reality that we are shut out from, must have been a very canny one. What it meant in practice was that death is less to be feared and avoided, than the loss of self-control. It is absolutely plain that Pyrrho did claim to *know* what the path to human happiness was. His philosophy was an *agōgē*, a *leading*. Reason could perceive nothing of reality; but it could perceive its own right to sovereignty over sensory consciousness and bodily conduct. Reason, knowing nothing, ought not to allow itself to be disturbed by anything; life ought always to be calm. Now, since what experience teaches is (in a nutshell) "self-preservation", this "most ancient" skepticism is indeed "turned against experience" as Hegel maintains [13]. (Pyrrho's *positive* doctrine of the human good was something of an embarrassment to the official "Pyrrhonians" later on. But it is important to us, because it shows that Pyrrho's skepticism did exist in the context of what Hegel calls a "speculative" doctrine. His *agōgē* was a form of the "primacy of practical Reason")

Hegel is certainly quite mistaken in thinking that the ten tropes (given both by Diogenes and by Sextus) were elaborated by Pyrrho or his direct disciples [31]. These tropes belong to a world of philosophical debate; but Pyrrho was not interested in arguing with others (engaging in disputes is disturbing). Instead, it is recorded that he habitually *talked to himself*. Talking was for him the way by which we can follow the "lead" of Reason; but one does not try to lead anyone who does not follow voluntarily.

4. The Ancient Skepticism: (b) The Academics

Just a few years after the death of Pyrrho, Arcesilaus was chosen to succeed Crates as head of the Academy (c.268 B.C.). He began at once to train all his students in the art of disputing all claims to empirical knowledge; and since he had already been teaching in the School for some years, they must have known what to expect when they elected him. Timon (the disciple of Pyrrho who did write books, and enjoyed controversy) and Ariston of Chios (an orthodox Stoic whose party was the main target of the Academic attack) claimed that Arcesilaus was imitating Pyrrho. But I see no reason to credit this claim. There is no sign that Arcesilaus accepted Pyrrho's moral "leading", or taught that the suspense of judgement is the key to happiness. For his own dialectical pursuit of wisdom, he needed no outside models, since he could appeal to the example of Socrates. His refusal to commit any opinions to paper could be justified, not only by the example of Socrates, but by the explicit declaration of Plato (in the Second Letter) that *his* philosophy was nowhere truly written, and that the Dialogues contained only an idealized portrayal of the Socratic example.[19]

The grounds of Arcesilaus' skepticism, on this view, are Heracleitean—for it was a Heracleitean view of sense experience that Plato adopted and taught. And the principal object of his attack was the dogmatic rationalism of Zeno—who used the doctrines of Heracleitus to defend the possibility of a truly comprehensive experience (kataleptikē phantasia). The whole subsequent history of Academic skepticism is taken up with an incessant criticism of Stoic positions— continually revised and moderated by the Porch until the two schools virtually collapsed into one stream of thought in the time of Cicero. The official vocabulary of skepticism, beginning with the word *epochē* (suspense of judgement) comes largely from Stoic sources.[20] It is possible to become wise according to Zeno, because we can suspend judgement until our rationally interpreted experience becomes *cataleptic*. Arcesilaus retorted that in that case the *epochē* ought to be absolute, since there is no infallible way of identifying any experience as *cataleptic*. The *epochē* itself, therefore, must be the goal of the wise man.

How did he mean this? Was he simply arguing dialectically about the proper behaviour for the Stoic Sage? More probably, he thought of it as a theoretical good, i.e., as the factual recognition of our actual situation, and hence as wisdom. Unlike Pyrrho, he did not see it as a practical good in itself. For, on the one hand, Sextus—who accuses

Arceilaus of holding the *epochē* to be good *dogmatically*—himself says "He says that the end is the *epochē* with which *we* say that *ataraxia* enters at the same time."[21] It is plain that Arcesilaus was not concerned about being unperturbed as a moral good. On the other hand, he was concerned about living a good life; and it involved for him, not just suspense of judgement, but the *subsequent* use of prudence (*phronesis*) to decide what was *reasonable* (*eulogon*).[22] Even this has recently been viewed as a dialectical lesson for the Stoics about the conduct of their wise man. But I cannot see why Arcesilaus should give them lessons in positive theory construction, unless he was himself Socratic enough to regard the conduct of life as a problem that the philosopher must face; and I do not see any necessary conflict between saying that no theoretic judgement is conclusively persuasive, and saying that we can still decide which course of action is more reasonable. (If Arcesilaus felt there was a conflict, I do not see how he could consistently offer this argument to the Porch; his doing so implies that he did not hold that it was illegitimate for the wise man to act upon an opinion without asserting it).

The claims of Sextus that Arcesilaus was a secret dogmatist (and that "he passed on to those naturally gifted the doctrines of Plato")[23] like the claims of his contemporaries that Arcesilaus imitated Pyrrho, must be regarded with reserve. But the echo of Plato's *Letters* is unmistakable, and I cannot help thinking, that although Arcesilaus was not (of course) a dogmatic Platonist—Plato himself was not that [26]—he was a Socratic seeker for the vision of the Good, which he knew could never be put into words.[24]

No such thought can be entertained about Carneades who became head of the Academy about 175 B.C.—i.e., sixty years after the death of Arcesilaus. He pursued the Stoic arguments in every detail; and because Chrysippus had refined and reformulated the whole doctrine in response to Arcesilaus, Carneades refined the attack.[25] Carneades himself often said that "if there had not been Chrysippus, there would not have been me"[26] and a comment of Cicero's makes it clear that he got the negative, as well as the positive side of the perfect rhetorical balances that he sought to set up, from Chrysippus.[27] Thus the comment of Carneades himself illustrates how Stoicism profited from Arcesilaus, and strove to comprehend its opposite; and also how the Academic skepticism was (in the Hegelian sense) a *determinate* negation. In Carneades the negative procedure itself became comprehensive. For whereas Arcesilaus trained students to argue on one side of a question (and typically *against* themselves, or on the side they were intuitively opposed to) Carneades would array *both* sides as equally as possible. He pursued the great encyclopaedic syntheses of Chrysippus in every direction, becoming for instance one of the great critics of the popular religion (which the Stoics sought to rationalize and accommodate). He reminds us irresistibly of the great Sophists, Protagoras and Gorgias. The sense of a Socratic quest is lost. His disciple Clitomachus (to whom we owe all that we know of him) said that he was never able to decide what Carneades really thought about the human *summum bonum*.[28] Thus the doctrine of the "trustworthy" (*pithanon*) and its degrees, which Sextus ascribes to Carneades, cannot be dogmatically his; it only teaches us what *Chrysippus* made out of Arcesilaus' gift of the *eulogon*, by combining it with Zeno's theory of the degrees of assent.

Since (like Arcesilaus before him) Carneades maintained that he did not *know* even that he did not know, it was natural for the Academy to be accused of being mere charlatans playing with words.[29] But the fact that they were serious is testified, above all, by their refusal to write. This is only explicable as a Socratic insistence on the care of one's own soul. With Carneades' refusal to commit himself to any view about what the philosophical activity aims at, however, the Socratic quest reaches an impasse. It is not surprising that the later Academics (after Clitomachus) retreated from this extreme. In Philo of Larissa (destined through Cicero's testimony to be philosophically canonized by Hume) we meet the first "mitigated skeptic". Recognizing that even skeptical assertions involve truth in some way, he taught that, although we cannot achieve the "cataleptic experience" we do know that things are not in themselves unknowable. Thus the senses can give *probable* knowledge and it is legitimate for the wise man to have opinions. In the Hegelian perspective we are now leaving speculation behind, and entering the comfortable territory of skeptical common sense.[30] Philo interpreted the whole history of the Academy (even including Plato, because he was held to have asserted only the Socratic ignorance) in terms of this mitigated skepticism.

5. The Ancient Skepticism:(c) The Skeptical School

With the admission that the philosopher could hold opinions, Academic skepticism collapsed. Antiochus of Ascalon, who succeeded Philo, was a dogmatic Platonist, scarcely distinguishable from the Middle Stoics. It is only now (or in the next generation) that the official school of the Skeptics becomes visible in the person of Aenesidemus. His dates cannot be fixed very definitely (the fact that Cicero does not refer to him suggests that his work became known some time after 50 B.C.). It is plausible to take him for an Academic rebel—a student, perhaps the leader of a group, who refused to accept the turn away from Carneades, and back to dogmatism. But it is also possible that the Skeptics had existed as a professional school for some generations. The Alexandrian scholars constructed a "succession" that starts with Ptolemy of Cyrene. Since the list includes known fellow-students of Chrysippus, the hypothesis that a group of Stoic students were radicalized into a skeptical stance by Arcesilaus is tenable.

Even if the school already existed, the hypothesis that Aenesidemus migrated from the Academy is attractive, because it provides a ready explanation of his "Heracleiteanism". Sextus reports that "those around Aenesidemus used to say that the skeptical leading was a way towards the Heracleitean philosophy".[31] Whatever it meant (and the students of skepticism will never find a satisfactory explanation of it as long as they view it through the eyes of Sextus) this view would occur much more readily to someone who read Heracleitus with Platonic spectacles, than to someone who read the Stoics (even as an opponent). For it is recorded that Cratylus (from whom Plato absorbed his skeptical version of Heracleitus) drove the doctrine to the limit of *aphasia*; and it is this same sense of the Logos as unspeakable, that I have suggested is present in the cognitive nihilism of Arcesilaus.

Because of this Heracleitean goal towards which the way of Aenesidemus leads, he must count as a *philosophical* skeptic in Hegel's scheme of things. But the school that he founded was, in the main, *un*philosophical in its tendency. The "ten tropes" are (probably) a codification of the technical armory developed by Carneades. Far from being directed against ordinary experience (as Hegel maintains) the tropes deploy that experience against the philosopher; and the philosophical schools against which the skeptical tropes are deployed are themselves decadent "schools of opinion". Hegel states the facts about the five tropes of Agrippa, and the simplified triad (of Sextus himself?) quite accurately [31, 33]: and once we take the first ten away from Pyrrho, what Hegel says about *all* of them expresses his distinction between the speculative and the dogmatic tradition of skepticism clearly.

The ascription of the first ten tropes to Pyrrho gives the first phase of skepticism a theoretical dimension that it probably did not have; apart from that Hegel distinguishes the three phases of skepticism with surprising accuracy. But his praise of the ancient skepticism ought not to embrace Sextus himself.[32] For, as he puts it, there is "the skepticism that is one with philosophy" (the Academy); "the skepticism that is not turned against Reason" (Pyrrho); and "the skepticism that is cut off from philosophy and turned against it" (Sextus) [30].[33] This "cutting off and turning against philosophy" occurs "as soon as philosophy became dogmatism".

Thus, in Hegel's analysis, it is the continuous dialogue between Stoicism and Skepticism that runs from Zeno and Arcesilaus to Philo and Antiochus of Ascalon that matters to the history of philosophy. This dialogue is completed by the *Phenomenology* which provides the *cataleptic phantasy*, the "science of experience" which comprehends why all of its failures are necessary elements in the truth itself. It is precisely the concept of a *criterion* by which the true appearance can be distinguished from the false that is the error that must be overcome. That there is, indeed, no such criterion is the essential *truth* of skepticism; and the integration of this truth into the "cataleptic phantasy" changes its character altogether. It becomes a "whole" which is both a "Bacchanalian revel" and a "highway of despair". The moment where skepticism emerges absolutely (i.e., not as a form of *determinate* negation) is Carneades, the philosopher who affirms nothing, but simply waits for Chrysippus to say "yes", in order to turn it into a "no" out of his own mouth. Carneades it is, who overthrows the old Gods; and in the person of Philo (who insisted, as we have seen, on the skeptical unity of the Academy as a whole) this skepticism is one of the figures waiting round the manger at Bethlehem for the truth to be reborn as subjectivity.

Aenesidemus is there too; but the school that he founded is only part of the intellectual flotsam of the succeeding centuries (like the work of the new Aenesidemus in Hegel's own time). Hegel does not want to admit this as a general proposition, because he does not want any of the "ancients" to be ranked with the new Aenesidemus. But the truth continually raises its head in his discussion of points of detail (except for the skeptical status of the *epochē* itself, about which, as Hegel rightly maintains, the Academy and Sextus were at one [24]). His misdating (and misinterpretation) of the ten tropes provides the main basis for his refusal to damn Sextus and the school-skeptics outright. But far from aiding his *philosophical* argument, this mistake (which is his worst historical error) only impedes our understanding of his classification of the types of skepticism. In the *Phenomenology* the truth has ceased to be inconvenient; for there it is *dogmatic* skepticism that provides a fixed *Gestalt* in its opposition to *Roman* Stoicism. The speculative tradition from Zeno to Arcesilaus is reincarnated in "the way of despair" itself.

6. God and Nature

In 1802 the project of a "comprehensive presentation" of the truth as spirit is still unborn, however. It comes to birth three years later, some time in the spring of 1805. For the moment, the project of the Identity Philosophy is Stoic in a much more abstract way. Logic, Physics and Ethics are to be united in the *intellectual intuition* of the God "in whom we live and move and have our being." The new Logic (or "transcendental philosophy" as it is now called in conscious homage to Kant, who is credited with having *almost* rediscovered speculative philosophy)[34] is in two main divisions. First there is critical logic, which performs the skeptical task of drowning all of our finite concepts in the infinity of speculative Reason; and then comes the new speculative logic (or "metaphysics") which begins with the concept of God. Thus the new speculation begins with the reinstatement of the Ontological Argument (which Kant stigmatized as a scholastic trick, or as the "plucking" (*ausklauben*) of the object's existence out of an Idea),[35] as the beginning of true philosophy.[36]

The God of Logic is *mirrored* in nature. Indeed the Identity Philosophy joined hands with the Stoic tradition in regarding the physical universe as the "body" of God; and this physical embodiment of God embraced the human world. In the new dispensation Ethics was the upper division of Physics itself. The "philosophy of nature" embraces "natural law" in both of its traditional senses. This is the reason why the essay on the "Relationship of the Philosophy of Nature to Philosophy in General" concentrates on ethical and religious issues, and hardly appears to be about what we understand by "natural philosophy" at all. The unspoken (or barely whispered) message is that Spinoza's approach to ethics is sounder than that of Kant and Fichte. But, of course, Spinoza's conception of "physics" was too close to that of Kant and Fichte to be sound either. The "nature" that is the image of God is the "everliving fire" of Heracleitus, or the "divine living thing" of the *Timaeus*. To comprehend nature under this aspect (including human nature as realized in the institutions of rational and civil life) is to form the "intuition" of God. This is the climax of the "transcendental realism" which complements the transcendental idealism of the Logic.

The conceptual unfolding of this intuition is the third, and highest "power" of the Identity Philosophy. Here in the realm of Art, Religion and Speculation we reach the level of "absolute" or free spirit. As a level of concrete experience which we all share, it is Religion. Art and Speculation are its handmaidens for they are modes of divine service.[37]

These are all views that are expressed (or obviously implied) in an essay which—like all of the formal published statements of the "transcendental realism" of the Identity Philosophy—was written by Schelling. Hegel's rather mystifying claims that the essay was "his" show, however, that he wanted to be identified with the positions that it sets up; and there is reason to believe that the religious perspective is peculiarly his. Also it was Hegel who regularly taught the "natural law" theory that forms the ethical division of the "philosophy of nature".[38]

It is a Trinitarian, but not yet a properly Christian perspective. For although the concept of Spirit is both primary and ultimate, the Incarnation of God does not yet take place properly in every singular human individual. God is incarnate in nature as a whole; and finite spirit is just the *second* nature, or the self-realization of *human* nature. Hegel always maintained the "transcendental realism" of the Identity Philosophy; and he continued to classify the philosophy of spirit together with the philosophy of nature as "Real Philosophy". But as soon as Schelling left Jena, the new "physics" and the new "ethics" fell apart into the "philosophy of nature" and the "philosophy of spirit" as autonomous disciplines; and very soon afterwards they took on the shape and relationship that we are familiar with in Hegel's mature theory.

This revolution occurred because Hegel for a time abandoned the theological starting point of the Identity Philosophy and went over to the problematic "standpoint of consciousness" that is the main theme of this volume as a whole. For a year and a half he tried to conceive the whole of philosophy as a phenomenology of consciousness.[39] Then finally he wrote his great work on this topic as the introduction to an ontological logic like that which he had conceived for the Identity Philosophy. This temporary desertion to the enemy is especially significant because it helps us to see that even the "transcendental realism" of the Identity Philosophy really is meant to be transcendental. The "philosophy of nature" is not a renaissance of Stoic dogmatism.[40] Hard as it may be to grasp how its theses can be interpreted "transcendentally", it is seriously meant as a study of the conditions of the possibility of human rational experience. If we begin (as Hegel insists we should) from the concept of "spirit", the possibility of a transcendental interpretation does become apparent. For to begin with "spirit" is to assert that the most basic condition of experience is a *community* of potentially rational consciousness. The philosophy of nature thus becomes an investigation of the natural (or physical) preconditions for such a community; and the claim that transcendental idealism must be matched by transcendental realism is the claim that a "disembodied" consciousness is not possible (at least in the sense that it could not be part of *our* community of consciousness).

I am only offering this defense of "transcendental realism" as a defense of the project in principle. I am not certain that we can state successfully what the necessary natural conditions of our rational consciousness are. Thus in the Identity Philosophy — as I read it — *light* becomes a primitive physical concept because of the analogy with the "inner light" of intellectual intuition. The *Phenomenology* (which begins with "now it is night") is an explicit rebellion against this intuitionism. But the skeptical insistence that we must begin now and here (where we find ourselves) means that absolute beginnings are hard to identify. We cannot here pursue the theme of transcendental skepticism into those higher and later reaches, however. Enough has surely been said already, to demonstrate that the discussion of the critical philosophy in the *Critical Journal* sounded the key note for a life's work.

Notes

1. Several of these essays have been translated by Fritz Marti, and published (with valuable notes and discussion which show everywhere a deep consciousness of the "difference" between Schelling and Fichte). See Schelling, *The Unconditional in Human Knowledge*, Lewisburg, Pa.: Bucknell, 1980.

2. *The System of Transcendental Idealism* appeared at Easter 1800. There is now an English translation (by P. Heath, Charlottesville: Univ. Press of Virginia, 1978). For the letters of Schelling and Fichte in October-November 1800, see Fichte, *Briefwechsel*, ed. Hans Schulz, (Vols. I, II, Hildesheim; Olms, 1967,) II, 284, 291-2.

3. Fichte began his long letter criticizing the new Identity Philosophy on 31 May, 1801. But he let the letter lie on his desk till 7 August before adding a postscript and sending it (Fichte, *Briefwechsel*, II, 322-9). Hegel probably began the *Difference* essay in May; and he finished it in July (see the Preface).

4. References in parentheses are to the texts in this volume.

5. See especially his essay on *Bruno* (*Werke*, IV, 307-29).

6. See Hegel, *The Difference between Fichte's and Schelling's System of Philosophy*, trs. W. Cerf and H. S. Harris, Albany: State University of New York Press, 1977, p. 87.

7. No doubt the main direct influence on Hegel's presentation was Schelling's *System of Transcendental Idealism*. But Beck's influence on *that* is probably worthy of some attention too.

8. *Faith and Knowledge*, trs. W. Cerf and H. S. Harris, Albany: State University of New York Press, 1977, p. 64.

9. Cerf and Harris, p. 65. (The Stoic origin of the "spark" metaphor deserves to be noticed).

10. See G. Nicolin (ed): *Hegel in Berichten seiner Zeitgenossen*, Hamburg: Meiner, 1970, report 58. Jacobi's temperate reaction to *Faith and Knowledge* is in report 65 (which is from a letter to Reinhold).

11. See Cerf and Harris, pp. 62-66 and 174-92.

12. The theses can be found either in Rosenkranz, (G. W. Fr. Hegels Leben, Berlin, 1844, pp. 156-9) or in Lasson's edition of Hegel's *Erste Druckschriften*, (Leipzig: Meiner, 1928, p. 404). The "Introduction" was probably written either *before* this time, or in October, for from August 15 to October 18 Hegel was urgently preoccupied with the preparation and submission of his Dissertation *On the Orbits of the Planets*. He had to

submit this before his lectures could begin. He delivered it (i.e., presumably a printed copy) on October 18 (see *Hegel-Studien* IV, 42-4 or *Briefe von und an Hegel*, Hamburg: Meiner, 1961, IV/I, 78-80). The first issue of the *Critical Journal* was at the press in November.

13. That this condemnation is itself sincere, is certified by the *Difference* essay (see Harris and Cerf, p. 111). Both *Difference* and *Faith and Knowledge* show what Hegel's sincere attitude to Spinozism was at this time.

14. Of course, Kant's skepticism is "imperfect", in that it is itself *scientific*, i.e., the "Dialectic of Pure Reason" does *demonstrate* the existence of a *limit*.

15. See Rosenkranz, p. 192. (*Faith and Knowledge*. Cerf and Harris, p. 11). Now that the fragment of the manuscript from which Rosenkranz was quoting has been recovered, we can say with fair certainty that this comes from the introductory lecture to Hegel's first course on "Logic and Metaphysics" (October 1801). (Heracleitus is, as I shall argue, more important to the dispute between the Stoics and the Academics than Parmenides; and certainly Heracleitus was important to the Identity Philosophy. But Hegel's view of the historical relation between Parmenides and Heracleitus was, of course, empirically mistaken.)

16. See especially the conclusion of *Faith and Knowledge*, (Cerf and Harris, p. 190).

17. It is just barely *possible*, I suppose—as it is possible also in the case of Socrates—that Pyrrho was only passively literate i.e., he could read but not write. But I do not myself *believe* this in either case. (Even if it were true, the element of policy must have been present. For the opportunity to learn was not lacking, and both Socrates and Pyrrho were determined characters!)

18. If we accept the tradition about Metrodorus of Chios and Anaxarchus, the Atomists themselves were complete sceptics— even to the point of denying that our ignorance could be asserted positively—before Pyrrho came into contact with them. There is every likelihood that Pyrrho found in Anaxarchus an ideal model of rational fortitude in ignorance who surpassed anything he was himself able to achieve. (See Diogenes Laertius IX, 58-60, and Cicero, *Academica* II, 73.)

19. 314c. To my nose both the Second and Seventh Letters have always exuded a strong smell of someone else's lamp-oil. I think they were forged in the Middle Academy (with skillful use of authentic letters to or from Plato, and of the *Dialogues*) to justify the *new way* of Arcesilaus. But the fact that *this* statement about the *Dialogues* goes a bit *too far*, is the only concrete evidence that I can offer for this suspicion. (Both letters, genuine or not, are marvellous apologias for what Arcesilaus did, and for his refusal to commit any view to writing.)

20. It seems probable that Pyrrho spoke of *aphasia* as the key to *ataraxia*—i.e., by continually telling himself and others that "things are no more this than that" he aimed to talk himself out of the need to talk at all. (The Indian inspiration, and the appalling difficulty that a voluble and gregarious Greek faced in seeking to achieve this Nirvana, of silence, are equally apparent.)

21. *Outlines of Pyrrhonism*, tr. R. G. Bury, Vols I-IV. Cambridge: Harvard University Press, 1933-1949, I, 232 (see further note 17).

22. *Against the Logicians* I, 158.

23. *Outlines of Pyrrhonism*, I, 234.

24. Cicero ascribes to him the view that there is "nothing that can be perceptually

distinguished (*cerni*) or understood (*intelligi*)" and explicitly says that "he denied there is anything that can be known, even the one thing that Socrates left to himself [i.e., that he knew nothing]" (*Academica*, I, xii, 45). This shows, certainly, that Sextus was wrong to accuse Arcesilaus of *asserting* the *epochē* as a dogma. I think that it also shows Arcesilaus' concern with Socratic *inwardness*. At any rate it transcends the simple skepticism of Sextus about "what is outside".

25. Here I am assuming the correctness of the view that we can detect two successive levels of complexity and sophistication in the arguments ascribed to the Academy by Cicero in *Academica* II, 79-87 (Arcesilaus) and II, 88-108 (Carneades). The introduction of Chrysippus (and the acknowledgement that it was *he* who furnished Carneades' dialectical armory) is the moment of transition (II, 87).

26. Diogenes Laertius, IV, 62.

27. *Academica*, II, 87.

28. *Academica* II, 139. The patron saint of Carneades' method is Protagoras (with his principle that "against every argument there is an equal and opposite argument") rather than Socrates. If the Skeptical school, which took this principle as a motto (see [21]) already existed, they may have influenced Carneades. But it is rather more probable that *his* adoption of the principle influenced *them* (either then or later). Gorgias, of course, was the first cognitive nihilist (and the School skeptics acknowledged him as a forerunner — see especially, *Against the Logicians* I, 65-87). But any reader of Plato's two dialogues will see that while Protagoras can be received into the company of "true seekers", Gorgias cannot. It is no accident that the *Gorgias* ends with a vision of the tyrants suffering for ever in Hell.

29. For the agnosticism of Carneades see *Academica* II, 78 and 139 (*inter alia*). I have not been able to discover whose testimony it is that supports Stäudlin's libels; but see "Skepticism" [26]. The Stoics, who were their main opponents, regarded the great Academic professors with immense respect (see especially the testimony of Zeno of Sidon about Carneades in Cicero *Academica* I, 46; if I am right about the genesis of the doctrine of the *pithanon*, the point hardly needs further proof for Arcesilaus).

30. See especially *Outlines of Pyrrhonism* I, 235. For the interpretation we must depend mainly on what Cicero asserts *in propria persona* (but his source is evident enough) — see *Academica* II, 64 ff.

31. *Outlines of Pyrrhonism*, I, 210.

32. What Hegel calls "the noblest side of skepticism" [45] is lacking in Sextus. But Hegel sometimes misstates the facts in order to make Sextus more of a speculative thinker than he was. One example is when he claims that the threefold classification into dogmatics, Academics, and skeptics shows that Sextus "by no means imagines that he has refuted the Academy too". [22] (In a highly qualified sense it *does* show that; but it does not show what Hegel wants, which is that — unlike Schulze — Sextus recognized the "third possibility, to wit, a philosophy".)

33. The only recent student of ancient skepticism who takes Hegel's contribution to the problem seriously is Mario Dal Pra. But he has not grasped these distinctions (see *Lo scetticism greco*, Bari: Laterza, 1975, I, pp. 1-8).

34. Compare *Difference*, 118: "[Fichte's philosophy] is the most thorough and profound speculation, all the more remarkable because, at the time when it appeared, even the Kantian philosophy had proved unable to awaken Reason to the lost concept of genuine

speculation." Also *Difference*, 79: "The Kantian philosophy needed to have its spirit distinguished from its letter, and to have its purely speculative principle lifted out of the remainder that belonged to, or could be used for, the arguments of reflection."

35. *KRV* A603; B631

36. This is the most important philosophical point in the Krug essay [100]. But obviously any purely "logical" approach to this "beginning" is open to the Kantian criticism (or misunderstanding); so again, we can see why the *Phenomenology* eventually emerged.

37. The principal documents which show that Hegel held these views are *Difference*, pp.170-2; *Faith and Knowledge*, p. 180-2; and *Natural Law*, tr. R. M. Knox, with an introduction by H. B. Acton, Philadelphia: University of Pennsylvania Press, 1975 (passim, but especially the conclusion). Compare also *System of Ethical Life* and *First Philosophy of Spirit*, trs. H. S. Harris and T. M. Knox, Albany: State University of New York Press, 1979, p. 143.

38. But, as I have shown in my notes to the essay, some of the modes of expression used in it are diametrically opposed to Hegel's.

39. The *First Philosophy of Spirit* (Harris and Knox, pp. 205-53) and the *Jena Logic and Metaphysics* (*Gesammelte Werke*, Vol. VII) are the major documents of this phase in Hegel's development.

40. Hegel does, of course, claim that the early Stoics were not dogmatic philosophers (37). But if that were taken to mean that the philosophy of nature need not be any more "transcendental" than the theory of Chrysippus (say) it would not help the cause of the Identity Philosophy much in the eyes of those of us who take Kant's achievement seriously.

The Critical Journal of Philosophy
Introduction
on The Essence of Philosophical Criticism
Generally, and its Relationship to the Present
State of Philosophy in Particular
[by G. W. F. Hegel (and F. W. J. Schelling)]

Kritisches Journal der Philosophie, I, no. 1 (1802) iii-xxiv

Translation and Notes by H. S. Harris

The Critical Journal of Philosophy (which this essay served to introduce) was Schelling's brainchild, and he was officially its principal
editor. It first appeared in the last months of 1801, and it disappeared
when Schelling left Jena with Caroline (the wife of A. W. Schlegel) in
the early months of 1803. But the junior editor, Hegel, actually wrote
well over half of what appeared in it (as well as doing almost all of
the editorial chores). In those early years he was universally regarded
as a mere "mouthpiece" of Schelling[1] —and although this view was
certainly mistaken, we must ask ourselves very seriously whether
Schelling himself did not actually regard his relation with Hegel in
this light at that time. He recommended this essay to A. W. Schlegel
in December 1802 almost as if it was his own;[2] and Caroline (who
must have known that Hegel was the main author, but who clearly
regarded him as a mere amanuensis for any essay that Schelling was
actively concerned about) asked her husband, the week after the issue
was sent, "Does not the introduction to the Journal seem to you to be
excellently composed and written?"[3] Yet there cannot be any real
doubt that the pen that wrote most of the words in the essay was
Hegel's; for Hegel included it in a list of his contributions to the *Critical
Journal* which he drew up in connection with his candidacy for a
professorship at Jena in 1804.[4]

The first editors of Hegel's works did not have this piece of
incontrovertible contemporary evidence. So it is not surprising that a
controversy arose. Schelling declared in a letter of 1838; "As far as
the Introduction to the *Critical Journal* is concerned, it was partly
written by Hegel but many passages which I could not precisely identify
on the instant, as well as the main ideas (*Hauptgedanken*) are by me;
there can surely be no passage which I have not at least revised".[5]

Now what I would call the *Hauptgedanken* of the essay are for the
most part distinctively Hegelian. But there could well be dispute about
what the *Hauptgedanken* are. The "main idea" of the Identity Philosophy
itself was certainly Schelling's; but I think that Hegel has here set his
own theory of criticism into that frame. Anyone who will read the
whole of the *Critical Journal* carefully, as I have done, will be obliged
to agree that Hegel's contributions embody and express the programme
of the "Introduction" much better than Schelling's do. If Schelling
remained convinced, when the two of them were discussing what
should be said in this opening salvo of their critical onslaught upon
the old ways of thought, that he was directing the attack, this only
makes the essay into the first document of an insidious influence of
Hegel upon him, which others, more thoroughly conversant with

Schelling's writings than I am, have fairly conclusively exhibited in works that he definitely wrote for himself.[6]

Having said that much, I shall leave the reader to ponder upon my Notes (remembering always that it is Hegel's thought that I am interested in, and that I have read Schelling only for the light his work throws upon that). Setting aside all arguments about whose ideas these are, and who influenced whom, what I take to have happened in the writing of the Introduction for what everyone agreed was "Schelling's Journal" is this. The two editors discussed what should be said (and discussed it at some length) before Hegel sat down and wrote a draft for Schelling's review and approval. Schelling, as senior editor, certainly went over that draft carefully and made revisions and additions, because he felt directly responsible for what was said. The ideas had to be his, by definition, because they were appearing in this initial proclamation. Hence he should certainly be regarded as a co-author of the piece.

Notes

1. The only *signed* statement in the *Critical Journal* was a footnote in which Hegel denied that he had acted like a ventriloquist's dummy in writing the *Difference* essay— see Hegel, *Gesammelte Werke*, IV, 190, note 1. More details about this incident will be found in my introduction to the *Difference* essay (p. 67, note 10).

2. G. L. Plitt, ed., *Aus Schellings Leben in Briefen*, Leipzig: Hirzel, 1869-79, I, 351: "I am sending you in the next post the first issue of a *Critical Journal for* (sic) *Philosophy* that I have undertaken with Hegel. In it you will find, apart from an introduction on the essence of philosophical criticism generally, and its specific relation to the present state of philosophy a five or six sheet essay of mine against and about Reinhold's idiocies, and after that some special reviews". (By a "sheet" — *Bogen* — Schelling means a printer's octavo sheet of 16 printed pages). The dialogue "On the Absolute Identity System and its relation to the latest (Reinholdian) dualism" actually fills pp. 1-90 in the first issue — which contained XXIV + 131 pages in all.)

3. E. Schmidt, ed., Caroline: *Briefe aus der Frühromantik*, Leipzig, 1913, II, 270.

4. The *curriculum vitae* is known to us only though Nohl's citation of it. Since his time it has been lost. He supplies the date September 1804. (See *Hegel's Theologische Jugendschriften*, Tübingen, 1907, pp. VIII-IX; or Hegel, *Briefe* IV, 1, 88-90.)

5. The full text of Schelling's letter to Weisse is in *Aus Schellings Leben*, Vol III.

6. See especially Klaus Düsing, "Speculation und Reflexion", *Hegel-Studien*, V (1969) pp. 95-128.

IN WHATEVER DOMAIN OF ART or [speculative] science it is   [iii]
employed, criticism requires a standard which is just as independent
of the person who makes the judgement as it is of the thing that is
judged—a standard derived neither from the singular [*ie.* the immediate
occasion for critical judgement] nor from the specific character of the
[*judging*] subject, but from the eternal and unchangeable model [*Urbild*]
of what really *is* [*die Sache selbst*].[1] Just as the idea of fine art is not
first created or discovered by art criticism, but is purely and simply
presupposed by it, so too in philosophical criticism the Idea of
philosophy is itself the precondition and presupposition without which
it would only be able to set one subjective view against another for
ever and ever, and never set the Absolute against the conditioned.

What distinguishes philosophical criticism from art criticism is not
the judgement of the capacity for objectivity that is expressed in a
[philosophical] work, but rather just // the object [of criticism]; [in   [iv]
other words] the Idea itself that is basic to the criticism, and which
cannot be anything other than the Idea of philosophy itself. As far as
the capacity for objectivity is concerned, philosophical criticism involves
the same claims to universal validity that art criticism does. So anyone
who wants to deny objectivity of judgement in philosophy in spite of
that, must claim not merely the possibility of distinct forms of one
and the same Idea, but the possibility of essentially distinct yet equally
true philosophies—a view of the matter [*Vorstellung*] which properly
deserves no consideration, for all its immense comfortableness. The
fact that philosophy is but one, and can only be one, rests on the fact
that Reason is but one; and just as there cannot be distinct Reasons,
so too a wall cannot be set up between Reason and its self-cognition,
through which its self-cognition could become essentially distinguishable
from its appearance. For Reason absolutely considered, and Reason
when it becomes object for itself in its self-cognition (and hence
philosophy) is again just one and the same thing, and therefore
completely equal.

The ground of a distinction within philosophy itself cannot lie in
its essence, which is strictly one, any more than it can be based on
the inequality of the capacity to shape [*gestalten*] the Idea of philosophy
objectively. For the fact is that in the philosophical perspective the
Idea itself is all that counts, while the capacity to set it forth that
comes additionally with its possession, makes only another side of
philosophy, and one that is not peculiar to it. Therefore, once
philosophy is defined as a cognition of the Absolute, the possibility
of infinitely many distinct reflections, // such that each has an equal   [v]

right to maintain itself against the others, each of them being essentially distinct from the others, could only result from thinking of the Absolute (whether as God or in some other aspect as Nature) as fixed in immovable and absolute opposition to cognition as subjective.

But even upon this view the distinction would have to suspend and ameliorate itself. For since cognition is here represented as something formal, it is thought of as completely passive in its relationship to the object; and it is required of the subject that is to be capable of this reception of the divinity, or of the purely objective intuition of nature, that it should close itself quite generally against every other relationship to any limiting factor at all, and restrain itself from any activity of its own, since that would upset the purity of the reception. Through this passivity of intake, and the equality of the object [in all such pure intuitions] what is represented as result, would have to be just the cognition of the Absolute, and a philosophy that sprang from this root must again be simply unique and in every respect the same.

It is because the truth of Reason is but one, like beauty, that criticism as objective judgement is possible in principle, and it follows evidently [vi] that it only makes sense for those // who have the Idea of the one identical philosophy present to their minds; and by the same token it can only be concerned with those works in which this Idea is expressed more or less clearly for cognition. The effort of criticism is entirely wasted on the people and the works that are deprived of the Idea. In the absence of the Idea criticism gets into the gravest difficulty, for if all criticism is subsumption under the Idea, then all criticism must necessarily cease where the Idea is lacking, and it can have no other direct relationship [to that with which it is concerned] than that of repudiation. But in this repudiation it ruptures altogether every connection between that wherein the Idea of philosophy is lacking, and that in whose service criticism exists. Since reciprocal recognition[2] is in this way suspended, what appears is only two subjectivities in opposition; things that have nothing in common with one another come on stage with equal right for that very reason; and in declaring that what is before it to be judged is anything else one likes, — which is tantamount to declaring it to be nothing at all, since philosophy is all that it aims to be — criticism transposes itself into a subjective situation and its verdict appears as a one-sided decision by violence. Since its activity ought to be objective, this situation directly contradicts its essence; its judgement is an appeal to the Idea of philosophy but since this Idea is not recognized by the adverse party, it is only a foreign court of judgement for him. There is no immediate escape from this relationship of criticism, which cuts unphilosophy[3] off from philosophy — criticism must stand on the one side and have unphilo-
[vii]   sophy on the opposite side. // Since unphilosophy takes up a negative

attitude to philosophy, and hence there can be no question of discussing it as philosophy, there is nothing to be done but recount how this negative side expresses itself and confesses its non-being (which in as much as it has a phenomenal aspect is called platitude), and since what is nothing to begin with, must unfailingly appear ever more clearly as nothing in its development, until it can be recognized [*erkannt*] as such by virtually everyone, through this completely executed construction [of evident nullity] from the primal nullity.[4] Criticism is reconciled once more with the incapacity [of the cultured public] which could see nothing in the original verdict [of the philosophical critic] but self-satisfied personal bias and caprice.

On the other hand, where the Idea of philosophy is actually present, there it is the concern of criticism to interpret the way and the degree in which it emerges free and clear, and the range within which it has been elaborated into a scientific system of philosophy.

As for this last point, if the pure Idea of philosophy is expressed with spirit, but naively and without scientific range—if it does not arrive at the objectivity of a systematic consciousness—we must still greet it with joy and delight; it is the mark of a beautiful soul, whose inertia guards it against falling into the original sin of thinking, but which also lacks the courage to hurl itself into that sin and to follow the path of its guilt, till the guilt is dissolved—and so // it has not arrived at the intuition of itself in an objective whole of science. The empty form of such spirits, however—those who aim to give the heart and essence of philosophy in short formulas without [living] spirit—this form has no scientific significance, and has no other interest either.[5] [viii]

But when the Idea of philosophy becomes more scientific it must be carefully distinguised from the individuality which will express its character without harm to the identity of the Idea of philosophy or to the purely objective exposition of it—the subjectivity or limitedness, that gets mingled in the exposition of the Idea of philosophy. Criticism has to apply itself especially to the way that philosophy looks when masked by this subjectivity—it must tear the mask off.

When it is shown to be the case that the Idea of philosophy is actually before the mind, then criticism can cleave to the requirement and to the need that is expressed, to the objective factor in which the need seeks its satisfaction, and can lay aside the limitedness of the shape through its own genuine tendency toward perfect objectivity.

But in this connection two cases are possible. In the first case consciousness has not properly developed beyond subjectivity. The Idea of philosophy has not risen to the clarity of free intuition, but stays hidden in a dark background, partly, perhaps, because some forms in which it finds itself largely expressed, // forms which possess great authority, still hinder the breakthrough to pure formlessness, or [ix] to be the highest form (which is the same thing). Even when criticism cannot allow the work and the deed to be valid as a shape of the idea, it will not ignore the striving [toward that]; the genuinely scientific concern here is to peel off the shell that keeps the inner aspiration from seeing daylight; it is important to be aware of the manifoldness of the reflections of the spirit, each of which must have its place in philosophy, as well as being aware of their subordinate status and their defects.[6]

In the second case it is evident that the Idea of philosophy has been more clearly cognized, but that subjectivity has striven to ward off philosophy in so far as this is necessary for its own preservation:[7]

Here what matters is not to set the Idea of philosophy off in relief, but to uncover the nooks and crannies that subjectivity makes use of in order to escape from philosophy, and to make the weakness, for which any limitation offers a secure foothold, visible both on its own account [für sich] and with respect to the Idea of philosophy *qua* associated with a subjectivity; for the true energy [i.e., actualization] of the Idea is incompatible with subjectivity.

[x] But there is still another way of proceeding upon which criticism must especially fasten; the one that gives itself out to be in possession of philosophy, which uses the forms and // vocabulary in which great philosophical systems are expressed, goes in for lengthy debates, but is at bottom only an empty fog of words without inner content.[8] This sort of chatter, though lacking the Idea of philosophy, gains for itself a kind of authority through its very prolixity and arrogance. Partly this is because it seems almost incredible that such a big shell should be without a kernel, and partly because the emptiness is in its way universally understandable. Since there is nothing more sickening than this transformation of the seriousness of philosophy into platitude, criticism must summon up all its forces to ward off this disaster.

These distinct forms [of philosophy and unphilosophy] are in general more or less dominant in the German philosophy of the present time to which this Critical Journal is addressed. But they [the forms] have the further peculiarity that every philosophical enterprise takes on the aspect of a science and the dimensions of a system, or at the very least takes its stand as the absolute principle of philosophy as a whole. Through the work of Kant, and still more through that of Fichte, the Idea of a science, and particularly of philosophy as a science, has been established. Philosophizing piecemeal [das einzelne Philosophieren] has lost all credit, and the possibility of counting for something as a philosopher through a variety of philosophical thoughts upon this or that topic, published perhaps in scholastic treatises, no longer exists. As a result a multitude of systems and principles is arising which gives that part of the public which does philosophy a certain outward similarity to the state of philosophy in Greece, where every prominent philosophical // mind elaborated the Idea of philosophy   [xi] in his own individual way. At the same time philosophical freedom— emancipation from authority and independence of thought—seems to have reached such a pitch with us, that it would be considered disgraceful to call oneself a philosopher after the fashion of a school that already exists; opinion has it that thinking for oneself can only proclaim its presence through originality—the invention of a system that is entirely novel and one's own.

When the inner life of philosophy comes to birth in an outward shape, it necessarily endows that shape with something of the form of its own peculiar organization; by so much is the original aspect of genius distinct from the *particularity* which takes itself for, and gives itself out to be, *originality*. For this particularity, upon closer examination, really keeps firmly to the common highway of culture, and can never boast of having arrived at the pure Idea of philosophy by leaving it; for if it had grasped this Idea, it would know [*erkennen*] it again in other philosophical systems, and *ipso facto* it would then be unable to label itself with the name of a *personal philosophy*, even though it must of course, preserve its own living form.[9] What the particular originality has created of its own upon that highway, is a particular form of reflection, seized upon from some singular, and hence subordinate, standpoint. This is easy enough to do in an era that has cultivated the understanding in so many aspects, and has, in particular, fashioned it into philosophy in so many ways. // An assemblage of   [xii] such original tendencies, and of the manifold efforts after a form and system of one's own, offers us the spectacle of the tortures of the damned, rather than that of the free upsurge of the most various living shapes in the philosophical gardens of Greece. Either they are for ever bound to their own limited position; or they must seize on one position after another, marvelling unstintedly at them all, and casting one after the other away.[10]

As for the labour of enlarging a *particularity of this kind into a system*, and setting it forth as the whole, this is a hard labour in good sooth, and the particular originality must surely come to grief over it, for how could what is limited be capable of extending itself into a whole, without *ipso facto* flying to pieces itself? The very quest for a particular principle is already committed to the goal of possessing something of one's own, something that satisfies one's self alone, and renounces any pretension to the objectivity of knowledge or to its totality. And yet the whole is, more or less, present in objective form, at least as raw material, as a mass of knowledge; it is hard to do it violence and to follow the thread right through it consistently with one's own peculiar concept; but at the same time, given that it [the whole] is indeed there, one is never permitted to stage it approvingly without coherence [with one's principle]; the cleverest way, it seems, is not to bother oneself on that account, and to set up one's own peculiar principle as the only thing that matters, leaving the rest of knowledge to bother itself about its coherence with the principle. It seems, of course, that [xiii] this is a // lower task altogether; to give to the basic principle its objective scientific range. But if, on the one hand, this range is not to be lacking, and on the other hand, one wants to spare oneself the effort of bringing the manifold array of knowledge into coherence with itself and with the limitedness of the principle, the way of proceeding that unites both of these requirements is that of "provisional" philosophizing, i.e., that which sums up what is present not in terms of the needs of a system of knowledge, but on the following ground: that it seems that what is present can have its use then too—to exercise our heads, for why else should it be there?[11]

In this respect the Critical Philosophy has performed an exceptionally important service. To wit, it has been proved therein—to express the matter in its own words—that the concepts of the Understanding only have their application in experience, that Reason as cognitive through its theoretical Ideas only involves itself in contradictions, and that its object must be given to knowledge generally by sensibility. All this is useful for getting us to renounce Reason in [philosophic] science, and give ourselves over to the most crass empiricism. The crudest concepts dragged into experience, and an intuition polluted by the rudest offspring of a spiritless reflection, have been given out as "inner and outer experience" and "actual facts of consciousness." Everything has been tumbled together under this heading upon an assurance received from anywhere, that it does occur in consciousness; and all this comes to pass by appeal to the Critical Philosophy, which [xiv] has // proved that experience and perception are necessary for cognition, and which allows Reason no constitutive relationship to knowledge, but only a regulative one. Apart from the fact that unphilosophy and anti-science [Unwissenschaftlichkeit], which philosophy used to regard with easy contempt, have taken on a philosophical form for their justification, the Critical Philosophy has in this way brought about even greater benefits; to wit, it has reconciled healthy common sense, and every limited consciousness, with philosophy[12]—along with their finest blooms, which are at times called the highest moral interests of humanity.

But if subjectivity, without regard for the further difficulty which it faces in setting itself forth as a system, because the Critical Philosophy has now made at least one great range of finite forms suspect or unusable,—if it is afflicted with insight into its limitedness, and by a kind of bad conscience, and is ashamed to set itself up as absolute, how can it be preserved and made valid in spite of its own better knowledge and the Idea of Philosophy that floats before its mind?[13]—In the first place, we must start with a form that is recognized as finite. It must represent nothing but what is, to all appearances, an arbitrary starting point, worth nothing indeed upon its own account, but it has to be granted for the moment because its utility will become evident soon enough. It is granted for the time being, on request, in a provisory, problematic, hypothetical way, without any special pretensions; it will soon legitimate itself later on.—If we once // arrive at what is true   [xv] having started from it, our gratitude for the sign post will recognize [erkennen] that arbitrary starting point as a necessary one, and see that it has been verified. However the true needs no leading-reins to guide us to it;[14] but must bear within itself the power to step forth on its own account; and the limited [starting point] is itself recognized here for just what it is, that is to say it does not have the stuff of its own subsistence in it, but is understood to be only something hypothetical and problematic, even though in the end it is due to be verified as a veritably true [being]. It is evident therefore that the salvation of finitude was the principal concern. But what is not supposed to be hypothetical later on, cannot be hypothetical in the beginning either; or else what is hypothetical at the beginning cannot become categorical later on. It might, of course, come forward as absolute straight away, but since it is, quite rightly, too timid for that, we need a roundabout way to sneak the Absolute in.

Making out that a finite starting point of this kind is a hypothesis for the time being only introduces one more deception. For the starter comes on stage pretending to have no pretensions: whether he comes forward modestly as a hypothetical [being] or right away as self-certain, both starts lead to the same result:[15] that the finite is preserved as what it is in its separateness, and the Absolute remains an Idea, a Beyond—in other words, it is afflicted with a finitude.

The certain starting point, which is taken up in its immediate consciousness in order that it may be certain, seems // through its   [xvi] immediate certainty to make up for what it lacks by reason of its finitude; and pure self-consciousness is just such a certainty since, *qua* starting point, it is posited as a pure [consciousness] in immediate opposition to the empirical [consciousness].[16] In and for itself the concern of philosophy cannot be with finite certainties of this kind. A philosophy which, in order to anchor itself to a certainty, begins from the most universally valid statements or activities ready at hand for every human understanding, is either doing something superfluous, since it must still transcend this limitation, and suspend it, in order to be philosophy at all (and ordinary common sense, which must thereby be led astray will take good note when its sphere is abandoned, and one wants to lead it into self-transcendence); or else, if this finite certainty is not to be suspended as such, but is to abide and subsist as something fixed, then it must, of course, recognize its finitude, and *require* infinity. However, the infinite then comes on the scene precisely and only as a requirement, as something thought of, *only as an Idea*. For although it is the necessary and comprehensive, all-inclusive, Idea of Reason, it is still, *ipso facto*, one-sided, since the Idea itself and that which thinks it [or: that which it thinks][17] (or whatever else the determinate was from which the start was made)[18] are posited separately. In this type of salvation for the limited the Absolute is exalted into the supreme Idea, but not at the same time into the unique being, so that the antithesis [of thought and being] remains dominant and absolute throughout the whole system of philosophy, since this is the point from which the science of philosophy first begins:[19] To a certain extent

[xvii] these salvation programmes // are what typifies our own recent philosophical culture: and almost everything that has been accepted as philosophy in our day falls within the scope of this concept. Even the highest manifestation of philosophy of the last generation has not overcome the fixed polarity of inner and outer, of here [in the sensible world] and yonder [in the noumenal one]. It allows two opposed philosophies to stand: one in which we can only approach towards the knowledge of the Absolute, and another which is within the Absolute itself—though this latter is, to be sure, only established under the title of faith. In this way the antithesis of dualism is given its most abstract expression and so philosophy is not led forth from the sphere of our reflective culture [*Reflexionskultur*][20]. As a result the most abstract form of the antithesis is of the greatest importance; and from this most acute extreme, the transition to genuine philosophy is all the easier. For the very idea of the Absolute that is set up itself rejects the antithesis, because the antithesis carries with it the form of an Idea, of an Ought, of an infinite requirement. We must not overlook how much the study of philosophy has profited from the manifold elaboration that antithesis in general has undergone—the antithesis which every philosophy aims to overcome—because a later philosophy was directed against the form of the antithesis that was dominant in an earlier one, and overcame it, even though the later philosophy fell back again, all unwittingly, into another form of antithesis; but at the same time we must also not overlook the variety of forms that the

[xviii] antithesis can assume. //

On the other hand, there is a prevalent manner of proceeding that has only unprofitable aspects: to wit, that which is at pains to make philosophical ideas *popular*, or more precisely, common, as soon as they appear on stage. Philosophy is, by its very nature, something esoteric, neither made for the vulgar as it stands [*für sich*], nor capable of being got up to suit the vulgar taste; it only is philosophy in virtue of being directly opposed to the understanding and hence even more opposed to healthy common sense, under which label we understand the limitedness in space and time of a race of men; in its relationship to common sense the world of philosophy is in and for itself an inverted world.[21] When Alexander, having heard that his teacher was publishing written essays on his philosophy, wrote to him from the heart of Asia that he ought not to have vulgarized the philosophizing they had done together, Aristotle defended himself by saying that his philosophy was published and yet also not published. In the same way philosophy [now] must certainly admit [*erkennen*] the possibility that the people can rise to it, but it must not lower itself to the people.[22] But in these times of freedom and equality, in which such a large educated public has been formed, that will not allow anything to be shut away from it, but considers itself good for anything — or everything good enough for it — in these times even the highest beauty and the greatest good have not been able to escape the fate of being mishandled by the common mob which cannot rise to what it sees floating above it, until it has been made common enough to be fit for their possessing; so that vulgarization has // forced its way into being recognized as   [xix] a meritorious kind of labour. There is no aspect of the higher striving of the human spirit that has not experienced this fate. An Idea, in art or in philosophy, needs only to be glimpsed in order for the processing to start by which it is properly stirred up into material for the pulpit, for text books, and for the household use of the newspaper public. Leibniz partly undertook these labours for his philosophy himself, in his *Theodicy*; his philosophy did not thereby gain a general *entrée*, but he made a great name for himself.[23] Nowadays, there is a ready supply of people trained for the job. With isolated concepts, it happens automatically; all that is necessary is to attach the concept-name to what has long been familiar in everyday [*bügerlich*] life. In its origin and its realized essence [*an und für sich*] the Enlightenment already expresses the vulgarity of the understanding and the vanity of its exaltation above Reason, and there was no need to change the meaning of the concepts [*Verstand* and *Vernunft*] in order to make them attractive and easy to grasp; but one can readily grant that the word "Ideal" carries nowadays the general meaning of that which has no truth in it, or the word "humanity" of that which is utterly dull.[24] — The seemingly opposite case — which is, however, just the same as this one at bottom — occurs where the matter is "popular" already, and where popular clichés (everyday ideas), which do not go even one step beyond the sphere of common concepts, have to be given the outward look of philosophy by philosophical and methodical processing. Just as in the first case the assumption is made, that // what is philosophical can   [xx] still be "popular" at the same time, so in the second [there is the assumption] that what is "popular" by nature, can in some way or other become philosophic.²⁵ Thus the compatibility of platitude and philosophy [is taken for granted] in both cases.

In a general way we can relate this variety of [philosophic] efforts to the spirit of unrest and instability that is everywhere astir. This spirit is the mark of our time. After long centuries of the toughest obstinacy, for which the casting off of an old form involved the most fearful convulsions, it has finally brought the German spirit to the point of tying even philosophical systems into the concept of the ever changing and the ever new; although we must not mistake this passion for change and novelty for the indifference of play which, in its extreme insouciance, is at the same time the most exalted and only true seriousness [Ernst].²⁶ For the restless impulse of our time goes to work with the extreme earnestness [Ernsthaftigkeit] of limitedness [as distinct from the only true seriousness]. Yet fate has of necessity given it a dim feeling of mistrust and a secret despair which very soon reveals itself because the earnest limitedness is without living seriousness, so that on the whole it cannot stake [setzen] much upon its concerns. Hence also it cannot achieve any great works—or [only] highly ephemeral ones.

Moreover, if we wish, we can also regard this present unrest as a process of fermentation through which the spirit strains upwards toward [xxi] a new // life out of the putrefaction of the deceased culture, and springs forth again in a rejuvenated shape from under the ashes of the old.²⁷ To be exact it was against the Cartesian philosophy and the universal culture that it expresses that philosophy like every other side of living nature had to seek a means of salvation. The Cartesian philosophy expounded [in a philosophical form] the universally comprehensive dualism in the culture of the recent history of our north-westerly world—a *dualism* of which both the quiet transformation of the public life of men after the decline of all ancient life, and the noisy political and religious revolutions are equally just different-coloured outward manifestations. What philosophy has done for its salvation has been greeted with fury where it was pure and openly expressed;²⁸ where it was more covert and more mixed up [with empirical considerations], the understanding has mastered it more easily and turned it round again into the earlier dualistic pattern [Wesen]. All the sciences have been founded upon this death, and the time itself has completely killed whatever was still scientific in them, and hence at least subjectively alive.³⁰ So that if it were not immediately the spirit of philosophy itself which feels the strength of its growing wings all the more when it is submerged and crushed together in this broad sea, the very tedium of the sciences would make the whole flat plain unbearable — this edifice built by an understanding abandoned by Reason which at its worst (under the borrowed title either of rational englightenment, or of moral reason) has even ruined theology in the end.[31] This tedium was bound to at least arouse a yearning of the // [dead] riches for a spark of fire, for a concentration of living [xxii] intuition, and, once the cognition of the dead had gone on long enough, for that cognition of the living which is only possible through Reason.

Belief in the possibility of such an actual cognition, and not just in the negative wandering along or the perennial springing up of new forms, is absolutely necessary if the effect to be expected from a critique of them is to be a true one, i.e., not a merely negative destruction of these limited forms, but one that results in a preparation of the way for the arrival of true philosophy. But in any case, even if it can only produce the former [merely negative] effect, it is quite proper that the pretensions of limited forms and the enjoyment of their ephemeral existence should be soured and cut short; and he who can, may well regard [philosophical] criticism as nothing but the ever-turning wheel, dragging down again every instant the shape that the surge had thrown up.[32] It may be that resting self-assured on the broad base of healthy common sense, he simply delights in this objective spectacle of appearance and disappearance, and takes comfort and confirmation from it all the more for his own banishment from philosophy, because by induction *a priori* he regards the philosophy upon which the limited comes to grief as just another limited form. Or again, it may be that he marvels over the coming and going of the forms in their fountain with profound sympathy and interest, grasping it with much // effort, [xxiii] and then watches their disappearance with a wise eye, and lets himself drift giddily.[33]

When criticism itself wants to maintain a one-sided point of view as valid against others that are likewise one-sided, it becomes partisan polemic. But even the true philosophy cannot protect itself from the outward look of polemic against unphilosophy. For, since it has nothing positive in common with the latter, and cannot engage with it in a [positive] critique of the common ground, only the negative activity of criticism is left — together with the construction of the inevitably singular manifestation of unphilosophy. Moreover, since this appearance follows no rule and takes on a different shape again in every individual, the construction of unphilosophy is the construction of the individual in which its manifestation has occurred.[34] — Now if one group has another group facing it in opposition, each of them is called a "party"; but when one of them no longer even seems to amount to anything, then the other ceases to be a party likewise. Hence, on the one hand, each side must find it unbearable to appear merely as a party, and must not spare itself the spontaneously appearing and disappearing semblance [of partisanship] which it acquires in the struggle, but must enter into the battle, which [even though it creates the semblance of partisanship] is at the same time, the emerging manifestation of the nullity of the opposed group. On the other hand, if a group wants to save itself from the danger of the battle, and from the manifestation of its own inward nullity, then in virtue of its declaration that the other side is *only* a party, it has recognized the opposition as something [real], and has renounced for its own part the universal validity in respect to which, what is actually [for the moment] a party, must not [xxiv]   be a // party but rather nothing at all. In so doing it has confessed itself to be a party, i.e. to be null and void for the true philosophy.[35]

Notes

1. *Urbild der Sache selbst*. In this first appearance of *die Sache selbst*, the conceptual context appears to involve a combination of Spinozist and Neoplatonic concepts (the One Substance and the Ideas as archetypes.)

2. *das gegenseitige Anerkennen* — the "struggle for recognition" is a distinctively Hegelian theme that makes its first appearance here. The reader will see as he proceeds, that the whole conception of criticism in the present essay depends upon the kind of recognition that is possible between author and critic. In this connection the relation of "philosophy" to "unphilosophy" is the first case of a master-slave dialectic. The awkward implications of this — which are still by no means apparent to Hegel himself as yet — will not escape any careful student of the *Phenomenology*.

3. *Unphilosophie* — the sense of active opposition, rather than merely neutral difference, is best captured by preserving the Latin prefix unchanged. The noun forms are unnatural in both languages; but the echo of the perfectly natural adjectives (*unphilosophisch*, unphilosophical) is appropriate.

4. "Construction" is Schelling's preferred technical term for the general method of the Identity Philosophy. At each level (*Potenz*) of life and knowledge the Absolute Identity has to be "constructed" as a "totality" that is the complete unfolding of an original unity. Critical "construction" is apparently the complete unfolding of an original nullity (i.e. it is what we would ordinarily call *destruction*). But at the end of the essay Hegel speaks of the "construction" of *individuality* — even in the case of the specific manifestations of "unphilosophy" — as if it were something positive, and not just a negative or destructive demonstration of philosophic nullity.

5. The target of this polemical remark is very probably Jacobi (who summed up Spinoza's theory as a set of short formulas). The whole paragraph deserves to be considered in the light of Hegel's discussion of Jacobi in *Faith and Knowledge*.

6. This "first case" is the situation of pre-Kantian or "dogmatic" metaphysics. The forms that "possess great authority" are typically those of theology which still has

philosophy as its handmaid, or of "Faith" dominant over "Reason." But the Enlightenment reaction against this dominance involved the same imperfection. Thus an example of a work which is "not valid as a shape of the Idea," but which nevertheless deserves philosophical appreciation, is provided by the *Système de la Nature* of Baron d'Holbach. (Compare *Difference*, p. 177.)

7. This is the post-Kantian case, and the paradigm for it is probably Fichte—though Kant himself would fill the bill.

8. Jacobi, Reinhold, and G. E. Schulze (against whom Hegel's "Skepticism" essay was directed) are all attacked in Hegel's later contributions to the *Critical Journal* for proceeding in this way.

9. Fichte is in the peculiar hybrid position of being by Hegel's standards a true original genius with a *personal philosophy* which cannot recognize itself in other systems (compare *Difference*, pp. 87-88)

10. Dante is often in Hegel's mind in this period—and it is quite likely that Schelling was responsible for this since there are no obvious references to Dante in Hegel's papers before the Jena period. The paradigm of Dantesque damnation here (being "for ever bound to his own limited position") is probably Jacobi. The philosopher who "seized one position after another, marvelling unstintedly at them all" is unquestionably Reinhold—compare *Difference*, pp. 178-79, 191. For other Dante references see *Faith and Knowledge*, pp. 146-47 and *Natural Law*, pp. 104-5.

11. It was Fichte who insisted on the absoluteness of his philosophical principle, and left experience to take care of itself. Reinhold laid great stress on the *provisional* character of all philosophizing; he also (apparently) thought of the study of earlier philosophies as being mainly useful as an exercise for our minds. Hegel seems here to be characterizing both of these attitudes (compare *Difference*, pp. 86-89, 108-9, 130-31; *Faith and Knowledge*, pp. 156-62).

12. "Healthy common sense" (*gesunde Menschenverstand*) had many spokesmen in this period. But one who spoke for it against a Kantian background, and whose work was criticized by Hegel in this same first issue of the *Critical Journal* under the heading "How Ordinary Common Sense Takes Philosophy," was W. T. Krug. (A translation of this essay follows herein).

13. This question, and the fairly careful exposition of the ambiguity involved in the answer, can be interpreted with considerable plausibility, as the reflection of a better understanding of Fichte's views than Hegel had when he wrote the *Difference* essay, a few months before the present introduction was drafted. The exposition of Fichte in the *Difference* essay is based on direct study of the *Science of Knowledge* of 1794. Hegel there takes Fichte as a "speculative" thinker, (i.e. one who expounds philosophy from an "infinite" or "absolute"—not from a "finite" or human—standpoint). In *Faith and Knowledge* (1802) he abandons this view entirely, and criticizes Fichte as a "reflective philosopher of subjectivity" (where "subjectivity" refers to the same finite, human standpoint that is referred to here). The change is most easily accounted for by assuming that after the publication of the *Difference* essay Hegel gained access (in some form) to the second version of the *Wissenschaftslehre*. This was the substance of Fichte's last lecture courses at Jena (1798) but it remained in manuscript until after 1930. Students who had attended the course could well have taken Hegel to task for misunderstanding the formal exposition of 1794, and assuming that the whole position was meant to be seen from the standpoint of the self-positing Ego which is placed first

on grounds of logical priority only. If they backed up their claim by producing their lecture notes, the sudden switch in Hegel's attitude toward Fichte would be fully accounted for. (One would think that Schelling would know what Fichte was saying in 1798, but if he did, he probably attached little importance to what he would have regarded simply as an experiment in Fichte's mode of exposition. He was always making such experiments himself without any important change in the views expounded. For that matter, Fichte did not change *his* views, either. He was impelled to seek a new mode of exposition in order to demonstrate his loyalty to his Kantian beginnings, and to make clear the difference between his view and the "speculative" theory of his supposed "disciple" Schelling. The *Wissenschaftslehre* of 1798 is the exposition which shows clearly that there was *always* a radical difference between Fichte and Schelling about the question of *how* philosophy is possible—about "The Possibility of a Form of Philosophy in General" as Schelling put it in the title of one of his earliest essays).

14. The French translator, B. Fauquet, believes that this metaphor originates in Rousseau's attack on the pedagogic use of leading reins for children (*Emile*, Book II, tr. Foxley, Everyman, p. 42). Kant took up Rousseau's point in his own *Reflections on Education* (tr. Churton, Ann Arbor, 1960, section 41, pp. 40-41); but then went on to use the image metaphorically with respect to the human faculty of judgement generally in the *Critique of Pure Reason* B 174. Hegel, like Kant, admired Rousseau, and read him carefully. But it is Kant—if anyone— who has suggested this metaphor to him.

15. The great proponent of the "hypothetical" and "problematic" starting point was Reinhold. But if the hypothesis in note 13 is correct Hegel may have been uncertain whether Fichte's actual starting point was to be regarded as problematic (in the Kantian sense) or as certain (in the Cartesian sense). There is this sort of ambiguity, I think, about the "I" of the *Vocation of Man*. So Hegel may here be considering Reinhold and Fichte together, or Reinhold alone—or, of course, there may be still other theorists in his mind either specifically or additionally. The important points to notice are: (i) he claims here that it makes no difference in the end whether the starting point is certain or problematic; (ii) that the *Phenomenology of Spirit* begins with a "self" whose status is ontologically ambiguous in just this way—but also Hegel insists that "we" who observe the "phenomenology of the Spirit" must be at home with the Absolute from the start.

16. This opposition is unmistakeably Fichtean. It is basic to Hegel's exposition of Fichte in the *Difference* essay.

17. *dasjenige, das sie denkt—sie (die Idee)* can be either the subject or the object of *denken* here; and I believe that the ambiguity is deliberate. That the Infinite Idea "thinks" all finite reality, and in particular it is the "pure Ego" which thinks the finite ego, expresses the standpoint of "speculative" philosophy. That the finite reasoner "thinks" the Infinite Idea of Reason— and finds himself involved in dialectical contradiction when he seeks to pass from "thinking" to "cognition"—expresses the "reflective" standpoint of Kant and Fichte. The French translator chooses the speculative interpretation here. But I think that the context requires rather the reflective one. We are, however, meant to be conscious of the "true" (speculative) interpretation, so I have inserted the alternative in brackets.

18. This clause indicates that Hegel means his discussion to embrace the theories of Reinhold, Jacobi and other "reflective" philosophers of finite experience generally. But the Idea which is "only an Idea" is the Kantian "Idea of Reason." So there can be no question that his principal targets are Kant and Fichte.

19. The antithesis of thought and being is the ultimate dualism which the Philosophy of Identity seeks to overcome. This is the opposition that is basic to the "reflective philosophy of subjectivity" (in which thinking is regarded as a mere "reflection" of "being"). (See further the next note.)

20. There is a deliberate echo here from the book of *Exodus*. Kant was often thought of as a philosophical Moses. But for the Identity theorists, the conception of thought as mere "reflection" of being was the philosophical "land of Egypt" or "house of bondage." Hegel's longest and most important critical essay, *Faith and Knowledge*, aimed to show that Kant, Jacobi and even Fichte, were all "reflective philosophers of [finite] subjectivity." The whole of that essay forms an extended commentary on the present passage.

21. This is the first occurrence of the concept of a "verkehrte Welt" in Hegel's work. In view of the way in which the "inverted world" appears in the *Phenomenology* as part of the dialectic of the Understanding, it is important to note that it appeared first as the crucial contrast between "healthy human understanding" and Reason." There is no contradiction here, since the dialectic of Understanding in the *Phenomenology* is the process by which ordinary perceptual consciousness becomes philosophical in the first instance. Thus the present passage illustrates how important the seemingly absurd byplay of the *Phenomenology* really is. Also it shows both the limited justification and the ultimate injustice (from Hegel's point of view) of Engels' complaint that Absolute Idealism turns the world upon its head. According to Hegel this is a necessary result of Kant's Critical Philosophy, but the further transition from critical Understanding to Reason turns things the right way up again. The Marxist critique of Hegel's Idealism ascribes to it the "reflective" opposition to "reality" which is the hallmark of the "subjective" standpoint which it set out from the first to overcome (but which was, by the same token, essential to its own genesis).

22. The insistence that philosophy is essentially esoteric belongs to Schelling more than to Hegel at this period. At the time of his arrival in Jena Hegel was preoccupied by the problem of how his philosophical ideals could be made "influential in the life of men." Aristotle's response to Alexander (that a philosophy may be at once published and yet still unpublished) represents the way in which he reconciled this concern of his own with his acceptance of Schelling's position. He agreed that philosophy could not be expressed in a "popular" form because of its opposition to the standpoint of the Understanding, and its dialectical treatment of the principles of common sense. But he insists that the *Volk* can "rise to philosophy" nevertheless. This contradicts Schelling's more rigorously aristocratic view that philosophy is *für sich* antipathetic to the vulgar. The *Phenomenology* was the eventual outcome of Hegel's effort to raise general cultural consciousness to the level of philosophy. It would perhaps, be generally agreed that that book is a paradigm case of a philosophy that remained unpublished in its publication.

The (spurious) correspondence of Aristotle and Alexander is cited and appealed to by Plutarch in his "Life of Alexander," chapter 7; compare Aulus Gellius, *Noctes Atticae* XX,5.

23. The term "popular philosophy" was apparently coined (in Germany) by Moses Mendelssohn (and he was the most notable member of the group of Enlightened thinkers in Berlin, who set out to write philosophy in the plain and simple manner of the French *philosophes*). But Hegel (rightly I think) sees that the kinship of these German "Enlighteners" is with the *Theodicy* rather than with *Candide*. Among those "trained

for the job nowadays" Hegel certainly included Bardili (called by Fichte a "formula philosopher") and Krug—and probably Schulze.

24. *Ideal* is Kant's name for the perfect exemplification of an *Idee*. *Humanität* is an ideal with which Herder made great play. Hölderlin and Hegel both took it over from Herder and remained much attached to it even in the last years of the eighteenth century, at a time when Schelling was openly contemptuous about it as being mere empty rhetoric. Hegel himself shows contempt for Herder's rhetoric in *Faith and Knowledge* (1802). Nevertheless I think that this example stems from Schelling.

25. Hegel regarded Fichte's *Vocation of Man* as belonging to this genre—and indeed the affinity with Leibniz' *Theodicy* is here obvious enough. The *Vocation of Man* is perhaps the clearest instance of "the seemingly opposite case"—see especially *Faith and Knowledge*, pp. 177-87. The same tendency is present in Kant according to *Faith and Knowledge*, pp. 94-95.

26. The true seriousness of "play" is insisted upon for the first time in Schiller's *Aesthetic Letters* (1795). The present passage testifies to the lasting importance of this work in Hegel's mind. The "playfulness" of the *Phenomenology* has certainly not been ignored, but it has not generally received the "serious" interpretation that it deserves.

27. The sense that 1789 was the dawn of a new age to which *Germany* must give its philosophical expression dominated Hegel's mind from 1793 onwards. The concluding pages of the Preface to the *Phenomenology* (the last pages of the book to be written) express this consciousness very explicitly. (The remarks here about the relation of the new idealism to Cartesian rationalism should be compared with *Difference*, pp. 91-93).

28. The reference here is probably to the general reputation of Spinoza as a "notorious atheist."

29. This may well be a reference to the way that Wolff's Scholastic system was derived from Leibniz.

30. The evil genius responsible for the "death" of living Nature into universal mechanism was Newton.

31. The currents of French Deism, Wolff's Eudaemonism and the "religion of Reason" in Kant and Fichte appear to be lumped together in this passage. Compare *Difference*, pp. 89-90, 193-95; and *Faith and Knowledge*, pp. 177-78.

32. Hegel is now considering the skeptical followers of the Critical Philosophy, especially G. E. Schulze (Aenesidemus).

33. Reinhold is the most notable example, but not the only one, of a philosopher who was bowled over by each new philosophical fashion in turn.

34. The relation of this historical "construction" to the method of "construction" in the system of identity itself is by no means clear (see note 4 above). But the project of a critical "construction" of each form of *unphilosophy* is certainly an important moment in the genesis of the *Phenomenology*, in which a series of quite *un*philosophical individualities are "constructed" in a way which shows that "appearance" does follow a rule after all. By this means, too, the opposition between philosophy and the unphilosophical is overcome so that although the movement toward the "true philosophy" is a "highway of despair" it is not a reduction of the unphilosophical forms to mere nullity.

35. This is perhaps the first appearance of the "life and death struggle" in Hegel's thought. We should note that it is a struggle for *recognition*, but that the essentially

equal and reciprocal character of effective recognition is not yet recognized. The struggle between philosophy and unphilosophy aims at the establishment of the "lordship" of the former and the "bondage" of the latter. Thus the analysis of "lordship and bondage" in the *Phenomenology* should be seen as a criticism of the inadequacy of the *aristocratic* position adopted here (compare note 2 above).

How the Ordinary Human Understanding
takes Philosophy
(as displayed in the works of Mr. Krug)
[by G. W. F. Hegel]

Kritisches Journal der Philosophie, I, no. 1 (1802) 91-115

Translation and notes by H. S. Harris

Wilhelm Traugott Krug was born, like Hegel himself, in 1770. He was not an important thinker, and there are only two reasons—as far as I can see—why he deserves a place in the scholarly footnotes of the history of German idealism. First, the challenge he issued that the new idealism should "deduce his pen"—which Hegel waxes so ironical about in this review—stuck in Hegel's mind. It is clear that he always regarded the demand as illegitimate; but in the context of the Identity Philosophy he could not clearly show what was wrong with it. The immediate response that he gives is important because it shows us how significant the Ontological Argument was for the new idealism from the very beginning. For this reason alone, Hegel's critical review of Krug deserves our careful attention. But the definitive answer to Krug's challenge comes only in the first chapter of the Phenomenology.[1] *As Aristotle had already laid down, philosophical science is not concerned with the knowledge of singulars. But Hegel could only show the relation of "Science" to "experience" properly by writing his "science of the experience of consciousness". Even in the Berlin years, he recurred to Krug's challenge as the irritant that forced him to deal with this problem.[2] So it is right to see this review of Krug as an important moment in the evolution of Hegel's mature system.*

Secondly, when Kant died in 1804 the Philosophical Faculty at Königsberg elected Krug to Kant's chair of logic and metaphysics. This is interesting because it reflects and symbolizes the aged Kant's own attitude towards his "idealistic" followers. Krug was outwardly a "Kantian", rather than an adherent of the Scottish philosophy of common sense. But, as the title of Hegel's essay suggests, Krug's work showed how the "common human understanding" can "take philosophy" upon itself as a disguise. The early followers of Reid, Oswald and Beattie, in Germany were mainly hostile to Kant (and he to them). This was only natural, since as Manfred Kuehn remarks, "If Scottish common sense had already succeeded in showing what Kant wanted to show, then Kant's difficult critical philosophy was really superfluous".[3] But when he was faced with the work of declared "followers" like Beck and Fichte— not to speak of Schelling who never acknowledged that he followed anyone—Kant preferred to align himself with the "popular philosophy" which he had effectively vanquished and driven from the field. In his "open letter" of August 7, 1799, he declared:

> Since some reviewers maintain that the *Critique* is not to be taken literally in what it says about sensibility and that anyone who wants to understand the *Critique* must first master the requisite "standpoint" (or Beck or Fichte) because Kant's precise words, like Aristotle's will kill the mind, I therefore declare again that the *Critique* is to be understood in accordance with the letter, and is to be understood exclusively from the point of view of common sense, which only needs to be sufficiently cultivated for such abstract investigations.[4]

It was ironically appropriate therefore that his successor was someone who had already been exposed (by the successors whom he rejected) as a thinker who was

was merely dressing up common sense in the stage costume of his "transcendental synthetism".

In 1809 Krug became professor of philosophy of Leipzig. Hegel *did not live to see the* Allgemeines Handworterbuch der philosophischen Wissenschaften nebst ihrer Literatur und Geschichte *that he published there in six volumes between 1832 and 1838 — but the reader of Hegel's review will be amused to note that in the end the philosophical literature and its Sachregister filled all of the promised Volumes! Krug himself died in 1842.*

Notes

1. *Gesammelte Werke*, Vol. IX, p. 66 (tr. A. V. Miller, Oxford; Clarendon Press, 1977, section 102)

2. *Enzyklopädie*, §250 (footnote): *Philosophy of Nature*, (trans. Miller) p. 23. Hegel returns there to the problem of the *quill* as part of the natural order.

3. M. Kuehn, "The Early Reception of Reid, Oswald and Beattie in Germany: 1768-1800", *Journal of the History of Philosophy*, XXI (1983) 485.

4. Kant, *Philosophical Correspondence*, p. 254 (I follow Kuehn's revised version of the last sentence.

I.   Letters on the Science of Knowledge. *Together with a treatise on the philosophical definition of religious faith essayed by the* Science of Knowledge. *Leipzig, Roch and Co., 1800*

II. Letters on the Newest Idealism. *A continuation of the "Letters on the Science of Knowledge". Leipzig, H. Muller's Bookshop, 1801.*

III. Outline of a New Organon of Philosophy, *or essay on the principles of philosophical cognition by Willhelm Traugott Krug, Member of the Philosophical Faculty at Wittenberg. TI PRŌTOV ESTIN ERGON TOU PHILOSOPHOUNTOS? APOBALEIN OIĒSIN. Arrian. Meissen and Lübben, K. F. W. Erbstein, 1801.*

Mr. Krug's philosophical efforts distribute themselves naturally into two categories; one group is polemically directed against transcendental idealism the other is concerned with his own philosophical convictions (as Krug himself calls them.)

So far as his polemical campaign is concerned, the standpoint that Mr. Krug adopts in his opposition to the // *Science of Knowledge*[2] is to be the standpoint of skepticism (I, p. 5 Preface) so that, as befits the skeptical stance, Mr. Krug argues from within the science of knowledge and not from his own convictions. (The *Letters on Transcendental Idealism* [i.e. II] and especially the *Organon* [III] where the author expounds his own convictions, offer him an occasion to tell us why he does not argue from his own standpoint). Mr. Krug intends his "letters" to be the introduction for a scientific inquiry. With respect to his subjective manner of expression, it is a true delight to hear the author's sobriety, equity and fair dealing speak out: "The Science of Knowledge", he say *has so far* been priggish enough, *to be sure,* and *in very large measure* has set its opponents right in a *somewhat* ungentle tone of voice. It is *not to be denied, however, that in many instances* it has only availed itself of the right to take fair revenge, *and if* in doing this, it has overstepped the *bounds* of that right *now and again,* this *may* perhaps arise more from the total commitment with which it marches into battle, than from a naturally hostile disposition. The author has taken no part in this conflict till now, because *he took it as his duty* to test any system *rather carefully on its own account,* before he issues the result of the test to the public"[3] With the nobly benevolent consciousness of this duty well done he now treats the *Science of Knowledge* "with *the respect due to it*; he has set solid grounds against it, not spiteful inferences [. . .] and *unless he is wholly* //*mistaken in his opponents,* he need fear no contrasting treatment himself; for he has too good an opinion of them not to expect to be treated in quite a different way than [. . .] etc. *But if* he should find that he was deceived in this hope of his, then he *would give up his investigations".*[4] The right minded and respectable reason for this is "because it is *but seldom* that *anything sensible* emerges from a leterary feud that is pursued with passionate heat, and in the end only a *scandal* is created for the audience *which brings both science itself and its promoters* (among whom Mr. Krug reckons himself as well) *into public disrepute".*

In the first letter Mr. Krug tells us what he finds worthy of approval in transcendental idealism. He declares on p. 14 that he does not find the ego by any means *so ridiculous* or *so unthinkable* as many people seem to find it. "For what is irrational", he asks, "what is there that could make *an intelligent man laugh, or even just* smile, if I call what I think of through *Abstrakzion* (Mr. Krug's own spelling) from everything that does not pertain to myself simply ego?" *Also he "finds the demand very reasonable:* 'Attend to yourself. Turn your gaze away from everything that surrounds you, and into your inner [life].' "[5] *Furthermore he has nothing against* etc. and *"finally he cannot regard* idealism as a philosophical theory *to be so dangerous* as it seems to be

[92]

[93]

[94]   considered by many people"[6] In // these respects he does not see
anything objectionable in transcendental *Idealisme* (Mr. Krug declines
"ism" words thus: *dem Organisme, dem Dogmatisme*; and in the genitive,
des Idealismes, des Organismes, des Realismes etc).[7] "*But whether it does
not have weaknesses in other respects* the sequel will show".[8]

What Mr. Krug gives his seal of approval to in transcendental idealism
constitutes the content of the first letter; but this self-conceited and
self-satisfied tone of righteousness and platitude, and this tediousness
of manner prevails throughout.

But what Mr. Krug brings up against the science of knowledge,
and what he calls on p. 79 a *thorough testing* extends from p.24 to p.
52. For in the second letter he only deals with idealism, dogmatism,
and realism nominally: "The main question does not depend upon
names [. . .] but through the opposition set up with dogmatism each
and every opponent of the science of knowledge is *to some extent*
condemned in advance, and for that reason alone all access to the
spirit of impartial testing—which is *so often* and so expressedly asked
for on its behalf *nevertheless*—is, *if not* quite prevented, *at the least*
impeded."[9] To stave off any such peril Mr. Krug divides dogmatism
in its material aspect into idealism, (which denies the reality of the
external world), and realism (if it *concedes* and *asserts* this reality). But
it is precisely transcendental idealism that is left out in this division;
for transcendental idealism does not just concede—it is not concessions

[95]   that are // at issue between philosophical systems— but asserts the
reality of the external world, just as much as its ideality; and the
theoretical part of the *Science of Knowledge* is concerned with nothing
else but a deduction of the reality of the external world.

The detailed examination (I, pp. 24-52) of the *Science of Knowledge*
is directed against one single point. Specifically, Mr. Krug cannot tolerate
the being bounded of the ego: The ego is to *bound* itself then, "and
that not *freely and arbitrarily* (what a fine pairing!) but *in accordance
with an immanent law of its own essence*";[10] and yet the basis for believing
in transcendental idealism is the interest in independence; and I, too,
says Mr. Krug, along *with* the friend to whom I am addressing these
letters, and *with* the author of the *Science of Knowledge*, have a great
interest in *my own* independence. That Fichte has associated himself
with Mr. Krug and his friend as one who shares the interest in Mr.
Krug's independence (as Mr. Krug tells us here) has not been publicly
acknowledged before. But it makes no difference at all to the interest
in Mr. Krug's independence, whether the ego necessarily acts as it
does through its outward or through its inward nature. Mr. Krug
compares the ego that acts from inward natural necessity with the
ego that gets determined through a nature outside us thus: that latter
is like a simple flute that a musician plays, the former like a mechanical
flute that produces harmonious sounds *all by itself*.[11]

"As a result it is *also* clear enough, // *of course* that the moral   [96]
dutifulness of the idealistic way of thinking is not such a serious matter
as all that";[12] a good will and a moral disposition can be bound up
with any philosophical theory. (On the other hand, the anthropomorphism of the imagination in polytheism, is for him such awful
abomination that, as he declares on p. 112, it is quite imcompatible
with morality). Never mind that "the interest of independence is not
adequately satisfied by transcendental idealism; for it involves an
uncommonly important advance for the *speculative* interest of Reason
in any case. Here everything is radiant and clear, the ego lets everything
arise before its eyes, and sees it all";[13] but the main problem is still
not solved. For Mr. Krug sees two men, one a European, the other a
Moor, and he feels compelled to represent the one to himself with
white skin, and the other with black. [. . .] Or he might save one man
from a perilous situation, but the torrents still rage, and the flames
still blaze etc."[14] The *Science of Knowledge* stays stuck in the
incomprehensibility of the boundaries, just as "*in all likelihood all
philosophy* [will]".[15]

Mr. Krug closes the last letter (in which he equitably and sensibly
opines about the consistency or inconsistency of the Kantian system
with the *Science of Knowledge* that it is best to refrain from judgement
on this head altogether), with the Latin tag: *ignavum, fucos, pecus a
praesepibus arce*.[16] This is certainly apposite to a great deal that Mr.
Krug was not thinking about when he wrote it out.

The polemical part of the // *Letters on the Newest Idealism* —which is   [97]
directed against Schelling's system of transcendental philosophy—is
just the same in content. But the author does say in his Preface that
"with respect to the *public* exposition of his own convictions he has
here gone one step further."[17]

It must also be reckoned as part of this public exposition that Mr.
Krug voices his objections more boldly in this case, and demonstrates
unforgiveable inconsistencies, palpable contradictions, *nonsense* and
so forth in Schelling's system—though how Mr. Krug can call him
"*our* transcendental idealist" is past all finding out.

Some light seems to have dawned for Mr. Krug about the original
limitedness, from the construction of the ego's modes of action out of
opposite activities, or from the original difference; and he is no longer
forthcoming about the absolute necessity of positing Reason as subject
and object, and hence the necessity to posit boundedness. But he
now clings all the more tightly to the *determinacy*, which will be admitted
as the inexplicable and incomprehensible thing in philosophy.

In the first place he finds a contradiction in the fact that nothing is
to be presupposed in philosophy at all, and yet the Absolute A = A
is presupposed as absolute identity, and as difference, from which all
boundedness is constructed.[18]

This contradiction is just the one which the common understanding always finds in philosophy. The common understanding posits the Absolute on // exactly the same level with the finite, and extends the range of the requirements that are made in respect of the finite to the Absolute. Thus it is required in philosophy, that nothing shall be established without proof; the common understanding at once discovers the inconsistency that has been committed, it sees that the Absolute has not been proved; the being of the Absolute is posited immediately with its Idea, but the common understanding is quite up to objecting that we can very easily think of something, form an Idea of something, without there being any necessity on that account that the thing we have thought of should straightaway have any existence; and so on. Presumably Mr. Krug will object to geometry that it is not an internally complete science (as it claims to be) since it certainly does not prove the existence of an infinite space, though it draws its lines in that space.—Or does Mr. Krug take God or the Absolute to be the kind of hypothesis for which philosophy makes itself responsible, just as one theory of Physics permits itself the hypothesis of an empty space, a magnetic or electrical matter and so on, in place of which another physical theory can posit still other hypotheses?

The *second* inconsistency that strikes Mr. Krug is that a promise is given that the whole system of our presentations will be deduced; and although he has himself already found a passage in the *Transcendental Idealism* in which the sense of this promise is explicitly clarified, [19] still he cannot help altogether forgetting again that it is philosophy we are talking about here. He cannot help understanding the question // like the most vulgar man in the street, and demanding that every dog and cat shall be deduced—yes and why not his own pen too.[20] And since this does not come to pass he thinks he must remind his friend about the mountain laboring and the tiny wee mouse coming forth: *one ought not to have* given the impression that one was going to deduce the whole system of presentations.[21]

It is comical to see how Mr. Krug is nonetheless gracious enough not to want to take the philosopher who puts on the air of being a master in philosophy, quite strictly at his word. Instead he asks just for *some small example*, just a deduction of one definite presentation, e.g. of the Moon with all its characteristics or of a rose, a horse, a dog, or of wood, iron, clay, an oaktree, or even just of his pen.[22] It looks as if Mr. Krug wants to make the problems easy for the idealists, when he makes these demands; for he only sets them the task of [deducing] one subordinate point in the Solar System (the Moon)—or as something even easier still by a lot, his own pen. So Mr. Krug does not comprehend then, that the determinacies which cannot be comprehended within transcendental idealism, belong—so far as they are a proper topic of philosophical discussion at all—as Mr. Krug's pen is *not*—to the philosophy of nature. He seems not to know anything about the distinction between natural philosophy and transcendental idealism; but in natural philosophy he can find a *Dedukzion* (the meaning of the word matters no more here than its spelling!) of one of the things that he proposes, to wit, of *iron*. But has Mr. Krug so little // conception of what philosophical construction is, as to suppose that the Moon could be comprehended apart from the Solar System as a whole, and has he such a trivial impression of the Solar System that he does not see that cognition of this system is the highest and most sublime task of Reason? If Mr. Krug had even the vaguest notion of the importance of this determinate task, how could it occur to him to demand from philosophy the deduction of his pen? Not to mention the task that touches the interest of philosophy most nearly at the present moment: to put God back again at the peak of philosophy, absolutely prior to all else as the one and only ground of everything, the unique *principium essendi* and *cognoscendi*, after all this time in which he has been put *beside* other finite things, or put off right to the end as a postulate that springs from an absolute finitude. A dog, an oak, a horse, a reed are higher things to be sure (like a Moses, an Alexander, Cyrus, Jesus and so on);[23] and both of the series of organic forms (*Organisationen*) are more germane to philosophy than Mr. Krug's pen and the philosophical works that it writes. The philosophy of nature gives him the clue regarding how he has to comprehend such organic forms as an oak, a rose, a dog or cat; and if he has the desire and the urge to contract his own human individuality to the vital level of a rose or a dog in order to comprehend their living being and grasp it completely, then he may make the attempt, but he cannot expect others to do it. It would be better for him to try to expand his own essence to the great // individualities of a Cyrus, a Moses, an Alexander, or a Jesus etc., or even just to that of the great orator Cicero; for then he cannot fail to comprehend *their* necessity, and to regard these singular men, along with the sequence of the manifestations of the world-spirit that we call history as capable of a construction. But to this end he must completely renounce the demand for a deduction of his pen, and not trouble his head any more about idealism's ignorance in such matters.

Mr. Krug believes he has made an extremely good find with this demand of his for the deduction of something determined in this way. He considers that with this he is fully equipped against idealism, and he opines that through the solution of this problem "the newest idealism could be securely established against all further objections". He, at least, would have no hesitation in underwriting the whole

[100]

[101]

system straight away once he has a deduced pen to write with. But he is "also convinced in advance that no idealist in the world will even just make an attempt" at the deduction.[24]

To the end that we may really understand his objection in the proper way he displays *samples* of his common sense (in II, pp. 34 ff.) in a series of naive problems which transcendental idealism will hardly be capable of resolving. These problems are such things as the fact that we are forced to represent to ourselves that we were born at a specific time, that we die at a specific time, that we even get news [102] daily through the newspapers about what happens in the world // in places where we are not, and so on. That if the organism is a product of intelligence, one cannot see how investigators can come upon regions where they discover new plants, or why they are forced to journey all over the earth, and so on; or again one cannot see how intelligence could produce someone born blind, or sickness and death.[25] In short it is quite stupid not to count oneself among the drones, and yet to talk purely in this tone of the most vulgar common sense. — Mr. Kurg declares that "no false shame shall keep him from advancing his objections, for he is sincerely seeking the truth. Because he quite simply cannot conceive an activity or a doing, without a being, it may be (says he) that I am *ipso facto* absolutely incapable of philosophizing, but I cannot help the fact that that is the case, and I would rather confess my incapacity than pretend to a conviction that I do not have."[26] But the alternative does not really exist of either pretending or else spilling one's common sense all over philosophy. — Apart from this wide-ranging contradiction that Mr. Krug discovers (that everything is supposed to be deduced in transcendental idealism yet the dog and the horse do not get deduced) he finds some other contradictions too, by putting together specific passages from the system where the discussion is conducted from quite distinct points of view. Then he cries out against the contradiction in the words of the Jews (as in II, p. 90): "What need have we of further witness that *our* system is a dogmatic transcendent idealism? For indeed we have heard it from [103] the system's own mouth".[27] In one of the passages that Mr. // Krug has picked out the discussion concerns specifically the original limitedness (i.e. the fact that the ego posits itself in opposition as subject and as object). In this connection, it is remarked that any system which sublated this ground would be a dogmatic transcendent idealism.[28] The other passage concerns the epoch in the development of self consciousness in which the subjective and the objective are divided for the ego itself. For this point of division, the limit lies neither in the ego (which is now defined as subjective) nor yet in the thing. It lies nowhere (this is expressly said); it simply is because it is. It will appear as strictly contingent, both in connection with the ego, and in connection with the thing.[29] Mr. Krug explains this thus: there is no ground of limitation at all.

From such pitiable things as this it is obvious that Mr. Krug is not even superficially acquainted with the system which he declared it was his duty to try out thoroughly before he ventured to give a public judgement upon it. Otherwise, once he was aware that consciouness was to be constructed, he would know in advance without hunting around for a particular passage, that an act of the intelligence must occur, in which the limit appears to be contingent (or without a ground) for the ego and the thing.

After this demonstration of Mr. Krug's way of testing things, it remains to mention that at the end of the *Letters on the Science of Knowledge* (from pp. 61 to the end) there is a treatise on religious faith; and this has both an appendix and a further addition.[30] All of it together is concerned with Fichte's essays on religion. Since Mr. Krug explicitly declares here // that in this inquiry he means to   [104] leave aside the transcendental standpoint (which is the only one proper for the philosopher as such) completely, [31] we have nothing whatsoever to say about these effusions of the heart and the common understanding. Without saying so, Mr. Krug leaves the transcendental standpoint out everywhere, and we find that in his detailed *testing* of it he has not talked about it at all. His outbursts of fiery zeal against the pagans are particularly emphatic. Their utterly crude superstition is directly contrary to the religion of conversion to the good life.[32] These outbreaks are directed against the assertion in one of the essays in the *Philosophical Journal* that [true] religion is just as consistent with polytheism or anthropomorphism as with other views.[33] In Mr. Krug's opinion there is a certain hardihood in this that does not befit the seriousness of the problem. "Look what risky adventures, even a really good head can be misled into through the ambition to produce brilliant paradoxes", he exclaims.[34]

As for Mr. Krug's *own convictions*, he asks us to "test them with special care since he is concerned precisely with a new *philosophy of foundations*, so that a really careful trial *might perhaps be quite appropriate*".[35] Mr. Krug first begins to pour forth these convictions in the *Letters on Transcendental Idealism* and the *Organon* (in Latin: *urceus exit*,[36] the jug pours it out). But the great pot that holds them properly is to be a work in eight volums on philosophy as a whole, seven of them for the contents and one for the topical index.[37] Mr. Krug is hanging out the sketch of the // *Organon* as a garland for it. In   [105] order to get hold of these convictions right at their centre, let us take up what Mr. Krug calls his system, or the main plank in those convictions of his. He holds that in our consciousness there is an original transcendental synthesis between the real and the ideal

(*Organon*, p. 75); and he "calls the system that recognizes without wanting to explain it (because in order to do that one must begin either from one side or from the other and must thereby sublate the synthesis) 'transcendental synthetism'. His system is thus an indivisible union of transcendental realism and transcendental idealism". These are expressions that do not sound bad. But we still have to investigate just how Mr. Krug really understands that synthesis of the real and the ideal; for the word "synthesis" does not constitute the thing itself. Now according to the *Organon* (p. 25) the original synthesis is consciousness; but consciousness is not the ego, rather it is *in* the ego.

Let us listen further to Mr. Krug about the ego: he is generally a warm patron of the ego against the opponents of the science of knowledge, "he has nothing against the ego as the starting point of philosophy; . . . all the jesting about it is petty and tasteless", etc.[38] Like Fichte he makes the ego into the real first principle of cognition;[39] he tells us how transcendental idealism is grounded on the independence of the ego, *or of Reason*, and that he has a real concern for this independence.[40] In Mr. Krug's work, however, the ego is separated from Reason; only in this story does the one term occur as an [106] explanation for the // other. Elsewhere in the three works before us, *even the word* 'Reason' is not employed by Mr. Krug—except that in the *Letters on the Science of Knowledge* it occurs a few times in the genitive (or on p. 45 in a similar sense).[41] (We are pointing this out to Mr. Krug, lest it should come to pass in the seven volumes of the philosophical sciences that Reason either does not occur at all, or only in the genitive, so that in the fact-index in the eighth this "fact" is not to be found). Mr. Krug has sublated this collocation of "the ego or Reason", because Reason cannot be made into a thing; that the ego is a thing, on the other hand, is one of the basic principles of this synthetism, and one which he proves often and earnestly. Thus (*Letters on Transcendental Idealism*, p. 80) "where we *perceive* as action", we *must* "also assume an agent, that is we must posit a subject with a certain reality, from whom the action proceeds *as it were*; or in the *Organon*: there is an ego, the subject of the activity exists, "*because* actual activity without a subject who acts is not thinkable—*as his own consciousness will teach anyone*" (Mr. Krug asserts) "*as soon as he will but try to think of something in that way.*"[42] That the *principium essendi* of cognition, or its real principle, is a cognising subject, for this Mr. Krug gives a kind of proof; "*for*", says he, "were there no such subject *there*, then there would be no cognition there either".[43]

Well now, it is in this *thing* that consciousness is, and this consciousness is an infinite collection of facts. Among them Mr. Krug lists a principle of contradiction, a certain practical principle (namely the ethical law), and a man named Alexander too, who was a great hero, a man named

Cicero who was a great orator, and an infinite array of things of that sort. In the *Organon* (p. 14) they are said to be plain facts that are none of them contained in the proposition "Ego = Ego" or "A = A", and the manifold actual facts of consciousness. Those infinitely manifold actual facts of consciousness do indeed all lie within the ego, into which they enter in an incomprehensible way, but chaotically of course, and without any unity or order:

> everything gets mixed with everything else,
> like mouse-dirt and coriander.[44]

Then a Reason in the genitive makes its entrance as well, introducing a formal unity (III, pp. 76-77), putting the muddle in order, and binding it down by "subordinating it under a certain principle as its point of union. This is not to be taken to mean that all the singular cognitions could or should be inferred from the point of union as far as their *content* is concerned. [. . .] Rather the singular cognitions in their multiplicity should be connected with it as a certain unity: *just as* every element in a vaulted roof is connected with the keystone as the last and highest point of union, even though this point cannot at the same time contain the foundation of the vaulting within itself". And *"perhaps"*, opines Mr. Krug // "this is just what the Science of Knowledge had in mind, when it set up the proposition 'Ego = Ego' at the apex of its inquiries", and this 'A = A' should be taken as "a symbolic displaying of that harmony, [. . .] the supreme formal principle of philosophy, but one which does, of course, presuppose other material principles, actual facts of consciousness grasped in concepts, and set forth in propositions."[45] That "perhaps" does honor to the prudence of Mr. Krug, for it is certain that he would not want to assert this positively. [108]

We see now too that when Mr. Krug attacked transcendental idealism on account of the original boundedness [of consciousness], it was not his concern to liberate [consciousness] from being bounded, but rather to find herein a license for the infinite multitude of boundaries in empirical consciousness, and to prove that the system of transcendental idealism is not one whit better than his "synthetism" which posits an infinite multitude of boundaries for empirical consciousness. Mr. Krug, "for his part, holds in this connection, that it does not in any way dishonor the philosophers, to admit right from the start, that there are things which are too high for any human wisdom", (*Letters on the Newest Idealism*); "[. . .] to want to go outside of his consciousness, or beyond and above it, seems to Krug, to amount exactly to sublating his consciousness, while yet wanting to retain it in that very same act by which it is sublated".[46] But what else does Mr. Krug mean by philosophical reflection, if not the sublation of consciousness and its retention, both together in one and the same act?

[109]   Mr. Krug believes he has every right to make the empirical // consciousness into the first principle of his speculation; and every right to assume too, that whatever he finds in his own empirical consciousness, and whatever he must think within it, is perfectly true; he must think of the ego as a thing, and therefore it is a thing. We "posit as actual whatever we must think as a necessary addition; that is how physicists and mathematicians have proceeded in their own field ever since men began to think (II, p. 82) "and no one has taxed them about this procedure to this day"; indeed transcendental idealism proceeds thus itself "in a hundred places!" "Why then are its opponents not allowed to do the same?" *ego homuncio non fecerim?* ["Why should a mere man like me not have done it?].[47] But Mr. Krug is forgetting that when mathematics, physics and idealism ask what has to be thought, they do not turn to the empirical consciousness in which the dogs and cats, Mr. Krug's pens, the great orator Cicero, and so on, carry on their affairs [*ihr wesen treiben*]. Using this model the "synthetism" of Mr. Krug has to be thought of as follows: One forms the image of a Krug jug in which Reinhold's pure-sweet [*Reinhold-isches*] water, beer that went flat in Kant's corner [*Kantisches abgestandenes*], enlightening syrup ('Berlin' brand) and other similar ingredients that just happen to be around, are contained as "actual facts"; the jug is the synthetic bond of all these – (= ego). Now someone comes in and introduces a unity throughout all that muddle, separating the things, by smelling and tasting them one after the other (or doing whatever is appropriate); but more especially he hears from others what has
[110]   come into fashion among them, and finally he makes a // report of it all. This, then, is the formal unity or philosophical consciousness.

This is the essence of the Krug-jug "synthetism"; and though it lies before us quite plain and undisguised, it is still none too easy to find it out because this system contains all the others at once within it (just as a true philosophical system must do). Since being and thinking are united within the empirical consciousness in an incomprehensible way, so that a just, sober and modest philosophy ought not to go beyond this experience, Mr. Krug regards his system as being at one with that of Jacobi;[48] the Kantian *a priori* concepts he does not lack; and as we have seen, he is also a warm patron of the ego of idealism.

Furthermore, with respect to the historical aspect of what is most distinctive in this system, we are inescapably reminded of the earlier quite similar system of Mr. Schmid (*Philosophical Journal*, 1795, Part 10): The reviewer of Krug's *Organon* in the *Jena Literary Times* has already remarked on this. One would never have thought that after the inventor of this system himself had abandoned any attempt to

work it out in detail, it would again be taken up by someone else after he had rejected it. What Fichte foretold at the time (*Philosophical Journal*, 1795, Part 12) has come true completely: "this discovery will undoubtedly be made use of; but it is to be hoped that those who use it will accord the honor of the invention to its true inventor (or as he prefers to say, the honor of the finding); and that they will behave better towards him than toward another famous philosophical author // whose writings are the original fountain of their Kantianism, yet to whom but few of them show the gratitude that they ought to".[49]   [111]
—Toward Reinhold Mr. Krug is not entirely guilty of this fault of ingratitude, but still he is a long way from doing full justice to him. On p. 33 of the *Organon* Krug says that when the *Theory* set up consciousness as the foundation of philosophical cognition it was *by no means so far* removed from the truth, as many of its critics have claimed". But it was only mistaken on one point (Mr. Krug has hit on the very spot): it presupposed that "the whole of philosophical cognition must be erected upon [. . .] or derived from one unique actual fact of consciousness".[50] The truth is, however, that Mr. Krug does Reinhold's *Theory* an injustice, for in virtue of the material character of presentations which is also involved in that one basic principle of consciousness, the whole mass of the actual facts of consciousness (just as endlessly manifold as Mr. Krug could ever desire them to be) - come in too.[51]

Fichte also said about this system of synthetism itself, that it answered exceptionally well to the most pressing needs of the time. The Kantian philosophy made a great stir, and there are many people looking for something special beyond it; through the system of synthetism all the difficulties are removed at one blow; the world is all there waiting without any help from Reason; critical idealism receives an interpretation that is *so easy* to grasp; nothing more is asserted by it than the *capacity to bring all our awareness into one system*.[52] All that remains remarkable, once we have achievèd this // outcome, is how so many alarms   [112]
could have arisen about nothing, and why Kant had to make such tremendous preparations just in order to establish the simple proposition that we can draw inferences about the things in the world. Mr. Krug has now done the same service for the Fichtean system that was then rendered in respect to Kant, in that he shows that "Ego = Ego" signifies the "principle of the original identity of the ego", about which only the consciousness of our own self can teach us, "which accompanies *all of my* activities, and through which I recognize them as *my* activity".[53] Or in short the identity has to be posited in this: that all of the actual facts of consciousness are *in me* and in no one else. But still Mr. Krug is cautious enough to preface this explanation of the "Ego = Ego" with a *perhaps*; for perhaps "Ego = Ego" could also express something else.

Mr. Krug lays the foundation stone soundly for this philosophy of his fundamental convictions in his third section, where he *proves* that there must be only *one* 'real principle' (the ego) but several ideal principles; he appeals later on (III, pp. 19 and 77) to the way that the plurality of the principles is established here. And yet the concluding footnote to this section (III, p. 15) begins thus: "I doubt very much whether anyone will ever get out of the magic circle into which the investigation of the principles of philosophical cognition transposes us, through the assumption of *one* supreme absolute principle [. . .] that would express the complete content and the complete form of [113] philosophy" etc. (from Schelling's essay "On the possibility of // a form of philosophy in general").[54] If Mr. Krug is ready to base an eight-volume system of the philosophical sciences upon his principle, how can his modesty and sobriety lead him so far astray that after he has proved this principle of his convictions, he is *only doubtful* about the opposed principle?

About one of the main actual facts of consciousness (the external world) Mr. Krug gets no further than this: on page 40 he draws the conclusion that although indeed "the assumption of the reality of the external world cannot, be directly proved, nevertheless *a great deal* can be *said* to justify our belief in it indirectly," i.e. through reflection upon the contrary supposition. Specifically this belief and presupposition "[. . .] is so natural and necessary to every man that the most resolute idealist cannot possibly free himself from it; *for he believes in it, as soon as he is not speculating". And on page 47 it follows just from this that the belief in the objective world is "far more rational,* than the asserting of the contrary".[55]

Mr. Krug has crammed all these facts and popular ideas about "philosophy as a "synthetism"" which we have set forth, into the Spanish boots of his real principles and his ideal principles (both the formal and the material ones); he cites the writings of Fichte and Schelling, the *Philosophical Journal*, and his own works diligently; he divides the whole argument into sections with their special notes 1, 2, 3, etc; by all of these devices, in short, he has deprived the substance of his ordinary common sense of part of the popularity and easiness that [114] belongs to it on its own // account. But popular easiness constitutes such a notable virtue of it, that if this plain common sense organized into numbered sections were really philosophy, one would have to lament the fact that our times and customs do not permit him to do as Socrates did, and try it on everyone, gentry and commoners alike; in no time at all Mr. Krug would succeed in arraying the whole of the uncultured public in philosophic robes; even for the skeptic this philosophy is good medicine, as Mr. Krug himself is aware; "if I have merely grasped the actual facts of my consciousness rightly", he says, "and expressed them intelligibly, then no philosopher in the world will be able to reject the philosophical principles I have established; even the skeptic will have to grant them".[56]

Mr. Krug announces at the end of his *Organon* (where we are also informed that this organon is still not properly speaking *the* organon) that, "if his basic propositions are fortunate enough to meet with the approval of connoisseurs, he would not be averse to the working out of a system of philosophy" in eight volumes ("as he has already given his friends to understand in a private communication").[57] On that account we bid him first merely to consider that although in seven volumes a fine big catalog of the actual facts of consciousness can be set out still it is hard to see how he can fit the *infinitely* manifold facts of philosophical consciousness all in (among which he even counts the fact that "there was a great orator by the name of Cicero, and a great warrior by the name of Alexander" etc); and secondly that if seven volumes will not // suffice for them, where will there still   [115] be room to philosophize about these facts laid to rest on their foundation, since the eighth volume (according to III, p. 112) is already bespoken for the philosophical literature, and for a factual index of the philosophical facts in the other seven?

Notes

1. "What is the first task of the philosopher? To cast out conceit" *Discourses* (of Epictetus) tr. W. H. Oldfather, Cambridge: Harvard University Press, 1925-1928, II, 17.

2. *Wissenchaftslehre* was the title of the textbook that Fichte published in connection with his lectures in 1794. Thus Fichte is the target of Krug's first volume of polemical letters, while Schelling's *System of Transcendental Idealism* is the target of the attack on the "newest idealism." (Hegel himself does not underline the references to Fichte's "science" and Schelling's "idealism" as book-titles. But I have done this wherever I felt that it would be helpful).

3. I, 5-6. The emphases are Hegel's. (Hegel also peppers all of his quotations with many superfluous commas, which can hardly be added in the translation. I think that an ironic, eyebrow raising, impression is, perhaps, intended).

4. I, 6-7 (the emphasis is Hegel's). Hegel put this passage in quotation marks; but it is partly a condensed paraphrase. (Where Hegel wrote "etc." Krug says he expects to be treated differently from mindless buffoons and sycophants". The implication of Hegel's breaking off at this point is clear enough. In the following sentence the quotation marks have been added by the translator. The marked passage — emphasis Hegel's — is

closer to a verbatim continuation of the quotation than the last sentence enclosed in Hegel's own marks).

5. These quotations were not marked as such by Hegel. The first is rather free. The second contains a citation by Krug from Fichte's "First Introduction to the Science of Knowledge" (*Werke*, I, 422; Heath and Lachs, p. 6).

6. Hegel omits what Krug (I, 17-18) "has nothing against" (probably because he is himself very much against exactly what Krug finds acceptable — the characterization of "necessity" as a "feeling"). Krug cites two of Fichte's formulations of the problem of philosophy here: "What is the ground of the system of presentations that are accompanied by the feeling of necessity and of this feeling of necessity itself? ("First Introduction", *Werke* I, 423; Heath and Lachs, p. 6) and "How do we come to attribute objective validity to what is never the less only subjective?" ("Second Introduction" *Werke* I, 455-6; Heath and Lachs, p. 31). Also Hegel does not mark his own quotation. What Krug actually wrote (I, 18-19) was: "Finally I cannot regard the idealism of the Science of Knowledge to be so dangerous merely *as a philosophical theory* as it seems to be considered by many people, though it would be most harmful *as soon as it passed over into practice*; it is not dangerous for the very simple reason *that it is not possible for it ever to pass over into practice*".

7. The form *Idealism* (in the title of II etc.) is not normal German. In Hegel's time and now, the Germans speak of *Idealismus*; and they treat these Latin forms as indeclinable. Krug's attempt to naturalize these words more completely may perhaps be a reflection of the Scottish influence upon his thought.

8. I, 20. Hegel does not mark this quotation. The emphasis is his.

9. I, 20-21. Hegel (or the printer) failed to mark the beginning of the quotation, but it is fairly close from the point here marked. The emphasis is Hegel's.

10. I, 27. Hegel did not mark the quote; and apparently he did not notice that Krug was quoting Fichte's *System der Sittenlehre* (see Fichte, *Werke* II, 100-1; the emphasis is Fichte's). So here Hegel's irony falls on the wrong target — or does it?

11. All of this is based on I, 29-31

12. I, 32 (not quite verbatim; Quotation marks mine.)

13. I, 36-7 (not quite verbatim; quotation marks mine.)

14. I, 45-6 (turned to oblique form; quotation marks mine.)

15. I, 48 (not verbatim; italics Hegel's, quotation marks mine.)

16. Virgil, *Georgics* IV, 168: "Keep the drones, the base herd, away from the mangers". (See I, 59)

17. II, 6 (italics Hegel's, quotation marks mine)

18. See II, 13-15.

19. II, 29. Krug here refers to the passage in Schelling, *Werke*, III, 398. (Heath, p. 50). For the "second inconsistency" see II, 16, 19 etc

20. Krug (II, 73) quotes Schelling, *Werke* III, 429: "No dogmatist has yet undertaken to describe or depict the nature and manner of this external influence etc." (Heath, p. 74) as the justification for his challenge. Examination of this passage in context will soon convince the reader that Krug did indeed miss the point of Schelling's argument.

21. These complaints of the mountain and the mouse and of false impressions are found earlier in Krug's discussion (II, 24, 28).

22. The challenge about his own pen is at II, 73. The other cases are offered earlier (II, 31-34).

23. A 'deduction' of these historic figures (and others) is asked for in II, 38-9.

24. Hegel did not mark these quotations from II, 32-33.

25. See II, 43-4, 47 ff

26. Hegel put this in quotation marks, but what he gives us in indirect speech is not a quotation. Krug does say (II 66-67) that he "quite simply cannot conceive (*denken*) an *activity* or a *doing* without a *being*". The rest of Hegel's quotation then follows as given in the text.

27. The echo is from Caiaphas (Matthew, 26, 65).

28. See Schelling, *Werke* III, 408 (Heath, p. 58).

29. Schelling, *Werke* III, 425 (Heath, pp. 71-72).

30. Krug's supplementary essay, with its appendages, deals with the essay of Fichte that occasioned the *Atheismusstreit*, and with Fichte's subsequent essay in his own defense.

31. I, 77-79.

32. I, 112-13.

33. I, 109. Here Krug is criticizing an essay by Forberg on the "Development of the Concept of Religion", *Philosophisches Journal*, VIII part 1, pp. 21-46.

34. I, 116. (Quotation marks added)

35. See II, 6. (Hegel marked the end of the citation).

36. Hegel is punning on Krug's name which means "jug" or "pitcher" in German.

37. See III, 112-4.

38. See II, 63. (Quotation marks added—as also for the quotation from II, 75).

39. See III, 16-18.

40. See I, 24 and 31.

41. In fact this claim is false. Krug uses the word *Vernunft* fairly often and not only in the genitive. Hegel is playing upon Krug's claim that Reason is not a "thing", but pertains to various "things", to suggest that it does not pertain to Krug's ego or his books.

42. See III, 64 (italics Hegel's, quotation marks mine).

43. See III, 17 (italics Hegel's, quotation marks mine.)

44. Goethe, *Ein Fastnachtsspiel vom Pater Brey*, (Act I), *Werke*, Berlin edition, 1960-1978, V, 160.

45. III, 77-9 (Hegel has eliminated most of Krug's italics and added his own. Quotation marks are mine).

46. II, 91 (quotation marks added)

47. The second sentence is from II, 83 (Quotation marks added). Hegel's classical tag is from Terence, *Eunuchus*, line 591 (tense changed from future to future perfect). (In the play the question asked is "If Jove may seduce Danae, then why may not a little guy like me do it too?")

48. For the language see III, 27. But Krug does not mention Jacobi. (His argument for the external existence of things, III 37-8, is very reminiscent of Jacobi however. Jacobi's view was modelled upon Hume).

49. See Fichte, *Werke* II, 439. (Hegel did not mark this as a quotation, but it is almost verbatim).

50. The reference is to Reinhold's famous early work: *Versuch einer neuen Theorie des menschlichen Vorstellungsvermögens* (Prague and Jena, 1789; reprinted, Darmstadt, Wissenschaftliche Buchgesellschaft, 1963). What Krug actually says at the end of this unmarked quotation is: "erected upon *one supreme principle*, or derived from it, and this principle must express one *single determinate actual fact of consciousness.*"

51. Compare Hegel's criticism of Reinhold's theory in *Difference* etc. pp. 178-95.

52. Fichte, *Werke*, II, 438.

53. See III, 78-79. (Quotation marks added.)

54. See Schelling, *Werke*, I, 94. (Marti, p. 43)

55. III, 40-41, 47 (italics Hegel's, quotation marks mine).

56. III, 30 (quotation marks added).

57. III, 113 (not quite verbatim; quotation marks added.)

On The Relationship of The Philosophy of
Nature to Philosophy in General
[by F. W. J. Schelling (and G. W. F. Hegel?)]

Kritisches Journal der Philosophie, I, no. 3 (1802) 1-25

Translated by George di Giovanni and H. S. Harris
Notes by H. S. Harris

The long excerpt that is translated above (see pp 105-33) from G.E. Schulze's first book Aenesidemus (1792) provides a clear picture of what his philosophical position was, and of how he sought to defend it. Hegel is here concerned with the major work that Schulze published nine years later (not eight as Hegel mistakenly says at the beginning). Schulze's own position has not changed, so the reader will be able to decide for himself how far Hegel's extremely trenchant criticism of Schulze himself is just.

But the review shows us that the historical topic of Schulze's book was far more important to Hegel than Schulze's own position (see the introductory essay, pp. 256-65 above). Schulze provided both a historical view of skepticism and a skeptical critique of modern philosophy from Descartes onwards. From Hegel's own critical reactions we can see that he studied both the ancient skeptics and the modern rationalists for himself. But his own view of the tradition to which Schulze himself belongs (and especially of Hume) probably owes a lot to Schulze. Even Hegel's interpretation of the thinkers whom he seeks to defend (e.g. Sextus Empiricus) is often quite obviously biassed by his determination to prove that Schulze is wrong about them. Thus Schulze the commonsensical skeptic, like his opposite number, W. T. Krug, the commonsensical idealist, has a greater negative (irritant) influence on the development of Hegel's speculative idealism, than Hegel himself recognizes.

Critique of Theoretical Philosophy, by Gottlob Ernst Schulze, Court [1] Councillor and Professor in Helmstädt. Hamburg: C. E. Bohn, 1801. Vol. I, xxxii + 728 pp.; Vol. II, vi + 722 pp.

EIGHT YEARS AFTER Mr. Schulz[e][1] came forth with great éclat against the Kantian philosophy, especially in the form it had acquired in the "Theory of the Representative Faculty",[2] he now takes hold of theoretical philosophy in general, in order to set it on fire by means of his skepticism and burn it all to the ground. The whole crew of modern skeptics rightly honor Mr. Sch[ulze] as their leading light, and this sandbag containing four alphabets (just for the present)[3] that Mr. Sch[ulze] has hurled against the fortress of philosophy assures him a good right to this first place.

The proper exposition and appreciation of this latest form of skepticism makes it necessary for us to deal with the relationship // [2] of skepticism in general, and of this form in particular, to philosophy; the different modifications of skepticism will define themselves

automatically according to this relationship, and at the same time the
relationship of this latest skepticism, which claims to stand on the
shoulders of the ancient tradition so that it can both see further and
be more rationally doubtful, will emerge; an explanation of the
relationship of skepticism to philosophy, and a cognition of skepticism
itself arising from that explanation, seems not without utility for this
further reason, that the concepts ordinarily current about it are
extremely formal ones, and the noble essence of it, when it is genuine,
is habitually inverted into a universal bolthole and talking-point of
unphilosophy in these latest days.

The "Introduction" gives us an account of the *subjective source* of
Schulzian skepticism. It develops the following line of thought: "if a
cognition that is supposed to be generated from Reason alone, cannot
secure for itself any universal and lasting assent, but those who labor
on it are in constant contradiction with one another [. . .] and every
new effort to endow this cognition with the stability of a science comes
to grief; [. . .] then the conclusion can be drawn with considerable
plausibility that at the basis of the quest for a cognition of this kind
[. . .] there must lie an unachievable goal, and an illusion shared by
all who work for it. [. . .] The observation of such success, as has
[3]   always attended the striving of so many // men distinguished for
their talents and for the zeal they have shown in the discovery of
hidden truths toward the goal of a scientific philosophy, has strongly
influenced the author's way of thinking about philosophy too "—and
to be universally distrustful of eulogies about the insight and wisdom
of Reason is a reproach to no one—"this has given his thought the
direction that gave rise to this critique of theoretical philosophy [. . .
] Every urge to employ his energies on the working out of whichever
one of these systems seemed to him to carry the surest guarantee of
truth and certainty, was always repressed once more as soon as he
made preparations to satisfy it, *most especially by pondering on the fate*
which has befallen every speculative involvement with the ultimate
grounds of our cognition of the existence of things; for *his confidence
in his faculties has never gone so far*, that he could entertain the hope
of actually achieving something, for which so many men endowed
with the greatest talents and the most manifold insights had striven
in vain."[4]

That is what is called speaking straight to men's faces and out of
their very mouths. —The Athenian lawgiver set death as the penalty
for political unconcern in the times when unrest broke out in the
State; philosophical unconcern, not taking sides, but being resolved
in advance to make submission to what may be crowned with triumph
and with universal acceptance by destiny, is of itself punished by the
death of speculative Reason. If indeed the pondering of fate could

become a [decisive] motive in one's respect for and commitment to a philosophy, then it would have to be not its universality, but rather its non-universality // that was a motive for acceptance; for it is [4] comprehensible enough that the most authentic philosophies are not those that are universally accepted, and that, quite apart from the universal acceptance obtained by bad philosophies, if more authentic philosophies also achieve it, then the aspect of them that is universally accepted is precisely the one that is not philosophical. So that even in the philosophies that enjoy what is called a happy destiny—which ought in truth to be counted as bad luck for them, if we can speak of lucky and unlucky destinies at all in this connection—it is the non-universal aspect that must be sought out in order to find the philosophy.[5]

But if Mr. Sch[ulze] has seen that the result of the striving that so many men distinguished for their talents and zeal have devoted to the discovery of the ultimate grounds of our cognition is equal misfortune all round, this estimate in its turn can only be rated as an extremely subjective point of view. Leibniz, for example, expresses quite a different point of view in the passage that Jacobi chose for one of his epigraphs:"j'ai trouve que la plupart des sectes ont raison dans une bonne partie de ce qu'elles avancent, mais non pas tant en ce qu'elles nient."[6] The superficial view of philosophical controversies lets only the differences between systems appear, but already the old rule, *contra negantes principia non est disputandum*[7] leads us to recognize that there is conscious agreement [Einigkeit vorhanden] about principles when philosophical systems contend with one another—it is another matter, to be sure, when philosophy is contending with unphilosophy —an agreement which is above all success and historic destiny, one which cannot be [re]cognized from the point of contention, and which escapes the vacant gaze of the man, who always // takes in the very [5] opposite of what is happening before his eyes. In the matter of principles, or of Reason, it has gone well for all those men distinguished for their talents and zeal; and the variation between them is all to be located in the higher or lower [level of] abstraction, with which Reason has expounded itself in principles and systems. If the frustration of speculative truth be not taken for granted, then there is no place for the modest humility and despair of attaining what only a superficial view declares that these distinguished men have been frustrated about; or again if the frustration is taken for granted, if modesty and distrust in one's faculties could make up the turning weight along with pondering on the success [of one's predecessors], still there is no question which modesty is the greater: not entertaining the hope for oneself of reaching that goal for which those men filled with talent and insight had striven in vain; or instead, as Mr. Schulz[e] says has happened to him, falling into the conjecture that there is a certain *original sin* that infects philosophy, which must have been transmitted from one dogmatic concern with it to the next (we shall see later that Mr. Sch[ulze] is only acquainted with skeptical and dogmatic philosophizing); that Mr. Sch[ulze] is confident that he has discovered this original sin, and is expounding what he has discovered about it, in the work we have before us, proves that he thinks as little of the motive of modesty in philosophy for his part, for all his talk of it, as we ought to think of the motive of success.[8]

[6]   The *discovery of the original sin* of all previous speculative philosophies is promised, then, in this work; // and Sch[ulze] says (Vol. I, 610) that all hope of successful speculation is *cut off for the future* by this discovery, since it would be foolish (oh yes indeed!) to hope for a change in the human cognitive faculties. What luckier discovery than this of an original sin of all speculation could be brought before the philosophy-craving community (*Volk*)?

Either this community continually justifies keeping its distance from speculating — which needs no justification of course, but still here is one — by pointing to the state of strife there; and proclaims itself disposed to adopt a system only when the day comes that a philosophical council or colloquium agrees unanimously on a universally valid philosophy. Or else it runs after all the philosophical systems (among which it reckons every wind egg) but its intellectual chemistry is so unfortunately organized that it has affinity only for the base addition that is alloyed with the noble metal of a mind-minting, and will only combine with that. This community is continually coming to realize that it is only being made a fool of; and it finally hurls itself despairingly into the moral realm, though still not without cares on the speculative flank.

For both of these parties what more fortunate discovery could there be than that of an original sin in the inmost essence of speculative philosophy itself? For the first group this provides the proof of having been the cleverest, because it never risked anything on speculative philosophy; and the second one finds comfort here for having always been made a fool of, since the blame for this is shifted from its shoulders onto those of philosophy, and its cares on account of speculative [7]   philosophy are taken from it. // It is no wonder, therefore, that this skepticism gains widespread if not universal acceptance, and in particular, that such rejoicing has arisen over the weighty elaboration of it that lies before us. A sample of this rejoicing will be found in our "news and notices" section.[9]

Mr. Schulz[e] excludes ethics and aesthetics from his skeptical elaboration of philosophy, and limits himself to the theory of knowledge [*theoretische Philosophie*]. Making an overall judgement, it seems that Mr. Schulz[e] regards only theoretical philosophy as speculative; but one cannot tell just how he regards the other parts. More precisely, we cannot see anywhere the slightest hint of the Idea of a speculative philosophy, which is neither specifically theoretical, nor practical, nor yet aesthetic. For the rest, Mr. Schulz[e] arrives at this [three-part] division of philosophy by way of empirical psychology; regardless of the fact that he himself excludes this from philosophy, he still uses it, oddly enough, as the source of his division of philosophy; in fact, "some important distinctions" are supposed to "occur between the actual facts of consciousness, they are either cognitions of objects, or utterances of the will, or feelings of pleasure and dislike, among which the feelings of beauty and the sublime also belong; [. . .] our insight into [the facts] goes far enough to tell us that they cannot be reduced to a single class, or derived from a single source" (a remark which we read word for word in Kant's *Critique of Judgment*, Introduction, p. xxii) "but they are essentially distinguished from one another by abiding marks,"[10] and so they give us the above named three parts of philosophy. — Here already, Mr. Schulz[e] diverges essentially from Sextus Empiricus, for in his critique of the //singular parts of philosophy   [8] and of the sciences Sextus does not make the division himself but takes it over as he finds it, and attacks it skeptically.[11]

We have to see, first of all, how Mr. Sch[ulze] comprehends this *theoretical philosophy*, and just what is the character of the enemy that he strikes to the ground. In the first section the essential marks of theoretical philosophy are sought out in a highly methodical way that takes pages and pages, and the following definition is produced: theoretical philosophy is "the science of the *highest and most unconditioned causes of all conditioned things whose actuality we are otherwise certain of.*"[12] — This other certainty about the conditioned apart from philosophy we shall learn about later. But the highest and unconditioned causes of things, or better the Rational itself, these Mr. Schulz[e] comprehends as *things [Dinge]* once more, things which lie outside and above our consciousness, something existing that is strictly opposed to consciousness. No idea [*Vorstellung*] of rational cognition occurs anywhere except this one (repeated *ad nauseam*) that through Reason a cognition of Things [*Sachen*] is supposed to be acquired, — Things which are supposed to lie hidden *behind* the shadow-pictures of things, that the natural human mode of cognition offers us; *existence* is supposed to be made *discoverable* by the aid of abstract principles and of *concepts*; what things may be, taken in their true but hidden *actuality* is to be *reconnoitered*; the tools that philosophy employs for this reconnoitering of things are *concepts*, abstract principles, // conceptual implications;   [9] and the bridge to those *hidden things* is built out of nothing but *concepts*.[13]

It is not possible to conceive speculation and the rational realm in a cruder way; speculative philosophy is consistently represented thus, as if ordinary experience in the unalterable form of its ordinary actuality lay stretched out before it unconquerable, as an horizon of adamant, and speculation surmised and wanted to seek out behind that, the *things* in themselves of its horizon, like the mountain of an equally ordinary actual world, which was bearing that other actuality [of our experience] upon its shoulders; Mr. Sch[ulze] simply cannot represent the rational [reality], the In-itself, to himself in any other way than as a mountainpeak under snow; for the Catholic the Host transforms itself into a living God; but what happens here is not what the Devil asked of Christ, the changing of stones into bread—instead of that the living bread of Reason is transformed forever into stone.

The positive side of Sch[ulze]'s skepticism stands opposed to this speculative philosophy which seeks for a cognition of things that are supposed to *exist outside of* our consciousness; for his skepticism does not just have its negative side which is concerned with the destruction of the brain-children of the dogmatists, and their attempts to achieve cognition of the *existence of hyperphysical* things.

The *positive side* of this skepticism consists, to be precise, in this: that it can be described in general as a *philosophy* which *does not go beyond consciousness*; and verily (p. 51) "the existence of what is given within the compass of our consciousness // has *undeniable certainty*; for since it is present in consciousness, we can doubt the certainty of it no more than we can doubt consciousness itself; and to want to doubt consciousness is absolutely impossible, because any such doubt would destroy itself since it cannot occur apart from consciousness, and hence it would be nothing; what is given in and with consciousness, we call an *actual fact* [*Tatsache*] *of consciousness*; it follows that the facts of consciousness are what is undeniably actual, what all philosophical speculations must be related to, and what is to be explained or made comprehensible through these speculations."[14]

[10]

Now then, may we not ask this philosophy, which posits indubitable certainty in the facts of consciousness, and limits all rational cognition (p.21) to the formal unity which is to be assigned to those facts, just like the most vulgar Kantianism, how it comprehends the fact that man does not content himself with this indubitable certainty which he finds in the perpetual glassy-staring perception of objects, and further how it hopes to comprehend that ordering of perceptions on the basis of perception alone? How is it that man proceeds beyond the bestial level of an existence of this kind, which—to put it Mr. Sch[ulze]'s way—consists in the perception of the real being of things,[15] and comes to the thought of what Mr. Sch[ulze] calls "metaphysics", the thought of a *grounding* of that real being, or of a logical derivation of this real being and of all that belongs to it from a *primal ground*, in order to make it comprehensible?[16] The "conscious-fact" philosophy has no answer save this // stupid one: that that striving after a [11] cognition that lies beyond and above the real, quite certain being of things, and is thus the cognition of things as uncertain — that striving, too, is a fact of consciousness. Mr. Sch[ulze] puts it thus (Vol. I, p. 21): "Thanks to the original constitution of our mind [*Gemüt*] we have in fact an urge to seek for the ultimate and unconditioned ground for everything that exists *according to our insight* into it *only* in a conditioned way."[17] But if every fact of consciousness has immediate certainty, then this insight that something exists only in a conditioned way is impossible; for 'to exist in a conditioned way' is synonymous with 'not being certain on its own account'. — The author expresses himself in the same way on p. 72, when he makes the transition from that bestial staring at the world with its indubitable certainty, to the problem of theoretical philosophy: "although the *being of things* is *quite certain* according to the verdict of consciousness, this in no way satisfies Reason." (here we shall learn what Reason consists in) "because with the *existing* things of our acquaintance *it is not self-explanatory, that they are, and that they are what they are.*"[18]

But what then is the status of that indubitable certainty of the fact in our immediate cognition of the being of things; (p. 57) "there are definitely no degrees in the actuality that we ascribe to the intuited facts, such that one fact would possess more of it than another." P. 62: "The intuiting subject cognizes the objects and their existence directly and as something which exists and subsists in complete independence // "of the workings of the presentative power just as [12] the cognitive subject exists and subsists independently."[19]

In view of this absolute certainty that things exist (and certainty of how they exist) how can it at the same time, be the case that *it is not self-explanatory* that *they are* and that *they are* what they are? Two cognitions are asserted simultaneously: one in which the existence and character of things is self-explanatory and another in which this existence and character is not at all self-explanatory. One could not devise a more complete contradiction between what goes before, and this way of making the quest for a rational cognition comprehensible, or a more oblique and tortuous transition to metaphysics.

After having clarified the positive side of this skepticism, let us pass onto its *negative side*, to which the whole third part of the first volume is devoted. Mr. Schulz[e] himself is sensible that a skepticism which ascribes an indubitable certainty to the actual facts of consciousness is scarcely consistent with the concept of skepticism which the ancient skeptics offer us; we must first hear Mr. Sch[ulze]'s own opinion about this difference. He explains his view of it in the introduction and the first section of the third Part.

To begin with he reminds us that "it has often been the case, that the man who first fell upon a thought on the way to the truth *understood much less* about its content, grounds, and consequences *than others* who investigated the origin and significance of it carefully after him; until now the true view of skepticism has been for the most part misunderstood, // etc."[20]

[13]

The skepticism that Mr. Sch[ulze] views as *true*, and as more perfect than the ancient one "is *related* to the judgments *peculiar* to philosophy; i.e., those which" (as Mr. Sch[ulze] formulates the final purpose of this science) "define the absolute or at least supersensible grounds of the something that is present in a conditioned way according to the testimony of our consciousness, i.e., the grounds present outside the sphere of consciousness."[21] But "the judgments belonging only *to* philosophy are no object to this skepticism; for they express either so-called facts of consciousness, or they are grounded on analytic thinking; hence their truth could be grounded and assured by this skepticism too"; on the other hand this skepticism claims as against theoretical philosophy that "nothing at all can be *known* about the grounds present outside the compass of knowledge", or as the author also puts it, "the grounds of the being of things that are not given in consciousness in the way they exist, or about the things which exist apart from the existing things".[22]

Mr. Sch[ulze] himself allows the objection to be made against this concept of skepticism, that according to it "*nothing* of what *experience teaches*, can be an *object of skeptical* doubt, and in particular *not the sum-total [Inbegriff] of external perceptions* and *only philosophy among all the sciences* (since none of the others has to do with the cognition of things outside the compass of consciousness)"; the ancient skepticism on the other hand ranged over both [experience and philosophy], and the most ancient extended at least to the teaching of experience.[23]

[14]

Mr. Sch[ulze] emphasizes especially that "the beginning // and development of skepticism was always determined by the pretensions of the dogmatists"; the ancient skeptics "admit that there is a cognition through the senses and a conviction thereby of the existence and of certain properties of things subsisting on their own account, a cognition by which every rational man has to be guided *in his active life*.[24]

From the fact that any such conviction was directed merely to the active life, it follows immediately that it has nothing to do with philosophy, that it and the limited consciousness, fulfilled with its 'facts', is not set up as the principle of an indubitable certainty in general opposition to Reason and philosophy, least of all as bragging against them. Rather this conviction was designed as the smallest possible tribute that could be paid to the necessity of an objective determining [world]. We should *not*, said the skeptics, choose this, or avoid that when dealing with things that are within our power, but the things that are not within our power, but according to necessity, these we cannot avoid, we [simply] hunger, thirst, get cold; for these things won't let themselves be put aside by Reason.[25]

But the ancient skeptic was far from elevating the consciousness that is involved with these necessary needs to the rank of a knowledge that is objectively asserted; since we cannot be completely inactive, "we live," says Sextus, "taking account of the phenomenon, in accord with the ordinary understanding of life," but without making any [theoretical] commitment [*Meynung*] or assertion.[26] For this [ancient] skepticism it is not a matter of a conviction of [the existence of] things and of their properties. The criterion of // skepticism, as Sextus expresses it, is what appears (*phainomenon*), by which we, in fact, understand its appearance (*phantasian autou*) hence the subjective; for since it [the appearance] lies in the conviction (*peisei* but not a persuasion of [the existence of] a thing) and in an involuntary being affected, there is no room for inquiry; it is *azētētos*[27] (the German term "Zweifel" [or the English "doubt"] used about [ancient] skepticism is always awkward and inappropriate).   [15]

As for the fact that the [ancient] skeptics declared all perception to be mere semblance, instead of ascribing indubitable certainty to it, and that they maintained that one strictly should [*müsse*] assert the opposite of what one has said about the object according to its appearance, one must just as much say the honey is bitter as that it is sweet[28] — that, as Mr. Sch[ulze] himself asserts, the first ten authentic "tropes" of the skeptics concerned only this uncertainty of sense perception — Mr. Sch[ulze] gives as the ground for this fact that even in the earliest period of speculative philosophy sensations were already given out by the dogmatists to be an *appearance*, which had something quite different as its ground; and "an agreement with what was supposed to be *discoverable behind* it as the authentic fact was conferred on the appearance, indeed cognition through sensations was in very many instances affirmed by them as a science of the *object lying hidden behind* sensation."[29]//   [16]

There is here expressed with regard to the ancient philosophers, the same extremely crass view that Mr. Sch[ulze] has of rational cognition; but the line of interpretation — that [ancient] skepticism attacked not sense perceptions themselves, but only the facts placed behind and beneath them by the dogmatists — is quite unfounded. When the skeptic said "The honey may be just as well bitter as sweet." there was then no thing placed behind the honey that was meant (*gemeynt*). —

"The fact that for the skeptics of Greece [. . .] *the propositions of all* [empirical scientific] *doctrines* that lay claim to validity for every human understanding were also an object of doubt testifies to an ignorance on their part about the true grounds of their doubt."[30] And *furthermore* the particular sources of the cognitions of each science, and the degree of conviction possible in it, had still not been investigated then as they have *today*; "many doctrines which *now set all reasonable urge to doubt at defiance* (such as *physics and astronomy*, for example) were then still only an ensemble of unprovable opinions and groundless hypotheses."[31] This trait perfects the character of this modern skepticism, and its differentia from the ancient form; apart from the actual facts of consciousness, the physics and astronomy of modern times would thus be the further sciences which set all reasonable skepticism at defiance; doctrines which, setting aside their purely mathematical parts,

[17]   which do not belong peculiarly to them, consist of // "forces", "matters" etc., in a science [*Wissen*] which claims objectivity throughout, yet is purely formal, and derived from a reporting of sense-perceptions, and their amalgamation with the concepts of the understanding.

This is a science, of which one part, the reporting of perceptions, has nothing at all to do with a scientific mode of knowing, and hence falls quite outside the range of skepticism too, so far as nothing but its subjectivity ought to be expressed in the utterance of perception; while the other part of it is the highest peak of a dogmatizing understanding. What would the ancient skeptics have said to a bastard offspring of this kind, a skepticism which can come to terms with the glaring dogmatism of these sciences?

Finally Mr. Sch[ulze] gets to the uncertainty and imcompleteness of our information about ancient skepticism. —Certainly we lack precise information about Pyrrho, Aenesidemus and others of the older skeptics who were famous; but, on the one hand, it emerges from the whole record [*Wesen*] of this skepticism that the polemical aspect of opposition to philosophical systems, which typified the skepticism of Aenesidemus, Metrodorus, and their successors, was absent from the skepticism of Pyrrho, to which the first ten "tropes" belong,[32] and on the other hand, it emerges likewise that in the tropes of Sextus Empiricus the universal essence of this skepticism is very truly preserved for us, so that every further development of skepticism could not be anything but the continual repetition in active use of one and the same universal mode.

In general, however, the concepts of skepticism which allow it to be viewed *only* in the particular form in which it comes on the scene as skepticism pure and simple, disappear in the face of a philosophic

[18]   standpoint from which // it can be found as genuine skepticism even *in those philosophical systems* which Sch[ulze] and others with him can only regard as dogmatic. Without the determination of the true relationship of skepticism to philosophy, and without the insight that skepticism itself is in its inmost heart at one with every true

philosophy, and hence that there is a philosophy which is neither skepticism nor dogmatism, and is thus both at once, without this, all the histories, and reports, and new editions of skepticism lead to a dead end. This *sine qua non* for the cognition of skepticism, this relationship of skepticism to philosophy, not to some dogmatism or other, this recognition of a philosophy that is not a dogmatism, in fine, therefore, the concept of a philosophy as such, this it is that has escaped Mr.Sch[ulze]; and if Mr.Sch[ulze] had not been able to put the Idea of philosophy completely to flight from the battlefield of those philosophies that he examines skeptically, then just the historical aspect of the ancient skepticism must surely have led him to the thought, at least, that philosophy may possibly be something other than the dogmatism which is all that he is acquainted with.

Diogenes Laertius remarks on it himself in his own way, saying that some people name Homer as the founder of skepticism, because he spoke of the same things differently in different relationships; and many dicta of the Seven Sages were skeptical, as for instance: "Nothing too much," and "Commitment goes hand in hand with corruption" (i.e. every bond with something limited contains its downfall in itself); but for good measure Diogenes cites Archilochus, Euripides, Zeno, Xenophanes, Democritus, Plato etc. as skeptics too;[33] in short those whose views // Diogenes repeats had the insight, that a true   [19] philosophy necessarily involves a negative side of its own too, which is directed against everything limited, and thereby against the heap of the facts of consciousness, and their indubitable certainty, and against the blinkered concepts [34] in those marvellous doctrines which Mr.Sch[ulze] regards as unassailable by rational skepticism – turned against this whole soil of finitude, upon which this modern skepticism founds its essence and its truth; and thus a true philosophy is infinitely more skeptical than this skepticism.

What more perfect and self-sustaining document and system of genuine skepticism could we find than the *Parmenides* in the Platonic philosophy? It embraces the whole domain of that knowledge through concepts of understanding, and destroys it. This Platonic skepticism is not concerned with doubting these truths of the understanding which cognizes things as manifold, as wholes consisting of parts, or with coming to be and passing away, multiplicity, similarity, etc. and which makes objective assertions of that kind; rather it is intent on the complete denial of all truth to this sort of cognition. This skepticism does not constitute a particular thing in a system, but it is itself the negative side of the cognition of the Absolute, and directly presupposes Reason as the positive side.

Hence, notwithstanding the fact that the Platonic *Parmenides* appears only from its negative side, Ficino, for example, [re]cognizes full well, that he who draws near to the sacred study of it, must prepare himself in advance through purification of mind [*Gemüth*], and freedom of spirit, before he dares to touch the secrets of the sacred work. But on [20] account of this utterance of Ficino, Tiedemann // only sees in him one who is stuck in the Neoplatonic mud, while in the works of Plato himself he sees nothing but a cloud of passably obscure sophisms, or a heap of passably acute ones (acute for the time of a Parmenides and a Plato though nauseating to a modern metaphysician).[35]

This weakness arises from the fact that metaphysical expressions had not yet been correctly defined by exact philosophers; anyone who has had some practice in metaphysical things, would find that concepts that are at opposite poles from one another are exchanged for one another. — In other words those otherwise acute folk, Plato and Parmenides, had not yet penetrated to the philosophy which finds the truth in the actual facts of consciousness, and everywhere else except in Reason, nor had they achieved clarity of concepts, as the understanding and a merely finite thought establishes it in the modern sciences of physics, etc. and expects [*meynt*] to get it from experience.

This skepticism that comes on the scene in its pure *explicit* shape in the *Parmenides*, can, however, be found *implicit* in every genuine philosophical system; for it is the free side of every philosophy; if in any one proposition that expresses a cognition of Reason, its reflected aspect — the concepts that are contained in it — is isolated, and the way that they are bound together is considered, it must become evident that these concepts are together sublated, or in other words they are united in such a way, that they contradict themselves; otherwise it would not be a proposition of Reason but only of understanding.

Spinoza begins his *Ethics* with the declaration: "By cause of itself I [21] understand that whose // essence involves in itself existence; or that whose nature can only be conceived as existing."[36] — But now then, the concept of essence or nature can only be posited, inasmuch as existence is abstracted from; the one excludes the other; the one is only definable as long as there is an opposition to the other; let both be posited bound together as one, and their bonding contains a contradiction, so that both are negated together. Or again, when another proposition of Spinoza reads thus: God is the immanent, not the transient cause of the world;[37] he has negated the concept of cause and effect. For in positing the cause as immanent, he posits it as one with the effect, — but the cause is only cause, inasmuch as it is opposed to the effect; the antinomy of the one and the many is equally sovereign [over the finite concepts]; the one is posited as identical with the many, substance as identical with its attributes.

In that every such proposition of Reason permits resolution into two strictly contradictory assertions, e.g., God is cause, and God is not cause; He is one and not one, many and not many; He has an essence which is itself eliminated once more, since essence can only be comprehended in antithesis to form, and His form must be posited as identical with His essence; and so on. Thus the principle of skepticism: panti logōi logos isos antikeitai ["against every argument there is an equal one on the other side"][38] comes on the scene at its full strength. The so called "principle of contradiction" is thus so far from possessing even formal truth for Reason, that on the contrary every proposition of Reason must in respect of concepts contain a violation of it. To say that a proposition is merely formal, means for Reason, that it is posited alone and on its own account, without the equal affirmation of the contradictory that is opposed to it; // and just for that reason it is   [22] false. To recognize the principle of contradiction as a formality, thus means to cognize its falsity at the same time. — Since every genuine philosophy has this negative side, or always sublates the principle of contradiction, anyone who has the urge can set this negative side in relief and set forth for himself a skepticism out of each of them.

It is quite incomprehensible that all through his study of Sextus the concept never entered the mind of Mr.Sch[ulze], even in the most general way, that apart from skepticism and dogmatism, there was still a third possibility, to wit, a philosophy. Right in his very first lines Sextus divides philosophers into dogmatists, academics and skeptics;[39] and if in his whole work he is dealing with the dogmatists, he by no means imagines that he has refuted the Academy too. This relationship of skepticism to the Academy has been convassed enough; it has occasioned a celebrated dispute in the history of skepticism; and this relationship of pure skepticism [to the Academy] with its embarrassment, is its most interesting side.

Not to be unjust to Mr.Sch[ulze], however, we should mention that through reading Sextus he has certainly been made aware of a relationship between the Academy and Skepticism. How then does he apprehend this relationship, and what Sextus says about it? In the note (Vol. I, p. 608) in which he disposes of the matter, Mr.Sch[ulze] says that "in the teaching" of Arcesilaus (the founder of the Middle Academy) "doubting the truth of the teachings of dogmatism was *now, indeed*, made into a procedure *stripped of all exployment of Reason*, since it cancelled itself again, and thereby heeded Reason // no   [23] more at all".[40] Mr.Sch[ulze] goes on to say that "Sextus (*Outlines of Pyrrhonism*, Book I, Chap. 33) *wanted to distinguish* the teaching of Arcesilaus from skepticism" quite radically because, according to the teaching of Arcesilaus and Carneades, "this proposition too, that every thing is uncertain, must in its turn be understood as uncertain;"[41] a doubting procedure of this kind, adds Mr.Sch[ulze] on his own account, is stripped of all Reason.

So far as the historical side is concerned, in the first place, one can hardly believe one's eyes when one sees such a ground for the exclusion of the teaching of Arcesilaus from skepticism attributed to Sextus. It is, indeed, the skeptics themselves, as Mr.Sch[ulze] himself mentions at the beginning of his note, who express themselves most explicitly on this point, that their habitual declarations (*phōnai*): "All is false, nothing is true;" "the one view has as little truth as the other" etc., apply to themselves as well (*sumperigraphein*), *Outlines of Pyrrhonism*, I, 7) and sublate themselves in turn (*huph heautōn autas anaireisthai emperigraphomenois peri hōn legetai* ["they are refuted by themselves, being included in the range of assertions of which they are spoken"]).[42] This doctrine was strictly necessary for them—apart from the fact that it is implicit in skepticism itself—in their outward commerce against the dogmatists, who threw up against the skeptics the objection that they too had a *dogma*: to decide nothing, or "no view is more true [than the one opposed to it]", and to distinguish themselves from other philosophers too, for example, (Chap. 30) from the school of Democritus, to whom the skeptical dictum: "One no more than . . . the other" belonged (e.g. "the honey is no more sweet than bitter").

The skeptics distinguished their own view by saying that there was an implicit dogma here: "the honey is neither"; while they on the other hand were showing by the // expression: "one no more than the other," that they did not know whether the phenomenon was both or neither of them. It is in this way that Sextus (Chap. 33) distinguishes the skeptics from the New Academy of Carneades too, whose basic proposition consisted in this, that "everything is incomprehensible";[43] perhaps, says he, the Academy is distinct just in this one particular, that they formulate this incomprehensibility as an assertion. What Mr.Sch[ulze] says to limit the range of that skeptical expression is "that Sextus only just wanted to teach that the skeptics do not decide anything about the transcendental character of things,"[44] either in a positive or in a negative manner. But in this there is no antithesis to be seen at all against that assertion of the skeptics and of Arcesilaus, that a skeptical expression includes itself in its own range of application, and so sublates itself; and what could the *transcendental character of things* mean in that case? Does not the transcendental lie precisely in this, that there is neither things nor a character of things?

So Sextus was far removed in every way from distinguishing the teaching of Arcesilaus from skepticism itself. Sextus himself says that "Arcesilaus and the Middle Academy seems to him to agree so well with the Pyrrhonian *logoi* that they are almost one and the same *agoge**

[24]

---

*Sextus explains that skepticism preferred to name itself thus, [as an *agōge*] rather than as a *hairesis*, because skepticism could only be called a school or a sect in the sense of a *logoi tini kata to phainomenon, akolouthousēs agōges* [a "leading that follows a certain view in accord with the phenomenon" (*Outlines of Pyrrhonism* I, 17)].

with that of the skeptics:"[45] even if one does not want to say that
Arcesilaus declared that the *epochè*[46] is good *according to nature*, but
that assent is evil. This makes the Academic position into an // asser-   [25]
tion, while the skeptics on the other hand, say nothing assertively on
this question too.[47]

The distinction, which in the opinion of Sextus can still be drawn,
has thus the directly opposite ground; according to Mr.Sch[ulze] the
Academy was shown up by Sextus as hyper-skeptical; but as we have
seen, Sextus finds it to be *not* skeptical *enough*. Apart from the
distinction we have mentioned, Sextus adds yet another more specious
ground, that depends on a scandal: to wit, that Arcesilaus, if we can
put credence in what is said about him, was only a Pyrrhonian in his
approach, but was in good sooth a dogmatist; that he only used the
skeptical method to test whether his students had the capacity for the
Platonic doctrine, and on this account he was regarded as a methodic
doubter; but to one found capable of it he taught the Platonic doctrine.[48]

Because of this difficult problem that was implicit for skepticism in
its relationship with the Academy, Sextus deals very thoroughly with
Plato and the Academies.[49] It is only because Mr.Sch[ulze] is completely
oblivious of the concept of the true ground of this difficulty (and of
the concept of philosophy) that he can hold himself to be dispensed
from taking account of the Academy by the idle chatter that he quotes
from Stäudlin's *History of Skepticism* in this very same note.[50] "It has
already been remarked lately by several authors, and especially by
Stäudlin," says Mr.Sch[ulze], "that the spirit that animated the Middle
and the New Academy was wholly distinct from that which guided
the Skeptics in their inquiries; the adherents of the Academy were
actually no more than *sophistic chatterboxes* who // produced nothing   [26]
but *fallacies and verbal illusions*,, and used philosophy, along with the
whole controversy between the skeptics and the dogmatists as it was
then pursued, only as a *means* to their main end, which was the *art* of
persuading others, *dazzling* them, and *making a sensation; they had no
feeling* [*Sinn*] *at all for the discovery of the truth for its own sake*.[51]
—Even if such an accusation were not generally as empty and revolt-
ing in and of itself as this is, there would still be the earlier Academy
and Plato himself, there would still be philosophy in general, which
is no dogmatism, and which should have been taken into consideration; but we have not been able to find any further consideration of
philosophy than what we have cited from this note.

In antiquity on the other hand there was a highly developed consciousness concerning this relationship of skepticism to Platonism; a
great controversy raged about it, in that one party gave Plato out as
a dogmatist, the other as a skeptic (Diogenes Laertius, *Plato*, 51).
Since the documents of the controversy are lost to us, we cannot
judge how far the true relationship of skepticism to philosophy came

to utterance in it, and how far the dogmatists, who defended Plato as one of them, as the skeptics did likewise, understood this relationship in the sense that skepticism itself belonged to philosophy, or in the sense that it did not. Sextus refers us to a fuller treatment of the question in his *Skeptical Commentaries* which have not come down to
[27]   us;[52] in the *Outlines* I, 222 he says // he intends to report the essence of the matter "according to the view of Aenesidemus and Menodotus who were the principals on the side of the skeptics" in the controversy; Plato was a dogmatist "because when he showed that the Ideas are, or Providence, or the advantage of a virtuous life over a vicious one, he either dogmatizes by recognizing these things as real beings; or else, when he gives assent to the more convincing arguments (*pithanōterois*) he falls away from the skeptical character because he prefers some one view to the other on account of conviction or the failure of it."[53]

This distinction between Platonism and Skepticism is either a merely formal [*formale*] nicety, complaining of nothing but the form of consciousness involved in the preference affirmed, since the obedience of the skeptic to [natural] necessity and to the laws of his country[54] was a preference of the same kind, save that it was without conscious assent; or else if it is directed against the reality of the Idea itself, it concerns the cognition of Reason through itself; and here it is the peculiar mark of the pure skepticism that separates itself from philosophy that must display itself.

Sextus comes to this cognition of Reason in his first book *Against the Logicians* (section 310) after having contested first [the possibility of] the criterion of truth generally in view of the dissensions of the philosophers about it, and then particularly, the truth of sense-cognition. What he says here against the proposition that Reason is cognizant of itself through itself (*hoti oud' heautēs epignōmōn estin hē dianoia, ho nous heauton katalambanetai* "that the intellect is not cognizant of itself [nor does] the mind comprehend itself")[55] is so barren that if modern skeptics want to attack the self-cognition of Reason, they must certainly
[28]   bring forward something better, unless they find it // more convenient to spare themselves this effort completely by ignoring Reason and its self-cognition altogether, sticking safe behind the Gorgon-shield and so transforming the rational into understanding (subjectively expressed) and objectively into stone, not by any malicious distortion or artifice, not as if they had already seen it, but meeting it face to face; and by calling whatever they suspect of transcending understanding and stone, romantic dreaming and imagination.—

But anyway, Sextus knows of Reason and its self-cognition. What he puts forward about its possibility is the following piece of trite rationalizing which he here supports with just those reflective concepts of "whole and parts", which like Plato in the *Parmenides*, he nullifies in his books *Against the Natural Philosophers*:[56] "If Reason comprehends itself, then in comprehending itself it must either be the whole that comprehends itself or not the whole, but it must use a part [. . .] But if it is the whole, that comprehends itself, then both the comprehending and the comprehended are the whole; but if the whole is what is comprehending, then there is nothing left over to be the comprehended; it is however quite irrational, that the comprehending should be, while what is comprehended is nothing. But Reason can also not use a part of itself for this; for how then shall the part comprehend itself? For if it is a whole then nothing is left over as what is to be comprehended; if it again is to be comprehended by a part, how shall this part again comprehend itself; and so on *ad infinitum*; so that the comprehending is without a principle, in that either no first is found, which undertakes the comprehending, or there is nothing which // is to be compre-   [29] hended."[57] —One can see that Reason is perverted into something absolutely subjective, which, when it is posited as a whole leaves nothing over as what is to be comprehended.

And now come still better grounds which drag Reason down to its phenomenal appearance in a definite place, just as before it was confined in the concept of whole and parts, and of an exclusive alternative of absolute subjectivity or absolute objectivity: "Again, if Reason comprehends itself, then it will also comprehend therewith *the place* in which it is; for every comprehending includes a definite place within its grasp; but if Reason comprehends together with itself the place in which it is, then the philosophers strictly ought not to be at odds about it, in that some say that that place is the head, others that it is the breast; and in precise terms, some say the brain, others the meningeal area, others the heart, others the gates of the liver, or still some other part of the body; about this the dogmatic philosophers are at odds. Hence Reason does not comprehend itself."[58]

This is what Sextus advances against the self-cognition of Reason; it is a specimen of all the weapons of skepticism against Reason; they consist in the application of concepts to it. After that it becomes easy enough to demonstrate that a Reason transposed into finitude and turned into things, in Mr.Sch[ulze]'s way, is one thing opposed to another, which likewise must be posited, but which is not posited by that singular [finite Reason]. The most familiar weapon of all, i.e., the appeal to the mutual disagreements of the philosophers is expounded at length by Sextus immediately after the passage cited above.[59] // It is a talking point against speculation that the moral   [30] dogmatists share with the skeptics, just as Xenophon already puts it in the mouth of Socrates,[60] and the superficiality of a view which gets mired down in the verbal disagreements is obvious to anyone. So although this skepticism has already isolated itself and torn loose from [genuine] philosophy, i.e., the philosophy that includes skepticism within itself as well, still it did recognize this distinction between dogmatism and philosophy—the latter being distinguished under the name of the "Academics"—as well as the great measure of agreement between the Academics and skepticism.

But apart from the Skepticism that is one with philosophy, the skepticism that is self-sundered from it can be divided into two forms, according to whether it is or is not directed against Reason. The genuine ancient skepticism sets itself into striking contrast with the shape in which Sextus presents to us the skepticism that is cut off from philosophy and turned against it. To be sure, the authentic skepticism does not have a positive side, as philosophy does, but maintains a pure negativity in relation to knowledge, but it was just as little directed *against* philosophy as *for* it; and the hostile attitude that it adopted later against philosophy on the one hand, and against dogmatism on the other hand, is quite separate. The turning of skepticism against philosophy, as soon as philosophy became dogmatism, illustrates how it has kept in step with the communal degeneration of philosophy and of the world in general, until finally in these most recent times it has sunk so far in company with dogmatism that for both of them [31] nowadays the facts of consciousness // have an indubitable certainty, and for them both the truth resides in temporality; so that, since the extremes now touch, the great goal is attained once more on their side in these happy times, that dogmatism and skepticism coincide with one another *on the underside*, and offer each other the hand of perfect friendship and fraternity. Schulzian skepticism integrates the crudest dogmatism into itself, and Krug's dogmatism carries that skepticism within itself likewise.[61]

Sextus presents us with the maxims of skepticism in seventeen tropes, whose diversity signalizes for us quite precisely the distinction between his skepticism and that of the old school. Certainly the older skepticism stood by itself without philosophical knowledge, but at the same time it falls completely within the domain of philosophy, and in particular, it is wholly identical with the older philosophy, which had less to do with subjectivity.[62]

The first ten of the seventeen tropes belong to this older skepticism. It was the skeptics of much later on—Sextus says simply "the moderns", while Diogenes specifically names Agrippa, who lived about five hundred years after Pyrrho—added five more. The other two that were added seem to be still later; Diogenes does not mention them at all, and Sextus puts them by themselves; they are not important.[63]

These ten articles, then, to which the old school was confined, are directed, like all philosophy generally, against the dogmatism of ordinary consciousness itself. They provide a basis for the uncertainty about the finite situations by which it is unconsciously prepossessed; and for the indifference of the spirit. In the face of this indifference everything that the phenomenal world, or the understanding offers, grows shaky, and in this shaking of everything // finite, according to the skeptics the ataraxia secured by Reason enters, "as the shadow follows the body." Just as Apelles, when he was painting a horse, could not bring off the representation of the foam, until, giving up hope he hurled the sponge which he used to wipe the colours from his brush, against the picture, and in that way achieved the reproduction of the foam.[64] Similarly, in the muddle of all appearances and thoughts, the skeptics find what is true, or the equanimity that is secured by Reason, the *natural* possession of which constitutes the differentia between beast and man. It was this that Pyrrho once showed to his companions aboard ship, when they were frightened in the raging storm; he pointed calmly to a pig, that was feeding in the ship, with the remark that the wise man must be undisturbed like that.[65] Thus this skepticism had its positive side wholly and only in character, and in its complete neutrality toward the necessity of nature. [32]

A brief mention of the ten points which provide the basis for the *epochē* of skepticism, will immediately bring out their polemical bearing upon the security of things and of the actual facts of consciousness; the uncertainty of all things and the necessity of the *epochē* is made out: (1) from the diversity of animals; (2) of men; (3) of the organization of the senses; (4) of circumstances; (5) of situations, distances, and places; (6) from muddles (in which nothing presents itself to the senses in purity); (7) from the diverse sizes and properties of things; (8) from the relationships (i.e., because everything stands in relationship to something else); (9) from the frequency or rarity of happening; (10) [from the diversity] of education, // of customs, of laws, of mythical faith, of prejudices.[66] [33]

Sextus himself remarks regarding their form, that all these tropes "can properly be reduced to a triad: one trope of the diversity of the cognitive subject, one of the cognized object, and one of both put together."[67] So they are necessarily bound to flow into one another in the discussion too — Sextus speaks already of the diversity of organs, which properly belongs to the third trope, in connection with the first two tropes, the diversity of animals and of men; the one with the most extensive range, he remarks, is the eighth, which concerns how every finite thing is conditioned by another, or the way that everything only exists in relationship to something else. We can see that they are raked together haphazardly and they presuppose an undeveloped reflection, or rather an absence of deliberation on the part of reflection in the matter of having a doctrine of one's own, and a clumsiness that would not be present if skepticism had already had to face the task of criticizing the sciences.

But the content of these tropes proves even more clearly how remote they are from an anti-philosophical tendency, and how they are simply and solely aimed against the dogmatism of ordinary common sense; no single one of them is concerned with Reason and its cognition; all of them concern only the finite, and the understanding, or the cognition of the finite throughout; their content is partly empirical, and in that measure it does not apply to speculation *a priori* [*schon an sich*]; partly it concerns relationship in general, or the fact that everything actual [34] is conditioned by another, and in that // measure it expresses a principle of Reason. Consequently this skepticism is in no way directed against philosophy, but against ordinary common sense, and that in a popular mode, not in a philosophical one; against the ordinary consciousness, which holds fast to the given, the fact, the finite (whether this finite is called "appearance" or "concept"), and sticks to it as certain, as secure, as eternal; the skeptical tropes show common sense the instability of this kind of certainty, in a way which is at the same time close to ordinary consciousness; that is, it likewise calls upon appearances and finite cases for help, and [re]cognizes their untruth, by way of their diversity, along with the equal right of all of them to count as valid, i.e. from the antinomy that is to be recognized in the finite thing itself. From this point of view it can be seen as the first stage for philosophy; for the beginning of philosophy must, of course, be elevation above the truth which ordinary consciousness gives, and the presentiment of a higher truth; so we ought to refer the most recent skepticism, with its certainty of the facts of consciousness, above all things, to this ancient skepticism and to this first stage of philosophy; or to common sense itself, which is very well aware [*erkennt*] that all the actual facts of its consciousness, and even this finite consciousness itself, passes away, and that there is no certainty therein; the distinction between this side of ordinary common sense and the [modern] skepticism consists in this, that common sense expresses itself thus: "Everything *is* transient"; while skepticism on the other hand, when a [35] fact is established as certain, understands how to prove that // that certainty is nothing. —

Furthermore, in ordinary common sense its skepticism and its dogmatism about finite situations, stand side by side, and its skepticism becomes thereby something merely formal [*formell*]; whereas the dogmatism is sublated by genuine skepticism, and thus the ordinary belief in the uncertainty of the facts of consciousness ceases to be something formal, in that skepticism elevates the whole range of actuality and certainty to the level of uncertainty, and nullifies ordinary dogmatism which belongs unconsciously in the context of particular customs and laws, and of other circumstances, the context of a power (*Macht*), for which the individual is only an object, and which comprehends him, too, among its single details, in the threads of its causal web. The ordinary dogmatism produces for itself an under-standing knowledge of this context, and thereby sinks only ever deeper into servitude under that power. Skepticism elevates the freedom of Reason above this necessity of nature, in that it cognizes this necessity as nothing; but at the same time it honors necessity supremely. For just as, for skepticism, there is no one of the *natural* details in the web that is something certain, but only natural necessity in its universality, so the skepticism *itself* as a single detail, does not transplant itself into the web as an absolute end, which skepticism would have liked to pursue there, as if *it* knew what is good; —skepticism anticipates in the individual what the necessity displayed serially in the finitude of time carries out unconsciously for the unconscious race. What counts for the race as absolutely One and the same, and as fixed, eternal and everywhere constituted in the same way, time wrenches away from it; most commonly [what does this is] the increasing range of aquaintance with alien // peoples under the pressure of natural necessity; as, for example, becoming acquainted with a new continent, had this skeptical effect upon the dogmatic common sense of the Europeans down to that time, and upon their indubitable certainty about a mass of concepts concerning right and truth. [36]

Well then, since [early] skepticism had its positive side in character *alone*, it did not give itself out for a decided option [*haeresis*] or school, but rather as we said above for an *agōgē*, an education for a way of life, a formative process, whose subjectivity could only be objective in this respect, that the skeptics [each] employed for themselves the same weapons [as the others] against the objective [web of necessity] and their dependence upon it; they [re]cognized Pyrrho as the founder of skepticism in the sense that they were like him not in doctrines, but in these "turnings" against the objective (homotropōs Diogenes Laertius, IX, 70). The "ataraxy" towards which the skeptics formed themselves, consisted in the fact that, as Sextus says (*Adversus Ethicos*, 154), no disturbance (tarachē) could be fearful for the skeptic, "for though it be the greatest possible, the blame falls not on us, who suffer it involuntarily and according to necessity, but upon nature which cares nothing for what men establish, and upon those who through opinion and a will [of their own] draw evil upon themselves."[68] From this positive side it is just as obvious that it is not alien to any [true] philosophy. The "apathy" of the Stoics and the "indifference" of the philosophers generally, must [re]cognize themselves in the skeptic "ataraxia".

Pyrrho was a creative individual [*origineller Mensch*] who, like any other first beginner of a school, became a philosopher off his own bat; but his original philosophy // was not, on that account, something [37] idiosyncratic, opposed to other philosophies necessarily and in principle; it was not so much that the individuality of his character imprinted itself upon his philosophy; rather his individuality was his philosophy itself, and his philosophy was nothing but freedom of character. How then could a philosophy stand opposed to this skepticism on *that* point? If the proximate pupils of great individuals such as he, adhered especially, as sometimes happens, to what was formally distinctive, then, certainly, nothing but the diversity was manifest; but once the weight of authority of the singular personality became increasingly blurred by time, and the philosophical interest emerged in its purity, the sameness of philosophy could once more be [re]cognized. Just as Plato integrated the Socratic, and the Pythagorean philosophies with that of Zeno, etc., in his own so it was too that Antiochus took over the Stoic philosophy into the Academy—and we have seen above that the latter essentially contained skepticism within itself. Cicero studied with Antiochus and if it were not obvious from his life that he was ruined for philosophy, no very favorable light would be cast on his teacher and on *that* integration of philosophies by *Cicero's* philosophical productions.

We need hardly say that what is at issue here is an integration that [re]cognizes the most inward heart of diverse philosophies as one and the same, not an eclecticism, that rambles round their fringes, and binds for itself a crown of vanity out of blooms picked at haphazard from all quarters.

[38]   It is an accident of the time, that later on the // diverse philosophical systems went apart from one another completely, and that "apathy" now became opposed to "ataraxy", and the dogmatics of the Porch counted for the Skeptics as their most direct opponents (*Sextus, Pyrrhonian Hypotyposes*, I, 65).[69] The *five later tropes* of skepticism, which make up the genuine arsenal of its weapons against philosophical cognition, are wholly and exclusively related to this complete separation of philosophies, and the complete fixation of their dogmas and dividing lines, and likewise related to the contemporary orientation of skepticism against dogmatism on one side, and against philosophy itself on the other. To justify our exposition, we shall discuss them briefly now.[70]

The first of these tropes of the suspense of judgement, is that of the *diversity*, no longer now of beasts or of men, as in the first ten tropes, but rather of common opinions, and of the teachings of philosophers, both in the opposition of the two groups, and internally within each group; this is a trope about which the skeptics are always very prolix— everywhere they look for and introduce diversity, where they would do better to see identity. The second is *that of the infinite regress*; Sextus uses it often, in the guise in which it has come to the fore in modern times as the "urge toward a ground"; it is the familiar argument that for one grounding [principle] a further ground is required, for this still another again, and so on *ad infinitum*. —The third was already there in the first ten, namely, the trope of relationship. The fourth concerns *assumptions*, —against the dogmatics who posit something as strictly first, and unproven, in order not to be driven to infinity. The skeptics straightaway // imitate them, by positing with equal right the [39] opposite of that assumption. The fifth is the *circular* argument, when that which is to serve for the proof of another [proposition], itself needs for its own proof, that same [proposition] that is to be proved by its means. —

There are still two other tropes, which Sextus says were also adduced, although Diogenes does not mention them. It is obvious at sight that they contain nothing new, but are only the preceding tropes reduced to a more general form: that what is comprehended, is comprehended either of itself, or through another;—but not of itself, for there is disagreement about the source and the organ of cognition, as to whether it is sense or understanding; nor yet through another, for then we fall either into the trope of infinite regress or into that of circularity.[71]

It is evident even in the repetition of some of the first ten tropes, namely (in part) those which are the first and the third of the five, and from their whole content, that the intent of these five tropes is quite distinct from the tendency of the first ten, and that they only concern the later orientation of skepticism against philosophy.

There are no better weapons against dogmatism on finite bases, but these tropes are completely useless against philosophy, since they contain plainly reflective concepts, they have a quite opposite significance when turned in these two different directions; directed against dogmatism they appear from the point of view where they belong to Reason, setting the other term of the necessary antinomy alongside the one asserted by the dogmatism; // directed against [40] philosophy on the other hand, they appear from the side where they belong to reflection. Against dogmatism they must necessarily be victorious therefore; but in the face of philosophy they fall apart internally, or they are themselves dogmatic.

The essence of dogmatism consists in this that it posits something finite, something burdened with an opposition (e.g. pure Subject, or pure Object, or in dualism the duality as opposed to the identity) as the Absolute; hence Reason shows with respect to this Absolute, that it has a relation to what is excluded from it, and only exists through and in this relation to another, so that it is not absolute, according to the *third* trope of relationship; if this other is supposed to have its ground in the first, while at the same time the first has its ground in the other, then there is a circle, and it falls into the *fifth* trope, the trope of reciprocal dependence; if no circle is to be committed, but

this other, as the ground of the first, is grounded in itself—if it is made into an ungrounded assumption, then because it is a grounding [principle] it has an opposite, and this opposite can be presupposed with equal right without being unproved or grounded, once [the problematic character of] the grounding procedure has been recognized, in accordance with the fourth trope (of presuppositions); or alternatively this other ground is again supposed to be grounded in another—but then this first [term] grounded on the infinity of reflection, will be driven to infinity in finite [terms]; so it is once more groundless, in accordance with the *second* trope. Finally that finite Absolute of dogmatism must also be a universal, but this will necessarily not prove to be the case, since it is a limited thing; and this is where the *first*
[41]   trope (of diversity) has its place.—//

Sextus employed these tropes with great success against dogmatism, which cannot overcome them; and especially against physical theory, a science which, like applied mathematics, is the veritable storehouse of reflection, of limited concepts, and of the finite—yet for the modern skeptics it counts, to be sure, as a science which bids defiance to all rational skeptical attack; it can be maintained, on the contrary, that the ancient physics was more scientific than the modern, and hence that it was less vulnerable to skepticism.

Against dogmatism these tropes are rational in this respect, that they let the opposite [moment], from which dogmatism has abstracted, come on stage against the finite [moment] of the dogmatism. But as directed against Reason, on the other hand, they retain as their peculiar [character] the pure difference by which they are affected; their rational aspect is already in Reason. So far as the *first trope* (of diversity) is concerned, the rational is always and everywhere, self-identical; pure inequality is possible only for the understanding; and everything unlike is posited by Reason as one [and the same]. Of course, this unity, and that unlikeness too, must not, as Plato says,[72] be taken in the common, childish way—e.g. that an ox, for instance, is posited as the one, of which it would be asserted, that he is at the same time many oxen. It cannot be proved about the rational, in accordance with the third trope, that it only exists within the relationship, that it stands in a necessary relation to another; for it is itself nothing but the relationship. Since the rational is relation itself, the [terms] stand in relation to each
[42]   other, which are supposed to ground one another, when // they are posited by the understanding, may well fall into the circle, or *into the fifth*, the trope of reciprocity; but the rational itself does not, for within the relation, nothing is reciprocally grounded. Similarly the rational is not an unproved assumption, in accordance with the *fourth* trope, so that its counterpart could with equal right be presupposed unproven in opposition to it; for the rational has no

opposed counterpart; it includes both of the finite opposites, which are mutual counterparts, within itself. The two preceding tropes both contain the concept of a ground and a consequent, according to which one term would be grounded by another; since for Reason, there is no opposition of one term against another, these two tropes become as irrelevant, as the demand for a ground that is advanced in the sphere of oppositions, and repeated endlessly (in the *second* trope, of the infinite regress). Neither that demand, nor the infinite regress, is of any concern to Reason.

Now, since these tropes all involve the concept of a finite [world], and are grounded on that, the immediate result of their application to the rational is that they pervert it into something finite; they give it the itch of limitedness, as an excuse for scratching it. The tropes are not, in and for themselves, directed against rational thinking; but when they are [willfully] directed upon it—an additional use that Sextus makes of them—they immediately alter the rational. Everything that skepticism advances against the rational can be comprehended from this point of view. We had an example above when it controverted the cognition of Reason by Reason;[73] // the skeptical attack makes Reason either [43] an absolutely-subjective, or an absolutely-objective [totality], and either a whole or a part; both [oppositions] are added on by skepticism in the first place. So when skepticism enters the field against Reason, we must at once reject the concepts that *it* brings with it, and repudiate its bad weapons [as] inept for any attack.—

What our most recent skepticism always brings with it, is, as we saw above,[74] the concept of *a thing*, that lies *behind* and *beneath* the phenomenal facts. When the ancient skepticism employs the expressions *hupokeimenon, huparchon, adēlon*, etc.,[75] they signify thus the objectivity whose essence it is not to be expressed; skepticism remains, on its own account, on the subjective side of appearance. But for skepticism, this phenomenal appearance is not a sensible *thing*, behind which yet other things, to wit the supersensible ones, are supposed to be asserted by dogmatism and by philosophy. Since it holds back altogether from expressing any certainty or any being, it does not, on its own account, have any thing, any conditioned[76] [being] of which it could have knowledge; and it is not obliged to shove either this [empirically] certain thing, or another one that would be behind it, into the shoes of philosophy, in order to bring about its fall.

Because of the orientation of skepticism against knowing in general, it is impelled, since it sets one thought against another, and so combats the "is" of philosophical thought, to sublate the "is" of its own thought likewise, and thus to keep itself within the pure negativity which is, *per se*, a pure subjectivity. How sickening the skeptics were about

[44]   this, // we have already seen above in the case of the New Academy,[77] who asserted that everything is uncertain, and that this proposition embraced itself within its own range; yet this is not skeptical enough for Sextus, he distinguishes the Academy from Skepticism, because even in asserting this, they are setting up a proposition and dogmatizing; yet that proposition expresses the height of skepticism so well that Sextus' distinction becomes something entirely empty. At this rate, it must even befall Pyrrho to be given out as a dogmatist by someone.[78] This formal [formell] semblance of an assertion it is, which the skeptics are regularly teased about; it is thrown back at them, that if they doubt everything, then this "I doubt", "It seems to me" etc., is certain; so that the reality and objectivity of the thinking activity is held against them, since they hold firm to the form of positing in every positing by thought, and in this way show up every expressed activity as involving dogmatism.

In this extreme of supreme consistency, the extreme of negativity, or subjectivity, which no longer limited itself to the subjectivity of character, which is also objectivity, but grew into a subjectivity of knowledge, which directed itself against knowledge, skepticism was strictly bound to become inconsistent; for the extreme cannot maintain itself without the opposite; so pure negativity or subjectivity, is either nothing at all, because it nullifies itself at the extreme, or else it must at the same time be supremely objective; consciousness of this is ready at hand, and it was this that opponents urged; just for that reason, as we mentioned above,[79] the skeptics made clear that their *phōnai*
[45]   "all is false, nothing true","neither more than the // other" were self-referential; and that the skeptics, in the utterance of their slogans, were only saying what appeared to them, only uttering how they were affected, not giving an opinion, or making an assertion about an objective being.

Sextus (*Outlines of Pyrrhonism* 7, and elsewhere, especially chapter 24)[80] expresses himself thus, that "just as he who utters 'peripato' says in truth 'I am walking' ", so one must in one's mind always add on to what the skeptic says: " 'according to us' or 'so far as I am concerned'. or 'as it seems to me' ". This purely negative attitude that wants to remain mere subjectivity and seeming, ceases *ipso facto*, to be something for knowledge. He who stays holding fast to the vanity of the fact that "it seems so to *him*," "that *he* is of the opinion that . . .," he who wants his utterances never to be taken as objective assertions of thought and judgement at all, must be left where he stands. His subjectivity concern no one else, still less does it concern philosophy, nor is philosophy concerned in it.

Summing up briefly, there emerges from this consideration of the different aspects of ancient skepticism, the distinguishing mark and the essence of our most recent skepticism.

To begin with, this modern skepticism lacks the noblest side of skepticism, its orientation against the dogmatism of ordinary consciousness, which is present in all of the three modifications we have pointed out, i.e., whether it is identical with philosophy and is just its negative side, or separated from philosophy but not turned against it, or turned against it. For the most recent skepticism, by contrast, the ordinary consciousness with its whole infinite range // of facts,[81] has an indubitable certainty. Reasoning on the basis of these facts, reflection and classification of them, which constitutes the business of understanding for this skepticism, gives us as its science, an empirical psychology on the one hand, and many other sciences produced by the application of analytical thought to the actual facts, sciences elevated above all rational doubt. [46]

Neither the earlier skepticism, nor materialism, nor even the most vulgar common sense, unless it is completely bestial, has been guilty of this barbarity of placing indubitable certainty and truth in the facts of consciousness; till these most recent times, it was quite unheard of.

Furthermore, according to this latest skepticism, our physics and astronomy, and analytical thought, bid defiance to all rational doubtfulness; and thus it lacks also the noblest side of the later ancient skepticism, i.e. its orientation against limited cognition, against finite knowledge.

What then is left of skepticism in this latest version of it, which places its truth and certainty in the most blatant limitedness both of empirical intuition, and of empirical knowledge, which transforms empirical intuition into reflection, and pretends only to analyse it, *not* to add anything to it? Nothing at all, of necessity, except the denial of the truth of Reason, and the transformation of the rational into reflection, (or of the cognition of the Absolute into finite cognition) to that end. The // basic form of this transformation, however, which is everywhere prevalent, consists in this, that the opposed counterpart of Spinoza's first definition, which was quoted above[82] (which explains a *causa sui* as that whose essence involves existence at the same time) is made into a principle and asserted as an absolutely basic proposition, to wit that what is *thought* of, since it is thought-object, does not at the same time involve a *being* in itself. [47]

This sundering of the rational, in which thinking and being are one, and the absolute insistence [*festhalten*] on this opposition, in other words the understanding made absolute, constitutes the endlessly repeated and universally applied ground of this dogmatic skepticism. This antithesis, considered on its own account, has the merit that difference is expressed in it in its supreme abstraction and in its truest form; the essence of knowledge consists in the identity of the universal and the particular, or of what is posited in the form of thought and of being; and science is, with respect to its content, an embodiment of that rational identity, and on its formal side a continual repetition of the same; non-identity, the principle of ordinary consciousness, and of the opposite of knowledge, is expressed in the most definite way in that form of the antithesis; a part of the merit will be taken from this form again, to be sure, because it is conceived only as [the] antithesis of a thinking subject and an existing object.

Considered in its relationship to the latest skepticism, however, the merit of this antithesis vanishes entirely; for the discovery of this antithesis is, in itself, older beyond question than this skepticism. Nor [48] does this latest skepticism deserve any credit // for having brought this antithesis home to the culture of our modern age; for as we all know, it is the Kantian philosophy—which from the limited standpoint from which it is idealism (in its deduction of the categories) does indeed sublate this antithesis; but which is otherwise inconsistent enough to make the antithesis into the supreme principle of speculation; the insistence [*festhalten*] on this antithesis comes out most explicitly and with infinite self-satisfaction against the so-called "Ontological Proof" of the existence of God, and as reflecting judgement against Nature; and especially in the form of a refutation of the Ontological Proof it has enjoyed universal and widespread good fortune; Mr. Sch[ulze] has accepted this form for his own use, and has not only made use of it generally, but has even repeated Kant's own words to the letter (See [Vol. I] p. 71 and elsewhere). Or again, he cries out in Kant's voice on page 618 of volume I: "If ever a striking effort has been made to link the realm of *objective actuality* immediately to the sphere of *concepts*, and to pass over from this last into the former exclusively through the aid of a *bridge* which is likewise *manufactured* out of *plain concepts*, this happened in the ontological theology; nonetheless recently (how blinded philosophy was then, before these recent times!) the empty subtlety and illusion which we are involved with in this attempt, has been completely exposed.[83]

So Mr. Sch[ulze] has done nothing except pick up this recent and most excellent discovery of Kant's, just as countless Kantians have done. [49] He brings this supremely // simple stroke of wit to bear left and right, in all directions, even against the father of the discovery himself. He attacks and dissolves all of his ingredients with one and the same acid.

The science of philosophy, too, only repeats for ever one and the same rational identity, but new cultural formations spring forth from the former ones in this repetition, out of which it builds itself up into a complete organic world, which is [re]cognized both as a whole and in its parts as this same identity. Whereas the eternal repetition of that antithesis which leads to organic breakdown and the *nihil negativum*, is on its negative side a perpetual pouring of water into a sieve[84], and from its positive side, it is the continual and mechanical application of one and the same rule of understanding, wherein no new form comes forth from the old, but always the same mechanical work is done; this application of the rule is like the labor of a woodcutter who ever strikes the same blow, or of a tailor who sews uniforms for an army.

Jacobi's opinion about knowledge in general, comes true here: the Nuremberg caprice-game is played over and over, "so that we get sick of it, once all the moves and turns are known and thoroughly familiar to us."[85] This skepticism has in its game, only one single move, and one turn altogether, and even that is not its own, but it has borrowed even that from Kantianism. We can make out this character of the latest skepticism most clearly from what it calls its grounds, and by an example of its application.//   [50]

It can be [re]cognized adequately from the way in which it has apprehended its object, the interest of speculative Reason—as the problem of *explaining* the *origin* of human cognition of things; to spy out for the conditioned existence, what exists unconditioned.[86] To begin with, 'things' are opposed to 'cognition' within [the context of] Reason here; and secondly an explanation of its origin [is asked for], and therewith the causal relationship is dragged in; the ground of cognition, then, is something other than what is grounded, the former the concept, the latter the thing, and when once this basically false picture of rational thinking is presupposed, then there is nothing further to be done, except to repeat for ever that ground and grounded, concept and thing are different modes; that all rational cognition aims just to *pluck* a being *out of* thinking, existence out of concepts, (as it is put in words that are likewise Kantian).[87]

According to this latest skepticism, the human cognitive faculty is a thing, which has concepts, and since it has nothing but concepts, it cannot go out to the things that are outside it; it cannot neither *search them out* nor *reconnoiter* them—for both of them (Vol. I, p. 69) are "*specifically* distinct; [. . .] no rational man will be under the illusion that in *possessing* the *image* of something he also *possesses* that thing itself."[88]

Nowhere is this skepticism outwardly disposed to be so consistent as to show that no rational man will be under the illusion that he *possesses an idea* [*Vorstellung*] of something; // for certainly since the idea is   [51] also a something, the rational man can only have the illusion of possessing the idea of the idea, not the idea itself; and then again not that either, since this idea of the second power [*Potenz*] is again a something, but only the idea of the idea of the idea; ans so on *ad infinitum*. In other words when once the matter is represented thus, that there are two distinct pockets, of which one contains the somethings that are "ideas", the other those which are "things" one can't see why the former should remain the full pocket, and the latter be the always empty one.

The reason why the first pocket *is* full, but we only have an illusion that the second one is full, could not be anything else than this: that the first is in the shirt, the second in the jacket of the subject; the idea-pocket is closer to hand, the Thing-pocket is harder to get to; but then the proof would be performed through the presupposition of what is to be proved; for the question at issue is precisely whether the subjective or the objective has the advantage of reality.

This fundamental skeptical assumption [*skeptischen Grundwesen*] that we should only reflect on its being the idea and not the thing that is represented, and not upon their both being identical, is scarcely consistent, to be sure, with what is claimed about the indubitable certainty of the facts of consciousness; for according to Mr. Sch[ulze] (Vol. I, p. 68) "the ideas are true and real, they constitute a cognition, inasmuch as they *completely agree* with that which they are related to, and which is represented through them, or inasmuch as they *offer* to consciousness, nothing else but what is to be found in what they // represent"; and (p. 70) "we continually presuppose an *agreement of this kind* as certain in our *everyday* life, without troubling ourselves in the least about its possibility,"[89] as the newer metaphysics does.—

[52]

Now what else does Mr. Schulze ground the indubitable certainty of the facts of consciousness upon, then, but the absolute identity of thought and being, of the concept and the thing?—and then again in an instant he explains that the subjective, the image, and the objective, the thing are of different species.

In everyday life, says Mr. Sch[ulze], we *presuppose* that identity; that it is a *presupposition* in everyday life, means that it is not present in ordinary consciousness; *the newer metaphysics seeks to give grounds for the possibility of this identity.*[90] But to say that the newer philosophy seeks to give grounds for the possibility of the identity *presupposed* in ordinary life is no true word in fact; for it does no more than to express and [re]cognize that presupposed identity; just because that identity is presupposed in everyday life ordinary consciousness always posits the object as something other than the subject: and it posits both the objective and the subjective [world] alike as an infinite manifold of [elements] absolutely distinct from one another; metaphysics brings this identity, which for ordinary consciousness is only presupposed, or unconscious, to consciousness; it is the absolute and unique principle of metaphysics. The identity would only be susceptible of an explanation, in so far as it is not, as Mr. Sch[ulze] calls it, one that is presupposed in ordinary life, but an actual identity, that is a thoroughly // determinate and finite one; [53] and hence too the subject and object are finite; but an explanation of this finiteness, inasmuch as it once more posits the causal relationship, falls outside of philosophy. —

About this agreement Mr. Schulz[e] says (p. 70) "its possibility is one of the greatest *riddles* of human nature, and in this riddle there is at the same time the secret of *the possibility of a cognition of things* a priori, *that is a cognition of them even before we have intuited these things*".[91] — Here we learn then, exactly what a cognition *a priori* is: the things are out there, inside is the cognitive faculty; when it has cognitions without looking at things, it does so *a priori*. — So as not to leave anything out from these three pages, 68-70, which contain the true quintessence of the concepts about philosophy offered by this latest skepticism, we must further remark that on the question of "what the authentically positive [aspect] of the agreement of ideas with their real objects consists in " Mr. Sch[ulze] says "that it does not permit of further description or indication in words; *every one* of my *readers* must seek to come to terms with it rather in this way, by observing it then when he is conscious of it (the positive [aspect]), and by *looking rather closely* at what he has perceived and grasped, when through the comparison of an idea that he formed for himself of a Thing in its absence, with the Thing itself, at the moment when it is intuited by him, he finds that the idea completely agrees with the Thing and represents it precisely."[92] What does this explanation amount to? Does the whole of the agreement (or non-agreement) of the idea with the object come // down again to a psychological distinction [54] between presence and absence, between actual intuition and the remembering of it? Ought the agreement of an idea with the object that is present in perception to elude the readers in the absence of a Thing, and should something else be *put before* their consciousness, than what *can be found* in the represented thing? —

To speak in Mr. Sch[ulze's] way, scarcely has the identity of subject and object, in which the indubitable certainty is posited, scarcely has it come into view, before it finds itself, one knows not how, transposed again at once into empirical psychology; it sinks back at times into a psychological meaning, so as to be wholly and completely forgotten in the critique of philosophy itself, and in the skepticism, and leave the field open for the non-identity of subject and object, of concept and thing.

This non-identity reveals itself as principle in what are called the *three grounds of skepticism*. Just as the ancient skeptics had no dogmas, or basic propositions, but called their forms "tropes" [turnings] ▬

which, indeed, as we have seen, is what they were; so Mr. Sch[ulze] likewise avoids the expressions, "basic propositions," "principles," and calls them just "grounds," regardless of the fact that they are completely dogmatic theses. The plurality of these grounds could have been dispensed with through a more complete abstraction; for they express nothing save the one dogma: that concept and being are not the same.

[55]   They read as follows (Vol. I, p 613 ff.): "*First Ground: in as much as philosophy* // *is to be a science, it needs basic principles that are unconditionally true. But basic principles of that kind are impossible.*"[93]

Is this not dogmatic? Does it look like the expression of a skeptical trope? A dogma of this kind: that unconditionally true basic propositions are *impossible*, requires its *proof* too. But because this dogmatism has had the wit to call itself a skepticism, the expression "proof" will again be avoided, and the word "clarification" [*Erläuterung*] is used instead; but how can such an external semblance change the fact?

As always, then, the *clarification* finds speculative philosophy guilty of believing that it could create from mere *concepts* its insight into the *existence* of supersensible things. The proof itself amounts to this: that in a proposition that is a bonding of images and concepts, neither in the bonding (*copula*), nor in the concepts of the proposition is an *agreement* of the *proposition* with what is *thought by its means* given as necessary; — the *copula* is only the relationship of the predicate to the subject *in the understanding* (hence something purely subjective), and by its very nature has absolutely no relation with anything outside the thought of the understanding; — in the concepts of predicate and subject nothing [is given as necessary], — for with the actuality of the concept in the understanding only the *possibility of it is given*, i.e., that it is not self-contradictory, but not that it *has a relation to something distinct from it*. This is just the place where the illusory nature and the

[56]   empty subtlety of the // Ontological Proof of the existence of God strikes Mr. Sch[ulze]. The "second ground" is nothing but a repetition of this "clarification":

Second Ground (p. 620): "*Whatever the speculative philosopher pretends to have cognized of the highest grounds of what is present in a conditioned way, he has apprehended and thought merely in concepts. But the understanding that is occupied with mere concepts is no faculty for making something to the measure of actuality even only in idea.*

In the *clarification* the author says that, among speculative philosophers or seekers for the existence of things on the basis of mere concepts, the *understanding* is rated so highly that anyone who casts the slightest doubt on that high rating makes himself liable to the suspicion and accusation of having little understanding or even

none at all. But on this point it is rather the contrary that is true, in that speculation holds the understanding to be thoroughly inept for philosophy. —Mr. Sch[ulze] goes on to say that we must bethink ourselves whether *Reason* can concede this perfect adequacy to the understanding. But what can Reason be doing here? Why has our author spoken in the second ground itself, only of the understanding, of which there is no question in speculation, and not of Reason? As if he was appropriating understanding for philosophy, and Reason for his skepticism. We find, however, that on the few occasions where the word "Reason" occurs, it is only used as an honorific word, one that will make an impression. What this Reason produces is never anything but "The // concept is not the thing". A Reason of this   [57]
sort is just what is called understanding by speculation.

Third Ground (p. 627): "*The speculative philosopher rests his pretended science of the absolute grounds of what exists in a conditioned way quite peculiarly on the inference from the constitution of the effect to the constitution of an appropriate cause. But there is no mode of inferring with any security at all from the constitution of the effect to that of the cause.*" —

In the *clarification* it is asserted that "unless one claims to have arrived at the cognition of what can lie at the foundation of everything conditioned *through some inspiration*,"[93] that cognition can only be one mediated by the principle of causality. —But this assumption about speculative philosophy, that the causality-relationship is peculiarly dominant in it is once again radically false; for on the contrary, the causal relation is wholly banned from speculative thought; if it seems sometimes to occur in the form of producer and product, then it is only the verbal expression for the relationship not the relationship itself that is employed; for the producer and the product are posited as equivalent, the cause is equivalent to the effect, one and the same [substance is posited] as cause of itself, and as effect of itself, so that the relationship is immediately sublated. There is simply no question in speculative philosophy of the unconditioned being *inferred* from the constitution of the conditioned. //   [58]

"This then (p. 643) is the schedule and the content of the general grounds upon which the skeptic denies certainty to the doctrines of all the systems of philosophy that have been established so far, or may yet be established in the future, and which lead him to the decision not to concede that any single one of these systems has warranted claims to truth."[94] But we have seen that these grounds have nothing to do with philosophy inasmuch as philosophy is not at all concerned with plucking a thing out of concepts, nor with reconnoitering a fact that lies beyond the range of Reason, it is not concerned either with what our author calls "concepts" or with "things", and it does not infer causes from effects.

On these grounds, says Mr. Sch[ulze] (p. 610), when the skeptic "weighs up the authentic goal" of philosophy, and its conditions, "and on the other side the *capacity of the human mind*, to arrive at a real and secure cognition, he finds himself disposed not to be able to see how a cognition of the supersensible could ever come to pass [. . .] as long as *the equipment* of the human cognitive faculty *does not change*, which *no rational man expects*,"[95] and which *it would be foolish* to nourish any hope for. Indeed it would be all the more foolish to nourish any such hope, since even with the equipment of the human mind standing as it does in the current year, a philosophy is possible.

These are the weapons with which the systems of Locke, Leibniz [59] and Kant, are combatted; // the systems of Locke and Leibniz specifically as systems of realism, the former sensualistic, the latter rationalistic; Kant's system, however, as a system of transcendental idealism; the later transcendental idealism is reserved for a third volume.[96]

The first volume contains the *exposition* of these systems (Locke's, pp. 113-40; Leibniz', pp.141-172). But pages 172-582 supply us with one more extract of the much-expounded Kantian *Critique of Pure Reason*; what follows to the end of the volume is devoted to the skepticism set forth above.

The second volume contains the critique of these systems in the light of the grounds elucidated above: – the critique of Locke, pp. 7-90; of Leibniz, pp. 91-125; six hundred pages are devoted to the critique of Kant.

As an example of how these skeptical grounds are applied to these systems, we offer the way in which our author controverts the "innate concepts" of Leibniz; this refutation of Leibniz takes the following course (Vol. II, p. 100): – "In general, since Leibniz has set the tone," with his doctrine "that the ground of necessary judgments lies simply in the mind itself, and hence that the understanding already contains a priori cognitions, it has been repeated countless times, of course, that necessary judgments can only originate from the cognitive subject himself; but so far, no single property of this subject has been demonstrated, in virtue of which it is quite specifically qualified to be the source of necessary judgments; and neither in its simplicity, nor [60] in its substantiality, nor even in its cognitive faculties // has the basis for any such qualification been found."[97]

Are the simplicity and substantiality of the soul qualities that this skepticism concedes to it then? – If the assertion of necessary judgments depended only on this, that we can point them out in a quality of the soul, then indeed there is nothing that needs doing except to say, the soul has the quality of necessary judgments."

Our author asserts then that "so far as our insight into our own cognitive Ego goes, we do not find anything in it which determines that it must be a source of necessary judgments;" yet he goes on immediately afterwards to say that "the objects of our thought are sometimes contingent, and sometimes necessary judgments; but one could not say that the necessary ones had more relation to the understanding and its nature, than the contingent, and that it belonged to the essence of our understanding to produce necessary judgments;"[98] but, indeed, one has only to admit that there are qualities of two kinds in the understanding, one quality being that of contingent judgments, the other that of necessary judgments; in this way the qualification of our mind for necessary judgments is just as well made out as the other qualities in an empirical psychology. Mr. Sch[ulze] certainly admits necessary judgments as an actual fact of consciousness.

"But what Leibniz says about *the truth* of innate concepts and the insights of pure Reason, is "in every way" more devoid of foundation, and one *must actually marvel*, how the man could have paid *so little attention //* to the precepts of *logic* [61] here, seeing that the requirements of a valid proof were *by no means* unknown to him."[99] Here, first of all, we learn what it is that Leibniz has failed in, namely attention to logic; and Mr. Sch[ulze] actually marvels at this; but what Leibniz did not fail in, what he had too much of, was genius, as we shall find a bit further on; and that is what one actually must still marvel at, too, that a man has genius.

To be precise: "it is not obvious in itself, that if there are innate concepts and basic principles in our mind, there is also something corresponding to them, outside of them, to which they relate, and which gives them a cognition, just as it is, according to its objective actuality; for *concepts* and *judgments in us* are *certainly not* the *objects themselves* which are thought by their means; and with the necessity of the relation of the predicate to the subject in our thought of it, the relation of thought to a real thing existing outside of it is by no means given, being *quite* different *in kind* from that."[100]

One can see that our author takes the innate concepts in the most blatantly crude way possible; according to his picture, a subject is born, with a packet of letters of exchange in his head, drawn upon a world existing outside of that head; the question then would be whether the letters will be accepted by this bank, whether they are genuine, not forged; or with a heap of lottery-tickets in the soul, about which we shall never find out, whether they are not all losing numbers; for there comes no draw afterwards, by which their fortune is decided. "This," continues the author, "has always been seen and admitted by the defenders of innate // concepts and basic principles in the human [62] soul, and hence they have tried to give a *proof* of the truth of these concepts and basic principles, *or at least* to define more precisely *the way* in which these concepts, should be related with real things."[101]

In his note it is alleged that "according to Plato, the concepts and basic principles which the soul brings with it innately into this present life, and whereby alone we are capable of cognizing the actual as it is, not as it appears to us through the senses, are simple recollections of those intuitions of the things in which the soul [. . .] participated during its sojourn with God. Descartes lets the matter be [. . .] appealing to the veracity of God; [. . . .] for Spinoza the thought of our understanding is true because it consists of the ideas and cognitions of the divinity, inasmuch as they are what make up the essence of our spirit; these cognitions of the divinity must completely agree with what is cognized through them, indeed they are one and the same thing with this cognized object."[102] "According to Leibniz the basic principles located in our minds *a priori*, and the ideas they contain, acquired truth and reality, because they are copies of the concepts and truths that are to be found in the understanding of the divinity, concepts which are the principle of the possibility, existence and constitution of all real things in the world."[103]

But even before he gets to criticism Mr. Sch[ulze] has at once distorted the problem by the way that he has presented it. For was it properly [63] the problem at issue for Plato, Spinoza, Descartes, // Leibniz to find a way of proving that a reality corresponds to the innate concepts or to Reason; or to define the way [it corresponds] when these philosophers posit God as the ground of their truth? According to Mr. Sch[ulze] the chain of argument is this: (a) [there are] subjective concepts, that are without reality on their own account; then (b) [there is] a reality lying outside of them; so (c) the question, how it comes together [arises]; (d) the proof of their truth in a [being] that is alien to both the concepts and the reality. Rather [it is the case that] those philosophers have [re]cognized, what Mr. Sch[ulze] calls that identity of concept and reality presupposed in everyday life, and they called it the understanding of God, in which actuality and possibility are one.

"We do not want to investigate," according to the author's judgment of the matter, "whether this argument for the truth and reliability of innate concepts is ultimately bound up with *theosophical fancies* about the kinship of our soul with the nature of God, and could have been derived from that; though one might infer this anyway from what Leibniz taught about the genesis of finite monads from the supreme monad."[104]

Now we have got the whole story then! The kinship of our souls with the nature of God is theosophical fancy, and, for politeness' sake no doubt, our author does not want to investigate how closely the argument for the truth of ideas is bound up with it. But these philosophers have laid it down, in accord with truth [*der Sache noch*], that the soul is nothing in itself, but is what it is *in God*; the shortest way to deal with this in discussion is to stigmatize the philosophy of these philosophers as dreamy enthusiasm and theosophical // fancies.   [64]

But Mr. Sch[ulze] puts on airs about wanting to deal with the ground of cognition; "But every one of our readers can certainly see this much," he continues, "that at this point, the question must necessarily be asked: *from what source* then, *do we know*, that our understanding possesses the exalted privilege of participating in copies of the eternal and real cognitions which are in God's understanding? Since the senses teach us nothing at all about God and his properties, Leibniz can only derive and generate his answer to this question from the understanding and from its *innate insights*; so that is what he did. In consequence, his proof of the truth of innate concepts is drawn round in a circle."[105] Quite right! and if he did not go in a circle, then he would have a causal relationship, and in accordance with the third ground the bridge from effect to cause would be built of plain concepts which have no reality. —

But it was not necessary to separate the truth and reliability of the so-called innate concepts on one side, from the exalted privilege of participation in the copies and the eternal and real cognitions of God on the other, and to make each of these into a particular quality (or whatever one wants to call it); on the contrary the two are one and the same thing. There is no question of proving the first on the basis of the second. So all circularity vanishes, and nothing is left over, but the assertion in two modes of expression, that Reason, according to Leibniz, is an image of the divinity, or that it has true cognition. This runs out into theosophical fancies, to be sure, but it cannot be denied all the same — to put it in the // language of this skepticism — that   [65]
that kinship of our soul with the nature of God, and the imaging [*Vorstellen*] of the divinity, was a fact of consciousness for those philosophers; but consciousness is for this skepticism the supreme court of certainty and truth; as we saw above,[106] what is present in consciousness can no more be doubted than consciousness itself — for to doubt that is impossible.

So then, since in the consciousness of some philosophers the reality of their Ideas, and the kinship of their nature with the nature of God occurs, while in that of others it does not, there is nothing to be done but to call those philosophers liars, which just won't do, — or else to demand of them that they should make their consciousness comprehensible, which again cannot be required, for the identity of idea and thing that is presupposed in everyday life is likewise not comprehended by the ordinary consciousness which could make this demand; so there is nothing left but to admit two races of consciousness, one that is conscious of that kinship, and another that explains that sort of consciousness as a theosophical fancy.

Then Mr. Sch[ulze] shows the groundlessness of the Idea that Reason has reality because it is a copy of the divine Reason, from what Leibniz himself says. For Leibniz admits that the concepts of finite essences are infinitely different from the concepts in the understanding of God.

[66]
But Mr. Sch[ulze] could very easily learn the concept of the Leibnizian antinomy of the finite and the infinite from his exposition // of Leibniz's system (in Vol. I); or rather it is once again Mr. Sch[ulze] who treats the antinomy of finite and infinite as an absolute one; in the exposition of Leibniz's system, section 28, we read that "the properties which constitute the ground of cognitions and of volitional capacity in the created monads, *correspond* to the properties of the divinity"; but in God "they are present in *infinite* degree and in *the highest perfection*; the *corresponding* properties in the created monads on the other hand are mere *likenesses* of them, according to the degree of perfection that they possess". Compare section 34 and the note there.[108]

Since perfections of the finite monads correspond to the perfections of the infinite one, the antithesis that Leibniz sets up between the infinite monad and the finite ones is not the absolute antithesis of finite and infinite, in the way that Mr. Sch[ulze] apprehends it—he could very well express his view of it by saying that the two are *specifically distinct*;[109] the fact that Leibniz posits the absolute monad as infinite, and the others as finite, and yet speaks of a likeness between the two, Mr. Sch[ulze] would probably count as one of the cases in which Leibniz has not been attentive enough to the *precepts of logic*.

Furthermore, according to Mr. Sch[ulze], Leibniz's proof "that the necessary judgments of the human understanding must also be present in the understanding of God", is derived from the fact "that those judgments, inasmuch as they constitute eternal truths, must be present
[67]
from all eternity // as determinations of an understanding that eternally thinks the same thought, and hence likewise exists from all eternity". Mr. Sch[ulze] asks whether "it must first have been made out in advance that an eternally *existing* understanding that is thinking certain truths without a break *actually exists* before it can be asserted that there are eternal truths valid for all times"; "eternal truths are those which, according to *our* insight, every understanding that is conscious of the judgment must think in just the way that we think them, and this has consequently no relation to the fact that an understanding which actually thinks these judgments has existed from

eternity".[111] Mr. Sch[ulze] here again apprehends the existence of the divine understanding as an empirical one, and the eternity as an empirical one too.

Finally, we cannot pass over what Mr. Sch[ulze] offers us regarding Leibniz's conception of clear and confused presentation'; "the intuition of external things," he say, "is a consciousness of the immediate presence of a *thing*, that is distinct from *our cognizing subject* and from its merely subjective determinations."[112] (It seems that Mr. Sch[ulze] distinguishes still between *himself* and *his subject*; one cannot help being curious to have an explanation of this distinction; depending on how it was developed it could certainly lead to theosophical fancies). "Hence the view that intuition arises from the confusion of the manifold characteristics [of the monads] in an image [*Vorstellung*] has no sense and significance at all"; the two are *in no way // akin* to one another.[113]   [68] (The question would be, what kinship is there then between the Ego and our subject which is to be distinguished from the Ego, and what kinship is there with its subjective and finally with its objective determinations).

"It stands within the power of every man, to bring forth within himself intuitions of things at his pleasure, and if he has thought something clearly, to transform his state of consciousness straightaway into the intuiting of an object. In order to intuit a chiliagon, or a piece of gold, a house, a man, the Universe, the divinity etc., as present nothing would be required, except that one should *properly confuse together* the characteristics found in the *representation* of the chiliagon, of gold etc., after one has turned one's attention aside from their distinctness; while to turn the intuition of a house, a man, a tree into a simple concept, on the other hand, nothing more would be necessary than that one should make clear to oneself the parts that occur in the so-called sense-presentation, by distinguishing them from one another in consciousness. *Hopefully*, however, *nobody* will *seriously* pretend, that *his* cognitive *subject*" (here we find *nobody* and *his subject*) "is in a position to perform such *unheard of conjuring tricks* through any such arbitrary transformation of the concepts of things into intuitions, and of intuitions into concepts."[114] Since Mr. Sch[ulze] does not blench here at dragging the speculative theory of the nature of the presenting activity that Leibniz proposes, // down to the solid soil and homely   [69] comfort of empirical presentation, and at dishing up for table against Leibniz trivialities of exactly the same kind that Nicolai and other such leading lights bring forward against idealism, we can be sure that the more recent idealism, to which Mr. Sch[ulze] means to devote a third volume has nothing else to look forward to, but the repetition of these same disgraces on his part.[115] This idealism will be given out as the assertion of an arbitrary power of producing things, and of changing concepts into things, it will be revealed as the most unheard of conjuring tricks.

This treatment of the Leibnizian philosophy by the new skepticism will be a sufficient sample of the way it carries on. And just as the Leibnizian philosophy already deserved in and for itself, to have been dealt with as a rational system, so the *investigation* of the *Kantian philosophy* could be made outstandingly interesting by the fact that this philosophy of understanding is elevated above its own principle, which it finds in reflection. The great Idea of Reason and of a system of philosophy which everywhere lies at its foundation could be dragged out [of the shadows] and set forth [openly, so that it appears] like a magnificent ruin, in which the understanding has claimed squatter's rights.[116]

The effective presence of this Idea is already visible in the outward scaffolding of its parts; but it also emerges more explicitly at the culminating points of its syntheses, especially in the *Critique of Judgment*. It is the spirit of the Kantian philosophy to be conscious of this supreme Idea, but to set to work expressly to root it out again. Thus we [can] distinguish two types of spirit that // become visible in the Kantian philosophy, one being that of the philosophy which is continually ruined by the system, the other that of the system which aims to do the Idea of Reason to death; this latter spiritless spirit still has, however, also a letter, and Mr. Sch[ulze] warns us that, in accordance with the express declarations of Kant, that his system must be taken according to the letter not according to the spirit, he [Schulze] has held to the letter.[117]

This then is the way in which he has arrived at the spiritless letter of the spiritless spirit of philosophy. This wholly formal essence, he has criticized with an equally essential formality. The Kantian philosophy is poured out in the crassest way possible, a view of it in which our author was altogether justified by the advance work of the Reinhold theory and of other Kantians; he has conceived it exclusively in the shape of the crassest dogmatism, which has a [realm of] phenomena and Things in themselves which lie *behind* the *phenomena* like wild beasts lurking in the bushes of appearance; and this is not just because the Kantians are to be tormented with this straw man image [*Bild dieser Krassheit*], but because, as we have already satisfied ourselves above, this skepticism, and the system of the indubitable certainty of the actual facts of consciousness cannot conceive it any other way.

For the Kantians who are nailed to the letter, this hard labor and the grim struggle that another formalism takes upon itself with the formalism of Kant, along with the straw man image (if they are still capable of being frightened by that) could have the effect of giving them a good fright. It is not just the image of the Kantian philosophy as it is put before them here [i.e. in Vol. II, part II] [that I mean], but

[70]

this image as it is so strikingly represented independently in the whole //   [71]
continuous run of these four alphabets.[118] Another thing that is
sufficiently demonstrated for them is the inability of the Kantian
formalism to deduce or to produce its own forms. But they would
seek in vain here for the concept of philosophy; for this has slipped
away in the press of the "actual facts" and of the "things" sought for
behind the "facts". Philosophy gets the blame for this quest, and in
that way the whole business of this skepticism ceases to bear upon it
in the slightest.

Finally we cannot refrain from picking out one piece of the empirical
psychology of this skepticism, namely the way in which it represents
the relationship of genius and fancy to philosophy. In the Preface (p.
xxiv) Mr. Sch[ulze] explains, with reference to his own mode of writing,
that "flowers of rhetoric are quite out of place in discussing the questions
of speculative philosophy, since they lead Reason [. . .] astray," and
get the fancy involved in its concerns;" so that even if it had been in
his power to enliven the exposition of this *Critique* more with eloquence
and a ready flow of metaphors, and thus make it more attractive, he
would have made no use of such means."[119]

About Leibniz our author says (pp. 91 f) that "if the concern of
Reason in philosophizing consisted in *surpassing even* the highest flights
that fancy can ever dream of, by bold and *delightfully* entertaining
poetic fictions about a *pretended* transcendental world *lying hidden behind*
the world of the senses, and giving these // poetic fictions unity   [72]
and consistency with the aid of concepts that are certain, then [. . .]
no other philosopher even approached Leibniz, not to speak of outdoing
him; [. . .] it seems that nature meant to show in him, [. . .] that the
attainment of the highest goal of the cognitive powers [. . .] was not
merely a matter of the possession of *great natural gifts*, and that a
thinker less *favored by nature*, if he just used his powers appropriately,
could not only *equal the genius in this field*, but *often probably even
surpass* him."[120] It is the opinion of Mr. Sch[ulze] that even if Leibniz
had developed his philosophical aphorisms into a system himself,
nothing much would have come of it save perhaps for "Neoplatonic
daydreams."[121]

About Kant, on the other hand, Mr. Sch[ulze] speaks with the greatest
respect, declaring that "the *Critique of Pure Reason* is the product of a
strenuous effort of the power of thought, one that shirks no obstacles,
and arises only from the free resolution of its author, and that *genius*
and *lucky chance* cannot claim the *slightest credit* in the execution of
the plan that lies at its foundation"[122] (as if there could be a lucky
chance for anyone else except a genius!).

Looking at this contempt for genius and great natural gifts, this
opinion that the fancy supplies nothing else save flowers of rhetoric

to the exposition of philosophy, as if Reason made fictions in the
sense in which newspaper-lies, for instance, are invented fictions, or
when it does offer inventions that pass beyond the range of ordinary
actuality, it produces castles in the air, religious dreams, or theosophical
[73]   fantasies, that it // can surpass fancy itself in poetic invention, even
in fancy's highest flights, one does not know which is more outrageous—
the ingenuous barbarity with which it applauds the absence of genius,
or the vulgarity of the concepts. When we call contempt for superior
natural gifts barbarity, we are not thinking of the natural barbarity
that lies outside of the range of culture; for the natural barbarian
honors genius as something divine, and respects it as a light that
penetrates the obscurity of his consciousness. We mean the barbarity
of culture itself, a savagery that is made, one that creates an absolute
boundary for itself, and despises the unbounded range of nature from
within this fenced enclosure; where it speaks cognitively it is
understanding. As for the concepts, they stem from the sort of empirical
psychology that disperses the spirit into mutually external qualities,
and hence finds no whole, no genius and no talent among these
qualities, but describes them as if they were a sack full of "faculties",
each of which is quite particular, one being a "Reason" that is without
intuition, and separate from the fancy; another a fancy that is without
Reason, one whose emptiness can only be filled with "facts" [Sachen]
at the cost of heavy labor, and which only has its proper worth in
factual and thing-filled fulfilment. The understanding too abides there
among the other faculties that dwell in the soul-sack of the subject,
the most eminent among them, because it understands how to change
everything into "facts"—concepts on one side, things on the other.
Hence this understanding runs also through the two alphabets of
criticism, with its monotonous process of tearing everything up into
concepts and things existing outside of them (just as it sets forth alien
"facts" in the two prior expository alphabets).[123]
[74]   The process lacks // all the quickening vitality of an Idea of
Reason; it carries on without the touch of fancy or of fortune, in a
resounding, sense-clouding, sleep-inducing, overwhelming tone,
producing the same effect as if one was wandering through a field of
henbane in bloom, the stupefying scent of which no efforts can
withstand, and where one is not aroused by any enlivening beam,
not even in the shape of an impending nemesis.

Notes

1. In spite of the correct heading Hegel only spells Schulze's name correctly once in the whole essay (below p. 52). For the most part he abbreviates it to "Sch." — but where he spells it out, he omits the final vowel. Perhaps the heading of the review was only added to the manuscript when it was otherwise ready in final form for the printer. But since Hegel may also be evincing a satirical contempt for the "facts of consciousness" I have made his abbreviations and omissions visible to the reader.

2. The reference is to *Aenesidemus*. For an excerpt from this work, see pp. 105-33 above.

3. Printers then (as now) used the letters of the alphabet to mark their sheets — each of which folds (in octavo as here) into sixteen printed pages. An "alphabet" contained twenty-three sheets. Schulze's *Critique* contained "four alphabets for the present" because it was not yet complete. He promised a third volume which never materialized.

4. All of this paragraph is freely quoted (in oblique form) from the direct text of Schulze (Vol. I, pp. 3, 6-7; quotation marks added).

5. A case very much in Hegel's mind here is that of Fichte. In the "Preface" to the *Difference* essay he says "one cannot say of Fichte's system that fortune has smiled on it"; he ascribes this partly to what he regards as its weaknesses and partly to "the unphilosophical tendencies of the age." But he also says that it "has caused so much of a stir . . . that even those who declare themselves against it . . . still cling to its principle." He believes there that "fortune's smile" is a sign that the system that receives it answers "some widespread philosophical need" (*Difference*, pp. 82-83). But in *Faith and Knowledge* he sets out to show that the principle that has made Fichte's work so widely acceptable is only the *un*-philosophical principle of *finite* subjectivity. The *speculative* or philosophical side of Fichte is there said to be despised even by Fichte himself (p. 167). The attitude expressed in the present essay is close to that of *Faith and Knowledge*.

6. "I have found that most sects are right in a good part of what they maintain, but not so much in what they deny." (*Trois lettres à Mr. Rémond de Montmort*, 1741). Jacobi put this motto on the title page of his *Letters on the Teaching of Spinoza* (1789).

7. "One must not dispute with those who deny principles," Aristotle maintained this only with respect to logical principles, especially contradiction (*Metaphysics*, Gamma, 4). It is more likely that Hegel understood Aristotle's position, than that he knew much of the Scholastic application of it to principles of all kinds. It was certainly from the disputes of the medieval schools that the Latin axiom descended to the logic books of Hegel's time. But from the way he goes on to use it as a support for the postulate of one true philosophy at the foundation of all "systems" we can see that Hegel thought of it as applying to the transcendental *logic* in terms of which all "systems" have to be interpreted.

8. The barb of Hegel's irony — here unveiled though still nameless — is that Adam's sin of disobedience was identified in traditional moral theology as the sin of *pride*. In his claim to have discovered the original sin of philosophers generally, Schulze is assuming

God's role in Adam's story. The promised demonstration that Schulze is not acquainted with *speculative* or *transcendental* philosophy is given below (pp. [17-26], [50-4], [69-71]).

9. At the end of each issue of the *Critical Journal* Schelling and Hegel planned to have, and usually did have a "news sheet" (*Notizenblatt*). Their object in this section was to satirize authors and works which they thought unworthy of serious attention, and sometimes (as here) to supplement their serious criticism with satire. One of their favorite techniques in the *Notizenblatt* was to quote passages which they found particularly amusing from books or reviews of books (either without comment, or with obviously ironic asides). In the case of Schulze they reprinted an ironic "blurb" composed by Hegel himself and printed (anonymously) in the *Oberdeutsche Allgemeine Literatur Zeitung* of Munich.

10. *Kritik*, Vol. I, 52; Kant *Critique of Aesthetic Judgement*, trans. Meredith, p. 15. (Hegel's reference is probably to the first edition, 1790; see Academy Ed. V, 177). Schulze wrote "Some important distinctions occur between the actual facts of our consciousness, and so far as we have investigated these distinctions till now, and learned to know them, these facts are either *cognitions of objects*, or *utterances of the will* or *feelings of pleasure and dislike*. But although these facts have a variety of standing connections with one another; still our insight into them goes far enough to tell us that they cannot be reduced to a single class, or derived from a single source, but are essentially distinguished from one another by abiding marks. Upon this distinct variety in the facts of our consciousness then, the division of philosophy into *theoretical*, *practical* and the *philosophy concerned with feelings* is grounded; this last, in so far as it deals with the feelings of the beautiful and sublime has had the name of *Aesthetics* in Germany.

11. See *Outlines of Pyrrhonism* II, 1; and *Against the Logicians* I, 1.

12. *Kritik*, I, 26-27. Schulze's formula says simply "the highest and unconditioned causes" and contains no "otherwise".

13. Hegel is not quoting directly but weaving together a tissue of Schulze's favorite expressions.

14. *Kritik*, I, 51. The quotation is not marked and is not quite word perfect.

15. See *Kritik* I, 56.

16. Compare *Kritik* I, 72-73. Hegel's language (and Schulze's) seems to indicate that the "metaphysics" most immediately in question is that of Reinhold, who was also a theorist of the *Tatsachen des Bewusstseins*, and the primary architect of the language. (Compare especially *Difference*, pp. 105, 178-86).

17. The quotation was abbreviated by Hegel (who did not use quotation marks for it).

18. This quotation (though not marked as such) is almost word perfect (the italics are Hegel's).

19. These two (unmarked) quotations are abbreviated.

20. *Kritik* I, 585. Unmarked by Hegel but almost word perfect.

21. *Kritik* I, 588. Again unmarked but almost exact.

22. See. *Kritik* I, 589 and 590-91 (italics Hegel's, quotation marks mine).

23. *Kritik* I, 593 (italics Hegel's, quotation marks mine). The French translator Fauquet claims that Hegel is in the wrong here and that truth is more on the side of Schulze. But he seems to me to have missed Hegel's point. It is not "the existence and presence of sense-presentations and feelings" that the ancient skeptics are here said to have

doubted but "what experience teaches". The question is about the attitude of ancient and modern skepticism toward two kinds of *knowledge*: empirical knowledge and rational (or speculative knowledge). Hegel claims that Pyrrho doubted at least the former, and the later sceptics doubted both; while Schulze doubts only the latter, and wishes to maintain the validity of the former. (See further the introductory essay, sections 3-5).

24. *Kritik* I, 595, 596-7 (not quite verbatim; italics Hegel's, quotation marks mine). Schulze refers to Sextus *Outlines of Pyrrhonism* I, 10. But compare ibid. I, 8.

25. Diogenes Laertius IX, 108: "for in matters which are for us to decide but happen of necessity; such as hunger, thirst and pain, we cannot escape, for they are not to be removed by force of reason." (trans. R. D. Hicks, Loeb Classical Library, II, 519).

26. *Outlines of Pyrrhonism* I, xi, 23; compare also I, xi, 21.

27. *ibid., I, xi, 22*: "Therefore we say that the criterion of the skeptical school is the phenomenon, and potentially we call the image (*phantasia*) of the [actual] phenomenon, the criterion. For since it lies in a conviction (*peisei*) and affection that is involuntary it cannot be questioned (*azētētos*). Clearly Sextus means that as a matter of psychological fact we cannot doubt the phainomenon that presents itself. But to the eye of skeptic reason it *remains* a mere phenomenon. We cannot help accepting it as the guide for our actions, but it may mislead us; our inescapable psychological conviction is no guarantee of truth. "That which cannot be questioned" is *not* equivalent to "that which cannot be doubted".

28. Hegel cites this from Sextus below. See *Outlines of Pyrrhonism* II, vi, 63. The origin of the example is in Atomism. See Democritus D.-K A. 135, p. 119, line 11; and Theophrastus *De sensibus*, 69.

29. *Kritik*, I, 593-4. Unmarked but almost word perfect.

30. *Kritik*, I, 599. Unmarked but almost word-perfect, except that Schulze wrote *Quellen* ("sources") not *Gründen* ("grounds"). The italics are Hegel's.

31. *Kritik*, I, 599. Hegel wrote "had been then" for Schulze's "were then" (which I have restored). Otherwise the quotation is almost word perfect though unmarked. The *italics* are Hegel's. The sentence between these two direct quotations is a paraphrase of the intervening context in Schulze.

32. Hegel's attempted reconstruction of the history of the "school" is almost certainly mistaken. There was probably little or no historical connection between the earlier skepticism of Pyrrho and the genuine "school succession" of Aenesidemus, Metrodorus etc., and the earliest *tropoi* certainly belong to the later school.

33. Diogenes Laertius IX, 71-73.

34. Either "welche" must be deleted (as earlier editors decided) or a verb must be supplied here. Buchner and Pöggeler supply "vorkommen". I have accepted the deletion rather than this amendment. The reader can see how little difference it makes which way the problem is dealt with by reading the sentence with "that «come up" inserted.

35. I have distributed the elements of what I take to be a deliberate chiasmus here. Hegel wrote: "nothing but a heap and a cloud of passably obscure, and for the times of a Parmenides and a Plato passably acute, but to a modern metaphysician nauseating sophisms."

Dietrich Tiedemann was the general editor of the edition of Plato that Hegel owned and habitually used (12 Vols., Zweibrücken, 1781-86). This edition provided Ficino's Latin version at the foot of the page. The Ficino quotation and Tiedemann's comment come from the supplementary *Dialogorum Platonis argumenta* supplied by Tiedemann.

36. *Ethics*, Part I, Def. I. Hegel did not use quotation marks.

37. *Ethics*, Part I, Prop. XVIII: "God is the immanent not the transient cause of all things."

38. Sextus, *Outlines of Pyrrhonism* I, 12, 18, 202-5.

39. *Outlines of Pyrrhonism*, i, 4.

40. *Kritik* I, 608 note. Not marked by Hegel (and somewhat free at the end).

41. *loc. cit.* Only the clauses that I have placed in quotes come directly from Schulze's text, but Hegel printed it all in spread type as shown.

42. *Outlines of Pyrrhonism*, I, 206; cf. I, 14

43. *Outlines of Pyrrhonism*, I, 226: *akatalēpta einai panta* i.e. no phenomenon is grasped by a "cataleptic phantasm", or no experience is self-certifying as knowledge beyond the possibility of doubt.

44. *Kritik* I, 607 note. Almost word perfect but not marked by Hegel.

45. Sextus (*Outlines of Pyrrhonism* I, 232) of course, wrote "seems to me" and "same agōgē ours". Otherwide Hegel is translating his text directly though he did not mark the quotation.

46. The *epochē* is the skeptical suspense of judgement.

47. From his later reference back to this passage, it appears uncertain that Hegel has rightly understood *Outlines of Pyrrhonism* I, 233: "He [Arcesilaus] also says that *epochē* regarding particulars is good, but assent regarding particulars is bad. Only one might say that whereas *we* make these assertions according to what appears to us and not positively, *he* asserts them as according to nature, so as to say that *epochē* is in itself good, and assent is evil." In point of fact Sextus was *wrong* about this (see the Introductory essay); but Hegel is, in any case, quite correct in maintaining as he now does, that, if we are to follow Sextus, as both sides claim to be doing, Schulze has got the official distinction between the Academic skeptics and the Pyrrhonian tradition completely backwards. It is the Academics who are said to be *dogmatically* skeptical—trusting their own reasoning and the Pyrrhonians who are skeptically skeptical (or "stripped of Reason" as Schulze prefers to say).

48. Compare *Outlines of Pyrrhonism* I, 33, 234.

49. *Outlines of Pyrrhonism* I, 220-35. Sextus allows for the distinction of no fewer than *five* Academies: The Old Academy (Plato); the Middle Academy (Arcesilaus); the New Academy (Carneades); The Fourth Academy (Philo of Larissa); and the Fifth (Antiochus of Ascalon). He discusses the *skeptical* credentials of the first four. (See further the introductory essay).

50. C. F. Stäudlin: *Geschichte und Geist des Scepticismus* (Vorzüglich in Rücksicht auf Moral und Religion), 2 vols Leipzig, 1794. Schulze refers in the following quotation to Vol. I, 306. (It is worth remembering that the Stäudlins were old friends of the Hegel family—see my *Toward the Sunlight*, pp. 59, 81, 116.)

51. *Kritik*, Vol. i, 608. Schulze wrote "which was to persuade others, etc. through their art . . . " (the italics are Hegel's, the quotation marks mine). The French translator Fauquet (p. 43, note 61) asserts that "On the precise point evoked by Hegel, Stäudlin has the authority of the texts on his side against Hegel." But Hegel is saying that *all* such criticism is worthless. And he is right. Fauquet *ought* to acknowledge (in any case) that the best texts are on *Hegel's* side (see the introductory essay).

52. *Outlines of Pyrrhonism* I, 222. Hegel learned from the note of Fabricius (whose edition of Sextus he owned and used) that the work Sextus refers to was one that had perished. But Sextus may mean the five books *Adversus Mathematicos* VII-XI (two books *Against the Logicians*, two *Against the Physical Philosophers* and one *Against the Ethical Philosophers*).

53. *Kritik* I, 222. Hegel did not mark this as a quotation but he has translated the Fabricius text of Sextus quite closely.

54. See for instance *Outlines of Pyrrhonism* I, 237 and Diogenes Laertius, IX, 108; also *Against the Ethical Philosophers*, 166

55. *Adversus logicos* I. 310.

56. Hegel probably means *Parmenides* 127a. Fauquet compares also Simplicius' account of Zeno in D-K. 29 A. In Sextus see *Adversus Physicos* I, 258-64; 308-58. (There are similar discussions in other works, but Hegel's reference points to these).

57. *Adversus logicos* I, 310-312. Hegel did not use quotation marks but his translation is fairly close.

58. *Adversus logicos* I, 313. The italics are Hegel's, the quotation marks mine.

59. See *Adversus logicos* I, 317-319.

60. See *Memorabilia*, I, 1, 13-14.

61. See Hegel's essay on Krug "How common sense etc."

62. We know from the earlier discussion that the philosophy with which true ancient skepticism is "identical" is Platonism. But Hegel seems here to have the Presocratic roots and sources of Platonism in mind. Compare Hegel's reference to the long history of "Skepticism" from Homer onwards, above. Socrates is certainly the turning point in the matter of "concern with subjectivity".

63. On the first ten tropes see note 32 above, and the introductory essay. For the ancient texts on which Hegel depends see Sextus, *Outlines of Pyrrhonism*, I, 36-179 and Diogenes Laertius IX, 79-88. (What he says here about the insignificance of the last two tropes is not borne out by his own later discussion).

64. This story, and the image of body and shadow, comes of course from Sextus—see *Outlines of Pyrrhonism* I, 28-29. The image itself may have come from Pyrrho.

65. This story comes from the "life of Pyrrho" in Diogenes Laertius, IX, 68.

66. Hegel takes this list directly from *Outlines of Pyrrhonism*, I, 36-37. He has inserted one or two explanations of his own.

67. *Outlines of Pyrrhonism* I, 38. The quotation marks are mine.

68. Actually this is from *Adversus ethicos*, 155-6. Hegel does not use quotation marks, but he is trying to translate the passage accurately into his own terms. Thus Sextus says that "Nature cares nothing for *nomos.*" Hegel cannot render this directly because he does not accept the reflective opposition of *phusis and nomos*. To write that "Nature cares nothing for *Sitten* (or *Gesetze*)" would be absurd, because the *Sitten* are natural, and Nature is a system of *Gesetze*. So he has to use the periphrasis "dasjenige, was die Menschen festsetzen" which expresses what the *skeptics* meant by *nomos*. (It is interesting that *kata krisin* in Sextus becomes "durch einen Willen").

69. Hegel's claims about early Stoicism are mistaken; and Antiochus must be counted as a mere "eclectic" by his standards, (see the introductory essay). Stoic "dogmatism" was always the primary target of skeptical attack.

70. See *Outlines of Pyrrhonism* I, 164-171, for Sextus' discussion of them.

71. Hegel paraphrases this from *Outlines of Pyrrhonism* I, 178-9.

72. See *Philebus* 14d-15a. Compare *Parmenides* 127e-128.

73. See [28-29]

74. See [8-9]. But there Hegel calls the transcendent *Sache* a *Ding*; he returns to this use in what follows here. *Sache* is intended as a rendering of the Greek *pragma*. For this see rather [15-6].

75. The expression *adēlon* (which comes from Anaxagoras) was used by the Academics. Hegel's view of what *they* meant is defensible. The other, more Aristotelian expressions which we find in Sextus refer to "things outside us" in much the same sense that Schulze speaks of them. I do not think that a distinction between Sextus and the modern Aenesidemus can be defended.

76. "kein Ding, keine be*dingtes*" – the verbal echo should always be remembered though it cannot be rendered in English without extreme artificiality.

77. Actually the earlier discussion referred to Arcesilaus and the Middle Academy [24-25]. Hegel simply refuses to admit that Sextus was biassed and mistaken. He wants (at least at this point) to make all of ancient skepticism *noble*. So he makes Sextus claim a distinction without a difference. But in fact Sextus falsely asserted a difference in order to make a distinction. (I think that perhaps Hegel misunderstood the Greek in the *Outlines of Pyrrhonism* I, 233 – see note 47 above).

78. Compare Diogenes Laertius IX, 88.

79. See [23].

80. More precisely: Book I, 13-15 and 198-199. The quotation I have marked comes from the latter passage. Hegel's "in Wahrheit" translates *dunamei* (implicitly); and he misunderstood, and so misplaced *kath' hēmas*. We *should* read: "always (according to us) add on to what the skeptic says: "So far as I am concerned etc.""

81. Translated literally, Hegel's text says: "its whole range of infinite facts." But it is clear that Hegel means the "bad infinite" of understanding – i.e. "its whole range of innumerable facts" (cf. Fauquet, p. 62); thus the right sense is given by making the infinity a character of the *range*.

82. See [20-21].

83. Hegel marked this quotation himself. Except for the parenthetical interjection it is fairly exact. (Compare also the *Critique of Pure Reason*, B. 618).

84. Compare *Difference*, p. 193.

85. *Jacobi an Fichte, Werke* III, 29-30 (the quotation marks are mine). The *Nürrenberger Grillenspiel* is a form of solitaire.

86. Formulations of this kind are frequent in Schulze's *Kritik* from the Introduction onwards.

87. See *Kritik* I, xxi. The expression *herauszuklauben* is Kantian (see *KRV* A 603, B 631).

88. The italics are Hegel's: the quotation marks mine.

89. The first quotation is exact, the second not quite. Schulze says "In everyday life, then, we continually presuppose, the actuality of an agreement of this kind et." Except for *"completely agree"*, the italics are Hegel's; the quotation marks are mine.

90. The quotation above (at note 89) continues: "The newer metaphysics, on the other hand, contains several attempts to investigate and give grounds for this possibility [i.e. of an agreement of our images with what they represent]".

91. *Kritik*, Vol. I, p. 70 (The italics are Hegel's, the quotation marks mine.)

92. *Kritik*, Vol. I, 69-70. (The italics are Hegel's, the quotation marks mine).

93. The quotation is exact. The spread type comes from Schulze also. He prints his three "grounds" in a larger font as headings.

93a *Kritik*, I, 627-8 (quotation marks mine).

94. Hegel himself uses quotation marks here (but he leaves the first three words outside the citation).

95. This much is direct quotation from *Kritik* I, 609-10. Schulze goes on to say simply "and upon which he [the rational man] will therefore also not ground the hope of the possibility of a science". A little further on he adds: "it would be foolish for any one to nourish the slightest hope" that the *Hauptzweck* of a scientific philosophy would be more successfully attained in the future than hitherto. (The italics are Hegel's, the quotation marks are mine).

96. This third volume never appeared.

97. Hegel has rearranged this verbatim quotation — *Kritik* II, 100 (quotation marks added).

98. *Kritik* II. 100-101 (quotation marks added)

99. *Kritik* ii, 104 (italics Hegel's, quotation marks mine)

100. *loc. cit.* (italics Hegel's, quotation marks mine)

101. *Kritik* II, 104-5 (italics Hegel's, quotation marks mine).

102. *Kritik* II, 105n. (Not quite verbatim. Quotation marks added).

103. *Kritik* II, 105 (Not quite verbatim. Quotation marks added).

104. *Kritik*, Vol. II, 105-6. (Italics Hegel's, quotation marks mine).

105. *Kritik*, Vol. II, 106. Almost word-perfect. (Italics Hegel's; quotation marks mine).

106. See [10].

107. See *Kritik*, II, 107-8.

108. *Kritik*, I, 160 (italics Hegel's, quotation marks mine). The note is on p. 163 and it simply refers us to *Monadology*, sections 58-61.

109. Compare [50].

110. *Kritik* II, 108 (quotation marks added)

111. *Kritik* II, 109 (italics Hegel's, quotation marks mine).

112. *Kritik* II, 112 (italics Hegel's, quotation marks mine).

113. *Kritik* II, 112 (italics Hegel's, quotation marks mine).

114. *Kritik* II, 113-4 (italics Hegel's, quotation marks mine).

115. Friedrich Nicolai (1733-1811) was one of the "leading lights" (*Gelichter*) of the German Enlightenment and its "popular" philosophy (which Hegel abominated, just as Goethe abominated the simplistic attitude of such "lights" toward literature). He satirized current or recent philosophical views by embodying them in the characters of his novels.

116. Hegel has here characterized briefly the object of his own critical reconstruction

of "Kantian Philosophy" as a rational system in *Faith and Knowledge*. Compare pp. 67-96.

117. See for instance *Kritik* I, xxvii; II, 506-7

118. See note 3 above.

119. Not quite verbatim (quotation marks added).

120. *Kritik* II, 91-2 (not quite verbatim); italics are Hegel's, quotation marks mine.

121. See *Kritik* II, 93-4 (quotation marks added).

122. *Kritik*, II, 137. The quotation is exact. (The italics are Hegel's, the quotation marks mine).

123. See note 3 above.

On The Relationship of The Philosophy of
Nature to Philosophy in General
[by F. W. J. Schelling (and G. W. F. Hegel?)]

Kritisches Journal der Philosophie, I, no. 3 (1802) 1-25

Translated by George di Giovanni and H. S. Harris
Notes by H. S. Harris

There was a great dispute about the authorship of this essay when the editorial committee of Hegel's friends were preparing the first edition of his collected works after his death. K. L. Michelet not only printed it as a work of Hegel's, but claimed to find in it the very moment where Hegel first went beyond Schelling. This interpretation was a reaction against his own original certainty that the essay come from Schelling's pen. He reported that when he had expressed this earlier view to Hegel, Hegel had contradicted him flatly, and had said that the essay was his. His account of the conversation carries complete conviction; what Hegel said had clearly made a great impression on Michelet, it overturned his ideas, and I do not think we can doubt that what he reported took place. (Also it is reliably reported that Hegel told Cousin the essay was his).

Nevertheless, Schelling said categorically, when he was appealed to in 1838, that "there is not a single letter from Hegel's pen in the essay, indeed he did not even see it before it was printed"[1] and the draft of Hegel's curriculum vitae of 1804, when it was found, showed that he did not claim the authorship at that time. So there cannot now be any real doubt that Schelling was the author.

We are left with a puzzle about what Hegel meant, and what he was remembering, when he spoke to Michelet and others in the 1820's. We can start by setting aside the claim that Hegel never saw the essay before it was printed. That simply cannot be true, because he was the one who saw the Journal through the press; and the printing of this issue of the first volume was delayed until after the first issue of the second volume was published. That issue was entirely filled (and indeed swollen out of due proportion) by Faith and Knowledge. Volume I, number 3, on the other hand, is entirely by Schelling. The natural hypothesis is that Hegel was not willing to give it his editorial attention until after he got is own work properly completed.

In view of the facts that can be definitely established, we must assume that Hegel's memories about the making of the Journal were less misty in the 1820's than Schelling's were in the late 1830's (and early forties). So, unless we are to brand Hegel as an outright liar (for which there is no other warrant in the published record), we must set aside even Schelling's more moderate statement (in 1844) that "Hegel had no part in the essay either with respect to the content or with respect to the forms."[2] Michelet originally claimed to identify the style and poetic enthusiasm of the essay as Schelling's; and Hegel was (minimally) contradicting the claim that the style was Schelling's. So I infer that at the very least, he edited the essay stylistically. Further, I think we must suppose that the content reflects his influence upon Schelling in conversation. And finally, of course, there is the basic fact that the Identity Philosophy was common to both of them. Whatever the grounds for Hegel's claims to authorship in the 1820's, there is no doubt that he wanted his students to regard the essay as a document of his spiritual evolution (and not to try to separate his

pen from Schelling's here.) Whether he deserves to be counted as a co-author in fact
is doubtful. I do not see how the doubt can ever be finally resolved, but I have
tried in my notes to point to some matters both of substance and of form in which
it is legitimate to see evidence of his influence.

Notes

1. G. L. Plitt, *Aus Schellings Leben* III, 142-3.
2. ibid. III, 187.

[1]   THE PURPOSE OF this essay is to put into their proper perspective
several prejudices and pronouncements against the Philosophy of Nature
and about it, which derive partly from a one-sided and false view of
philosophy, and partly from superficiality and a total lack of scientific
sense.

Though it is granted here that there is a relationship between the
Philosophy of Nature and philosophy in general, this relationship is
not to be conceived in any way as one of subordination. Whatever is
philosophy is philosophy totally and undividedly; what is not philosophy
in this sense, but only borrows its principles from it, and otherwise
stands aloof from the philosophical concern and pursues quite
unphilosophical goals, cannot be called philosophy, or even a
philosophical science in the stricter sense.

All the distinctions that are made in this regard are empty and
[2]   merely conceptual: that is to say, there is only one // philosophy
and one science of philosophy; what we call different philosophical
sciences are only presentations of the one undivided whole of
philosophy under different conceptual [*ideell*] determinations—or, to
use the familiar expression right away, of philosophy in its distinct
'powers'.[1]

The complete manifestation of philosophy emerges only in the totality
of powers. For this reason, the principle of philosophy itself as the
point where all the powers are identical has necessarily no power;
but this indifference-point of absolute unity lies in its turn within
each particular unity separately [*für sich*], just as in each they all repeat
themselves; philosophical construction does not aim at the construction
of the powers as such and hence as different, but only at the display
of the Absolute in each, so that each is on its own account the whole
again. The relation of the individual parts within the closed and organic
whole of philosophy is like that of the different shapes in a perfectly
constructed poetic work where each, although it is a member of the
whole, is nevertheless inherently absolute and independent because
it is a perfect reflection of it.

One can lift an individual power out of the whole and treat it on its own account; this presentation is itself philosophy, however, only in so far as one actually displays the Absolute in it; in any other case where one treats it *as particular*, and lays down for it laws and rules as particular, it can only be called the theory of a certain object as [for instance] the Theory of Nature or Theory of Art. To grasp this universally, we might remark generally that all antitheses and differentiations are // only different forms [of the one whole], which   [3] have no essence of their own *qua* distinct, but are only real in their unity; and since the unity of all cannot in turn be a particular, the different forms are real only inasmuch as each represents the absolute whole, the universe within itself. Whenever one formulates laws for a particular *qua* particular, one removes one's object *eo ipso* from the Absolute, one's science from philosophy.

As such, therefore, the Philosophy of Nature is philosophy whole and undivided; and in so far as nature is objective *knowledge*, and the expression of the indifference-point is *truth*, so far as it lies in nature (just as it is beauty so far it lies in the ideal [*ideell*] world)—to this extent, the whole of philosophy viewed from the theoretical side can be called Philosophy of Nature.

That the Theory of Nature too (as speculative physics) takes its principles from the Philosophy of Nature does not concern us here; and in another respect we exclude this reference altogether for present purposes. What is at issue is Philosophy of Nature as such and *in itself*— and *not* what is only derived from it (although this last is almost universally confused with it).

By these standards, we can only speak of a relationship of the Philosophy of Nature to philosophy in one of two senses: either the idea of a Philosophy of Nature is connected with something which is [falsely] held to be philosophy, or it is dealt with according to its absolute essence (*Absolutheit*), i.e., as an integral and necessary part of the whole of philosophy.

Philosophy itself, however, can in its turn be considered from two points of view: either from the purely *scientific* side, or in // its reference   [4] to *the world*. And this has just two aspects: there is the reference to religion, insofar as religion is speculation itself that has turned into immutable, objective intuition; and the reference to morality, insofar as the latter is an objective expression of speculative Ideas in conduct.[3]

Poetry too, as long as it has not yet become the concern [*Sache*] of the [human] genus or at least of a whole race, and the 'one-and- all' of a nation is considered only in particular connections. The only unconditional and universally valid points of reference are the two that have been given; for this reason we want to restrict ourselves to these two in the present study.

I

The misguided judgements to which the Philosophy of Nature has been subjected at the hand of what people like to call "philosophy" are so deeply implicated in the fundamental error that has lurked unchallenged at the base of almost all recent [philosophic] efforts (and even at the base of the attempted reforms) that in order to evaluate them properly we must go back to the error itself.[4]

Since the error is in a certain way the focal point of our whole modern culture as well, a philosophy that originates in the range of general ideas derived from our culture has no point of access to it. The historical thread that would otherwise lead many individuals from one form of philosophy to another breaks off at this point; to find the point of access, they would have to go back to a much earlier [5] time than that which is familiar to them. But on the one // hand those who are actually philosophers normally have no other principle of judgement than that of their own limited position; and [on the other hand], those who are not philosophers, though they plume themselves on their reputation for it, have no principle other than that of historical comparison and opposition; there is no possible way, therefore, to rectify the opinion held by either side about the Philosophy of Nature, apart from the disclosure of the very point which they must all master, above all else, before they will be in a position to pass judgement concerning its foundation and import.

This point, which they have not been able to get past so far, is—to state it as concisely as possible—the unconditional requirement that *the Absolute be kept outside oneself.* This is not the place to discuss at greater length what effect Christendom, in defining the entire culture of the later world as its universal sovereign, produced; how from the assimilation of the Absolute into innermost subjectivity a directly opposite result arose to that intended, namely the complete expulsion of the divine from a world that grew rigid as its life principle was being withdrawn from it.[5] Nor is it necessary to make the depth of the requirement, and how ineradicably implanted it was, more comprehensible. It committed itself utterly to the highest form of irreligiosity. For on the one hand there was the belief that the highest tribute of piety had been paid to God by withdrawing him from the world, as an otherworldly and transcendent substance; while on the other hand, a freer hand was obtained in this world, since it could be both [theoretically] regarded and [practically] made use of according to the most common form of understanding.

It is perhaps recognized widely enough that all dogmatism generally, and especially in most recent times the preaching of Jacobi and the proclamations of Reinhold, have no other cause than that quenchless // desire. Until now the fact that the simple conversion of the re- [6] quirement—in other words that *the Ego be held outside the Absolute* —guarantees the very same result for philosophy has been less widely recognized. And the reason why this has not been so generally noticed is as follows: One can reintroduce the Absolute as faith into philosophy through the back door, without prejudice to the first principle—yet in such a way that, when viewed theoretically, the Absolute is always just *in* the Ego and *on account of* the Ego, and is only *independent* of the Ego or outside of it when considered *practically*. Thus we gain the advantage of assuming an attitude of denial that rules out the dogmatic claim that the Absolute is outside us, without keeping the Absolute truly *in* the Ego nevertheless; for that would be impossible without abolishing the Ego as particular form.[6]

The concealed inner ground for positing the Absolute outside the Ego in dogmatism, is the requirement that the Ego must remain outside the Absolute. It is self-evident that the positing of the Ego outside the Absolute, when it is agreed to, and made into a *principle*, reciprocally entails by a very simple necessity the relegation of the Absolute outside the Ego. That this *result* is, in its turn, the inner motive of the principle will perhaps become clear from what follows.

By this move, which is of course a matter of turning dogmatism around, the '*in-itself*' is denied in theoretical philosophy—the Ego neither genuinely posits it within itself, nor genuinely posits itself in it; rather // the '*in-itself*' is simply superseded, its reality is entirely disavowed [7] *on the ground that it can always be posited once more in the Ego as ens rationis, and is to this extent a product of the Ego.*

Here the requirement is thus openly declared. In order to be genuinely real [*reell*] the '*in-itself*' must be independent of the *Ego outside it*. In other words, the whole presupposition of dogmatism is expressed as clearly as daylight.

It is a quite peculiar confusion to hold a philosophy to be precisely *idealism*, to pass it off as idealism, and perfect idealism at that, because (1) it *denies* the '*in-itself*' in general (the absolute Ideal), and (2) it denies it *on the ground* that it appears to be thinkable only as thing in *itself*, as something outside the Ego, and hence in a dogmatic-realistic mode. Apart from the tradition of Kant (who incidentally, had quite a different right—as could be demonstrated—to name his philosophy "idealism") this kind of argument probably derives its strength mainly just from the sheer impressiveness it has for the ordinary understanding when the latter is reassured that singular, sensible things do not exist outside it; but equally from the hidden importance accorded to the reality of these things in the fact that they can *be denied* — their denial can be taken for what is characteristic of a particular philosophy, and the philosophy can earn for itself the name of "idealism" through this denying alone.

But according to the whole intention of this *idealism*, the Ego should remain in its empirical integrity; for the 'in-itself' is removed simply [8]   because for the sake // of the Ego which ought to subsist *per se*, it too must be thought *outside it*. Idealism makes it a law for itself, quite generally, to recognize pure consciousness only in so far as it is given in the *empirical* one. But this empirical consciousness does not occur without the affections of objects; it is necessary, therefore, that through an *impact* which is theoretically *incomprehensible*, (or alternatively also in virtue of *incomprehensible bounds* that constrain the Ego,) as many affections be posited in the Ego as will correspond to the objects. This side of the Ego is the sensuous one that is at the same time practical in virtue of intuition. Hence in the Ego a quality as intelligence whose inner activity is a moving to and fro, the qualities of smoothness, sweetness or bitterness are posited in space, which is the universal form of the movement to and fro outwardly intuited; they are spread out over surfaces and, in a word, moulded into concrete things.

It is obvious enough that common places of this sort, as well as any conception of nature which would make it consist of affections, like green and yellow, etc., and of round and angular objects produced for the sake of these affections—all this makes a Philosophy of Nature something that can rightly be dispensed with. But the fancy of having abolished nature because one has preserved the accidents in their entire empirical reality, and has merely implanted in the Ego the essence or the substance in which they inhere, is particularly noteworthy—as if they were not properly seated there from the very beginning, and were not quite ineradicable.[7]

There can be no doubt why neither nature, in general, is established [9]   in this form of philosophy, nor a Philosophy of // Nature. As for the latter, the reason is not really, as this philosophy likes to pretend, because philosophy of nature justifies an empirical realism, but rather because it reduces the empirical realism founded upon the affections of the Ego described above to nothing, and aims at what is "in-itself" or [purely] intelligible in nature. It is not because the Philosophy of Nature asserts an antithesis between nature and the Ego (a being of nature outside the Ego), but because it asserts an absolute identity between the two in which *both* are submerged together—hence because the Philosophy of Nature does not (re)cognize any true bound either in the [alleged] incomprehensible impact or in the [alleged] incomprehensible bounds. In a word, it is *absolute idealism*.

We must look still more closely at the practical side of this type of philosophy in order to see clearly how its idealism stands with respect to dogmatism.

The claim is this: From the theoretical standpoint, philosophy is idealism; at the practical level, *realism* is restored, and comes into its rights again.

In this claim no consideration is given in any way to a genuine lifting of idealism to the absolute status by virtue of which it would already comprehend realism; accordingly, no consideration is given to a genuine dissolution of the antithesis between the two. Moreover, since the declared practical standpoint still has its own theoretical aspect too—and only what is speculatively asserted in the light of it can verily be actual philosophy—the whole is (even on this side) necessarily reduced once more to the idealism that holds the Ego *outside* the Absolute, and by the same token holds the Absolute outside the Ego also. // [10]

To put the question as plainly as possible: What is it, exactly, that drives this idealism to seek realism in practical philosophy? It is its concept of *realism*, according to which the Ego, if it is to be genuinely *real (reell)* must have the Absolute *outside itself, independent of itself.*

For this idealism, there is no reality of the Absolute, save in the relationship of slavery and subjection of the Ego under it. If its notion of reality is to be realized, the Absolute must appear in the shape of absolute command, and the Ego in that of unconditional acceptance of it and receptivity to it. (The categorical [aspect] of duty does not allow the same game to be played with it that is played in theoretical philosophy, i.e., its being posited over and over again in the Ego as an *ens rationis* and in this way its product comes to be; i.e. because it retains in this relationship the quality of standing absolutely outside the Ego it is actually real.)

It pertains to this relation, however, that it never gets to the absolute acceptance of that categorical and infinite [law of duty] in the Ego; for if it did, the antithesis between the Ego and the Absolute, which is unavoidably necessary and desirable, would be superseded; the Absolute, would indeed be posited *in the Ego*, but in consequence it would no longer be truly real *(reell)*. *If the system is to remain* it is therefore necessary that the relationship should be extended into an infinite progression; but it is thus also impossible that eternity should be in time, and the finite should anticipate the infinite inherently.

However, since the sensations and the affections of the Ego also contribute to its being preserved as something empirical,—and hence // also in opposition to, and in merely relative unity with, the pure [11] Ego which is pure willing itself—these affections must further be so determined in advance as to conform to the practical ends of rational beings. Light is no irruption of the divine principle in nature, no symbol of the eternal, primordial knowledge imaged by nature. It is rather that through which rational beings that have been put together physically out of enduring and pliable matter can, while speaking to one another, at the same time see one another—just as air is that through which, while seeing one another, they can at the same time speak to one another. These rational beings are bounded appearances of absolute Reason in their turn; and they are just as empirical as anything else. It is not possible, from their doings and strivings, to make out any reason whatever why they should claim the priority that they are accorded; but on this view they have the universal stock in the universe upon which the entire [mass of] finitude is grafted. What sort of absolute identity it is, however, that pre-determines for each rational being its universal and particular boundary, and in virtue of which alone nature can finally be comprehended too, will emerge in the following discussion.

Just as nordic barbaric languages have no expression for the Absolute that is not derived from property, so (in a simple paraphrase) the moral world-order, is the expression of a similar poverty—not linguistic, but philosophical; in that the Absolute acquires, instead of its speculative meaning, a purely moral one, the meaning that it has necessarily rises above everything. It is meaningless to say that the universe too is [12]   reduced to a morally conditioned world, and that all the // remaining beauty and majesty of nature is dissolved in moral references of the sort, since nature still consists for the most part only of smoothness and roughness, of green and yellow, for which we then first contribute the 'smooth' and 'rough', the 'yellow' and 'green'.

There is no other idea of God than the one mentioned, since it is only in this relationship (of duty) that he remains forever outside the Ego. Also it is only within an ethical order that nature can be delineated and have reality, for only therein can the universal and particular boundary be determined for each individual, in virtue of which he is able to project his own world for himself; for his is in principle the sphere of his duty, and without the categorical imperative there is no world at all.

Thus the genuinely speculative question remains still unanswered, namely, how the absolutely One, the absolutely simple and eternal Will, from which all things flow, expands into a multiplicity and into a unity re-born from multiplicity, i.e., into a moral *world*. Displaying the absolutely One as a *Will* does not help to resolve this problem at all. Conceptual determinations of this sort are quite accidental to philosophy, and fail to advance speculation.

The question would be an indispensable and unavoidable problem if this philosophy actually made what is for it the Absolute into a principle as well—but it carefully guards itself against this. It lets the whole of finitude be given to it, very conveniently, along with the Ego; it has this point in common with dogmatism too, that the Absolute is for it a result, something that needs justification. But, where dogmatism // concludes to God from a world which it would not [13] comprehend without him, this form of philosophy called "idealism" only assumes God in order to be able to harmonize the moral ends instead—thus not for *God's own sake* at all. God might just as well not be, if we were only able to manage without him in the moral world—just as in dogmatism, he might as well not be if we could account for the world without him. God exists, not for the sake of his absolute nature, as the Idea of all Ideas—the Idea which of itself comprehends absolute reality within itself immediately—but in a connection with rational beings which is still one-sided towards them [i.e. it is for their sake].

What is characteristic of this philosophy is just that it has given a *new* form to the age-old dichotomy [between the infinite and the finite]; but such forms may be legion—none lasts, each carries impermanence within itself. I cannot found anything permanent. An enthusiasm that fancies itself to be great if it sets its own Ego up (in its thoughts) against the wild storm of the elements, the thousand thousand suns and the ruins of the whole world,[8] makes this philosophy popular; and also makes it dumb and hollow otherwise—a fruit of the age whose spirit has for a time exalted this empty form, until the age itself sinks back as its own ebb sets in, and the fruit along with it.

What *abides* is only what supersedes all dichotomy; for only that is in truth One and unchangeably the same. From it alone can a true universe of knowledge evolve, an all-encompassing structure. Only what proceeds from the absolute unity of the infinite and finite is immediately capable *per se* of // symbolic presentation—capable [14] also, therefore, of what every true philosophy strives after, i.e., of becoming in religion, or objectively, an eternal source of new intuition, and a universal model of everything in which human action endeavours to express and portray the harmony of the universe.

II

The preceding indicates clearly the relation of the Philosophy of Nature to this kind of idealism, which does indeed deny sensible reality, but which, for the rest, remains burdened with all the antitheses of dogmatism.

Setting aside a few important phenomena which [are not and] cannot be our target here, since they have been universally misunderstood and persecuted,[9] it can be shown that all the more recent innovations in philosophy and in our view of the universe, since the dualism of Descartes (in which the dichotomy that had long been present only

came to conscious and scientific expression) are just different forms of a single opposition, thus far unsurmounted and indeed insurmountable by our culture. The Philosophy of Nature, on the contrary, simply cannot proceed from anything but a system of absolute identity, and can only be comprehended and understood [*erkannt*] within such a system. It is not surprising, therefore, that it meets everywhere with rejection, even on the part of what is generally called the "universal interest of mankind", and constitutes the general heritage of philosophy
[15]   as it were. // To conclude that because we must absolutely reject the religious and ethical connection given to philosophy in these earlier systems, we therefore reject the connection altogether, is a total misinterpretation of the aim of our philosophy. The exact opposite is the case; for since we do not even recognize as philosophy any view which is not already religion *in its principle*, we reject any cognition of the Absolute which emerges from philosophy only as *result*—we reject any view which thinks of God in Himself, but in some empirical connection; precisely because the spirit of ethical life and of philosophy is for us one and the same, we reject any doctrine according to which the object of the intellect (*das Intellectuelle*) must like nature be just a means to ethical life,[10] and must on that account be deprived, in itself stripped of the inner substance of that life.

For the understanding of what follows take note that it is impossible for us to think of religion as such without historical reference. There will be nothing alarming in this if one has become at all accustomed to regard historical [reality] from the point of view of higher concepts, and to rise above the relationships of empirical necessity that common knowledge discerns in history to the unconditional and eternal necessity through which everything in it, like everything that becomes actual in the course of nature is determined in advance. It is no accident, nor is it a conditional necessity, that the universal spirit of the religion of the modern world is determined as it is; and if it has its antithesis in a spiritual tendency that belonged to a world which perished before
[16]   us, this too is pre-appointed and founded in the universal // plan of the world's destinies and in the eternal laws that determine the course of human history.

The germ of Christianity was the feeling of a separation of the world from God; its aim was reconciliation with God—not through a raising of finitude to the infinite, but through the infinite's becoming finite, or through God's becoming man. In the first moment of its appearance Christianity set up this union as an object of faith. Faith is the inner certainty that anticipates infinity for itself; and by bringing the infinite back in this way Christianity intimated that it was itself a seed that would have its development only with the [successive] definitions of the world in the infinity of time. Singular deviations from the [basic] trend of this faith, and transitional positions generally, cannot enter into our consideration here as far as the whole pattern is concerned; we must fasten our eyes only on the universal and important manifestations.

All the symbols of Christianity exhibit the characteristic that they represent the identity of God with the world in images. The peculiar tendency of Christianity is that of intuiting God in the finite; this tendency arises from its inmost essence and is possible only in it—for the fact that this tendency is also to be found in isolated instances before Christianity, and outside it, only provokes that it is universal and necessary, and that the historical antitheses just like all the others, rest only upon a predominance.

We can call this directing of attention upon the intuiting of the infinite in the finite general mysticism.[11] // Nothing proves that   [17] mysticism is the necessary mode of intuition prescribed by the inmost spirit of Christianity more strikingly than the fact that it broke through even in what was most opposed to it, as Protestantism was; it broke through again in new forms and even to some extent in darker ones. The mystics of Christianity were rejected by the predominant belief; they were even considered heretical, and were driven out; but this was because they were converting faith into vision and they wanted to pluck the still unripe fruit of the time too soon. The general aspiration of the modern age has progressed to the point of preserving subjectively, in a lack of faith, the antithesis which subsists objectively in the faith that is not knowledge. In this way it preserves it whole. But that does not prove anything against the first tendency which even in faith pointed toward vision as something assured, in the future.

Mysticism constitutes the highest extreme in the antithesis between Christianity and Paganism. In Christianity the esoteric religion is itself the public religion, and *vice versa*; in the mystics of the pagans, on the other hand, a great many of the representations were themselves mystical in nature; if we abstract from the more obscure objects of the latter, the whole of Greek religion, like poetry, was free of mysticism altogether.[12] And just for the sake of a more complete implementation of its original tendency it was perhaps necessary to Christianity that the crystal-bright mysticism of Catholicism, which was constantly getting closer to poetry, should be driven back by the prose of Protestantism, within which mysticism would thus be born for the first time in its most perfectly implemented form.//   [18]

The definite opposition of Christianity and Paganism allows us to consider them as two unities that stand opposed to one another, distinct from one another only by their orientation. The unity of Paganism was the immediate divinity of the natural, the absolute assimilation or imagining of the finite in the infinite. If we can speak of one single orientation where the two antitheses immediately converge, then both the religious and the poetic intuition of Paganism started from the finite and ended in the infinite. If one grasps Greek mythology from its finite side, it appears throughout merely as a schematization of the finite or of nature; it is symbolic only in the unity which it had concurrently achieved even in its subordination of finitude. The character of Christianity, grasped from the side of the infinite, is the character of reflection; its unity is the imagining of the infinite in the finite, the intuition of the divine in the natural. That the task of Christianity lies further off, and that its solution appears to require an indefinite time, lies in its very nature. The unity which lies at the base of Greek mythology can be viewed as a still undissolved (*unaufgehobene*) identity; it is the one from which the first intuition proceeds; like the age of innocence, its dominion can last only for a short time; it has to appear as irretrievably lost. The task of Christianity already presupposes absolute scission; the finite within the infinite is the inborn [innocence]; through freedom the finite is antithetic to finitude, and if it cuts itself off, it cuts itself off absolutely. The // moment of union cannot coincide with that of division; between the scission, and the recalling of the infinite concept from its infinite flight, there are necessary intermediate stages that cannot determine the meaning and the direction of the whole.[13]

[19]

Just as, quite generally, all opposites cease to be opposites, as soon as each is on its own account absolutely self-contained, so it is not to be doubted that even in the direction pre-ordained for Christianity the other unity (i.e., that of the assimilation of the infinite into the finite) could be transfigured into the joy and the beauty of Greek religion. Christianity as an antithesis is only the pathway to fulfillment; in the moment of fulfillment it transcends itself as opposite; heaven is then truly regained once more, and the absolute gospel is proclaimed.[14]

There is no religion without one or the other of the two intuitions, without the immediate divinization of the finite, or the seeing of God in the finite. This antithesis is the only one that is possible in religion; for this reason there are only Paganism and Christianity — apart from these two there is nothing but the absoluteness that is common to both. Paganism sees the natural immediately in the divine and in the spiritual prototypes; Christianity sees through nature, as the infinite body of God, all the way to his inmost [essence] and to his spirit. For both of them, nature is the ground and source of the intuition of the infinite.

Whether the present moment in time, which has become such a remarkable turning point for everything // shaped by time, and for the sciences and the works of man, will not also be a turning point for religion; and whether the time of the true gospel of the

[20]

reconciliation of the world with God is drawing near to the stage where the temporal and merely outward forms of Christianity disintegrate and disappear—this is a question that must be left for each and every one who understands the signs of the future, to answer for himself.

The new religion, which already announces itself in revelations to single individuals[15] is a return to the first mystery of Christianity, and a fulfillment of it. It will be discerned in the rebirth of nature as the symbol of eternal unity. The first reconciliation and resolution of the age old discord [between Paganism and Christianity] must be celebrated in the philosophy whose sense and significance is only [rightly] grasped by those who recognize in it the life of the divinity newly arisen from the dead.

III

For many, the study of philosophy from the universal historical standpoint would at least have the advantage of making clear to them how narrow the philosophical frameworks are within which they claim to have staked out the limits of universal spirit. For others, unable to rise to [the level of] Ideas by their own free initiative, it would at least offer a more universal standard of judgement than an acquaintance with the forms and tendencies of philosophy // restricted to the [21] narrow circle of the present time.

The approach to nature that predominates in recent times was determined by the same turn of events that has made absolute scission into the principle of philosophy. And in the relation that the science of the ancients had to nature their still untranscended identity is expressed. That ancient science restricted itself to observation, because only observation assimilates objects in their integrity and undividedness. The art of isolating, and of observing nature in artfully devised combinations and separations, is a discovery of our later culture. But although the ordinary procedure of empiricism is a completely blind one, still the first ray of light which awakened it generally and which has sustained the nobler impulse to investigate nature, was the instinct, deeply ingrained in the feelings of the later world, to bring back to nature the life that had escaped from it. The enthusiasm with which the moderns accepted all the living manifestations of universal nature as so many vessels of the life locked up in it, and which the ancients hardly knew and paid little attention to—this enthusiasm certainly shows, on the one hand, the primitive coarseness of the moderns in contrast to the culture of the ancients, but at the same time also the irresistible necessity with which this new attitude toward nature was forced upon the human spirit.

There is no prospect of returning once more, from the uncultured earnestness and the gloomy sensitivity of the modern approach to nature, back to the cheerfulness and the purity of the Greek intuition [22] of nature, by any path save one: // the restoration through speculation of the lost identity and the transcending of the division at a higher power—for to return to the identity of the first power once it has been surpassed is denied to us.

The narrow spirits who do not comprehend the large-scale coherence of universal culture, and of the forms in which culture expresses itself, may for the time being pronounce the verdict of irreligion over the Philosophy of Nature, or call for such a verdict; nonetheless, the Philosophy of Nature will become a new source of intuition and cognition of God. Even cheaper the charge of amorality, or immorality with which a spineless, and impotent rhetoric of morality, from which any Idea of God is far removed, having first supplanted religion seeks now to supplant philosophy as well. With its accompanying scientific crudity, this moralizing conceives the unity of the Ego with nature empirically, as an expression of naturalism, and interprets the Philosophy of Nature in the light of that assumption just as, on the other side, it interprets idealism as a form of egocentricity.[16] A philosophy that derives totally from Reason and consists only in Ideas must spring from a more genuinely ethical energy; but that way of shoving ethical life forward is directed against reason and speculation. Ethics is in principle the liberation of the soul from what is alien and matter-like; it is elevation to the state of being determined through pure reason alone and unadulterated. This same purification of the soul is the condition of philosophy. To this extent the ethical and the intellectual reference of all this is one and the same thing again; it is their reference to pure, strictly universal reason, without material and without [23] intermediary or alien mediation.//

The genuinely ethical treatment of nature is thus also the genuinely intellectual treatment of it, and *vice versa*. An ethical reference that excludes the intellectual one ceases to be ethical as well. Both of them are in principle *one*; neither truly precedes or follows the other; only empirically does it appear to do so; in the context of our temporal becoming, the ethical comes first; and through it we embark upon the intellectual world and are cognizant of ourselves in it. Innate knowledge is only an imagining of the infinite or the universal in the particularity of our nature; the ethical command is immediately and spontaneously directed to the projection of our particularity with the pure universal, the essence, the infinite. But this antithesis between [innate] knowledge and ethical [formation] holds, only between knowledge and action in time. *True* knowledge turns away from the mere mirroring of the infinite in the finite towards the '*in-itself*' or the primordial knowledge; and it cannot go in this direction without a complete assimilation or resolution of the particular in the universal, i.e., without ethical purity of soul. In short, without the soul being at home in the world of Ideas, and dwelling in it as in its own domain, the true ethical life (which is not merely negative) would be impossible. The ethical life that cuts itself off from the intellectual [world] is necessarily empty,for only from the latter does it draw the material for its action. Whoever has not purified his soul to the point of partaking in the primordial knowledge, has not attained the ultimate ethical fulfillment either. The pure, unconditional universal is something external for him; for his part, he is still mired in impurity, therefore— still beholden to the particular and empirical.//   [24]

"Purification," says Plato (*Phaedo*, p. 152) "consists in separating the soul as much as possible from the body, and accustoming it to gather and withdraw itself into itself on all sides away from the body, and to dwell by itself as much as possible. *Death* is what we call this release of the soul from the body. Those who strive the most for this release are *genuine lovers of wisdom.*"[17] Thus ethical life and philosophy meet in this striving for purification. The path to this liberation is not the merely negative concept of finitude, i.e. the concept of it as a restriction of the soul; for this conception of finitude does not overcome it. A positive concept is needed and a like intuition of the '*in-itself*'; for he who knows that the natural is separated from the divine only in semblance, that the body is only body as distinct from the soul in an incomplete cognition, but that in the '*in-itself*' the body is the same as the soul—he who knows this will practice most the dying of that death, so praised by Socrates, which is the entrance to eternal freedom and true life. Those, however, who insert something of an alien nature, a material form or the like, between the pure universal or infinite and the soul (whether this happens consciously, or because they fail altogether to rise to the consciousness of what they are doing)—they are never genuinely freed from that restriction, but forever drag the finite and the body along with them as something positive and genuinely actual. The true triumph and final liberation of the soul lies in absolute idealism alone, in the absolute death of the real (*reellen*) as such.//   [25]

The blasphemers who slander the ethical principle of philosophy know neither the goal of the soul nor the stages through which it attains purification. What the soul experiences first is longing; for in order to receive the imprint of the immortal Being (*Wesen*) nature must necessarily be at the same time the grave of perfection. The soul that has become aware of the loss of the highest good speeds like Ceres to kindle the torch at the flaming mountain; it quests to and fro upon the earth, spying out all the depths and the heights, but in vain, till at last, it arrives worn out in *Eleusis*. This is the second stage. But only the all-seeing sun reveals Hades as already the dwelling place of the eternal good. The soul that encounters this revelation passes over to the final recognition that it must turn [back] to the eternal Father. Even the King of the gods cannot loosen the indissoluble chain; but he allows the soul to rejoice over the lost good in the images which the beam of eternal light, through the soul's mediation, wrest from the dark womb of the deep.[18]

Notes

1. *Potenzen:* the word comes from mathematics. At each level of nature there are three "powers"; and the whole of nature is a chain of these cubes. Schelling used the concept in different ways over many years. Hegel illustrates how it applies at this period in the *Difference* essay (see pp. 59-60 and 168-9); and the *System of Ethical Life* exemplifies *his* conception of the chain of *Potenzen*. The *third* power of each level is an achieved equilibrium which is therefore referred to as the "indifference point".

2. As an equilibrium of motion or tension every *Potenz* is also a *Gestalt*. (We have here the origin of the conception of the "shapes of consciousness" in the *Phenomenology*; and the Identity Philosophy, as the organization of a chain of *Gestalten* is incipiently "phenomenological" in Hegel's sense).

3. Thus religion and morality are the two aspects of Reason as a reality that can be *intuited*; speculation is the conceptualization of this intuition. This view is perfectly reflected in the *System of Ethical Life* — except that there it is religion and *Sittlichkeit* (not *Moralität* as here) that are the higher and lower degrees of the intuitable reality of Reason. Compare also the essay on *Natural Law* (especially Knox and Acton, pp. 112 for the relation of *Moralität* to *Sittlichkeit*, and pp. 132-3 for the transition from *Sittlichkeit* to *Religion*. The conclusion of the *Natural Law* essay should be read as the description of a religious experience rather than a speculative one).

4. Schelling's commitment to the speculative possibility of a philosophy of nature, was the main cause of his breach with Fichte. There were, of course, many other critics of this new departure from the bounds of critical rationality as established by Kant. But it *must* be Fichte whose "reform" of philosophy is here accused of failing because of this prejudice. (This "failure" is one of the main topics of the *Difference* essay).

5. The discussion of this problem "at greater length" eventually becomes one of the main themes of Hegel's *Phenomenology*.

6. The thesis of this paragraph (and those that follow) is closely connected both with the main argument of *Faith and Knowledge*, and with Hegel's critique of the sundering of philosophy into the extremes of skepticism and dogmatism in the "Skepticism" essay. The "dogmatists" (Reinhold and Jacobi) are named. The unnamed "skeptic" is Fichte.

7. This is a summary repetition of the critique of Fichte's conception of nature in *Faith and Knowledge* (see especially pp. 175-190).

8. This is an echo from Fichte's *Appeal to the Public* (*Werke* V, 237). The same echo occurs at the end of Hegel's "System Fragment" (Frankfurt, Sept. 1800; *Early Theological Writings*, Trs. T. M. Knox and R. Kroner, Chicago: University of Chicago Press, 1948, p. 318); and twice in *Faith and Knowledge* (pp. 174, 177).

9. It is a highly plausible hypothesis that the terminology of "expansion" and "contraction" comes to the Identity Philosophy from Jacob Boehme. Thus his theosophy may be one of the *grosse Erscheinungen* that has been "universally misunderstood and persecuted."

10. Fichte regarded nature as the essential scenery and intruments for the achievement of *Moralität*. Earlier *Moralität* was coupled with *Religion* in the way that Hegel couples *Sittlichkeit* with Religion; here *Sittlichkeit* is used for the *dominance* of the moral law over nature. Here, therefore, we have a complete reversal of the way Hegel used the terms *Sittlichkeit* and *Moralität* (and as the references given in note 3 above will show, Hegel's usage was already fixed and constant.)

11. Thus when a writer like Michael Rosen calls Hegel's conception of Reason 'mysticism' he is returning to Schelling's name for the *intuitive* (i.e. religious) awareness of it. Even in the context of the Identity Philosophy, the term is therefore rather one-sided. When we come to the liberated *conceptual* theory which Hegel founded upon the 'comprehensive presentation' of Reason as a *phenomenon* (i.e. and object of *intuition*) in the *Phenomenology of Spirit*, we can see, at once, that there is something wrong with the characterization of Hegel's *Logic* as "speculative Neo-Platonism" (*Hegel's Dialectic and its Criticism*, Cambridge, The University Press, 1982, p. 179.)

12. This was never Hegel's view (from the writing of the poem 'Eleusis', in 1976, onwards). The word 'mystic' comes to us from the Greek Mysteries; and Hegel always insisted both on the *importance* of the 'mystic' component in Greek religion, and on the fact that there was nothing 'obscure' about it. He *did* agree, however, with the contrast between Catholic 'poetry' and Protestant 'prose'; and probably with the opposition of 'crystal-bright mysticism' and the 'obscure mysticism' of Protestantism. (But only his agreement about Protestant mysticism can be definitely documented - see Rosenkranz, 182-3; translated in the Harris and Knox, p. 257). See further note 18 below.

13. This talk of cultural *union* and dichotomy or *scission* (*Vereinigung* and *Entzweiung*) is very typical of Hegel in 1801, in the *Difference* essay, and—as the newly discovered fragments show—in his lectures too. We cannot, of course, be sure who originated it; but it is one of the things that makes Hegel's puzzling claim that this essay is really his worth pondering upon. See especially *Difference*, pp. 90-4.

14. That the philosophical revolution would give birth to a new religion was a theme of Hegel's lectures in 1801-3. See especially Rosenkranz, pp 140-1 (translated in Harris and Knox, pp. 185-6).

15. Like Michelet, I find it hard to believe that Hegel would write like this about his own intuitions. But in Schelling's mouth the words may be either (mildly ironical) reference to Hegel's aims and effort, or a quite unironical reference to his own inspirations (or both!) (There is also, of course, Novalis; and the whole circle of Boehme enthusiasts— especially Franz von Baader—to be considered).

16. The reference here is to the revival in the Identity philosophy of Spinoza's doctrine of the unity of God and Nature—and of the "unity of the mind with the whole of nature" as the human good. The insistence (in what follows) on the identity

of the ethical and the intellectual good continues this same theme.

17. Actually this is an abbreviated citation from *Phaedo* 67 c-d in the standard Stephanus pagination. (Schelling gives us the actual page number in the Bipontine edition).

18. This use of the myth of the Mother questing for the Daughter at Eleusis is hardly in keeping with what is said earlier (see note 12) about the relative unimportance of the mystical in Greek experience. (One wonders whether "the poetic conclusion" which Michelet took for Schelling's was indeed Hegel's as Hegel definitely implied).

WORKS AND EDITIONS CITED

Alexander, W. M. *Johann Georg Hamann, Philosophy and Faith.* The Hague: Nijhoff, 1966.

Allgemeine Deutsche Biographie. Vols. I-LXVI. Leipzig: Duncker & Humblot, 1875-1912.

Allison, Henry E. *Lessing and the Enlightenment.* Ann Arbor: The University of Michigan Press, 1966.

Altmann, Alexander. *Moses Mendelssohn.* Alabama: The University of Alabama Press, 1973.

Atlas, Samuel. *From Critical to Speculative Idealism: The Philosophy of Solomon Maimon.* The Hague: Nijhoff, 1964.

Baumanns, Peter. *Fichtes Wissenschaftslehre, Probleme ihres Anfangs.* Bonn: Bouvier, 1974.

Baumgarten, Alexander Gottlieb. *Metaphysica.* Halle: Renger, 1739.

Beck, Jakob Sigismund. *Erläuternder Auszug aus den Kritischen Schriften des Hernn Prof. Kant, auf Anraten desselben.* Vol. 1, *Erster Band, welcher die Kritik der spekulativen und praktischen Vernunft enthält.* Riga: Hartknoch, 1793.

Vol. II, *Zweiter Band, welcher die Kritik der Urteilskraft und die metaphysischen Anfangsgründe der Naturwissenschaft enthält.* Riga: Hartknoch, 1794.

Vol. III, *Dritter Band, welcher den Standpunkt darstellt, aus welchem die Kritische Philosophie zu beurteilen ist: Einzig möglicher Standpunkt, aus welchem die Kritische Philosophie beurteilt werden muss.* Riga: Hartknoch, 1796. Reprinted, *Aetas Kantiana.* Brussels: Culture et Civilization, 1968.

Beck, Jakob Sigismund. *Grundriss der Kritischen Philosophie.* Halle: Renger, 1796. English Tr., *The Principles of Critical Philosophy.* Richardson, J. Tr. London, Edinburgh & Hamburg, 1797.

Beck, Lewis White. *Early German Philosophy, Kant and His Predecessors.* Cambridge, Mass.: Harvard University Press, 1969.

Bergman, Shmuel Hugo. *The Autobiography of Solomon Maimon with an Essay on Maimon's Philosophy.* London: The East and West Library, 1954.

_____.*The Philosophy of Solomon Maimon.* Tr. from the Hebrew by Jacobs, Noah J. Jerusalem: The Magnes Press, Hebrew University, 1967.

Berkeley, George. *The Theory of Vision Vindicated and Explained,* 1733. *The Works of George Berkeley, Bishop of Cloyne.* Luce, A. A. and Jessop, T. E. eds. Vols. I-IX, London: Nelson, 1948-1957. Vol. I.

_____.*A Treatise Concerning the Principles of Human Knowledge,* 1710. 2nd ed. 1734. *The Works of George Berkeley,* Vol II.

Breazeale, Daniel. "Between Kant and Fichte: Karl Leonhard Reinhold's 'Elementary Philosophy'." *The Review of Metaphysics,* XXXV (1981-1982), pp. 785-821.

————."Fichte's *Aenesidemus* Review and the Transformation of German Idealism." *The Review of Metaphysics*, XXXIV (1980-1981), pp. 545-568.

Cassirer, Ernst. *Das Erkenntnisproblem in der Philosophie und Wissenschaft der neueren Zeit.* Vol. I-III. Berlin: Bruno Cassirer, 1923.

Cicero. *De Natura Deorum and Academica.* Rackham, H. tr. Cambridge, Mass.: Harvard University Press, 1933.

Clark, Robert T. Jr. *Herder, His Life and Thought.* Berkeley & Los Angeles: The University of California Press, 1969.

Cloeren, H. J. "Philosophie als Sprachkritik bei K. L. Reinhold, Interpretative Bemerkungen zu seiner Spätphilosophie." *Kant-Studien*, LXIII (1972), pp. 225-236.

Crusius, August. *Entwurf der notwendigen Vernunftwahrheiten.* Leipzig: Gleditsch, 1745. Reprinted, *Die philosophische Hauptwerke.* Tonelli, Giorgio, ed. Vols. I-III. Hildesheim: Georg Olms, 1964. Vol. II.

————.*Weg zur Gewissheit,* 1747. *Die philosophische Hauptwerke.* Vol. III.

Dal Pra, Mario. *Lo scetticismo greco.* Vols. I-II, 2nd ed. Bari: Laterza, 1975.

de Vleeschauwer, Herman-J. *La déduction transcendentale dans l'oeuvre de Kant.* Vol. I-III, Paris: La Haye, 1934-37. Abridged English tr. *The Development of Kantian Thought.* Duncan, A. R. C. tr. London: Nelson & Sons, 1962.

Diels, Hermann and Kranz, Walther (eds). *Die Fragmente der Vorsokratiker,* Vols. I-III, 7th edn. Berlin: Weidmannsche Verlagsbuchhandlung, 1954. (D.-K).

di Giovanni, George. "Kant's Metaphysics of Nature and Schelling's *Ideas for a Philosophy of Nature.*" *Journal of the History of Philosophy,* XVIII (1979), pp. 197-215.

Düsing, Klaus. "Spekulation und Reflexion." *Hegel-Studien,* V (1969), pp. 95-128.

[Eberhard, Johann August?]. "Ueber das Gebiet der reinen Vernunft." *Philosophisches Magazin.* Eberhard, Johann August, ed. I (1789), pp. 263-289. Reprinted, Vol. I-IV. *Aetas Kantiana.* Brussels: Culture et Civilization, 1968. Vol. I.

————."Ueber die Entscheidung der Urteile in Analytische und Synthetische." *Philosophisches Magazin,* I (1789), pp. 307-343. Reprinted, Vol. I-IV. *Aetas Kantiana.* Brussels: Culture et Civilization, 1968. Vol I.

Epictetus. *The Discourses as Reported by Arrian, the Manual, and Fragments.* Oldfather, W. H. tr. Vols. I-II. Cambridge, Mass.: Harvard University Press, 1925-1928.

Feder, Johann Georg Heinrich. *Ueber Raum und Causalität, zur Prüfung der Kantischen Philosophie.* Göttingen: bei Joh. Chr. Dietrich, 1787. Reprinted, *Aetas Kantiana.* Brussels: Culture et Civilization, 1968.

Fichte, Johann Gottlieb: [Rezension:] Ohne Druckort: *Aenesidemus, oder . . .* 1794. *Gesammtausgabe der Bayerischen Akademie der Wissenschaften.* Lauth, R. and Jacobs, H. eds. Stuttgart-Bad Cannstatt: Fromann, 1965-. Vol. I, 2. French tr. "La recension de l'Enesidème par Fichte." Druet, P. Ph. tr. *Revue de Métaphysique et de Morale,* LXXVIII (1973), pp. 363-384.

_____.*Apellation an das Publikum*, 1799. *Sämmtliche Werke*. Fichte, I. H. ed. Vols. I-VIII. Berlin: Veit & Co., 1845/1846. Vol. V.

_____.*Die Bestimmung des Menschen*, 1800. *Sämmtliche Werke*. Vol. II. English tr. *The Vocation of Man*. Smith, W. tr. Chisholm, R. M. ed. The Library of Liberal Arts. Indianapolis and New York: Bobbs-Merrill, 1956.

_____.*Eigne Meditationen über Elementarphilosophie*, 1793/1794. *Gesammtausgabe*, Vol. II, 3.

_____.*Erste Einleitung in die Wissenschaftslehre*, 1797. *Sämmtliche Werke*, Vol. I. English tr. *Fichte: Science of Knowledge with First and Second Introduction*. Heath, Peter and Lachs, John trs. New York: Appleton-Century-Crofts, 1970; re-issued, Cambridge University Press, 1983

_____.*Grundlage der gesammten Wissenschaftslehre, als Handschrift für seine Zuhörer*, 1794/1795. *Gesammtausgabe*, Vol. I, 2. *Sämmtliche Werke*, Vol. I. English tr. *Fichte: Science of Knowledge with First and Second Introduction*.

Fichte, Johann Gottlieb. *Das System der Sittenlehre nach den Principien der Wissenschaftslehre*, 1798. *Gesammtausgabe*, Vol. I, 5. English tr. *System of Ethics*. Kroeger, A. E. tr. London: Trubner, 1897.

_____.*Ueber den Begriff der Wissenschaftslehre oder der sogenannten Philosophie, als Einleitdungschrift zu seiner Vorlesungen über diese Wissenschaft*, 1794. *Gesammtausgabe*, Vol. I, 2.

_____.*Versuch einer neuen Darstellung der Wissenschaftslehre. Einleitung. Zweite Einleitung für Leser, die schon ein philosophisches System haben*, 1797/1798. *Gesammtausgabe*, I, 4.

_____.*Die Wissenschaftslehre in ihrem allgemeinen Umrisse*, 1810. *Sämmtliche Werke*. Vol. II. English tr. The Science of Knowledge in its General Outline (1810). Wright, Walter E. tr. *Idealistic Studies*, VI (1976) pp. 106-117.

_____.*Zweite Einleitung in die Wissenschaftslehre*, 1798. *Sämmtliche Werke*, Vol. I. English tr. *Fichte: Science of Knowledge with First and Second Introduction*.

Gellius, Aulus. *The Attic Nights of Aulus Gellius*. Rolfe, John C. tr. Vols. I-III. Cambridge, Mass.: Harvard University Press, 1927.

Goethe, Johann Wolfgang von. *Ein Fastnachtspiel vom Pater Brey*. Noelle, Annemarie, ed. Berliner Ausgabe. Vols. I-XX. Berlin: Aufbau Verlag, 1960-1978. Vol. V (1964).

Guéroult, Martial. *L'évolution et la structure de la Doctrine de la Science chez Fichte*. Vols. I-II. Paris: Société d'Edition, 1930.

_____.*La philosophie transcendentale de Solomon Maimon*. Paris: Société d'Edition. 1930.

Hegel, Georg Wilhelm Friedrich. *Briefe von und an Hegel*. Hoffmeister, Joh. and Flechsig, Rolf, eds. Vols. I-IV. Hamburg: Meiner, 1961. Vol. IV, 1 & 2, 2nd ed., Nicolin, Fr. ed., 1977. English tr. *Letters*. Butler, Clark and Seiler, Christiane trs. Bloomington: University of Indiana Press, 1984.

_____.*De Orbitis Planetarum*, 1801. *Erste Druckschriften*. Lasson, Georg, ed. Leipzig: Meiner, 1928.

Hegel, Georg Wilhelm Friedrich. *Differenz des Fichteschen und Schellingschen Systems der Philosophie*, 1801. *Gesammelte Schriften*. Vol. IV. *Jenaer Kritische*

Schriften. Buchner, Hartmut and Pöggeler, Otto, eds. Hamburg: Meiner, 1968. English tr. *Hegel, The Difference between Fichte's and Schelling's System of Philosophy.* Cerf, Walter and Harris, H. S. trs. Albany: State University of New York Press, 1977.

_____.*Enzyklopädie der philosophischen Wissenschaften* (1830) F. Nicolin and O. Pöggeler eds. Hamburg, Meiner, 1959.)

_____."Glauben und Wissen." *Kritisches Journal der Philosophie.* Hegel, G. W. F. and Schelling, F. W. J. von eds. Vol I, 1 (1802), pp. 1-189. Reprinted, Vols. I-II. Hildesheim: Georg Olms, 1967. Critical edition, *Gesammelte Schriften*, Vol IV. English tr. *Faith and Knowledge.* Cerf, Walter and Harris, H. S. trs., with introduction and notes. Albany: State University of New York Press, 1977.

_____.*Logik, Metaphysik, Naturphilosophie* (1804/5), *Gesammelte Werke* Vol. VII. English tr. *Jena Logic and Metaphysics.* J. Burbidge, G. di Giovanni, et al. trs. Montreal/Kingston: McGill-Queen's University Press (in press).

_____.*Natural Law.* Knox, T. M. tr., with an introduction by Acton, H. B. Philadelphia: University of Pennsylvania Press, 1975.

_____.*Phänomenologie des Geistes*, 1807. Hamburg: Meiner, 1952; Critical edition *Gesammelte Werke*, Vol. IX. English tr. *Phenomenology of Spirit.* Miller, A. V., with an introduction and analysis by Findlay, J. N. Oxford: Clarendon Press, 1977.

_____.*Philosophy of Nature*, Miller, A. V. tr. Oxford, Clarendon Press, 1977.

_____.*System der Sittlichkeit*, 1802/03. Lasson, George, ed., 2nd ed., 1923. Reprinted, Hamburg: Meiner, 1967. English tr. *System of Ethical Life and First Philosophy of Spirit.* Harris, H. S. and Knox, T. M. trs., with an introduction and notes by Harris, H. S. Albany: State University of New York Press, 1979.

_____.*Das System der spekulativen Philosophie*, 1803/05. *Gesammelte Schriften*, Vol. VI, *Jenaer Systementwürfe* I. Hamburg: Meiner, 1975.

Hegel, Georg Wilhelm Friedrich. *Theologische Jugendschriften.* Nohl, Hermann, ed. Tübingen: Mohr, 1907. Reprinted, 1968. English tr. *Early Theological Writings.* Knox, T. M. and Kroner, Richard, trs. Chicago: University of Chicago Press, 1948. Reprinted, Philadelphia: University of Pennsylvania Press, 1975.

_____."Ueber das Wesen der philosophischer Kritik." (Introduction for) *Kritisches Journal der Philosophie*, I, 1 (1802), pp. iii-xxiv. Reprinted, Vols. I-II. Hildesheim: Georg Olms, 1967. Critical edition, *Gesammelte Schriften*, Vol. IV.

_____."Ueber die wissenschaftlichen Behandlungsarten des Naturrechts." *Kritisches Journal der Philosophie*, II, 3 (1803), pp. 1-88. (For English translation see *Natural Law* above.

_____."Verhältniss des Skeptizismus zur Philosophie." *Kritisches Journal der Philosophie*, I, 2 (1802), pp. 1-74. French tr. *La relation du scepticisme avec la philosophie, suivi de L'essence de la critique.* Fauquet, B. tr. Paris: Vrin, 1972.

_____.*Werke.* Complete edition edited by a committee of his friends. 2nd ed. Vols. I-XV. Berlin: Duncker & Humblot, 1841-54. Vol. I, *Philosophische Abhandlungen.* Michelet, K. L., ed.

_____."Wie der gemeine Menschenverstand die Philosophie nehme,— dargestellt an den Werken des Hernn Krugs." *Kritisches Journal de Philosophie.* I, 1 (1802), pp. 91-115.

Holbach, Paul H. D. Baron d'. *Système de la nature.* Paris, 1770.

Hume, David. *An Enquiry Concerning Human Understanding,* 1748. *Enquiries.* Selby-Bigge, L. A., ed. Oxford: Clarendon Press, 1902. German tr. *David Humes Untersuchungen über den menschlichen Verstand, neu übersetzt von M. W. G. Tenneman, nebst einer Abhandlung über den philosophischen Skepticismus von Herrn Prof. Reinhold.* Jena: Akademische Buchhandlung, 1793. *A Treatise of Human Nature,* 1739. Selby-Bigge, L. A., ed. Oxford: Clarendon Press, 1967.

Jacobi, Friederich Heinrich. *Werke.* Köppen, Fr. and Roth, Fr. Vols. I-VI. Leipzig: bei Gerhard Fleischer, 1812-1825. Reprinted, Darmstadt: Wissenschaftsliche Buchgesellschaft, 1968.

_____.*An Fichte* Hamburg: Perthes, 1799. *Werke,* Vol. III.

_____.*Ueber die Lehre des Spinoza in Briefen an den Herrn Moses Mendelssohn.* Neue vermehrte Ausgabe. Breslau: Loewe, 1789. *Werke,* IV, 1.

Kant, Immanuel. *Briefwechsel. Kants Gesammelts Schriften,* Vols. X-XIII. Berlin: Königliche Preussische Akademie der Wissenschaften, 1902—; later volumes published by Georg Reimer & Walter de Gruyter. English tr. *Kant's Philosophical Correspondence,* 1759-99. Zweig, Arnulf tr., with an introduction and notes. Chicago: University of Chicago Press, 1967.

_____.*Handschriftlicher Nachlass. Kants gesammelte Schriften,* Vols. XIV-XXII.

_____.*Kritik der reinen Vernunft.* Riga: Hartknoch, 1781; 2nd revised ed. 1787. The two editions collated by Schmidt, R. Hamburg: Meiner, 1930. English tr. *Immanuel Kant's Critique of Pure Reason.* Smith, Norman Kemp, tr. New York and Toronto: Macmillan, 1929.

Kant, Immanuel. *Kritik der Urteilskraft.* Berlin and Libau: Lagarde & Friederich, 1790; 2nd ed. 1793. *Kants gesammelte Schriften,* Vol. V. English tr. *Critique of Aesthetic Judgement.* Meredith, J. C. tr. Oxford: Clarendon Press, 1911.

_____.*Prolegomena zu einer jeden künftigen Metaphysik die als Wissenschaft wird auftreten können,* 1783. *Kants gesammelte Schriften,* Vol IV. English tr. *Prolegomena to Any Future Metaphysics.* With an introduction by Beck, Lewis White, The Liberal Arts Library, New York: Bobbs-Merrill, 1950.

_____.*Die Religion innerhalb der Grenzen der blossen Vernunft,* 1793; 2nd ed. 1794. *Kants gesammelte Schriften,* Vol. VI. English tr. *Religion Within the Limits of Reason Alone.* Greene, T. M. and Hudson, H. H. trs. with a new essay by Silber, John R. New York: Harper & Brothers, 1960.

_____.*Ueber eine Entdeckung, nach der alle neue Kritik der reinen Vernunft durch eine ältere entberlich gemacht werden soll,* 1790. *Kants gesammelte Schriften,* Vol. VIII. English tr. *The Kant-Eberhard Controversy.* Allison, Henry E. tr., with an introduction and notes. Baltimore and London: The John Hopkins Uni versity Press, 1973.

_____.*Reflections on Education*. Churton, Annette, tr. Ann Arbor: the University of Michigan Press, 1960.

Klemmt, Alfred. *Karl Leonhard Reinholds Elementarphilosophie, Eine Studie über den Ursprung des spekulativen deutschen Idealismus*. Hamburg: Meiner, 1958.

Krug, Wilhelm Traugott. *Allgemeines Handwörterbuch der philosophischen Wissenschaften nebst inter Literatur und Geschichte*. Vols. I-VI. Leipzig, 1832-8.

_____.*Briefe über den neuesten Idealismus*. Leipzig: H. Müller, 1801. Reprinted, *Aetas Kantiana*. Brussels: Culture et Civilization, 1968.

_____.*Briefe über die Wissenschaftslehre*. Leipzig: Roch & Co., 1800. Reprinted, *Aetas Kantiana*. Brussels: Culture et Civilization, 1968.

_____.*Entwurf eines neuen Organons der Philosophie*. Meissen and Lübben: K. F. W. Erbstein, 1801. Reprinted, *Aetas Kantiana*. Brussels: Culture et Civilization, 1968.

Kuehn, Manfred. "The Early Reception of Reid, Oswald and Beattie in Germany 1768-1800." *Journal of the History of Philosophy*, XXI (1983), pp. 479-497.

_____.*Scottish Common Sense Philosophy in Germany, 1768-1800*. Ph.D. Thesis. McGill University, 1980.

Kuntze, Friederich. *Die Philosophie Solomon Maimons*. Heidelberg: Carl Winter's Universitätsbuchhandlung, 1912.

Laertius, Diogenes. *Lives of Eminent Philosophers*. Hicks, R. D. tr. Vols. I-II. Cambridge, Mass.: Harvard University Press, 1925.

Lauth, Reinhart. "Genèse du 'Fondement de toute la Doctrine de la science' de Fichte à partir des ses 'Meditations personnelles sur l'élementarphilosophie'." *Archives de Philosophie*, XXXIV (1971), pp. 51-79.

_____.ed. *Philosophie aus einem Prinzip, K. L. Reinhold*. Bonn: Bouvier, 1974.

Leibniz, Gottfried Wilhelm von. *Essais de Theodicée*. Neufville, M. L. de ed. Vol I-II. Amsterdam, 1734.

Leibniz, Gottfried Wilhelm von. *Opera Omnia*. Dutens, L., ed. Geneva, 1768.

Léon, Xavier. *Fichte et son temps*. Vols. I-III. Paris: Colin, 1954.

Locke, John. *An Essay Concerning Human Understanding*, 1690. Frazer, A. C., ed. Vols. I-II. New York: Dover, 1959.

Maimon, Solomon. "Einleitung zur neuen Revision des Magazin sur Erfahrungsseelenkunde." *Magazin zur Erfahrungsseelenkunde*, IX (1792), pp. 1-29. Reprinted, *Gesammelte Werke*. Verra, Valerio, ed. Vols. I-V. Hildesheim: Georg Olms, 1970. Vol. III.

_____.*Kritische Untersuchungen über den menschlichen Geist oder das höhere Erkenntniss-und Willensvermögen*. Leipzig, 1797.

_____.*Lebensgeschichte*. Berlin: Vieweg, 1792/93. Reprinted, *Werke*, Vol. I. English tr. *Solomon Maimon: An Autobiography*. Ed. and with an epilogue by Moses, Hadas. New York: Schocken Press, 1947. English tr. *Solomon Maimon: An Autobiography with Additions and Notes*. Murray, Clark J. tr. Paisley: Alexander Gardner, 1888.

_____.*Philosophischer Briefwechsel, nebst einem demselben vorangeschickten Manifest.* In *Streifereien im Gebiete der Philosophie.* Berlin: Wilhelm Vieweg, 1793. Reprinted, *Werke,* Vol. III.

_____."Ueber die Welt-Seele, Entelechia Universi." *Journal für Aufklärung,* VIII (1789), pp. 99-122.

_____.*Versuch einer neuen Logik oder Theorie des Denkens.* Berlin: bei Ernst Felisch, 1794; 2nd ed. 1798. Reprinted, Darmstadt: Wissenschaftliche Buchgesellschaft, 1963. Reprinted, *Werke,* Vol. V. Critical edition: Engel, Carl B. ed. Kantgesellschaft. Berlin: Reuther & Reichard, 1912.

_____.*Versuch über die Transcendentalphilosophie.* Berlin: Voss & Sohn, 1790. Reprinted, Werke, Vol. II.

Moore, G. E. *Principia Ethica.* Cambridge: University Press, 1903.

Nicolin, Günther, ed. *Hegel in Berichten seiner Zeitgenossen.* Hamburg: Meiner, 1970.

Plato. *Opera Omnia.* Tiedemann, Dietrich, ed. Vols. I-XII. Zweibrücken: 1781-86.

Plattner, Ernst. *Philosophische Aphorismen.* Leipzig, 1776; 2nd ed. 1784.

Plutarch. *Lives. The Dryden Plutarch.* Revised by Clough, A. H. Vols. I-IV. London: Dent, 1910.

Pupi, Angelo. *La Formazione della filosofia di K. L. Reinhold, 1784-1794.* Milano: Vita & Pensiero, 1966.

Reinhold, Ernst. *Karl Leonhards Leben und literarisches Wesen, nebst einer Auswahl von Briefen Kants, Fichtes, Jacobis und andrer philosophierenden Zeitgenossen an ihn.* Jena: Fromann, 1825.

Reinhold, Karl Leonhard. *Ausführliche Darstellung des negativen Dogmatismus oder des metaphysischen Skeptizismus.* In *Beiträge zur Berichtigung bisheriger Missverständnisse der Philosophen.* Vols. I-II. Jena: Mauke, 1790 and 1794. Vol. II, pp. 159-206.

_____.*Auswahl vermischter Schriftzen.* Vols I-II. Jena: Mauke, 1797.

_____.*Briefe über die Kantische Philosophie.* Vols. I-II. Leipzig: beig Georg Joachim Goschen, 1790 and 1792.

_____.*Erörterungen über den Versuch einer neuen Theorie des Vorstellungsvermögens. Beiträge,* Vol. I, pp. 373-404.

_____.*Korrespondenz, 1773-1788.* Lauth, R., Heller, E., and Hiller, K., eds. Stuttgart-Bad Cannstatt: Friederich Fromann Verlag, Günther Holzboog & Verlag der Oesterreichischen Akademie der Wissenschaften, 1983.

Reinhold, Karl Leonhard. *Neue Darstellung der Elementarphilosophie. Beiträge,* Vol. I, pp. 167-254.

_____.*Ueber das Bedurfniss, die Moglichkeit und die Eigenschaften eines allgemeingeltenden ersten Grundsatzes der Philosophie. Beiträge,* Vol. I, pp. 91-164.

_____.*Ueber das Fundament des philosophischen Wissens.* Jena: Mauke, 1791. Reprinted, Schrader, W. H., ed. Hamburg: Meiner, 1978.

_____.*Ueber das Verhältniss der Theorie des Vorstellungsvermögens zur Kritik der reinen Vernunft. Beiträge,* Vol. I, pp. 255-388.

_____.Ueber das vollständige Fundament der Moral. Beiträge, Vol. II, pp. 206-294.

_____.Ueber den Unterschied zwischen dem gesunde Verstande und der philosophierenden Vernunft. Beiträge, Vol. II, pp. 1-72.

_____.Ueber die Möglichkeit der Philosophie als strenge Wissenschaft. Beiträge, Vol. I, pp. 339-372.

_____.Versuch einer neuen Theorie des menschlichen Vorstellungsvermögens. Prague and Jena: Widtmann & Mauke, 1789; 2nd ed. 1795. Reprinted, Darmstadt: Wissenschaftliche Buchgesellschaft, 1963.

Rosenkranz, Karl. Georg Wilhelm Friedrich Hegels Leben. Berlin, 1844. Reprinted, Darmstadt: Wissenschaftliche Buchgesellschaft, 1963.

Rousseau, Jean-Jacques. Emile. Foxley, B. tr. London: Everyman, 1911.

Schelling, Friedrich Wilhelm Joseph von. Aus Schellings Leben: In Briefen. Plitt, G. L., ed. Vols. I-III. Leipzig: Hirzel, 1869-79.

_____.Briefe und Dokumenta. Fuhrmans, H., ed. Vol II (Zusatzband). Bonn: Bouvier, 1973.

Schelling, Friedrich Wilhelm Joseph von. On the Possibility of a Form of Philosophy in General, 1794. Marti, Fritz, tr. In The Unconditional in Human Knowledge. Lewisburg, Pa.: Bucknell University Press, 1980.

_____.System des Transzendentalen Idealismus, 1800. Sämmtliche Werke. Schelling, K. F. A. ed. Vols I-XIV. Stuttgart and Ausburg: Cotta, 1856-1861, Vol. III. English tr. System of Transcendental Philosophy (1800). Heath, Peter, tr., with an introduction by Vater, Michael. Charlottesville: University Press of Virginia, 1978.

Schiller, Johann Christian Friedrich. Sämmtliche Schriften. Goedeke, K., ed. Stuttgart: Cotta, 1867-76.

_____.On the Aesthetic Education of Man. Snell, Reginald, tr., with an introduction. New York: Ungar, 1971.

Schmidt, E. ed. Caroline: Briefe aus der Frühromantik. Vols. I-II. Leipzig, 1913.

Schulze, Gottlieg Ernst. Aenesidemus, oder über die Fundamente der von Herrn Prof. Reinhold in Jena gelieferten Elementar-Philosophie. N.p.p., 1792. Reprinted, Aetas Kantiana. Brussels: Culture et Civilization, 1969. Critical edition: Liebert, Arthur, ed. Kantgeselischaft. Berlin: Reuther & Reichard, 1911.

_____.Kritik der theoretischen Philosophie. Vols. I-II. Hamburg: C. E. Bohn, 1801. Reprinted, Aetas Kantiana. Brussels: Culture et Civilization, 1968.

Sextus Empiricus. Opera. Fabricius, J. A., ed. Leipzig, 1718.

_____.Sextus Empiricus. Bury, R. G. tr. Vols. I-IV. Cambridge: Harvard University Press, 1933-1949.

Spinoza, Benedict. Opera Omnia. Paulus, E. E. G., ed. Vols. I-II. Jena: Akademische Buchhandlung, 1802-03.

Stäudlin, C. F. Geschichte und Geist des Sceptizismus. Vols. I-II. Leipzig, 1794.

Teichner, Wilhelm. *Rekonstruktion oder Reproduktion des Grundes, Die Begründung der Philosophie als Wissenschaft durch Kant und Reinhold.* Bonn: Bouvier, 1976.

Ulrich, Johann August. *Institutiones logicae et metaphysicae, scholae suae scripsit Joh. Aug. Ulrich.* Jena, 1785.

Verra, Valerio. *F. H. Jacobi, dall'illuminismo all'idealismo.* Torino: Edizioni di filosofia, 1963.

Wallner, Ingrid. *Jacob Sigismund Beck's Phenomenological Transformation of Kant's Critical Philosophy.* Ph.D. Thesis. McGill University, 1979.

ANALYTICAL INDEX